A Modern Guide to Financial Shocks
and Crises

ELGAR MODERN GUIDES

Elgar Modern Guides offer a carefully curated review of a selected topic, edited or authored by a leading scholar in the field. They survey the significant trends and issues of contemporary research for both advanced students and academic researchers.

The books provide an invaluable appraisal and stimulating guide to the current research landscape, offering state-of-the-art discussions and selective overviews covering the critical matters of interest alongside recent developments. Combining incisive insight with a rigorous and thoughtful perspective on the essential issues, the books are designed to offer an inspiring introduction and unique guide to the diversity of modern debates.

Elgar Modern Guides will become an essential go-to companion for researchers and graduate students but will also prove stimulating for a wider academic audience interested in the subject matter. They will be invaluable to anyone who wants to understand as well as simply learn.

Titles in the series include:

A Modern Guide to the Economics of Happiness
Edited by Luigino Bruni, Alessandra Smerilli and Dalila De Rosa

A Modern Guide to Economic Sociology
Edited by Milan Zafirovski

A Modern Guide to National Urban Policies in Europe
Edited by Karsten Zimmermann and Valeria Fedeli

A Modern Guide to Wellbeing Research
Edited by Beverley A. Searle, Jessica Pykett and Maria Jesus Alfaro-Simmonds

A Modern Guide to Philosophy of Economics
Edited by Harold Kincaid and Don Ross

A Modern Guide to the Urban Sharing Economy
Edited by Thomas Sigler and Jonathan Corcoran

A Modern Guide to the Digitalization of Infrastructure
Edited by Juan Montero and Matthias Finger

A Modern Guide to Sports Economics
Edited by Ruud H. Koning and Stefan Kesenne

A Modern Guide to Labour and the Platform Economy
Edited by Jan Drahokoupil and Kurt Vandaele

A Modern Guide to Financial Shocks and Crises
Edited by Giovanni Ferri and Vincenzo D'Apice

A Modern Guide to Financial Shocks and Crises

Edited by

Giovanni Ferri

LUMSA University, Italy

Vincenzo D'Apice

LUMSA University, Italy

ELGAR MODERN GUIDES

Cheltenham, UK • Northampton, MA, USA

Published by
Edward Elgar Publishing Limited
The Lypiatts
15 Lansdown Road
Cheltenham
Glos GL50 2JA
UK

Edward Elgar Publishing, Inc.
William Pratt House
9 Dewey Court
Northampton
Massachusetts 01060
USA

Paperback edition 2023

A catalogue record for this book
is available from the British Library

Library of Congress Control Number: 2021947689

This book is available electronically in the **Elgar**online
Economics subject collection
http://dx.doi.org/10.4337/9781789904529

MIX
Paper | Supporting
responsible forestry
FSC
www.fsc.org   FSC® C013604

ISBN 978 1 78990 451 2 (cased)
ISBN 978 1 78990 452 9 (eBook)
ISBN 978 1 0353 2029 5 (paperback)

Typeset by Cheshire Typesetting Ltd, Cuddington, Cheshire
Printed and bound by CPI Group (UK) Ltd, Croydon, CR0 4YY

Contents

Tables

Contributors

Christophe André, OECD

Elias Bengtsson, University of Gothenburg

Paola Bongini, University of Milano Bicocca

Giorgio Caselli, University of Cambridge

Eugenio Cerutti, International Monetary Fund

Jérémie Cohen-Setton, Independent Evaluation Office of the International Monetary Fund

Alex Cukierman, Tel-Aviv University

Vincenzo D'Apice, LUMSA University

E. Philip Davis, Brunel University

Giovanni Ferri, LUMSA University

Alexandre Garel, Audencia Business School

Aneta Hryckiewicz, Kozminski University

Dilruba Karim, Brunel University

Maria Nikolaidi, University of Greenwich

Tommaso Oliviero, University of Naples Federico II

Valerio Pesic, Sapienza University

Arthur Petit-Romec, TBS Business School

Giovanni W. Puopolo, University of Naples Federico II

Ornella Ricci, University of Roma Tre

Emanuele Rossi, University of Milano Bicocca

Francesco Saverio Stentella Lopes, University of Roma Tre

Haonan Zhou, Princeton University

Preface

"Systemic Financial Shocks" – henceforth simply "Financial Shocks" – have the power to wrench the macroeconomy. They matter for two main reasons. First, even when they come from imbalances external to the financial sector, financial shocks may unnerve society, by impairing asset values and encumbering economic growth. In this case, we may label them as first type – or exogenously determined – financial shocks. Second and more nastily, when their origin comes from finance itself, financial shocks acquire a stronger taint, as they also expose the inner fragility and instability of capitalist systems, building a wide sense of insecurity with possible contagion and domino effects, up to jeopardise the proper functioning of payments systems. Here, we can label them as second type – or endogenously bred – financial shocks. Whatever their origin, it is important to study financial shocks trying to answer the following questions. What causes them? Which channels may exacerbate their impact? What policies may help avoid their occurrence or, when they occur, limit their negative effect on the economy and society?

Answering these questions has become more and more crucial over the latest decades, when financial shocks have become more frequent, their intensity has escalated, their focal point has moved from the periphery to the centre of the world economy, and their nature has been upgraded from first to second type financial shocks. Indeed, from the post-Second-World-War up to the 1970s financial shocks had become extremely rare, if not absent. And even thereafter, financial shocks had been main characters only in developing and emerging countries. Up until 2007, one could be led to think that suffering a financial shock was the prerogative of developing and emerging economies, while rich countries – excluding the crises of Japan and the Scandinavian countries in the early 1990s – were rather immune from financial shocks. Hence, it was possible to believe that financial crises were due to more widespread market imperfections and lower quality of institutions outside the developed world. This tenet was, of course, rebuffed when the Global Financial Crisis (GFC) of 2007–09 erupted from America's Wall Street. Moreover, while almost all the previous systemic crises were associated with type one – or exogenously determined – financial shocks, this time around the GFC was clearly triggered by a second type – endogenous – financial shock. The GFC, in fact, came about under the initial impetus of the subprime crisis, where a large segment of innovative securities – leveraged on the backing of subprime mortgages, that is, mortgages entrusted to clients with low or no ability to repay – turned sour. Moreover, the GFC was followed by a second wave of instability caused by a broad reassessment of sovereign risks throughout Europe inducing a euro sovereign crisis. Indeed, after the GFC investors discontinued the previously held view that eurozone member countries all shared an analogous and common sovereign risk. As some of the chapters will debate later, the massive market reassessment of sovereign risks, together with some institutional fragilities within the eurozone, caused new intense financial shocks in some member countries. Again, this was a further blow to the naive view that financial crises were reserved to emerging and developing countries.

PLAN OF THE BOOK

This book consists of four parts: I. *Financial Instability after the Global Financial Crisis: Taxonomy and Models*; II. *Main Channels of Transmission of the Financial Shock*; III. *The Role of Public Policies*; IV. *Learning from Past Financial Crises to Prevent Future Ones*.

Part I – Financial Instability after the Global Financial Crisis: Taxonomy and Models – includes three chapters. In Chapter 1 – *The Global Financial Crisis* – D'Apice and Ferri recapitulate the chronology of the GFC and articulate the various concurrent factors behind it. In turn, in Chapter 2 – *Minsky's financial instability hypothesis* – Nikolaidi outlines how Minsky's hypothesis – something that had fallen into oblivion but was soon rejuvenated since 2008 – can help explain how the GFC came about. Moreover, Nikolaidi also explains how Minsky's analysis can be used to understand climate-induced financial instability, in the rapidly expanding area of climate-related financial risks. The first part ends with Chapter 3 – *Financial accelerator framework* – where Oliviero and Puopolo synthesise the main aspects of the Financial accelerator and delineate how the financial sector can amplify financial shocks through the economy.

Next, Part II – Main Channels of Transmission of the Financial Shock – consists of five chapters. In Chapter 4 – *The role of the household balance sheets* – André expresses the channels of transmission though which households played a major role in the GFC. Then, two chapters are devoted to encapsulate how contagion across banks contributed to the GFC. Specifically, in Chapter 5 – *The European network of cross-border lending* – Ricci and Stentella Lopes focus their analysis on interbank contagion across banks in Europe, while in Chapter 6 – *International banks and the transmission of financial shocks* – Cerutti and Zhou study contagion among banking networks at the global level. In turn, in Chapter 7 – *The role of bank ownership types and business models* – Caselli highlights the value of banking diversity, stressing how stakeholder-oriented and/or traditional banks contributed less to the build-up of systemic risk before the GFC. The second part ends with Chapter 8 – *The role of market valuation in financial crises* – where Bongini and Rossi discuss the role of market valuation rules at the time of the GFC and throughout its aftermath.

Part III – *The Role of Public Policies* – includes five additional chapters. In Chapter 9 – *Reflections on the shifting consensus about monetary and fiscal policies following the GFC and the COVID-19 crises* – Cukierman, building on his top-level expertise in the field, debates how the GFC and the COVID-19 crises seem to have drastically shifted the mainstream view about the role of monetary (and fiscal) policies to combat financial shocks. In Chapter 10 – *Fiscal policy lessons since the Global Financial Crisis* – Cohen-Setton elucidates how the role of fiscal policies has been magnified after the GFC and the euro sovereign crisis. In turn, the next two chapters expand on the role of the government when financial shocks hit the economy. Namely, in Chapter 11 – *The government as lender of last resort and temporary owner* – Hryckiewicz explains and provides empirical evidence that government intervention to save banks can be helpful through financial crises. Instead, in Chapter 12 – *The sovereign-bank nexus* – Ferri and Pesic deal with the negative link between a government and its national banking system, where the health of government finances may be strongly intertwined with the health of national banking systems, as substantiated by the euro sovereign crisis. The third part of the book ends with Chapter 13 – *Financial reforms* – where Garel and Petit-Romec formulate a detailed review of the main regulatory gaps evidenced by the GFC and what has been done in the following years to remedy the situation.

Finally, Part IV – *Learning from Past Financial Crises to Prevent Future Ones* – comprises two chapters. In Chapter 14 – *Looking back: a historical perspective on European crises* – Bengtsson draws on an extensive review of financial crises in Europe since the 1970s to synthesise the main recurrent factors. The book ends with Chapter 15 – *Looking ahead: early warning systems* – in which Davis and Karim discuss the evolution of early warning systems, a tool that may be particularly useful to forecast incoming financial crises.

INTERCONNECTIONS ACROSS THE CHAPTERS

The 15 chapters of the book are strongly intertwined as shown by the matrix of the cross references (Table 0.1). Naturally, Chapter 1 on the GFC builds the most intense network of 20 links, expressing ten 'active' links to other chapters and receiving ten 'passive' references from other chapters. Second comes Chapter 2 – Minsky's model – with 15 links, nine active and six passive, followed by Chapter 13 – financial reforms – with 13 links (nine active and four passive) and by Chapter 9 – monetary policy – with 11 links (four active and seven passive).

LOOKING AT THE FUTURE

This book was planned before the COVID-19 pandemic hit the world. The necessary adaptation of the manual to the new situation is entrusted to the individual chapters for which the new scenario caused more important changes. However, there is something general that we can say by comparing the COVID-19 and GFC mega crises. Although the pandemic triggered an enormous financial shock – as testified by the plummeting of the main stock market indices in March 2020 (e.g., between 20 February and 20 March 2020 the Dow Jones Industrial Average lost close to one-third of its value), this is again a mega financial shock of the first type. In other words, in this case the financial shock came about because of the exogenous occurrence of the pandemic and was not originated from inside the financial sector, as happened with the GFC.

While the pandemic continued to take dramatic tolls in terms of mounting deaths and of GDP losses around the world, can we be comforted by observing that the financial shock provoked by COVID-19 was of the first type and not of the second type? Strictly speaking, yes. In reality, the repair actions via expansionary fiscal and monetary policies could work more swiftly than they had done in 2008 – and, indeed, by the end of December 2020 the Dow Jones Industrial Average had fully recovered its pre-pandemic level. However, type two financial shocks could still be around the corner, especially if we consider that more than a decade of Quantitative Easing (QE) and close to zero interest rates may have resulted in more systemic risk build-up. The fact that unconventional monetary policies may turn into what Nickolaidi, in Chapter 2, calls "destabilising stability" seems to be receiving some support in the literature. To name a few, Lamoen et al. (2019) find that periods of QE coincide with exuberant investor behaviour in Europe, even after controlling for improving macro fundamentals, while Libich (2020) argues that monetary policy, especially

Table 0.1   *Matrix of cross references among chapters*

From/To	Ch. 1	Ch. 2	Ch. 3	*Part I*	Ch. 4	Ch. 5	Ch. 6	Ch. 7	Ch. 8	*Part II*	Ch. 9	Ch. 10	Ch. 11	Ch. 12	Ch. 13	*Part III*	Ch. 14	Ch. 15	*Part IV*	Total
Chapter 1		1	1	*2*	1	1	1	1	1	*5*	1	1	1			*3*				10
Chapter 2	1		1	*2*	1	1	1	1		*4*	1	1		1		*3*				9
Chapter 3	1	1		*2*	1					*1*										3
Part I	*2*	*2*	*2*	*6*	*3*	*2*	*2*	*2*	*1*	*10*	*2*	*2*	*1*	*1*		*6*				*22*
Chapter 4	1	1	1	*3*		1	1	1		*3*					1	*1*				7
Chapter 5	1			*1*							1					*1*				2
Chapter 6	1	1	1	*3*				1		*1*										4
Chapter 7	1	1		*2*			1			*1*										3
Chapter 8	1			*1*																1
Part II	*5*	*3*	*2*	*10*		*1*	*2*	*2*		*5*	*1*				*1*	*2*				*17*
Chapter 9	1		1	*2*									1	1		*2*				4
Chapter 10																				0
Chapter 11														1	1	*2*				2
Chapter 12															1	*1*				1
Chapter 13	1			*1*		1	1	1	1	*4*	1	1	1			*3*	1		*1*	9
Part III	*2*		*1*	*3*		*1*	*1*	*1*	*1*	*4*	*1*	*1*	*2*	*2*	*2*	*9*	*1*		*1*	*17*
Chapter 14	1	1	1	*3*		1				*1*	2	1				*3*		1	*1*	8
Chapter 15													1		1	*2*				2
Part IV	*1*	*1*	*1*	*3*		*1*				*1*	*2*	*1*	*1*		*1*	*5*		*1*	*1*	*10*
Total	10	6	6	*22*	3	5	5	5	2	*20*	7	4	4	3	4	*22*	1	1	*2*	

the unconventional measures (QE) implemented in the post-2008 period, has likely contributed to feed major asset bubbles with markets responding to bad news about the economy's fundamentals by stock price increases as if it was good news: in anticipation that loose monetary measures (injections of liquidity) would continue. In turn, studying the effects of interest rate cuts on investment behaviour in an experimental setting, Conrad (2019) finds that decreasing interest rates encourage risk-taking and excessive risk-taking ensues when there are no capital costs, thus leading to encourage financial bubbles and overinvestments or wrong investments under QE policies. In addition, Xu and de Haan (2018) show that the relationship between reduced credit spreads – as a result of QE – and future employment growth weakened after the Fed introduced QE. Finally, using option implied volatility indices Yang and Zhou (2017) and Yang et al. (2020) detect systemic risk spillover effects coming from US QE to the global economy.

Overall, we can reasonably hold that financial shocks will be a permanent trait in the future as well, even more so if market economies will continue in the process of expanding financialisation of the latest decades. Those readers who concur with this view will find food for thought by reading the following chapters.

REFERENCES

Conrad, C.A. (2019). The effects on investment behavior of zero interest rate policy, evidence from a roulette experiment. *Applied Economics and Finance*, 6(4): 18–27.

Lamoen, R., de Vette, N., & Hudepohl, T. (2019). Quantitative easing and exuberance in stock markets: Evidence from the Euro Area. De Nederlandsche Bank Working Paper No. 660.

Libich, J. (2020). Can money turn bad news into good news? *World Economics*, 21(2): 165–82.

Xu, Y., & de Haan, J. (2018). The time-varying relationship between credit spreads and employment growth. *Applied Economics*, 50(41): 4387–401.

Yang, Z., & Zhou, Y. (2017). Quantitative easing and volatility spillovers across countries and asset classes. *Management Science*, 63(2): 333–54.

Yang, Z., Zhou, Y., & Cheng, X. (2020). Systemic risk in global volatility spillover networks: Evidence from option-implied volatility indices. *Journal of Futures Markets*, 40(3): 392–409.

Acknowledgments

This book would not have been possible without the very valuable contribution of the co-authors. The editors are very grateful to them for the effort and the passion put into this project.

PART I

Financial instability after the global financial crisis: taxonomy and models

1. The Global Financial Crisis

Vincenzo D'Apice and Giovanni Ferri

1.1 INTRODUCTION

The Global Financial Crisis (GFC) of 2007–09 was the most severe crisis induced by a financial shock since the Great Depression. Although the more recent crisis caused by the COVID-19 pandemic has had even greater economic consequences, the GFC remains paradigmatic of the effects which systemic financial crises may provoke. In the United States (US), millions of families lost their homes and their wealth as a consequence of the GFC. Around the world, financial markets suffered huge losses, the credit market crashes, and the world economy experienced the worst recession in the post-war period. The magnitude of the losses was so high that economists define this episode as the "Great Financial Crisis". For these reasons, we decided to devote the first chapter of the book to it. More precisely, Section 1.2 describes the chronology of the crisis in its peculiar features. Section 1.3 explains the macro causes of the crisis, while Section 1.4 focuses on the micro ones.[1, 2]

1.2 CHRONOLOGY OF THE CRISIS

The roots of the GFC are to be found in the US financial deregulation waves, whose harmful effects have been exacerbated by the improvident monetary policy undertaken by the FED after the collapse of the "new economy". In fact, between January 2001 and June 2003, decreasing policy rates, which dropped from 6 to 1 per cent, encouraged US households – who expected the real estate appreciation to continue – to increase their borrowings to buy real estate properties. As a result, real estate prices skyrocketed triggering two feedback processes, which have amplified the effects of monetary policy and fed the speculative bubble. The first process involved the real estate market: as a result of rising property prices, more credit was granted to households, which reinforced the real estate appreciation. The second process, which was closely related to the spreading out of securitisation, took place in financial markets: rising real estate prices increased the value of the securities backed by mortgage loans, making the balance sheet of intermediaries stronger; thus banks could raise more funds to buy those securities, which reinforced their appreciation and guaranteed abundant liquidity to the primary mortgage market.

The growing real estate value and the increased ratio between issuance of mortgage-backed securities (MBS) and origination of mortgage loans led to a significant lowering of the credit standards. At the same time, financial authorities did not recognise the negative effects of excessive borrowing. Hence, a growing share of new loans was granted to individuals with very low repayment capacity, the so-called subprime clients. The solvency of this new category of borrowers depended almost exclusively on the continuous increase in the value of the collateral (i.e., the house) getting more credit to roll-over the debt at maturity.

However, between June 2004 and June 2006, the US policy rate increased from 1 to 5.25 per cent, jeopardising the sustainability of mortgage debts. Thus, the insolvencies started to increase, especially for subprime mortgages. Consequently, the demand for houses slowed down curbing the house price appreciation. Moreover, in 2006, reset options started to align the low initial mortgage rates to market rates, so increasing even further the servicing cost of mortgages. At the same time, the decreasing value of the houses made it very difficult to get a re-financing loan to remain solvent. In spring 2007, the insolvency rate on the *subprime* mortgages exceeded 16 per cent, thus speeding up the property price drop.

Defaults in the subprime segment soon affected financial markets because many insolvent loans, or loans at risk of insolvency, provided the cash flow of structured bonds (i.e., asset-backed securities – ABS – and collateralised debt obligations – CDOs) in the hands of a multitude of international investors. In addition, between June and July, as a result of many downgrades announced by the major rating agencies, markets lost confidence in the ability of ratings to estimate structured bonds' default probability. Financial markets worldwide panicked, as it became suddenly clear that no sufficient information was available to evaluate those securities in the changed environment.

The international financial crisis, that blew out in August 2007, went through five stages (BIS, 2009): (i) from the beginning to the Bear Stearns' rescue (August 2007–mid-March 2008); (ii) from the Bear Stearns' rescue to the bankruptcy of Lehman Brothers (mid-March 2008–mid-September 2008); (iii) from the bankruptcy of Lehman Brothers to the collapse of the international financial markets (mid-September 2008–end-October 2008); (iv) from the collapse of the financial markets to the world recession (end-October 2008–mid-March 2009); (v) from the world recession to the first signs of recovery (mid-March 2009–onwards).

1.2.1   Phase 1

On 9 August 2007, the subprime crisis became global: three European investment funds were frozen because it was impossible to determine the value of the securities linked to the US subprime mortgages in their portfolios. Therefore, panic became widespread on international financial markets. The high degree of opacity of structured financial instruments (mainly traded on unregulated or over-the-counter markets) made it impossible to single out just those assets related to subprime mortgages. Hence, a wide range of securities were no longer traded, liquidity disappeared from several markets, prices collapsed, bid-ask spreads increased, and stock markets recorded mounting losses.

The market for asset-backed commercial papers (ABCP) was the first one to be hit by the crisis. Rising insolvency rates on subprime mortgages reduced the quality of collaterals, thus increasing the interest rate spread on those securities, and also caused a significant drop in market transactions.

Hence, intermediaries operating in the shadow banking system could no longer roll-over short-term borrowing on commercial paper markets and were forced to draw on their credit lines with several US and European banks. Then, the crisis also affected commercial banks, whose difficulties became clear in the interbank market as counterparts were no longer willing to grant liquidity because of the fear they might need it too. Interbank interest rates (Euribor and Libor) rose to the point that central banks had to be involved. On 9 August 2007 the European Central Bank (ECB) undertook a short-term liquidity initiative worth 45 billion Euro, followed by five more initiatives, for a total value of 250 billion Euro. The FED also took similar measures. Nonetheless, interbank and commercial paper interest rates remained very high for the rest of the month.

On 19 September the crisis hit Northern Rock. The British bank was heavily relying on wholesale short-term funding and the lack of liquidity on international financial markets was challenging its solvency. Panicking depositors made long queues outside the bank's branches evoking movies recalling the Great Depression.

Market turmoil was temporarily eased by sovereign wealth funds' recapitalisation of the banks worst hit by the crisis. However, in November the situation got painful again as it became clear that total losses caused by the subprime mortgage crisis (approximately 200 billion dollars) were largely underestimated.

At this juncture, extraordinary measures were needed to avoid a dangerous deflationary spiral (see also Chapter 2 for how this relates to Minsky's instability hypothesis). Two options were available: (a) giving brokers the liquidity they needed, so that they would not be forced to sell some of their assets; (b) buying the securities that brokers were willing to sell, thus preventing a drop in prices. Initially the FED followed the first option, but lacking visible improvement, shortly after it followed the second option too. Moreover, the FED implemented various new monetary policy instruments to support financial markets. For instance, on 12 December it launched a Term Auction Facility (TAF) programme, targeted to commercial banks, with significant advantages compared to discount operations. As this instrument is used by the ECB on a regular basis, the ECB just made more short-term liquidity available to European banks, without changing its policy rate (see Chapter 9).

Following these initiatives, short-term interest rates recorded a significant reduction, but the situation got worse again at the end of January 2008. Financial markets were shocked by the potential downgrade of some major bond insurers. This prospect scared the markets which, between 21 and 22 January, reported unprecedented losses and forced the FED to further reduce its policy rate by 75 basis points in the first emergency meeting ever called since 1982.

After a period of apparent calm, new fears emerged in March. The liquidity crisis affected an increasing number of banks and on 11 March the FED announced a new credit line called Term Securities Lending Facility (TSLF). Moreover, a few days later, the FED, with the Primary Dealer Credit Facility (PDCF), committed itself to granting short-term loans also to investment banks. As the rate on this type of operation was the same applied to commercial banks at the discount window, this initiative marked the opening of FED facilities also to investment banks. This decision came under heavy scrutiny because investment banks were not subject to FED regulations and, in theory, would not be entitled to use public funds. During those days, markets experienced significant strains because of the difficulties of Bear Stearns. One of the five most important investment banks was in trouble because it could not roll-over its short-term loans due to the deterioration of its assets. Bear Stearns was a counterpart in many derivatives transactions and its bankruptcy might have started a dangerous domino effect. Thus, on 24 March JP Morgan Chase received 29 billion dollars from the FED to buy Bear Stearns and partially reassure the markets.

1.2.2   Phase 2

During this phase, the US financial system faced significant challenges. Liquidity problems turned into solvency problems, because subprime mortgages were just the tip of the iceberg and the prolonged downturn in house prices forced many investors to write-down a wide range of securities. Fannie Mae and Freddie Mac, the mortgage market giants, were badly hit by the crisis and in just a few months their market value went down by more than 70 per cent. So, on 7 September the US Treasury had to nationalise the two financial companies, which held more than 50 per cent of the mortgage loans originated in the US. The collapse of Fannie Mae and Freddie Mac intensified concern on the stability of the US financial system and operators shifted their attention to large investment banks. Lehman Brothers suffered the most because of its exposure to the real estate market through complex derivatives transactions. Markets were looking forward to some initiatives by US authorities, similar to the ones they had already undertaken for Bearn Stearns, but no such measure was taken. On 15 September Lehman Brothers, after being in business for 150 years, announced the largest bankruptcy in US history with 613 billion dollars liabilities.

1.2.3   Phase 3

Lehman's bankruptcy marked the beginning of the worst period of the crisis. On 16 September, the FED was forced to lend 85 billion dollars to AIG (American International Group). The largest insurance company in the world was on the edge of bankruptcy due to its hazardous dealing in Credit Default Swaps (CDS) derivatives offering counterparties insurance against default on many structured securities linked to the US real estate market.

Later on, the FED authorised Morgan Stanley and Goldman Sachs, the last two "pure" investment banks after Merrill Lynch had been bought by the Bank of America, to turn into commercial banks. This put an end to a form of capitalism that had been dominating Wall Street for more than 30 years (see Chapter 6 on the different contribution to financial instability by the various bank business models).

It became clear that resorting to ad hoc actions could not solve the crisis. In fact, a comprehensive strategy was needed to tackle the problem. During the last week of September, the Treasury Secretary Henry Paulson submitted a plan whereby the Government would buy the financial market securities that were causing the bankruptcy of many banks up to 700 billion dollars. The US Congress did not initially approve the plan, with subsequent losses on all international stock exchange markets (see Chapter 8 on how the drop in asset prices weakened financial intermediaries). The state of agitation continued even after the second week of October, when the plan was eventually passed.

At the end of September, the crisis hit the European financial system too. Lack of liquidity forced Iceland to nationalise the Glitnir bank, Germany to support Hypo Real Estate, Benelux to rescue the financial giant Fortis and support Dexia Group, the UK to nationalise Bradford & Bingley, Ireland to guarantee the deposits of the six main national banks (see also Chapter 7 for the role of international banks in the global transmission of the initial shock and Chapter 5 for this issue within the European context). On 8 October the British Government announced a plan to nationalise a significant portion of its banking system, worth more than 460 billion Euro (see Chapter 11 on government rescues of troubled financial intermediaries).

Between October and November, the subprime crisis completed its world tour contaminating also Asia and Latin America. The brisk global economic slowdown, through a sudden drop in the demand for raw materials, negatively impinged on those export-oriented economies like Chile, Peru, Argentina, Brazil and Venezuela; but even Australia, Japan and Singapore did not go unscathed.

1.2.4   Phase 4

In spite of timely and heavy government interventions, this phase was characterised by a significant degree of uncertainty on the stability of the international financial system.

Public financial stability plans encouraged stock markets' recovery, but the continuity of the recovery was still hindered by lack of specific details on the actions, the effects of the crisis on the real economy and the high degree of uncertainty about financial intermediaries' balance sheets. In January 2009, the International Monetary Fund (IMF) estimated 2,200 billion dollars of total write-downs related to the financial crisis.

Bearing in mind the experience of the Great Depression, central banks reacted jointly and consistently to the crisis. Within the context of a significant drop in aggregate demand and a drop in the inflation rate, policy rates were slashed to almost zero.

1.2.5   Phase 5

This phase was characterised by a slow return to normality in many key market segments: volatility abated, equity markets improved and the premium on corporate bonds decreased.

This retreating trend has been triggered by the fiscal and monetary efforts deployed to stop the crisis (see Chapter 10). More specifically, markets have welcomed the implementation of non-conventional monetary policies. On this front, central banks have resorted to three main instruments: (i) additional liquidity; (ii) establishment of extra reserves in commercial banks (quantitative easing); (iii) outright purchase of public or private bonds (credit easing). The first measure was undertaken already during the first three phases of the crisis to ease the liquidity crisis, while the last two were undertaken during phase 4 and phase 5 to reduce the medium and long-term interest rates.

In the summer of 2009 some encouraging signals (green shoots) emerged, indicating that probably the recession–deflation spiral had stopped. The oil price was rising again, industrial production had resumed growing in many areas in Asia and also business confidence bounced back. One of the most favourable signals was the Organisation for Economic Co-operation and Development (OECD) leading indicator, whose downtrend stopped. The indicator became again positive for the Euro zone and, though still negative, it showed some signs of improvement in the US and Japan.

1.3   ORIGIN OF THE CRISIS: MACRO ELEMENTS

Why did the crisis occur? For the sake of exposition, we classified the causes of the crisis as macroeconomic and microeconomic. Macroeconomic causes deal with global imbalances and low interest rates, while microeconomic causes address the impact of securitisation processes, financial regulation and the rating agencies.

1.3.1   Role of the Global Imbalances

Global imbalances are the first macroeconomic cause of the crisis. This problem was generated by the high and long-lasting current account deficit in the main industrialised countries, particularly the US, which was funded by massive capital inflows from the emerging economies.

The causes of the global imbalances remain the subject of a lively discussion. Some claim that the current account deficit might be due to the low savings ratio in industrialised countries, namely, the US, which requires the inflow of foreign capital to fund investments. Another option is that global imbalances – and the US deficit in particular – were caused by expectations of significant income growth in the US, which led the private sector to incur debts in order to smooth income over time. The third opinion is that insufficient domestic demand in the rest of the world, and in Asia in particular, caused an enormous capital inflow into industrialised countries. According to the fourth and most accredited explanation, the large current account deficits in developed countries were mainly due to: (i) increasing surplus in the raw material exporting countries, resulting from growing prices; (ii) increasing economic growth in Asia where saving propensity is high; (iii) increasing currency reserves of the Asian central banks to avoid another crisis, like the 1997 one. So, between 1997 and 2007, these trends significantly contributed to boost international savings, to the point of exceeding real investment potentials in these countries and causing a "saving glut", which then moved to industrialised countries (Bernanke, 2005).

Although the discussion on the causes of global imbalances is still open, the financial globalisation – that is, international financial markets being increasingly integrated – allowed surplus savings to flow to many industrialised countries, such as the US, the UK, Spain and Ireland. Having very low interest rates in these countries, investors searched for higher yields in different markets and real estate markets in particular. For example, Aizenman and Jinjarak (2009) analyse the situation in 43 countries (25 of which were OECD countries) between 1990 and 2005 and find a very strong positive correlation between current account deficits and real estate price increases: on average, a 4 per cent deficit increase is associated, over the years, with a nearly 10 per cent increase in real estate prices. Specifically, in the US house prices increased even more: while the current account deficit went up from 1.5 to above 6 percent of GDP over 1995–2005, household sector borrowings grew from 71 to 100 per cent of GDP and house prices more than doubled over 2000–06 (see also Chapter 4).

Besides fuelling a strong increase of real estate prices, the inflow of foreign capitals also weakened the relation between short-term interest rates, affected mainly by the domestic policy rate set by the central bank, and long-term rates influenced much more by international factors. The first signs of this weakness and its perils emerged a few years before the beginning of the crisis. Between 2001 and 2004, the possibility to cash the difference between the market value of property and the loan value, by using different types of funding such as home equity loans, allowed many American households to afford levels of consumption that would have otherwise been impossible. Thus, after the first half of 2004, the risk of deflation caused by the burst of the "dotcom" bubble seemed a distant memory; and there were even signs of overheating. To keep inflation under control, the FED raised the policy rate but, contrary to other phases of monetary tightening, long-term rates remained low and, to a large extent, neutralised the effectiveness of monetary restrictions. Even then, the president in charge of the FED, Alan Greenspan, was surprised and called the gap between the policy rates and long-term rates a conundrum (Wu, 2006). As a result, the costs of the fixed-rate loans remained substantially unchanged, the property boom continued, and the speculative bubble kept inflating.

1.3.2   Role of the FED's Monetary Policy

The overly easy monetary policy by the FED is the other macroeconomic cause of the financial crisis. The policy rate was kept too low for too long by the FED to ease the recessionary consequences following the burst of the "dotcom" bubble.

Two feedback mechanisms amplified the perverse effect of the overly easy monetary policy (see also Chapter 3).

The first circular mechanism, the balance sheet channel, is at work in the real estate market, where the supply of loans is closely related to the value of collateral assets. Specifically, very low interest rates reduced the cost of debt and increased the demand for houses. Therefore, real estate prices increased allowing households to get more credit, thanks to the rise of collateral values, which, in turn, inflated house prices even more. This because, in the short term, rapid growth of the demand for houses collides with a limited supply. In fact, at the beginning of the year 2000, in spite of the increasing efficiency of the US building sector, the technical time to build new houses was still long. As a result, house prices ballooned as shown by the Case-Shiller index that grew by more than 100 per cent between 2000 and 2006 (Figure 1.1).

The increasing employment rate following the 2001 recession, low interest rates and easier access to credit played a very important role, but were not enough to explain the huge house prices appreciation. Yale economist Robert Shiller claims that this is a typical example of a speculative bubble in which property prices increase so much because households and investors expect them to increase even more in the future. In his famous book *Irrational Exuberance*, Shiller describes a simplified model of bubbles based on the interaction between prices and expectations. According to the author, with a supply of houses relatively inelastic, that is, hardly reactive to the short-term price, fundamental factors like the increasing rate of employment and the availability of credit increase the demand and generate a remarkable growth of the market price. At this point, people searching high yield push up the demand for houses, because the gains grow very rapidly in the initial stages of the bubble. Thus, demand grows more than supply and paves the way to a period of steady price increases. Because of their irrational exuberance, some subjects believe that the price of property will keep growing indefinitely. Hence, more people invest in

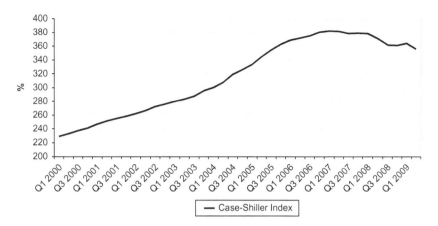

Source: Authors' elaborations on Thomson Datastream Data.

Figure 1.1   US home price indices

real estate, prices and appreciation expectations go up and the speculative bubble keeps inflating.

The second circular mechanism, the bank lending channel, is strictly linked to the spreading out of securitisations and is at work in financial markets: rising real estate prices increase the value of the financial assets originated via the securitisation of mortgages, in turn allowing financial intermediaries to raise additional funds to be invested in acquiring more assets. Usually, these new investments are in mortgage-securitisation-originated securities and, thus, contribute to raise the funds for granting new mortgages on the primary market.

This mechanism was very important in the subprime crisis and the following example is very useful to understand it (Adrian and Shin, 2008). Let's assume that a financial intermediary uses mark to market accounting (whereby the value of a financial instrument reflects the current market value of that instrument) and wishes to keep a leverage (defined as the ratio of total assets to equity) of 10. For example, he might have assets worth 100 Euro funded with 10 Euro of equity and 90 Euro of debt. Let's now have a look at the relationship between leverage and balance sheet size. If, for example, the value of the securities (assets) grows by 1 per cent, from 100 to 101 Euro, keeping the value of the bonds unchanged, the value of the equity gets to 11 Euro (10 + 1% of 100 = 11), while leverage drops to 9.18 (101 €/11 €). To keep leverage unchanged, the bank has to get funds and issue bonds to buy more securities, so that: total assets/shares = (101 + new securities)/11 = 10. The equation shows that the bank has to issue 9

Euro worth of bonds and use them to buy 9 Euro of securities. Hence, the 1 per cent security price increase has allowed the bank to issue new bonds, which have increased the assets value by 9 Euro.

As the price of securities goes up, the demand for them increases, rather than going down as would say the law of supply and demand. The growing demand increases securities price even more, thus triggering a process that, by reducing the leverage, pushes the price of securities up. The bank's balance sheet is now as follows: assets 110 Euro (securities), liabilities 110 (shares 11 € and bonds 99 €). If the price of securities drops to 109, keeping the value of the bonds unchanged, equity makes up for the reduction in the assets value and the bank's balance sheet is as follows: assets 109 Euro (securities) and liabilities 109 (shares 10 € and bonds 99 €). Leverage is now too high: (109/10) = 10.9 and, in order to get it back to 10, the bank has to sell securities that are worth 9 Euro and use the funds to pay off some of the issued bonds (deleverage), so that the values of the balance sheet are as follows: assets 100 Euro (securities) and liabilities 100 Euro (shares 10 € and bonds 90 €).

Also this mechanism is not in line with the law of supply and demand, because the price of securities goes down, but their supply increases. A negative sloped supply curve may trigger a circular process contrary to the one that was previously described: a drop in securities price increases the leverage level, pushes supply up and brings their price further down. This is the reason why the leverage of some intermediaries may cause pro-cyclical effects: during periods of price growth, increasing assets value pushes the demand for securities up, thus amplifies the upward trend. On the contrary, when prices drop, decreasing assets value pushes the supply of securities up amplifying the effect of the downward trend. Hence, leverage can be notably pro-cyclical and amplify the financial cycle. During the economic expansion between 2002 and 2006, US interest rates increased the banks' assets value and generated a surplus that had to be invested somehow, possibly on high-rating and high-yield instruments, such as senior tranches of CDOs, obtained from the securitisation of real estate loans.

The strong demand for these instruments made enormous amounts of new funds available for investments in real estate, but it also increased the market value of these securities, thus swelling financial operators' balance sheet. The availability of funds on the real estate market was so ample that mortgage originators, seeking loans available for securitisation, accepted significantly reducing their credit standards. As a consequence, rapid product and process innovation radically changed the US primary loan market. Before the beginning of the subprime crisis, it had become very common to obtain loans covering 100 per cent (or more) of the real estate value, to have loans granted for property already mortgaged (i.e., second line mortgage) and to obtain home equities loans. In particular, this last type of loans is quite usual at times of significant growth in real estate prices, as clients obtain funding – equal to the difference between the market value of the property and the value of the mortgage – to sustain their consumption.

From the loan origination point of view, the main innovation was in the Internet, which prevented many clients from going to banks and allowed them to provide limited documentation (low doc loans) or, in some cases, even unreliable documentation (liar loans). Mortgage brokers were very active in this field: they were not subject to strict financial supervision and, at the end of 2006, accounted for nearly 80 per cent of the new loans, twice the figure in 1996. As they profited to a large extent from commissions paid on the origination of loans, they did not have a long-term relation with their clients and were focused more on loan quantity than on loan quality. In addition, the possibility of grouping loans and selling them to other brokers relieved them of the burden to select clients accurately.

Without detailing all the products available in the US market, a differentiation should be made between prime mortgages, alternative-A mortgages and subprime mortgages. Prime mortgages are granted to clients with good payback features, while alternative-A mortgages go to those clients who declare high credit standards, but do not provide the needed documentation to prove it, so they might in effect be covert subprime mortgages. Finally, subprime mortgages are given to clients with low payback ability that are poor credit standards, which are considered as very risky clients. According to the most accredited definition provided by the Interagency Expanded Guidance for Subprime Lending Programs, typical subprime borrowers generally display a range of features, including one or more of the following: (a) two or more 30-day delinquencies in the last 12 months; (b) one or more 60-day delinquencies in the last 24 months; (c) judgment, foreclosure, repossession or charge-off in the prior 24 months; (d) bankruptcy in the last five years; (e) a credit score (FICO) of 660 or below; (f) debt service-to-income ratio of 50 per cent or greater. The growth of subprime and Alt-A mortgages, and related securities, was huge. For example, between 2001 and 2006, the value of originations increased by 215 per cent for subprime mortgages and by 566 per cent for alternative-A mortgages; likewise the issuance/origination ratio went up from 46 to 75 per cent for subprime mortgages and from 19 to 91 per cent for alternative-A mortgages (Ashcraft and Schuermann, 2008). Thus, the higher the number of originations, the fewer the loans in the balance sheets of those who originated them.

1.4   ORIGIN OF THE CRISIS: MICRO ELEMENTS

The subprime crisis also identified several microeconomic issues in the international financial system. The main problems are about securitisation processes, financial regulation and the rating agencies.

1.4.1   Securitisation Processes

Securitisation drastically changed the banking industry. Many financial intermediaries shifted from the "originate to hold" (OTH) to the "originate to distribute" (OTD) business model (Figure 1.2).

In the first model, loan origination is a simple operation that involves just two subjects: a bank and a borrower. The bank gets the funds from depositors and originates loans that it holds until their maturity. As the bank is exposed to the credit risk, it has strong incentives to accurately select borrowers (screening) and follow up their behaviour once the loan is granted (monitoring). On the contrary, in the second model loan

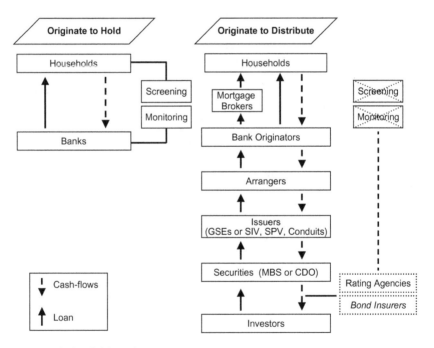

Source: Authors' elaborations.

Figure 1.2   Banking business models

origination is a more complex operation, similar to a production process, which involves several subjects. Upstream of the production chain, investors provide the funds that are needed to originate the loans; downstream, the bank grants loans to clients. Along this chain, many subjects – each of them specialised in a specific phase of the production process – use complex financial instruments to transfer the funds from investors to the bank and credit risk from the bank to investors. The main advantages of this business model are specialisation and risk distribution. On the one hand, specialisation favours: (i) a more efficient use of a bank's capital; (ii) a reduction of loan's cost; (iii) a high degree of financial innovation; (iv) an enlargement of clients eligible for a loan. On the other hand, the fact that many financial instruments – with different risk/return combinations – are issued renders the financial system more stable and allows investors to diversify their portfolios.

But the increase in efficiency has a cost, which sometimes could be very high. The transfer of the credit risk from banks to investors may distort the incentives of the "originate to distribute" model and create more low-quality loans. Moreover, due to their complexity, the risk of the financial instruments resulting from securitisations is very often difficult to evaluate. Errors made by the rating agencies in estimating the default probability of these instruments – which were too complex even for them – and investors' undue self-confidence in underwriting them reduced the stability of the international financial system.

In this framework, the US financial deregulation not only favoured the development of new loan types – questionable as they may be (for example the ninja mortgages granted to clients with no income, no job and no asset) – but also complicated the estimate of potential credit losses and the identification of the most exposed subjects. Therefore, it is not surprising that the defaults of the last link in the complex US financial chain (subprime clients) rapidly affected the whole sector. Lack of transparency of the instruments and players involved hindered the reduction of the exposure to the subprime mortgages and also entangled those intermediaries and financial instruments that were not closely related to the real estate market. Hence, the crisis started in a small segment of the US real estate credit market soon expanded to the whole US credit system and the wind of globalisation soon spread it to all the international markets.

Technical aspects of securitisation
Securitisation processes greatly exacerbated the effects of the US real estate bubble burst. Since the 1980s, this financial technique had been growing exponentially and expanded from real estate loans to many other sectors of the US financial system, such as credit card loans or loans to buy a car.

The securitisation can be divided into three phases: (a) identification of a group of homogeneous credits in the portfolio of a financial institution that – possibly through a broker – originated them (originator); (b) sale of credits to an ad hoc vehicle (conduit, SIV or SPV); (c) placement, by this vehicle, of asset-backed securities (ABS), whose interest rate payment and repayment when due depend on the cash flow generated by the underlying credits. For instance, in the case of securitisation of real estate loans, in phase 1 a bank (originator) issues the loans, which are then sold to another broker (arranger), who will also be entitled to get the cash flows of the loans and the collateral asset rights. In the second phase, the arranger groups the purchased loans and sells them to another subject (issuer), who has been specifically established to perform securitisation operations. In the third phase, the issuer issues the bonds backed by the purchased loans, whose cash flows match loan cash flows.

The bonds issued during the third phase are called structured bonds and can be classified as follows:

- Asset-backed commercial paper (ABCP);
- Mortgage-backed security (MBS) with residential mortgage-backed security (RMBS) or commercial mortgage-backed security (CMBS) depending on the collaterals type;
- Collateralised debt obligation (CDO) in which the ABS or MBS portfolios are securitised once again and are sliced into tranches. Depending on the type of collateral security, they can be further sub-classified as follows:
  - Collateralised mortgage obligation (CMO) guaranteed by residential mortgages;
  - Collateralised loans obligations (CLO) guaranteed by business loans;
  - CDO squared obligations, CDOs guaranteed by CDO obligations;
  - CDO cubed obligations, CDOs guaranteed by CDO squared obligations;
  - Synthetic CDO guaranteed by credit default swaps (CDS) portfolios. This instrument allows the special-purpose entity not to buy bonds, but rather to commit itself to paying back the nominal value of the MBS or CDO in case of default; receiving in exchange a quarterly premium.

Issuers can meet the different investors' risk propensity by splitting the bond issue into multiple tranches, each one with its specific risk-return profile. Junior tranches get higher yields, but are first in line to absorb losses, should borrowers default. Mezzanine tranches get lower yields than junior tranches, but are attacked only when the collateral security defaults exceed the junior tranche value. Finally, senior tranches get the lowest yields, but losses are recorded only if the default exceeds junior and mezzanine tranche values.

The tranching activity creates structured financial products whose risk is lower than that of the securitised assets average. This is the main justification to the significant growth in the issue of CDOs, whose senior tranches, also thanks to the triple A granted to them by rating agencies, were perceived by investors as risk-free bonds, with yields higher than those of the corporate obligations with equivalent ratings.

Specifically, the risk class of each tranche depends on two variables: degree of subordination and credit enhancement. The degree of subordination of a tranche is given by the total value of the lowest seniority tranche, while the most common level of credit enhancement is over-collateralisation. A common type of over-collateralisation is the creation of a tranche equity that is not placed on the market, but remains in the vehicle and is the first one to get losses, in case of a collateral default. Another type of over-collateralisation can be the creation of excess spread, resulting from the difference between the total yield of collateral securities and the yield of the obligations issued by the vehicle. In such a case, the first losses will be absorbed by this buffer and, should the losses be less than the excess spread, the difference will be assigned to the equity tranche; if the losses exceed the excess spread, the equity tranche does not get any premium and the other obligations will be attacked (according to their degree of subordination).

The possible relations between these instruments are shown in Figure 1.3. Initially, a special-purpose entity buys the subprime mortgages (1) and issues the mortgage-backed securities. The MBS are then bought by other entities, which use them as collateral securities to issue CDOs. High-quality tranches are used to issue high-grade CDOs (2), while low-quality ones are used to issue mezzanine grade CDOs (3). Finally, the low-quality tranches of the mezzanine CDOs are bought by another vehicle that uses them as collateral securities to issue the squared CDOs (4).

It should be kept in mind that senior tranches are less risky than other tranche types, only if the correlation between the collaterals default is low. For example, if the assets are 100 loans, all of them issued to very low-income households in the suburbs of New York, it is very likely that all the families will default at the same time should an economic slow-down occur. As a consequence, even the CDO senior tranches will probably get losses. On the contrary, should the 100 loans be issued to different clients, with very low to very high incomes in 100 different cities, the likelihood that all the clients default concurrently, should an economic slow-down

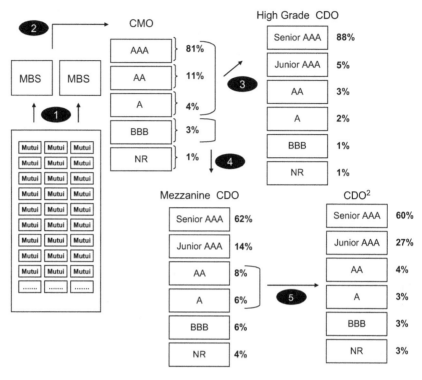

Figure 1.3   *MBS: mortgage-backed security, CMO: collateralised
                mortgage obligation, CDO: collateralised debt obligation*

occur, is much lower. In such a case the senior tranches are less risky than
the others.

Government-Sponsored Enterprises (GSEs) were the first issuers of
mortgage-backed securities. These government companies, like Fannie
Mae and Freddie Mac, buy loans from the originator banks and issue
MBS guaranteeing the cash flows on these instruments, in case of borrowers' default. For a long time this mechanism had granted liquidity
to banks on the primary market, and also developed a large secondary
market of MBS. Thanks to their crucial role, GSEs had always benefited
from the implicit guarantee of the US Treasury, which became explicit in
July 2008, allowing them to collect funds by issuing bonds (agency debt)
at a rate only slightly higher than that on Treasury bonds. However, to
minimise moral hazard behaviour, the US Treasury allows the GSE to

buy just conforming loans, that is, good-quality loans which meet specific requirements, for instance, in terms of size and loan to value ratio.

Until the mid-1990s, Fannie Mae and Freddie Mac controlled almost all the market of MBS. However, later on a shadow banking system emerged, challenging GSEs. Non-bank intermediaries like SIVs, SPVs, Conduits, investment banks and hedge funds got in the securitisation business. Most of the intermediaries that operate in the shadow banking system use short-term funding to make long-term investments, such as structured bonds. They share with traditional banks many features, such as asset maturity transformation, but operate in the shadow of the financial regulation. Their low degree of capitalisation gives them a powerful leverage effect, but also renders them very fragile. This explains why the liquidity crisis erupted in August 2007, exactly in the shadow banking system, turned quickly into a solvency crisis with enormous systemic effects, amplified by opacity of the instruments, financial techniques and operators involved.

1.4.2 Financial Regulation

Basel I regulation contributed to the growth of securitisation by assigning lower capital charges to securitised assets (Demirguc-Kunt and Serven, 2010). Hence, to reduce regulatory capital in the years before the crisis, many US banks established some special-purpose entities to which they could sell the originated loans through securitisation (Acharya and Richardson, 2009). Special-purpose entities funded the procurement of the loans by using ABCP guaranteed by the sponsoring bank. This guarantee has two important effects: first, the special-purpose entity can collect funds with low interest rates because the rating agencies give high rates to ABCP thanks to the bank's guarantee. Second, no capital charge is expected from the bank if the guarantee refers to ABCP with a less than 12-month maturity (the most common on the market).

1.4.3 Credit Rating Agencies

Financial regulation's reliance on ratings gave a significant contribution to the development of securitisation and, as a consequence, to the activity of the rating agencies.

The capital charge of banks, insurance companies, broker-dealers and pension funds depend on the rating level of their assets: the higher the rating, the smaller the regulatory capital they need. The demand for high rated and high yield instruments encouraged the growth of structured bonds, because by creating different types of tranches it is possible to issue many bonds with a rating higher than that of the average pool of securitised assets. In 2007 outstanding structured bonds amounted to almost 11,000 billion dollars, circa 35 per cent of the total US bond market; 60 per cent of them were triple A. This is a very high value if one considers that less than 1 per cent of the corporate bonds had such a rating (Fitch Ratings, 2007).

However, since July 2007, the quality of structured bonds rapidly decreased: in November of that year there were more than 2,000 down-grades, with 500 tranches downgraded more than ten notches (i.e., from AAA to BB+, since the one notch downgrade is between two contiguous grades). The downtrend continued in 2008, too, with more than 11,000 downgrades of structured bonds that had been given a triple A (Benmelech and Dlugosz, 2009). CDOs were the most badly hit; in fact, they were the core cause of loss of the main international financial institutions involved in the crisis. Because of the numerous downgrades, investors no longer trusted the rating system and the demand for structured bonds, which is highly dependent on the rating, collapsed. In 2008 private MBS, CDO and ABS issues decreased by 96, 88 and 82 per cent, respectively.

The main rating agencies were harshly criticised for declaring some bonds nearly risk-free (triple A), which then defaulted a few months later. The main cause of this debacle is probably the deep conflict of interest in the rating industry. On agencies' side, receiving the fees from the subjects who ask the rating can be an incentive to overestimate the quality of the bonds in order to meet the issuers' rather than the investors' needs (in literature this phenomenon is referred to as rating inflation). On firms' side, the possibility to be rated by multiple agencies and communicate only the highest rating to the market is like going shopping for the agency that is willing to grant the best rating. Moreover, some agencies also provide con-sulting services on how to organise the issues and structure the tranches to get the highest possible rating.

NOTES

1. This chapter partly draws on a more comprehensive explanation of the GFC published in V. D'Apice and G. Ferri (2010), *Financial Instability: Toolkit for Interpreting Boom and Bust Cycles*, Palgrave Macmillan Studies in Banking and Financial Institutions.
2. The pandemic crisis triggered by the spread of the COVID-19 virus is not analysed in depth in this book. Indeed, the shock originated outside the financial system and thus cannot be classified as a financial shock. However, given its importance, many parts of the book analyse its possible effects on the financial system.

REFERENCES

Acharya V.V., and Richardson M. (2009), Causes of the Financial Crisis, *Critical Review*, 21, pp. 195–210.

Adrian T., and Shin S.H. (2008), Liquidity and Financial Cycles, BIS working paper no. 256.

Aizenman J., and Jinjarak Y. (2009), Current Account Patterns and National Real Estate Markets, *Journal of Urban Economics*, 66 (2), pp. 75–89.

Ashcraft A.B., and Schuermann T. (2008), Understanding the Securitization of Subprime Mortgage Credit, Federal Reserve Bank of New York Staff Reports, no. 318.

Benmelech E., and Dlugosz J. (2009), The Alchemy of CDO Credit Ratings, *Journal of Monetary Economics*, 56 (5), pp. 617–34.

Bernanke B.S. (2005), The Global Saving Glut and the US Current Account Deficit, Remarks at the Sandridge Lecture, Virginia Association of Economics, Richmond (VA).

BIS – Bank for International Settlements (2009), *79th Annual Report: 1 April 2008–31 March 2009*, Basel, 29 June.

D'Apice V., and Ferri G. (2010), *Financial Instability: Toolkit for Interpreting Boom and Bust Cycles*, Palgrave Macmillan Studies in Banking and Financial Institutions, Houndmills, Basingstoke.

Demirguc-Kunt A., and Serven L. (2010), Are all the Sacred Cows Dead? Implications of the Financial Crisis for Macro and Financial Policies, *The World Bank Research Observer* 25 (1), pp. 91–124.

Fitch Ratings (2007), Inside the Ratings: What Credit Ratings Mean, http://www.securitization.net/pdf/Fitch/CreditRatings_7Aug07.pdf (accessed 10 August 2008).

Shiller R. (2000), *Irrational Exuberance*, Princeton University Press, Princeton.

Wu T. (2006), Globalization's Effect on Interest Rates and the Yield Curve, Federal Reserve Bank of Dallas, Economic Letter no. 9.

2. Minsky's financial instability hypothesis

Maria Nikolaidi

2.1 INTRODUCTION

Since the Global Financial Crisis, Minsky's financial instability hypothesis (FIH) has been receiving growing attention in macroeconomic analyses and policy making. Many commentators termed the Global Financial Crisis a 'Minsky moment' (e.g. The Economist, 2016). More recently, the former Governor of the Bank of England, Mark Carney (2015), talked about the possibility of a 'climate Minsky moment' as a result of an abrupt transition to a low-carbon economy.

Minsky developed his FIH primarily in the 1970s and the 1980s. A key aim of Minsky was to conceptualise the inherent instability of the economic system that stems from debt relationships and continuous institutional change. By doing so he departed from conventional approaches that analyse economic and financial issues through an 'equilibrium' lens. Since the 1980s, many economists have modelled different dimensions of the FIH and have further developed the theoretical underpinnings of Minsky's framework, taking into account the transformations and developments in the global financial system that we have seen over the last decades. More recently, research has attempted to examine empirically specific aspects of the FIH, while the interest in climate-induced financial instability à la Minsky is constantly increasing.

The aim of this chapter is to discuss Minsky's FIH based on Minsky's original writings and the rich Minskyan literature. I first explain the key perspectives of the FIH (Section 2.2) as well as the different aspects of financial fragility and the factors that can lead to an endogenous increase in this fragility (Section 2.3). I then focus on how policy interventions can tame (or not) financial instability (Section 2.4) and I explain how Minsky's framework can be useful for understanding the financial instability that might emerge from climate change (Section 2.5). Section 2.6 outlines avenues for future research on Minsky's FIH.

2.2 'STABILITY IS DESTABILISING'

Minsky's FIH can be summarised by the phrase 'stability is destabilising' (see Minsky, 1975, 1982, 1986 [2008], 1992; Wray and Tymoigne, 2009). There are two reasons why stability can be a source of instability. The first one is linked to the way that financial agents form expectations. During boom periods, when economic growth is high and the economy is perceived to be stable, both banks and firms tend to have euphoric expectations that induce them to participate in more debt contracts. This can result in higher indebtedness.

Minsky captured this by making a distinction between three finance regimes: hedge, speculative and Ponzi. A hedge finance regime refers to the case in which an economic unit has monetary inflows that are expected to be higher than the sum of the interest payments and principal repayments. As a result, debt financing is not necessary for the repayment of the accumulated debt – this is why the hedge regime is considered to be the more stable one. A speculative unit has expected inflows that can cover the interest payments but not the principal repayment. As a result, a speculative unit is expected to take on new debt in order to cover part of its repayment commitments. A Ponzi unit is a unit that can fulfil neither the interest nor the principal repayment commitments. Such a unit is therefore the most financially fragile one.

In Minsky's framework periods of stability lead both borrowers and lenders to take more risks. Consequently, hedge units are gradually transformed into speculative or Ponzi ones. The higher the proportion of speculative and Ponzi units in the economy, the more financially fragile such an economy can be. Once the level of indebtedness has been sufficiently high, some borrowers might be unable to repay their debt triggering a period of financial instability. During this period asset prices are declining, default rates are increasing and economic activity is contracting. Without proper government intervention, this period of financial instability can be transformed into a prolonged recession.

The second reason why stability is destabilising is institutional transformation. Stability can bring about instability not only because of behaviour-driven credit expansions, but also because it can cause institutional and policy changes that might render the system more fragile. For example, Minsky focused a lot of attention on how the post-World War II stability led to a gradual transformation of the global financial system towards 'money manager capitalism' whereby private financial institutions (like investment banks, hedge funds and money market funds) are the dominant actors in the economic system and tend to destabilise it through activities that seek high financial returns (Palley, 2011; Wray, 2011).

Such institutional transformations can be analysed with reference to what Minsky termed 'thwarting mechanisms': government interventions, policy regimes and customs that intend to stabilise the macrofinancial system (see Ferri and Minsky, 1992; Palley, 2011; Dafermos et al., 2020). Thwarting mechanisms include counter-cyclical fiscal policy, financial regulation, wage policies or policy frameworks that are meant to control inflation. Although these thwarting mechanisms can initially be successful in achieving stability, they might gradually be eroded for example because of innovations made by profit-seeking economic agents or because the designers of these institutions decide to make the institutions and policy interventions less strict due to the general sense of 'stability'.

Dafermos et al. (2020) argue that the endogenous change in the effectiveness of thwarting mechanisms can give rise to institutional supercycles. At the initial phase of a supercycle, the institutional and policy setting is able to prevent a significant increase in macrofinancial fragility and can ensure that recessions caused by real or financial factors do not lead to depressions. However, as thwarting mechanisms become less effective, it is more likely that economies will experience a severe economic and financial crisis. After such a crisis, a new supercycle might kick off if a new set of thwarting mechanisms is established.

There are three key features in Minsky's FIH that make it unique compared to conventional approaches to the causes of financial crises. First, Minsky views the financial system as a network of interconnected balance sheets that interact dynamically with macroeconomic factors within a non-equilibrium setting (see also Gabor, 2020 and Chapters 5 and 7). Financial instability is the endogenous result of this dynamic interaction. Although exogenous shocks can play a role in triggering financial instability, in the Minskyan framework financial crises are primarily explained by the endogenous increase in financial fragility. This, for example, departs from the way that financial issues have been analysed in Dynamic Stochastic General equilibrium (DSGE) models, which represent the dominant way of thinking about the macroeconomy. In a recent review of the DSGE literature Galí (2018, p. 107) pointed out that:

> none of the extensions of the New Keynesian model proposed in recent years seem to capture an important aspect of most financial crises – namely, a gradual build-up of financial imbalances leading to an eventual 'crash' characterized by defaults, sudden-stops of credit flows, asset price declines, and a large contraction in aggregate demand, output, and employment. Most of the extensions found in the literature share with their predecessors a focus on equilibria that take the form of stationary fluctuations driven by exogenous shocks.

Second, in Minsky's framework money is endogenous (see Wray, 2015). In other words, banks endogenously create money whenever they decide to provide credit to creditworthy borrowers (see Lavoie, 2014; McLeay et al., 2014). In a world of endogenous money, financial fluctuations are much stronger since the changes in the willingness of borrowers and lenders to enter into new debt contracts has strong effects on consumption and investment. This is not the case in conventional accounts of money and finance where banks are viewed as financial intermediaries – this by definition restricts their impact on economic activity (see Jakab and Kumhof, 2019 for a discussion on this).

Third, in Minsky's FIH, institutional change and policies interact with macroeconomic and financial factors. Typically, models of financial instability confine their attention to how financial crises might happen within a given institutional setting. On the contrary, Minsky provides a much deeper understanding of financial instability that takes explicitly into account evolutionary changes that affect the stabilising role of institutions and the profit-seeking behaviour of economic agents (see Wray, 2011; Argitis, 2019; Dafermos et al., 2020).

2.3 THE DIFFERENT SHADES OF FINANCIAL FRAGILITY

How can economies become financially fragile? Financial fragility is connected with the accumulation of debt. The Minskyan literature has focused on three types of debt: (i) corporate debt; (ii) household debt; and (iii) external debt.[1] I will explain what can drive the rise in each of these types of debt and how debt accumulation can lead to instability.[2]

2.3.1 Corporate Debt

Most Minskyan macroeconomic models have analysed the fragility that stems from corporate debt using this setting as a starting point: Firms undertake investment driven primarily by expected sales and profitability. The part of investment spending that is not covered by retained profits is financed through loans. Banks typically provide these loans on demand. Households consume part of their income without taking on consumer debt.

Why do firms over-accumulate debt in this setting and how can this over-accumulation lead to financial instability? Consider first the case in which the interest rate is constant. In a period in which there is high perceived economic stability and the default rate is relatively low, firms have a tendency to increase their debt-financed investment.[3] This can cause an increase in firms' leverage, which is a proxy of financial fragility. Once the leverage ratio has reached a sufficiently high level, there is a negative impact on investment which causes a reduction in economic activity. This dynamic interaction between leverage and investment can give rise to instability (see e.g. Jarsulic, 1990; Dutt, 1995; Lavoie, 1995; Charles, 2016) and real-financial cycles (see e.g. Foley, 1987; Semmler, 1987; Jarsulic, 1989; Skott, 1994; Yilmaz and Stockhammer, 2019).

In the Minskyan literature, the fragility of firms has not only been analysed through firm leverage ratios. Many macro models have made an explicit distinction between hedge, speculative and Ponzi finance regimes using either aggregate macro models (see e.g. Lima and Meirelles, 2007; Charles, 2008a; Ferri and Variato, 2010; Nishi, 2012; Sasaki and Fujita, 2012) or agent-based models (see e.g. Michell, 2014; Caiani et al., 2016; Di Guilmi and Carvalho, 2017; Jump et al., 2017; Pedrosa and Lang, 2018; Reissl, 2020).

The Minskyan theoretical framework about corporate debt-driven financial fragility raises three empirical questions: (i) is the leverage ratio of firms pro-cyclical?; (ii) does firm leverage have a negative impact on investment?; (iii) can we observe cycles that are driven by corporate debt?

The pro-cyclicality or not of the leverage ratio (or proxies of it) has been the subject of many empirical studies. The results are quite mixed. Wolfson (1990) showed that ahead of the US stock market crash in 1987 there was an increase in the corporate net interest payments to gross capital income. However, Lavoie and Seccareccia (2001) did not find any supportive evidence for an increasing leverage ratio for the G-7 countries over the period 1971–97, while Pedrosa (2019) showed that there was no increase in the aggregate leverage ratio for the US between 1970 and 2014. Similarly, Isenberg (1989) did not find any evidence of increasing financial fragility (which was measured by various debt ratios) at the aggregate level for the US for the period ahead of the Great Depression, but found some supportive evidence of Minsky's FIH for small firms. The lack of a pro-cyclical leverage in some empirical studies has often been linked with the 'paradox of debt': although firms increase their debt-financed investment, the positive macroeconomic impact of higher investment on the sales of firms can actually reduce firm's indebtedness (see Lavoie and Seccareccia, 2001; Toporowski, 2008; Passarella, 2012; Lavoie, 2014).

How about empirical studies that have used Minsky's distinction between hedge, speculative and Ponzi firms? Their results are mixed as well.[4] Focusing on the US, Mulligan (2013) found that between 2001 and 2009 the proportion of speculative and Ponzi firms increased over the upturn and declined over the downturn of the business cycle in some industries, like mining, manufacturing and transportation, but not in other industries, like agriculture, utilities and real estate. Davis et al. (2019) analysed the US economy over the period 1970–2014 and did not find a strong relationship between aggregate downturns and the probability of being Ponzi. This is broadly corroborated by Pedrosa (2019) who also used data for the US over the same period. However, it is interesting that Davis et al. (2019) documented a secular increase of Ponzi firms since the 1970s. In the case of Japan (1975–2015), Nishi (2019) did not find evidence of a pro-cyclical increase in Ponzi finance.

Regarding the impact of indebtedness on investment, Ndikumana (1999) showed that the debt service ratio negatively affected investment in the US over the period 1972–91. Arza and Español (2008) found that sufficiently high leverage ratios had a negative impact on investment in Argentina over the period 1992–2001. Similarly, Caldentey et al. (2019), whose empirical analysis covered large Latin American countries over the period 2009–16, showed that the leverage ratio had a negative effect on investment once the leverage ratio passes a threshold.

Stockhammer et al. (2019a) investigated simultaneously the pro-cyclicality of the leverage ratio and the effects of the leverage ratio on investment, in an attempt to identify whether corporate debt cycles have emerged in seven Organisation for Economic Co-operation and Development (OECD) economies. They found evidence in favour of such cycles in Canada and the UK over the period 1970–2015. In a similar study, Stockhammer et al. (2019b) focused on the US (1889–2015) and the UK (1882–2010), finding supportive evidence of corporate debt cycles only for the US.

How does the story about corporate debt-driven financial fragility change when an endogenous interest rate is considered? An endogenous interest rate can act as an additional source of financial fragility since it can increase the interest payments of firms during the upturn of the economic cycle. Minskyan models have assumed that the interest rate is a positive function of the leverage ratio of firms (e.g. Keen, 1995; Asada, 2001; Charles, 2008a; Lojak, 2018; Giri et al., 2019; Reissl, 2020), of economic activity (e.g. Lima and Meirelles, 2007; Fazzari et al., 2008) or of the financial position of both the lenders and the borrowers (Delli Gatti et al., 2010). Stockhammer et al. (2019a) have found evidence in favour of real-financial cycles between GDP and interest rate for Australia and the US over the period 1970–2015.

Interest rate-driven economic fluctuations in a Minskyan framework share some similarities with the ones that can be found in the financial accelerator literature (see e.g. Bernanke and Gertler, 1990; see also Chapter 3). In the financial accelerator framework changes in the external finance premium can amplify and propagate shocks to the macroeconomy.[5] This is so because the external finance premium depends inversely on the net worth of borrowers. Since borrowers' net worth is pro-cyclical, the external finance premium goes down during upswings and goes up during downturns. Although the financial accelerator framework has been developed within New Keynesian models where output is supply-driven and money is not endogenous, financial accelerator-type mechanisms can also be found in Minskyan demand-side models (see e.g. Delli Gatti et al., 2010; Giri et al., 2019; Reissl, 2020).

Financial fragility has also been analysed within more sophisticated Minskyan frameworks in which stock prices change in an endogenous way, wages change during the economic cycle, the retention rate of firms is endogenous and banks play a more active role in the provision of credit. I briefly describe these additional sources of financial fragility in turn.

Some Minskyan models have focused explicitly on the role of stock prices and the interaction of stock prices with corporate debt (see e.g. Franke and Semmler, 1989; Delli Gatti and Gallegati, 1990; Delli Gatti et al., 1994; Ryoo, 2010, 2013a; Chiarella and di Guilmi, 2011).[6] During boom periods, investors might increase their demand for stocks given that they expect that prices will go up. This boosts stock prices, working as a self-fulfilling prophecy. Higher stock prices have macroeconomic effects since they can positively affect the consumption of households via a wealth channel and they can increase investment via Tobin's Q. Moreover, higher stock prices can induce more corporate debt expansion.

Many Minskyan models have investigated the way that corporate debt might interact with endogenous changes in income distribution, in particular the distribution of income between wages and profits (see e.g. Keen, 1995; Grasselli and Costa Lima, 2012; Sordi and Vercelli, 2014; Stockhammer and Michell, 2017; Bastidas et al., 2019). In line with the analysis of Goodwin (1967), cycles might arise because of the impact that economic activity and employment might have on wages. For example, during the upturn of the economic cycle, a relatively low unemployment rate induces workers to demand higher wages, putting a downward pressure on the profits of firms, on top of the pressure placed by higher interest payments.

The dividend policies of firms can be an additional source of financial fragility. In some Minskyan models firms are portrayed to increase the dividends that they provide to shareholders when their profitability is high and/or their indebtedness is low (see e.g. Charles, 2008b; Yilmaz and Stockhammer, 2019; Reissl, 2020). By doing so they can gradually increase their reliance on debt, contributing to the rise of financial fragility. The pro-cyclicality of dividends is in line with the findings of empirical studies (see e.g. Benito and Young, 2003; Abdulkadir et al., 2016).

In other Minskyan models the behaviour of banks plays a prominent role (see Ryoo, 2013b; Nikolaidi, 2014). The key argument is that banks affect in an active way the accumulation of corporate debt. During periods of perceived stability, credit supply increases because banks feel more confident about both their own and the borrowers' financial position. The opposite holds when the economy undergoes a recession. This endogenous change in the quantity credit rationing of banks can amplify economic cycles.

2.3.2 Household Debt

Minsky did not analyse household debt in his FIH. However, household debt has been the focus of many Minskyan models. To begin with, there are Minskyan models that analyse the way through which household debt interacts with income distribution (see Palley, 1994, 1997; Dutt, 2006; Charpe et al., 2009; Kapeller and Schütz, 2014; Ryoo and Kim, 2014; Kapeller et al., 2018; Giraud and Grasselli, 2021). In these models it is typically assumed that low-income households take on debt to increase their spending. They do so since they wish to emulate the consumption of high-income households.[7] Although this has initially a positive effect on aggregate consumption (since low-income households have a higher propensity to consume out of income), the accumulation of debt and the increase in the interest payments of low-income households increases financial fragility. Interestingly, the more low-income households take on debt to cover consumption expenditures, the higher *ceteris paribus* is the reduction in their disposable income due to interest payments. At the same time, the interest paid on consumer debt might increase the income of high-income households (since the high-income households might receive the distributed profits of banks). This increases income inequality, inducing a further increase in the propensity of low-income households to take on debt. Once the indebtedness of low-income households has reached a sufficiently high level, economic activity starts going down, for example because banks might decide to reduce the provision of new consumer loans or because the interest rate charged to households might start increasing.[8]

This story is in line with the empirical evidence provided by Palley (1994) and Kim (2013, 2016) which shows that a rise in household debt has initially a positive effect on economic activity, but this effect becomes subsequently negative. It is also in line with the analysis in Cynamon and Fazzari (2008, 2016) and Barba and Pivetti (2009) who argue that increasing income inequality contributed to the rise in the indebtedness of the US household sector (see also Chapter 4).

Moreover, Minskyan models have paid attention to the interaction between the housing market and household debt.[9] One such model has been developed by Ryoo (2016). In this model households' investment in the housing market is induced by the belief that housing prices will go up (see also Chapter 1 on how, in the run-up to the Global Financial Crisis, only the expectation of constantly rising housing prices could deliver mortgages to subprime clients, who may be viewed as Ponzi borrowers). As investment in the housing market increases, housing prices go up even further, increasing the value of houses that are used as a collateral for bank borrowing. As bank borrowing increases, the demand for houses increases even more. In that way, housing prices and household credit reinforce each other. Higher household indebtedness can be a source of financial fragility and cycles.

Nikolaidi (2015) has modelled the interaction between household debt, housing prices and income distribution, focusing on the role of securitisation. In this model an increase in the use of securitisation can kick off an endogenous process that makes the economy more financially fragile, leading ultimately to instability. More precisely, an increase in the securitisation of mortgage-backed securities (MBSs) induces banks to provide more loans to low-income households. At some point, the indebtedness of low-income households becomes sufficiently high, inducing banks to reduce their credit provision since the demand for MBSs goes down. Once this happens, housing and MBS prices start declining and economic activity becomes lower, triggering financial instability. When the increase in securitisation is accompanied by a decline in the wage share, the expansionary period is shorter and instability is reinforced. Botta et al. (2021) have also developed a similar model which shows that the securitisation of household debt can lead to both higher financial fragility and higher inequality.

2.3.3 External Debt

External debt, and especially foreign currency denominated debt, can be a significant source of financial fragility in an open economy framework. Many scholars have analysed this source of fragility by extending Minsky's closed economy framework to an open economy setting.

Kregel (1998) and Arestis and Glickman (2002) have explained that when a domestic economy, which is open to capital inflows, experiences an economic boom combined with domestic currency appreciation, both the domestic private sector and foreign lenders might reduce their desired margins of safety. This is so because there is an increasing confidence that the economy will continue to perform well, increasing the appetite for more risky credit expansion, a large proportion of which is in the form of foreign denominated debt.

However, as the economy expands, the current account balance deteriorates and external debt is accumulated, financial fragility increases and instability might emerge. For instance, at some point, the increasing external debt might raise doubts among lenders about the ability of borrowers to repay it. This can result in capital outflow that can lead to exchange rate depreciation. Moreover, as argued by Kaltenbrunner (2015), the accumulation of foreign denominated debt increases the demand of borrowers for the foreign currency since they need to ensure that they will manage to repay their debt without problems. This can reinforce the depreciation forces especially in countries that have a subordinated position in the international monetary hierarchy.

Currency depreciation can reduce the ability of domestic borrowers to repay their foreign denominated debt. The situation might become worse if the monetary authorities respond to the depreciation by increasing the interest rate. In this case, interest payments might go up, increasing the number of Ponzi economic units in the economy.

Kregel (1998) and Arestis and Glickman (2002) used such a Minskyan perspective to explain the 1997–98 Southeast Asian financial crisis. De Paula and Alves (2000) and Gallardo et al. (2006) used similar Minskyan insights to analyse the 1998–99 Brazilian currency crisis and 1994 financial crisis in Mexico, respectively. A key argument of these studies is that, while such financial crises can be magnified by exogenous shocks, they should primarily be seen as the result of endogenous processes.

Kohler (2019) has recently developed a Minskyan model that shows how endogenous cycles can arise in emerging market economies (EMEs) through the interaction between flexible exchange rate dynamics and balance sheet effects. In this model currency appreciation results in an investment boom since this appreciation improves the financial position of domestic firms, inducing capital inflows. However, the investment boom triggers an increase in imports, deteriorating at some point the trade balance. This ultimately leads to currency depreciation and capital outflows, causing a decline in investment.[10]

However, endogenous cycles à la Minsky can arise in an open economy framework even in the case in which the exchange rate is not flexible. For instance, Foley (2003) has developed a model in which an endogenous change in the interest rate (because of central bank policy) is sufficient to trigger refinancing problems for firms that rely on external debt. Moreover, Dafermos (2018) has shown how endogenous cycles can emerge as a result of endogenous changes in the target debt ratio of the domestic private sector. These changes in the target debt ratio are driven by the expectations of both the foreign lenders and the domestic borrowers.

2.4   HOW CAN AN UNSTABLE ECONOMY BE STABILISED?

Both Minsky and Minskyan scholars have suggested several policies that can prevent financial fragility and contain financial instability. First, in Minskyan analyses the government needs to be large enough to be in a position to play a stabilising role by increasing spending and reducing taxes during periods of high economic activity, and doing the opposite during economic booms when the expectations of lenders and borrowers are euphoric (see also Chapter 10). Many Minskyan models have shown that counter-cyclical fiscal policy can indeed play a stabilising role (e.g. Keen, 1995; Nasica and Raybaut, 2005; Nikolaidi, 2014; Dafermos, 2018; Kapeller et al., 2018; Reissl, 2020). However, while counter-cyclical fiscal policy can reduce economic fluctuations, it does not necessarily eliminate them.

Second, employment programmes are a key component of Minsky's policy recommendations (see Minsky, 1986 [2008]; Papadimitriou and Wray, 1998). In particular, Minsky was an advocate of employer of last resort (ELR) programmes that guarantee a public sector job to those who are unable to find a job in the private sector. Minsky was more in favour of such programmes instead of transfer payments. He was of the view that the provision of public employment at a wage rate that is lower than the one provided in the private sector would be less inflationary and stabilising than the provision of transfers. This is so primarily because the latter tend to increase aggregate demand without necessarily increasing supply; on the contrary, employment programmes generate directly additional output.[11]

Third, Minsky viewed the lender-of-last-resort interventions of central banks as a significant stabilising mechanism (see also Chapter 9). However, he emphasised at the same time that central banks should take action in preventing speculative and Ponzi finance. Otherwise, their interventions might validate financial innovations that destabilise the financial system (see Argitis, 2013, 2017; Kregel, 2014a). Minsky was always in favour of a 'macroprudential' approach to financial regulation, according to which the interactions between the macrofinancial system and individual financial institutions are analysed as a whole. Since the Global Financial Crisis, such an approach has become fashionable (see also Basel III and Chapter 13). However, as explained by Kregel (2014b), the Basel III regulatory framework has not explicitly incorporated Minsky's view on the crucial role of endogenous evolutionary change and the endogenous tendency of the financial system to instability.

Minskyan models have examined the effects of specific aspects of macroprudential regulation. For example, Ryoo (2013b) has shown that Minsky's (1986 [2008]) proposal about the containment of bank leverage through the control of banks' dividend policy can be conducive to stability. Kapeller et al. (2018) have developed a Minsky-Veblen model in which they analyse the impact of a financial regulatory reform that increases household credit provision to changes in bank leverage. They show that such a reform reduces household indebtedness. Although this makes lower the amplitude of the cycles, it increases their frequency.[12]

Fourth, Minsky was in favour of policies that support small and medium-sized firms and a decentralised banking system with many small and independent banks (see Minsky, 1986 [2008] and Papadimitriou and Wray, 1998). He argued that a decentralised banking system where small banks finance small and medium-sized firms encourages more stable and sustainable borrower-lender relationships than what is the case in systems in which big banks play a dominant role (see also Chapter 6). In this context, he developed proposals about community development banking (see Minsky et al., 1993). He also argued that industrial policies that favour smaller firms are conducive to high employment – a key target of Minsky's policy recommendations – since such firms tend to use less capital-intensive production techniques.

All these Minskyan policy recommendations should, however, be viewed with caution. Minsky was not of the view that a static implementation of his policy proposals would safeguard long-run stability in capitalism even if some of these policies are initially effective. As he explains:

> Even as I warn against the handwaving that passes for much of policy prescription I must warn the reader that I feel much more comfortable with my diagnosis of what ails our economy and analysis of the causes of our discontents than I do with the remedies I propose. We need to embark on a program of serious change even as we need to be aware that a once and for-all resolution of the flaws in capitalism cannot be achieved. Even if a program of reform is successful, the success will be transitory. Innovations, particularly in finance, assure that problems of instability will continue to crop up; the result will be equivalent but not identical bouts of instability to those that are so evident in history. (Minsky, 1986 [2008], p. 319)

2.5   MINSKY MEETS CLIMATE CHANGE

Central banks and financial supervisors have recently paid attention to the financial instability that might arise from climate change (see Scott et al., 2017; Campiglio et al., 2018; NGFS, 2019; BIS, 2020). In a famous speech about climate change, Mark Carney, the former Governor of the Bank of England, talked about the possibility of a 'climate Minsky moment'. He used this phrase to refer to the implications of the so-called climate transition risks (see also Campiglio et al., 2019). A climate Minsky moment can arise because of abrupt changes in climate policies (e.g. a sudden increase in carbon prices) or because of sudden changes in energy-related technologies and environmental preferences that can result in a change in the climate-related expectations of financial actors. This in turn can lead to a revaluation of financial assets related to carbon-intensive companies and a tightening of credit provision to these companies. Given that many of these companies typically have an important position in the production system (see e.g. Cahen-Fourot et al., 2019) and interact with financial networks (see e.g. Battiston et al., 2017), the tightening of the financial conditions for these companies can lead to financial instability (see also Semieniuk et al., 2021).

Dafermos and Nikolaidi (2019) have modelled a specific dimension of a climate Minsky moment using an ecological stock-flow consistent model. They have shown that an abrupt increase in carbon taxes can reduce the profitability of firms, making investment and economic activity lower. This in turn can deteriorate the financial position of firms leading to higher defaults. The effects on economic activity are reinforced by the impact that a higher default rate can have on the capital of banks. This induces the latter to reduce credit supply, worsening the financial implications of the transition.

However, climate-induced financial instability might also result from the physical effects of climate change. Climate-related events (like hurricanes, typhoons and droughts) and global warming can affect both the supply-side and the demand-side of the economies. For instance, they can lead to lower labour productivity, capital destruction, lower consumption and lower investment. Dafermos et al. (2018) and Lamperti et al. (2019) have modelled the long-run implications of climate change for default rates and asset prices.

Both the physical and the transitions risks are typically viewed as exogenous shocks to the financial system. How can this be reconciled with the Minskyan perspective that emphasises endogenous forces in the emergence of financial instability? There are three ways to connect climate-induced financial instability with broader endogenous financial forces.

First, climate shocks can interact with endogenous financial dynamics, altering the severity of their impact. For instance, a disruption in carbon-intensive finance might cause more financial problems when a climate transition shock hits an economy that experiences a financial boom where leverage is already very high. In this case, the destabilising endogenous forces that are at play can reinforce the effects from the decline in carbon-intensive asset prices and the rise in the default rates.

Second, specific climate policies might induce a specific type of credit expansion that can gradually lead to more financial fragility. For instance, the European Commission has recently discussed the possibility of introducing a 'green supporting factor' in financial regulation, that is, a reduction in capital requirements related to 'green' loans (see HLEG, 2018). Although this might be beneficial for carbon emissions, it can also lead to an increase in bank leverage (see Dafermos and Nikolaidi, 2021) and can induce a green credit bubble that can increase the financial fragility of the economic system.

Third, climate-induced financial instability can be analysed from a broader long-run perspective that takes into account the interactions between the macroeconomy, the financial system and the ecosystem (see Dafermos et al., 2017). From this viewpoint, climate change can be conceptualised as a secular endogenous outcome of carbon-intensive financial and economic activities. For many decades, the provision of finance to carbon-intensive companies contributed to the generation of carbon emissions. However, cumulative carbon emissions were not sufficiently high to cause significant feedback effects on the economy and the financial system. This is no longer the case: cumulative carbon emissions have now been very high and continue increasing. The transition and physical effects that cumulative emission cause should not be viewed independently of the provision of carbon-intensive finance over the last decades.

2.6   CONCLUSION

Minsky provided us with a rich framework for analysing the macroeconomic implications of debt relationships in modern capitalism. Minsky's FIH focuses on the role of interconnected balance sheets that interact dynamically with macroeconomic factors within a non-equilibrium setting. This dynamic interaction, combined with evolutionary change in social norms and institutions, gives rise to financial fragility and endogenous cycles. Since the 1980s, Minsky's FIH has been expanded in several directions that capture the increasing expansion of global finance and the multiple sources of financial fragility that this expansion has created.

Although Minsky paid attention primarily to corporate debt, many Minskyan frameworks and models have been used to analyse the role of household and external debt, which have been at the core of financial crises seen over the last decades. A significant amount of research has also been conducted on Minsky's policy proposals, broadly verifying the stabilising role of his suggested policy reforms.

Minsky's rich framing of macroeconomic dynamics has not yet found its way into the approaches to macro modelling used by international organisations, governments and central banks. It is important that this happens in the coming years. Equally important is the need for more empirical work on the sources of financial fragility analysed by Minskyan theoretical frameworks. In addition, it is worth mentioning that the channels of transmission of financial fragility from high-income countries to emerging and developing economies, in the context of global shadow banking, are still under-explored. Moving forward, the investigation of these channels should be at the core of Minskyan theoretical and empirical research.

More crucially, in the era of climate change, Minskyan perspectives can illuminate the complex dimensions of climate-induced financial instability, both in terms of transition and physical risks. A Minskyan account of these risks can provide a more integrated understanding of their sources and financial implications. Such an understanding might be crucial for the design of a smooth transition to a low-carbon economy.

NOTES

1. From a Minskyan perspective, public debt is not in general a significant source of financial fragility. Actually, a high public debt is often considered necessary to stabilise economies that undergo a recession (see e.g. Wray, 2006). However, the analysis of the financial fragility of the government sector makes sense for countries that are not monetarily sovereign. Ferrari-Filho et al. (2010), Argitis and Nikolaidi (2014) and Terra and Ferrari-Filho (2020) have developed Minsky-inspired indices that analyse the financial fragility of the government sectors in Brazil and Greece.
2. Part of the analysis of Section 2.3 relies on Nikolaidi (2017) and Nikolaidi and Stockhammer (2017).
3. Euphoric expectations are modelled either explicitly or implicitly. For models that formalise euphoric expectations explicitly see Nasica and Raybaut (2005), Ferri and Variato (2010), Lojak (2018) and Cafferata et al. (2020).
4. There are other papers that have employed the hedge, speculative and Ponzi finance regime but without focusing explicitly on the pro-cyclicality of financial fragility. Schroeder (2009) documented a shift from hedge and speculative to Ponzi finance in the New Zealand firm sector during the period 1990–2007. Torres Filho et al. (2019) showed that the number of Ponzi Brazilian electricity distribution firms increased over the period 2008–13. Caldentey et al. (2019) found that there was a rise of speculative and Ponzi firms and a decline in hedge firms in Latin American countries between 2009 and 2016.

5. The external finance premium is equal to the cost of the borrower of raising funds externally minus the opportunity cost of internal funds.
6. Taylor and O'Connell (1985) have developed a Minskyan model without corporate debt in which stock prices is the only cause of financial fragility. See also Bhattacharya et al. (2015) for a model which analyses more broadly how investors' strategies in the financial markets are driven by expectations formation à la Minsky.
7. For the links between emulation and inequality see, for example, Palley (2010).
8. In the New Keynesian-style models of Eggertsson and Krugman (2012) and Benigno et al. (2020), which formalise the debt relationships between 'patient' and 'impatient' households, the decline in economic activity, described as a 'Minsky moment', is triggered by an exogenous decline in the quantity of debt that impatient households can borrow.
9. There is also some empirical research that has focused on the financial fragility associated with the interaction between housing prices and household debt. For example, Tymoigne (2014) developed an index of home finance fragility that he has applied to the US, the UK and France over the period before the Global Financial Crisis. The index clearly shows that growing financial fragility in the run-up to the crisis.
10. Note though that capital outflows in EMEs can also be triggered by developments that are independent of the domestic economy conditions. For example, Bonizzi and Kaltenbrunner (2019) have used a Minskyan perspective to show that the demand of insurance companies and pension funds for emerging market assets is driven by changes in the liability structure of these institutions and the search for high yields, which are largely unrelated to the conditions in EMEs.
11. Note that ELR has been the subject of considerable debate. See, for example, Sawyer (2003, 2005) and Mitchell and Wray (2005).
12. See also the Minsky-inspired empirical analysis of Greenwood-Nimmo and Tarassow (2016) for the US which shows that a credit-constrained macroprudential policy shock that is combined with active monetary policy can reduce financial fragility.

REFERENCES

Abdulkadir, R.I., Abdullah, N.A.H. and Wong, W.C. (2016) Dividend payment behaviour and its determinants: The Nigerian evidence. *African Development Review* 28(1): 53–63.

Arestis, P. and Glickman, M. (2002) Financial crisis in Southeast Asia: Dispelling illusion the Minskyan way. *Cambridge Journal of Economics* 26(2): 237–60.

Argitis, G. (2013) Veblenian and Minskian financial markets. *European Journal of Economics and Economic Policies: Intervention* 10(1): 28–43.

Argitis, G. (2017) Evolutionary finance and central banking. *Cambridge Journal of Economics* 41(3): 961–76.

Argitis, G. (2019) *Evolutionary Financial Macroeconomics*. London: Routledge.

Argitis, G. and Nikolaidi, M. (2014) The financial fragility and the crisis of the Greek government sector. *International Review of Applied Economics* 28(3): 274–92.

Arza, V. and Español, P. (2008) Les Liaisons dangereuses: A Minskyan approach to the relation of credit and investment in Argentina during the 1990s. *Cambridge Journal of Economics* 32(5): 739–59.

Asada, T. (2001) Nonlinear dynamics of debt and capital: A post-Keynesian analysis. In Y. Aruka (ed.), *Evolutionary Controversies in Economics* (pp. 73–87). Tokyo: Springer-Verlag.

Barba, A. and Pivetti, M. (2009) Rising household debt: Its causes and macroeconomic implications – a long-period analysis. *Cambridge Journal of Economics* 33(1): 113–37.

Bastidas, D., Fabre, A. and Mc Isaac, F. (2019) Minskyan classical growth cycles: Stability analysis of a stock-flow consistent macrodynamic model. *Mathematics and Financial Economics* 13(3): 359–91.

Battiston, S., Mandel, A., Monasterolo, I., Schütze, F. and Visentin, G. (2017) A climate stress-test of the financial system. *Nature Climate Change* 7(4): 283–90.

Benigno, P., Eggertsson, G.B. and Romei, F. (2020) Dynamic debt deleveraging and optimal monetary policy. *American Economic Journal: Macroeconomics* 12(2): 310–50.

Benito, A. and Young, G. (2003) Hard times or great expectations? Dividend omissions and dividend cuts by UK firms. *Oxford Bulletin of Economics and Statistics* 65(5): 531–55.

Bernanke, B. and Gertler, M. (1990) Financial fragility and economic performance. *The Quarterly Journal of Economics* 105(1): 87–114.

Bhattacharya, S., Goodhart, C.A.E., Tsomocos, D.P. and Vardoulakis, A.P. (2015) A reconsideration of Minsky's financial instability hypothesis. *Journal of Money, Credit and Banking* 47(5): 931–73.

BIS (2020) The green swan: Central banking and financial stability in the age of climate change. Bank for International Settlements.

Bonizzi, B. and Kaltenbrunner, A. (2019) Liability-driven investment and pension fund exposure to emerging markets: A Minskyan analysis. *Environment and Planning A: Economy and Space* 51(2): 420–39.

Botta, A., Caverzasi, E., Russo, A., Gallegati, M. and Stiglitz, J.E. (2021) Inequality and finance in a rent economy. *Journal of Economic Behavior & Organization* 183: 998–1029.

Cafferata, A., Dávila-Fernández, M.J. and Sordi, S. (2020) (Ir)rational explorers in the financial jungle: Modelling Minsky with heterogeneous agents. Working Paper No. 819, Department of Economics, University of Siena.

Cahen-Fourot, L., Campiglio, E., Dawkins, E., Godin, A. and Kemp-Benedict, E. (2019) Capital stranding cascades: The impact of decarbonisation on productive asset utilisation. Working Paper Series No. 18/2019, WU Institute for Ecological Economics.

Caiani, A., Godin, A., Caverzasi, E., Gallegati, M., Kinsella, S. and Stiglitz, J.E. (2016) Agent based-stock flow consistent macroeconomics: Towards a benchmark model. *Journal of Economic Dynamics & Control* 69: 375–408.

Caldentey, E.P., Favreau Negront, N. and Méndez Lobos, L. (2019) Corporate debt in Latin America and its macroeconomic implications. *Journal of Post Keynesian Economics* 42(3): 335–62.

Campiglio, E., Dafermos, Y., Monnin, P., Ryan-Collins, J., Schotten, G. and Tanaka, M. (2018) Climate change challenges for central banks and financial regulators. *Nature Climate Change* 8(6): 462–8.

Campiglio, E., Monnin, P. and von Jagow, A. (2019) Climate risks in financial assets. Council on Economic Policies. Discussion Note No. 2019/2, Council of Economic Policies (CEP).

Carney, M. (2015) Breaking the Tragedy of the Horizon – climate change and financial stability. Speech given at Lloyd's of London, 29 September, 220–30.

Charles, S. (2008a) Teaching Minsky's financial instability hypothesis: A manageable suggestion. *Journal of Post Keynesian Economics* 31(1): 125–38.

Charles, S. (2008b) Corporate debt, variable retention rate and the appearance of financial fragility. *Cambridge Journal of Economics* 32: 781–95.

Charles, S. (2016) Is Minsky's financial instability hypothesis valid? *Cambridge Journal of Economics* 40(2): 427–36.

Charpe, M., Flaschel, P., Proaño, C. and Semmler, W. (2009) Overconsumption, credit rationing and bailout monetary policy: A Minskyan perspective. *European Journal of Economics and Economic Policies: Intervention* 6(2): 247–70.

Chiarella, C. and Di Guilmi, C. (2011) The financial instability hypothesis: A stochastic microfoundation framework. *Journal of Economic Dynamics & Control* 35(8): 1151–71.

Cynamon, B.Z. and Fazzari, S.M. (2008) Household debt in the consumer age: Source of growth – risk of collapse. *Capitalism and Society* 3(2): 1–32.

Cynamon, B.Z. and Fazzari, S.M. (2016) Inequality, the Great Recession and slow recovery. *Cambridge Journal of Economics* 40(2): 373–99.

Dafermos, Y. (2018) Debt cycles, instability and fiscal rules: A Godley-Minsky synthesis. *Cambridge Journal of Economics* 42(5): 1277–313.

Dafermos, Y. and Nikolaidi, M. (2019) Fiscal policy and ecological sustainability: A post-Keynesian perspective. In P. Arestis and M. Sawyer (eds), *Frontiers of Heterodox Macroeconomics* (pp. 277–322). Basingstoke: Palgrave Macmillan.

Dafermos, Y. and Nikolaidi, M. (2021) How can green differentiated capital requirements affect climate risks? A dynamic macrofinancial analysis. *Journal of Financial Stability* 54, 100871.

Dafermos, Y., Gabor, D. and Michell, J. (2020) Institutional supercycles: An evolutionary macro-finance approach. Working Paper No. 15, Rebuilding Macroeconomics Working Paper Series.

Dafermos, Y., Nikolaidi, M. and Galanis, G. (2017) A stock-flow-fund ecological macroeconomic model. *Ecological Economics* 131: 191–207.

Dafermos, Y., Nikolaidi, M. and Galanis, G. (2018) Climate change, financial stability and monetary policy. *Ecological Economics* 152: 219–34.

Davis, L.E., De Souza, J.P.A. and Hernandez, G. (2019) An empirical analysis of Minsky regimes in the US economy. *Cambridge Journal of Economics* 43(3): 541–83.

De Paula, L.F.R. and Alves, A.J. (2000) External financial fragility and the 1998–1999 Brazilian currency crisis. *Journal of Post Keynesian Economics* 22(4): 589–617.

Delli Gatti, D. and Gallegati, M. (1990) Financial instability, income distribution, and the stock market. *Journal of Post Keynesian Economics* 12(3): 356–74.

Delli Gatti, D., Gallegati, M. and Gardini, L. (1994) Complex dynamics in a simple macroeconomic model with financing constraints. In G. Dymski and R. Pollin (eds), *New Perspectives in Monetary Macroeconomics* (pp. 51–76). Ann Arbor, MI: University of Michigan Press.

Delli Gatti, D., Gallegati, M., Greenwald, B., Russo, A. and Stiglitz, J.E. (2010) The financial accelerator in an evolving credit network. *Journal of Economic Dynamics & Control* 34(9): 1627–50.

Di Guilmi, C. and Carvalho, L. (2017) The dynamics of leverage in a demand-driven model with heterogeneous firms. *Journal of Economic Behavior & Organization* 140: 70–90.

Dutt, A.K. (1995) Internal finance and monopoly power in capitalist economies: A reformulation of Steindl's growth model. *Metroeconomica* 46(1): 16–34.

Dutt, A.K. (2006) Maturity, stagnation and consumer debt: A Steindlian approach. *Metroeconomica* 57(3): 339–64.

Economist, The (2016) Minsky's Moment, 30 July. Available at: https://www.economist.com/schools-brief/2016/07/30/minskys-moment (last accessed: 31 August 2021).

Eggertsson, G. and Krugman, P. (2012) Debt deleveraging, and the liquidity trap: A Fisher-Minsky-Koo approach. *The Quarterly Journal of Economics* 127(3): 1469–513.

Fazzari, S., Ferri, P. and Greenberg, E. (2008) Cash flow, investment, and Keynes-Minsky cycles. *Journal of Economic Behavior & Organization* 65(3–4): 555–72.

Ferrari-Filho, F., Terra, F.H.B. and Conceição, O.A.C. (2010) The financial fragility hypothesis applied to the public sector: An analysis for Brazil's economy from 2000 to 2008. *Journal of Post Keynesian Economics* 33(1): 151–68.

Ferri, P. and Minsky, H.P. (1992) Market processes and thwarting systems. *Structural Change and Economic Dynamics* 3(1): 79–91.

Ferri, P. and Variato, A. (2010) Financial fragility, the Minskian triad, and economic dynamics. *International Journal of Political Economy* 39(2): 70–82.

Foley, D.K. (1987) Liquidity-profit rate cycles in a capitalist economy. *Journal of Economic Behavior & Organization* 8(3): 363–76.

Foley, D.K. (2003) Financial fragility in developing economies. In A.K. Dutt and J. Ros (eds), *Development Economics and Structuralist Macroeconomics: Essays in Honor of Lance Taylor* (pp. 157–68). Cheltenham, UK and Northampton, MA USA: Edward Elgar.

Franke, R. and Semmler, W. (1989) Debt financing of firms, stability, and cycles in a dynamical macroeconomic growth cycle. In W. Semmler (ed.), *Financial Dynamics and Business Cycles: New Perspectives* (pp. 38–64). New York and London: M.E. Sharpe.

Gabor, D. (2020) Critical macro-finance: A theoretical lens. *Finance and Society* 6(1): 45–55.

Galí, J., (2018) The state of New Keynesian economics: A partial assessment. *Journal of Economic Perspectives* 32(3): 87–112.

Gallardo, J.L., Moreno-Brid, J.C. and Anyul, M.P. (2006) Financial fragility and financial crisis in Mexico. *Metroeconomica* 57(3): 365–88.

Giraud, G. and Grasselli, M. (2021) Household debt: The missing link between inequality and secular stagnation. *Journal of Economic Behavior & Organization* 183: 901–27.

Giri, F., Riccetti, L., Russo, A. and Gallegati, M. (2019) Monetary policy and large crises in a financial accelerator agent-based model. *Journal of Economic Behavior & Organization* 157: 42–58.

Goodwin, R.M. (1967) A growth cycle. In C.H. Feinstein (ed.), *Socialism, Capitalism and Economic Growth: Essays Presented to Maurice Dobb* (pp. 54–8). Cambridge: Cambridge University Press.

Grasselli, M.R. and Costa Lima, B. (2012) An analysis of the Keen model for credit expansion, asset price bubbles and financial fragility. *Mathematical Financial Economics* 6(3): 191–210.

Greenwood-Nimmo, M. and Tarassow, A. (2016) Monetary shocks, macroprudential shocks and financial stability. *Economic Modelling* 56: 11–24.

HLEG (2018) Financing a Sustainable European Economy, Final Report 2018 by the High Level Expert Group on Sustainable Finance Final Report, European Commission.

Isenberg, D. (1989) The financially fragile firm: Is there a case for it in the 1920s? Working Paper No. 15, The Levy Economics Institute of Bard College.

Jakab, Z. and Kumhof, M. (2019) Banks are not intermediaries of loanable funds – facts, theory and evidence. Staff Working Paper No. 761, Bank of England.

Jarsulic, M. (1989) Endogenous credit and endogenous business cycles. *Journal of Post Keynesian Economics* 12(1): 35–48.

Jarsulic, M. (1990) Debt and macro stability. *Eastern Economic Journal* 16(2): 91–100.

Jump, R.C., Michell, J. and Stockhammer, E. (2017) A strategy switching approach to Minskyan business cycles. Manuscript.

Kaltenbrunner, A. (2015) A post Keynesian framework of exchange rate determination: A Minskyan approach. *Journal of Post Keynesian Economics* 38(3): 426–48.

Kapeller, J. and Schütz, B. (2014) Debt, boom, bust: A theory of Minsky-Veblen cycles. *Journal of Post Keynesian Economics* 36(4): 781–814.

Kapeller, J., Landesmann, M.A., Mohr, F.X. and Schütz, B. (2018) Government policies and financial crises: mitigation, postponement or prevention? *Cambridge Journal of Economics* 42(2): 309–30.

Keen, S. (1995) Finance and economic breakdown modelling Minsky's 'financial instability hypothesis'. *Journal of Post Keynesian Economics* 17(4): 607–35.

Kim, Y.K. (2013) Household debt, financialization, and macroeconomic performance in the United States, 1951–2009. *Journal of Post Keynesian Economics* 35(4): 675–94.

Kim, Y.K. (2016) Macroeconomic effects of household debt: An empirical analysis. *Review of Keynesian Economics* 4(2): 127–50.

Kohler, K. (2019) Exchange rate dynamics, balance sheet effects, and capital flows: A Minskyan model of emerging market boom-bust cycles. *Structural Change and Economic Dynamics* 51: 270–83.

Kregel, J. (1998) Yes, 'it' did happen again. Working Paper No. 234, The Levy Economics Institute.

Kregel, J. (2014a) Economists and depression: Did it happen again? On Minsky's financial macroeconomics. *History of Economic Ideas* 22(3): 137–45.

Kregel, J.A. (2014b) Minsky and dynamic macroprudential regulation. Public Policy Brief No. 131, The Levy Economics Institute.

Lamperti, F., Bosetti, V., Roventini, A. and Tavoni, M. (2019) The public costs of climate-induced financial instability. *Nature Climate Change* 9(11): 829–33.

Lavoie, M. (1995) Interest rates in post-Keynesian models of growth and distribution. *Metroeconomica* 46(2): 146–77.

Lavoie, M. (2014) *Post-Keynesian Economics: New Foundations*. Cheltenham, UK and Northampton, MA, USA: Edward Elgar.

Lavoie, M. and Seccareccia, M. (2001) Minsky's financial fragility hypothesis: A missing macroeconomic link? In P. Ferri and R. Bellofiore (eds), *Financial Fragility and Investment in the Capitalist Economy: The Economic Legacy of Hyman Minsky* Vol. 2 (pp. 76–96). Cheltenham, UK and Northampton, MA, USA: Edward Elgar.

Lima, G.T. and Meirelles, A.J.A. (2007) Macrodynamics of debt regimes, financial instability and growth. *Cambridge Journal of Economics* 31(4): 563–80.

Lojak, B. (2018) The emergence of co-existing debt cycle regimes in an economic growth model. *Metroeconomica* 69(3): 526–45.

McLeay, M., Radia, A. and Thomas, R. (2014) Money creation in the modern economy. *Bank of England Quarterly Bulletin* 54(1): 14–27.

Michell, J. (2014) A Steindlian account of the distribution of corporate profits and leverage: A stock-flow consistent macroeconomic model with agent-based microfoundations. Working Paper No. 1412, Post-Keynesian Economics Study Group (PKSG).

Minsky, H.P. (1975) *John Maynard Keynes*. New York: Columbia University Press.

Minsky, H.P. (1982) *Inflation, Recession and Economic Policy*. New York: M.E. Sharpe.

Minsky, H.P. (2008) *Stabilizing an Unstable Economy*. New York: McGraw-Hill. Originally published 1986.

Minsky, H.P. (1992) The financial instability hypothesis. Working Paper No. 74, The Levy Economics Institute.

Minsky, H.P., Papadimitriou, D.B., Phillips, R.J. and Wray, L.R. (1993) Community development banking: A proposal to establish a nationwide system of community development banks. Public Policy Brief No. 3/1993, The Levy Economics Institute.

Mitchell, W. and Wray, L.R. (2005) In defense of employer of last resort: A response to Malcolm Sawyer. *Journal of Economic Issues* 39(1): 235–44.

Mulligan, R. (2013) A sectoral analysis of the financial instability hypothesis. *The Quarterly Review of Economics and Finance* 53(4): 450–59.

Nasica, E. and Raybaut, A. (2005) Profits, confidence, and public deficits: Modeling Minsky's institutional dynamics. *Journal of Post Keynesian Economics* 28(1): 136–54.

Ndikumana, L. (1999) Debt service, financing constraints, and fixed investment: Evidence from panel data. *Journal of Post Keynesian Economics* 21(3): 455–78.

NGFS (2019) Macroeconomic and financial stability: Implications of climate change. Network for Greening the Financial System, June.

Nikolaidi, M. (2014) Margins of safety and instability in a macrodynamic model with Minskyan insights. *Structural Change and Economic Dynamics* 31: 1–16.

Nikolaidi, M. (2015) Securitisation, wage stagnation and financial fragility: A stock-flow consistent perspective, Greenwich Papers in Political Economy No. 27, GPERC.

Nikolaidi, M. (2017) Three decades of modelling Minsky: What we have learned and the way forward. *European Journal of Economics and Economic Policies: Intervention* 14(2): 222–37.

Nikolaidi, M. and Stockhammer, E. (2017) Minsky models: A structured survey. *Journal of Economic Surveys* 31(5): 1304–31.

Nishi, H. (2012) A dynamic analysis of debt-led and debt-burdened growth regimes with Minskian financial structure. *Metroeconomica* 63(4): 634–60.

Nishi, H. (2019) An empirical contribution to Minsky's financial fragility: Evidence from non-financial sectors in Japan. *Cambridge Journal of Economics* 43(3): 585–622.

Palley, T.I. (1994) Debt, aggregate demand, and the business cycle: An analysis in the spirit of Kaldor and Minsky. *Journal of Post Keynesian Economics* 16(3): 371–90.

Palley, T.I. (1997) Endogenous money and the business cycle. *Journal of Economics* 65(2): 133–49.

Palley, T.I. (2010) The relative permanent income theory of consumption: A synthetic Keynes–Duesenberry–Friedman model. *Review of Political Economy* 22(1): 41–56.

Palley, T.I. (2011) A theory of Minsky super-cycles and financial crises. *Contributions to Political Economy* 30(1): 31–46.

Papadimitriou, D.B. and Wray, R. (1998) The economic contributions of Hyman Minsky: Varieties of capitalism and institutional reform. *Review of Political Economy* 10(2): 199–225.

Passarella, M. (2012) A simplified stock-flow consistent dynamic model of the systemic financial fragility in the 'New Capitalism'. *Journal of Economic Behavior & Organization* 83(3): 570–82.

Pedrosa, Í. (2019) Firms' leverage ratio and the Financial Instability Hypothesis: An empirical investigation for the US economy (1970–2014). *Cambridge Journal of Economics* 43(6): 1499–523.

Pedrosa, Í. and Lang, D. (2018) Heterogeneity, distribution and financial fragility of non-financial firms: An agent-based stock-flow consistent (AB-SFC) model. hal-01937186.

Reissl, S. (2020) Minsky from the bottom up – formalising the two-price model of investment in a simple agent-based framework. *Journal of Economic Behavior & Organization* 177: 109–42.

Ryoo, S. (2010) Long waves and short cycles in a model of endogenous financial fragility. *Journal of Economic Behavior & Organization* 74(3): 163–86.

Ryoo, S. (2013a) Minsky cycles in Keynesian models of growth and distribution. *Review of Keynesian Economics* 1(1): 37–60.

Ryoo, S. (2013b) Bank profitability, leverage and financial instability: A Minsky-Harrod model. *Cambridge Journal of Economics* 37(5): 1127–60.

Ryoo, S. (2016) Household debt and housing bubble: A Minskian approach to boom-bust cycles. *Journal of Evolutionary Economics* 26(5): 971–1006.

Ryoo, S. and Kim, Y.K. (2014) Income distribution, consumer debt and keeping up with the Joneses. *Metroeconomica* 65(4): 585–618.

Sasaki, H. and Fujita, S. (2012) The importance of the retention ratio in a Kaleckian model with debt accumulation. *Metroeconomica* 63(3): 417–28.

Sawyer, M. (2003) Employer of last resort: Could it deliver full employment and price stability? *Journal of Economic Issues* 37(4): 881–907.

Sawyer, M. (2005) Employer of last resort: A response to my critics. *Journal of Economic Issues* 39(1): 256–64.

Schroeder, S. (2009) Defining and detecting financial fragility: New Zealand's experience. *International Journal of Social Economics* 36(3): 287–307.

Scott, M., van Huizen, J. and Jung, C. (2017) The Bank of England's response to climate change. *Quarterly Bulletin* 2017 Q2.

Semieniuk, G., Campiglio, E., Mercure, J.F., Volz, U. and Edwards, N.R. (2021) Low-carbon transition risks for finance. *WIREs Climate Change* 12: 1–24.

Semmler, W. (1987) A macroeconomic limit cycle with financial perturbations. *Journal of Economic Behavior & Organisation* 8(3): 469–95.

Skott, P. (1994) On the modeling of systemic financial fragility. In A.K. Dutt (ed.), *New Directions in Analytical Political Economy* (pp. 49–76). Aldershot, UK and Brookfield, VT, USA: Edward Elgar.

Sordi, S. and Vercelli, A. (2014) Unemployment, income distribution and debt-financed investment in a growth cycle model. *Journal of Economic Dynamics & Control* 48: 325–48.

Stockhammer, E. and Michell, J. (2017) Pseudo-Goodwin cycles in a Minsky Model. *Cambridge Journal of Economics* 41(1): 105–25.

Stockhammer, E., Jump, R.C., Kohler, K. and Cavallero, J. (2019a) Short and medium term financial-real cycles: An empirical assessment. *Journal of International Money and Finance* 94: 81–96.

Stockhammer, E., Gouzoulis, G. and Jump, R.C. (2019b) Debt-driven business cycles in historical perspective: The cases of the USA (1889–2015) and UK (1882–2010). Working Paper No. 1907, Post-Keynesian Economics Society (PKES).

Taylor, L. and O'Connell, S.A. (1985) A Minsky crisis. *Quarterly Journal of Economics* 100 (Supplement): 871–85.

Terra, F.H.B. and Ferrari-Filho, F. (2020) Public Sector Financial Fragility Index: An analysis of the Brazilian federal government from 2000 to 2016. *Journal of Post Keynesian Economics*: 1–25.

Toporowski, J. (2008) Minsky's 'induced investment and business cycles'. *Cambridge Journal of Economics* 32(5): 725–37.

Torres Filho, E.T., Martins, N.M. and Miaguti, C.Y. (2019) Minsky's financial fragility: An empirical analysis of electricity distribution firms in Brazil (2007–2015). *Journal of Post Keynesian Economics* 42(1): 144–68.

Tymoigne, E. (2014) Measuring macroprudential risk through financial fragility: A Minskian approach. *Journal of Post Keynesian Economics* 36(4): 719–44.

Wolfson, M.H. (1990) The causes of financial instability. *Journal of Post Keynesian Economics* 12(3): 333–55.

Wray, L.R. (2006) Extending Minsky's classifications of fragility to government and the open economy. Working Paper No. 450, The Levy Economics Institute of Bard College.

Wray, L.R. (2011) Minsky's money manager capitalism and the global financial crisis. *International Journal of Political Economy* 40(2): 5–20.

Wray, L.R. (2015) Minsky on banking: Early work on endogenous money and the prudent banker. Working Paper No. 827, The Levy Economics Institute of Bard College.

Wray, R. and Tymoigne, E. (2009) Macroeconomics meets Hyman P. Minsky: The financial theory of investment. In G. Fontana and M. Setterfield (eds), *Macroeconomic Theory and Macroeconomic Pedagogy* (pp. 234–51). Basingstoke: Palgrave Macmillan.

Yilmaz, S.D. and Stockhammer, E. (2019) Coupling cycle mechanisms: Minsky debt cycles and the multiplier-accelerator. Working Paper No. 1904, Post-Keynesian Economics Society (PKES).

3. Financial accelerator framework

Tommaso Oliviero and Giovanni W. Puopolo

3.1 INTRODUCTION

All economic crises pose two important questions to economists and poli-cymakers: (i) how far is the economy from its full potential? and (ii) what are the determinants of the wedge between post-crisis economic outcomes and their efficient levels? Answering these questions provides necessary conditions to take timely and effective interventions that guarantee a rapid recovery.

The Global Financial Crisis (GFC) of 2007–09 has highlighted the key role of financial imperfections in shaping the amplitude and the persistence of the wedge between actual and potential economic outcomes. In fact, the GFC featured a banking sector overwhelmed by non-performing loans, an interbank market suffering a significant freeze, an insufficient level of bank capital and falling firms' creditworthiness due to high leverage and declining asset values. All these factors cannot simply be viewed as passive reflections of the economic collapse, rather they have largely contributed to the depth of the recession. In this work, we investigate the reasons why the economic literature has reached these conclusions.

The theoretical foundation of the general idea that economic disruptions may be generated or amplified by deteriorating credit-market conditions goes under the name of "financial accelerator framework" (FAF). In this regard, the seminal idea that financial conditions may prevent the economy from reaching its potential is contained in the pioneering work of Ben Bernanke (1983), who formalized and expanded some of the original insights of Fisher (1933). In the early 1980s, in fact, by investigating the determinants of the Great Depression (1929–33), Bernanke proposed an explanation based on the development of microeconomic theories on asymmetric information and principal-agent theory. According to Bernanke (1983), the ultimate nature of financial market imperfections is information-based (e.g. information asymmetry between lenders and borrowers) and this gives rise to market frictions. Since financial markets are incomplete, the relationship between some classes of borrowers (e.g. small private firms) and savers is mediated by the presence of information-gathering services (e.g. screening and/or monitoring activities) that are usually provided by the financial intermediaries at some cost – *the cost of credit intermediation.*

In a recession, ever more borrowers turn insolvent rising the cost of credit intermediation and banks may react either by charging higher interest rates to clients, whence possibly triggering the undesired effect of increasing borrowers' risk of default, or by cutting credit to people who would have been granted it in normal times. When credit stops flowing to borrowers or becomes too expensive, private investments collapse. This effect is expected to be larger for firms with limited access to external sources of finance different from intermediated loans (e.g. smaller firms). The gap between potential and effective low investments can persist over time according to how long it takes to re-establish pre-recession levels of information between lenders and borrowers. In other words, it depends on the time it takes to restore efficiency in the financial intermediation market.

Bernanke (1983) and his successive works – which will be discussed in the next section of this chapter – have outlined that financial frictions amplify the economic consequences of recessions in two ways. The first way is directly through the banking sector. More precisely, banks' defaults destroy the borrower-lender informational capital, thus reducing credit availability. In turn, this inhibits consumer spending and/or firm capital investment, generating an economic contraction. The second way is indirectly related to financial markets and operates through borrowers' creditworthiness. That is, reductions in the value of available collateral and/or in borrowers' cash flows impair their creditworthiness. This, in turn, raises the external finance premium (i.e. the difference between the cost of external and internal funds to a borrower), tightens financial constraints and ultimately limits the possibility to exploit investment opportunities. The existence of the external finance premium may be determined by imperfect information between borrowers and lenders, credit rationing resulting from the scarcity of bank capital (Holmstrom and Tirole, 1997), or adverse selection in the capital markets (Bolton and Freixas, 2000).

Even though the reasoning behind the FAF was originally developed for a better understanding of the Great Depression, it is easy to see that the theory can be applied to other crisis episodes: in particular, it helps provide a foundation for the macro-finance issues that followed the 2008 GFC. Thus, in light of this brief summary on how the FAF operates, it is not surprising that, after the occurrence of the GFC, this theory has been rejuvenated. The renewed interest by researchers, in fact, combined with the recent availability of microeconomic data and the development of micro-econometric techniques in the last decades, has provided a flourishing ground for empirical tests of the theory. In this regard, many authors have provided formal tests of the mechanisms behind the financial accelerator (FA).

Accordingly, the purpose of this work is to highlight the empirical applications that, in the last decade, have employed the FAF as a reference point for their studies. Our general conclusion is that the predictions of the financial accelerator theory (FAT) are valid and quantitatively important in explaining various aspects of firms' and households' dynamics, especially in relation to the years around the GFC.

Finally, in the last section of this chapter, we also provide a brief discussion of the recent COVID-19 pandemic. Unlike the GFC that originated in the financial sector, the COVID-19 crisis originated in a health shock whose large effects on the economy and the financial sector are due to full or partial lockdowns designed to moderate the spread of the virus. At present, it is very difficult to predict the impact of this economic crisis. However, firms' liquidity and financial frictions are expected to be still central to understand the length and depth of the current economic crisis. In this regard, the FAF can still provide useful insights for predicting firms' dynamics and the financial conditions that can favour a fast recovery.

The chapter is organized as follows. Section 3.2 describes the theoretical foundations of the FAF and discusses the empirical predictions of the theory. Section 3.3 features a comprehensive review of the empirical literature that followed the GFC and provides validation of the theoretical channels using microeconomic data and techniques. Section 3.4 discusses the issues of FA in the context of the COVID-19 crisis and the concluding remarks are reported in Section 3.5.

3.2   THE THEORETICAL PREDICTIONS OF THE FINANCIAL ACCELERATOR FRAMEWORK

Before describing the recent contributions and applications of the theory, it is important to provide a brief review of the seminal stream of research that originated from the pioneering contribution of Bernanke (1983). The basic ideas of the financial accelerator were applied to a different macroeconomic context already in the 1980s, and although the paper of Bernanke (1983) contained the main ingredients of the theory, the label "financial accelerator" explicitly appeared several years later, in Bernanke et al. (1996). In this paper, the authors explore the mechanisms through which small shocks can lead to large fluctuations, or equivalently, could translate, under certain conditions, into large economic disruptions. The authors highlight that, while a real or monetary shock may represent the initial spark of a small fire, the "acceleration" from a small to a big fire is potentially related to the functioning of the financial markets. In fact, when the initial small shock impacts the agency cost of external finance for borrowers, access to credit for affected borrowers becomes limited, and this in turn affects real investment.

One of the most notorious applications of the FAF regards monetary policy. Within this context, the literature has usually distinguished two main channels of monetary policy transmission through a FA mechanism (Bernanke and Gertler, 1995): the balance sheet channel and the bank-lending channel.

The balance sheet channel predicts that changes in interest rates due to monetary policy shocks affect the values of firms' assets and cash flows, and thus their creditworthiness. In particular, the increase (decrease) of interest rates affects borrowers' external finance premium and ultimately impacts on their investment through the decrease (increase) in their access to external finance. In this perspective, the balance sheet channel of monetary policy is an extension of the FA prediction that can be applied to all other sources of shocks, both idiosyncratic (e.g. firms' cash flows) and aggregate (e.g. a collapse in real commodity values such as housing), that affect the borrowers' creditworthiness. Accordingly, in a real business cycle framework, Bernanke and Gertler (1989) show how the effects of a productivity shock can be amplified through the FA channel. They assume that positive/negative productivity shocks can positively/negatively affect borrowers' net worth, which is ultimately related to the agency cost of debt. In the presence of financial constraints that limit the ability of borrowing by entrepreneurs, productivity shocks affect the final level of output to the extent that the limits are binding. The paper also shows that these effects not only can be larger than in the absence of financial frictions, but they are also persistent even if the initiating shock has no intrinsic persistence.

The bank-lending channel, instead, is related to the hypothesis that, by affecting the supply of loans offered by financial intermediaries, monetary policy indirectly impacts on borrowers' investment. The reasoning behind this idea was firstly presented in Bernanke and Blinder (1988) using a canonical IS/LM framework with the inclusion of a loan market. In this framework, monetary tightening (loosening) results in a shrinkage (expansion) of banks' balance sheets. This impacts the banks' ability to supply loans to borrowers which may have ultimate implications for their spending and economic activities.

Notice that the original idea of Bernanke and Blinder (1988) does not consider the potential impact of monetary policy on the cost of banks' funding and their net worth. Banks, in fact, may themselves be subject to dynamics in their external finance premia that depend on their perceived creditworthiness. As a consequence, an additional extension of the bank-lending channel is related to the possibility that all types of shocks, both monetary and not-monetary, by affecting the intermediation efficiency and/or the net worth of banks, may ultimately impact on their ability in converting their liabilities into loans. In other words, the theoretical predictions from the bank-lending channel of monetary policy can be extended to all other contingencies where banks are subject to idiosyncratic or aggregate external disturbances (e.g. changes in regulation or net worth shocks). For instance, drops in the value of bank capital, especially when capital buffers are not larger than what is required by the regulation, may impair intermediaries' ability to funnel resources to the corporate sector. The scarcity of bank capital for the allocation of intermediated debt, as in Holmstrom and Tirole (1997), is then compatible with the presence of a FA mechanism independently of (or even interactively with) changes in interest rates due to monetary policy interventions.

The mechanisms characterizing the FAT, in particular the balance sheet and the bank-lending channel, can refer to various economic environments which embed the presence of a non-negligible financial sector. A key assumption for the theory to hold in practice, in fact, is the presence of non-negligible financial frictions that, under certain circumstances, prevent the efficient flow of financial resources from borrowers to savers. In other words, we need to assume that the presence of financial constraints must be binding for some borrowers when a shock hits the economy.

To better understand these issues, we illustrate the effect of collateral-driven credit constraints with the underpinnings of the theory of Bernanke and Gertler (1995). We do not need to explicitly model the theoretical foundation of the collateral constraint that, as highlighted above, may ultimately be ascribed to asymmetric information in the financial market. It is worth underlining that the hypothesis that a borrower can obtain a fully collateralized loan is only a general way of modelling the contract arrangements arising in the borrower-lender relationship in the presence of strong asymmetric information. Since financial contracts are endogenous to institutions and types, in fact, a unique formalization that holds for all borrower-saver relationships hinges on a number of arbitrary restrictions on the nature of the financial arrangements. Nevertheless, the benefits stemming from assuming a simple framework with collateral constraints in the current context are twofold: (1) it provides the ground for outlining the predictions from the theory; (2) it represents the most used tool by the recent literature that embeds the FA features in a macroeconomic context.

The collateral constraint usually takes the following form:

$$(1 + r)\, L \leq m\, (qK),$$

that is, the borrower's total amount of loan L (gross of interest rate r) cannot exceed a fraction m of the discounted value of her assets, represented by asset volume K multiplied by its price q. In this context, the collateral value qK reflects a measure of the borrower creditworthiness and proxies for her ability to access the credit market. The interest rate r, instead, reflects the safe interest rate under no default conditions and proxies for the monetary policy regime. Finally, the parameter m can be considered a function of institutional factors that affect the intermediation efficiency of banks, or a function of regulatory constraints that impact on the risk attitude of the lender. It is important to consider such parameter because its changes reflect shocks to the banking sector that are independent of borrowers' collateral value.

The basic mechanism behind the FA hinges on the hypothesis that the financial sector is not just a veil. More precisely, it is required that a non-negligible fraction of borrowers does not own sufficient resources to finance its economic activity. Let us assume that, at some point, a negative shock, even temporary and external to the single borrower, hits the economy and makes the constraint on the collateral binding. In this case, even though the borrowers' marginal return on their investment is larger than the interest rate, an external finance premium arises. This limits the borrower's additional investment, production and spending which, in turn, negatively affects the aggregate level of economic activity and further propagates through time. The equilibrium condition is given by a negative spiral in which the constraint becomes even more binding, the external finance premium keeps increasing, and the borrower's activity is further negatively affected. This dynamic loop is at the core of the FAF.

As explained above, while the trigger of the FA mechanism is related to various sources of shocks, a necessary condition for its development is that there exists an external finance premium (due to, say, a binding collateral constraint) and that the latter is large enough (or involves a large fraction of borrowers) in order to be quantitatively important, and consequently observed empirically.

The ultimate nature of shocks that affect the borrowers' ability to access the financial market may regard different dimensions of the economy. Shocks to the collateral value or level (qK), shocks to the financial intermediation technology (m), or a monetary policy shock that affects the interest rate (r) may all have real impacts on the borrowers' activity by triggering a FA mechanism.

Empirically, both borrower-level and macro-level shocks may provide the basis for observing the FA at work. As suggested in Bernanke et al. (1996, p.1), in fact, "Testing for the existence of a financial accelerator raises difficult identification problems. A promising avenue for circumventing these problems is to examine cross-sectional implications of the theory." In this regard, the dynamics of developed countries' aggregate economy in the years around the 2008 GFC provided an extreme generous ground of experiences that allow for testing various aspects of the FAT.

We conclude this section by highlighting the three main testable hypotheses that will be investigated in the next sections. Moreover, consistently with the developments of the theory, we consider separately the predictions that pertain to monetary policy shocks from the ones that regard borrowers and lenders.

Testable prediction 1: When a negative (resp. positive) shock occurs to the value of assets used as collateral in the bank-firm relations (e.g. real estate prices), the economic activity of credit constrained borrowers should reduce (resp. expand) more than the corresponding one of unconstrained borrowers. This prediction is strictly related to the balance sheet channel of monetary policy even though the original shock does not pertain to the monetary authority. For this reason, in line with the related empirical literature, we refer to this mechanism as "the collateral channel".

Testable prediction 2: When a negative (resp. positive) shock occurs to the net worth of financial intermediaries, the economic activity of borrowers linked to affected banks should decrease (resp. increase) more than the ones linked to unaffected banks. Again, this prediction hinges on the hypothesis that borrowers face binding financial frictions and are not able to hedge the effect of a bank-specific shock, by immediately switching their main lenders. The ultimate nature of the shocks that affect the financial intermediation sector may be related to regulatory changes, to banks' investment or their funding ability. In other words, all disturbances that affect the intermediation technology of banks and their leverage capacity may give rise to a dynamic real impact on borrowers' economic activity. This prediction is a more general corollary of the bank-lending channel of monetary policy, which has been previously discussed in this section. Notice that, for this last channel to operate, we also need to assume that financial intermediaries are subject to some financial constraint that limits their ability in raising external funding when necessary. The presence of financial constraints on the intermediary side ultimately affects the supply of loans, under binding circumstances.

Testable prediction 3: When a negative (resp. positive) monetary shock occurs (e.g. an increase in the interest rates), credit supply to borrowers with tighter credit conditions should decrease (resp. increase) more than the supply of credit to other borrowers. In this regard, the presence of tighter credit conditions may be proxied, for example, by the availability of collateral or the quality of information exchange in the borrower-lender relation. According to this view, a tightening of monetary policy that reduces the net worth of borrowers should imply a reduction in credit to borrowers that is larger for less creditworthy borrowers. By contrast, an expansionary monetary policy should imply an increase in the credit allocated to less creditworthy borrowers relatively to other borrowers.

3.3   EMPIRICAL RESULTS IN THE LITERATURE

As highlighted above, the GFC inspired a renewed interest towards the FAF and its ability to explain the dynamics of the aggregate economy (see also Chapter 1). At the same time, the GFC provided a large ground for testing empirically the implications of the theory, favoured also by the diffusion of detailed microeconomic data among economists and the developments of micro-econometric techniques that allow a more reliable causal inference.

On the contrary, in the 1990s, despite its popularity, the FAT has seen relatively few empirical applications using disaggregated data at firm or bank level. The most important exception is the paper by Gilchrist and Himmelberg (1995) which studies the role of firms' cash flow on investments as a means to slack financial constraints. The authors compare the sensitivity of investment to cash flows of firms with easier access to capital markets (proxied by the access to commercial paper and bond market) with respect to firms with limited access to capital markets (indicated by the lack of participation in public debt markets). Consistently with the theoretical predictions of the FAF, they find that cash flows predict investment only for the second group of firms. In line with this evidence, Fazzari et al. (1988) find that firms' cash flows are a good predictor of investments for companies that are more likely to be financially constrained. The tightness of financial constraints is measured by the propensity to distribute dividends, or symmetrically, by the retention of internally generated financial resources. The authors find that cash flows, which proxy for the ability of companies to generate financial resources internally, are more likely to predict investments in firms characterized by more difficulties in raising external finance and, consequently, paying less dividends.

These papers not only provide the first empirical evidence on the importance of the FA using microeconomic data, but they also highlight the various identification challenges that empiricists face when testing the theory. In particular, the first challenge is related to the identification and isolation of the FA effect over and above the direct impact of borrowers' shocks on their economic activity. For example, considering the results in Gilchrist and Himmelberg (1995), the empirical link between cash flows and investments for firms with limited access to capital markets may arise because cash flows proxy for unobserved factors, like the future return on investment, that would be relevant to firms' investment decisions even in absence of capital-market frictions. Thus, the identification of the FA channel in a microeconomic setting requires that the shocks that affect the borrowers must be unrelated to their initial financial conditions and orthogonal to possible unobserved firms' characteristics. For instance, when identifying the transmission effects of bank-related shocks that influence the supply of credit to firms, it is crucial to account for the possible confounding effect of firms' credit demand; in other words, the identified effect on the credit supply must be disentangled from changes in firms' credit demand. Furthermore, it is required that the empirical setting provides enough variation in initial financial conditions of borrowers in order to estimate the impact of the binding/slack financial constraints.

The second empirical challenge regards the inability of the econometrician to directly measure the external finance premium of all potential borrowers in the economy. Two separate concerns must be highlighted about this point. The first one regards the empirical proxy used to measure the degree of the constraint. For instance, considering the hypothesis in Fazzari et al. (1988), the propensity to pay dividends may provide an inaccurate proxy: if dividend payments are used as a signal tool to the market, many financially unsound companies may be tempted to still pay dividends despite their contingency. In this regard, the incorrect measurement of financial constraints may lead to inconsistent conclusions even in the presence of a correctly identified shock to firms' net worth. Secondly, in some cases it is impossible to observe a borrower external finance premium; in other words, it is not always possible to identify the occurrence of a binding financial friction in a given state. For instance, in the presence of credit rationing, it is difficult to observe the interest rate that a bank would have charged to finance a project that has not been financed in reality. This creates a selection problem when measuring borrowers' credit conditions, simply because "unrated" or "unbanked" borrowers are not observed. As we will see in the banking context, the literature has faced this selection issue by using detailed data on loan applications or survey data regarding the occurrence of credit rationing.

A further identification challenge relates to the inherent nature of the borrower-lender relationship that is characterized by repeated interactions and information flows between a bank and a firm. The bank-firm relation is usually based on the exchange of information that is not observable and verifiable by third parties; this information specificity impacts on the degree of borrower's financial frictions and it is challenging to control or abstract from it in an empirical test.

Keeping in mind the predictions stemming from the theory, in the next sections we describe how the recent literature has addressed the above-mentioned empirical challenges and their contribution to the FAT. We separate the contributions in three groups following the sets of testable predictions we have highlighted in the previous section: (i) the balance sheet channel in the presence of firms' related shocks; (ii) the bank-lending channel in the presence of banks' related shocks; and (iii) the impact of monetary policy shocks within the FA context.

3.3.1   Empirical Test of the Collateral Channel

As explained above, one of the key testable predictions of the FAT regards the effect of changes in the borrowers' creditworthiness on the real economic activity. In this regard, it is important to highlight that the empirical literature has mainly focused on identifying exogenous changes in borrowers' creditworthiness that relate to the availability and/or the value of pledgeable collateral. This is not surprising since, as shown in Section 3.2, changes in the value of pledgeable collateral provide a variation in creditworthiness that is very close to the modelling assumptions of the theory. Furthermore, for identification purposes, changes in the values of collateral, under certain circumstances, can be immediately interpreted as shocks that are orthogonal to individual borrower's activities.

In this regard, Gan (2007) provides one of the first examples in the literature of a natural experimental setting applied to the "collateral channel" of the FAT. The paper exploits the variation in the value of Japanese firms' collateral that is due to the land market collapse in the early 1990s. The identifying hypothesis is that the real estate shock was unexpected and unrelated to firms' land holding prior to the shock; the intensity of the effect of the collapse is then pre-determined and does provide exogenous variation in the value of firms' collateral. The paper shows that larger collateral losses cause a reduction in credit availability for affected firms; this ultimately results in significant and sizeable reductions in firms' investment, in line with the FA mechanism.

Other empirical papers have adopted similar strategies based on variation in land and property values observed in the years around the GFC.

For instance, exploiting the impact of rising property values in the US in the years that preceded the GFC, Chaney et al. (2012) analyse the effect of increasing collateral values on firms' capital expenditure. The authors find that positive shocks to the collateral values, identified through an instrumental variable strategy that combines changes in interest rates with local constraints on land supply, have produced a large and significant impact on firms' investment, especially those that are more likely to be credit constrained. Working on a similar mechanism but exploiting different outcomes, Adelino et al. (2015) analysed the role of the collateral lending channel for entrepreneurship in the US in the period 2002–07. The authors exploit exogenous variation in local house prices due to housing supply elasticity and find that large increases of collateral values allowed individuals to start small businesses or to become self-employed. This effect is not present for large businesses and for firms belonging to non-tradable sectors, ruling out the spurious impact of booms in house prices on local demand shocks.

Other recent contributions have analysed similar empirical questions in different contexts. Jiménez et al. (2019) have exploited Spanish credit registry data in the years 2001–09. They show that credit supply booms induced by dynamics in the real estate market have led to modest positive real effects for borrowers, but at the same time, have positively affected the bank risk-taking attitude. Spanish banks, in fact, have softened lending standards and extended new loans to borrowers more likely to default during the downturn from 2007. This result points to the undesirable impact of credit booms, to the extent that they slack financial constraints to *ex ante* riskier borrowers. More recently, Bahaj et al. (2020), using UK data, highlight that increases in the value of residential real estate of firms' directors have a positive and significant impact on firms' investment by relaxing financial constraints.

This last result lies at the intersection of the collateral channel effect applied to the business sector and the one applied to the household sector (see also Chapters 4 on the macro effects of households' excess indebtedness). More generally, the literature has also emphasized the presence of a collateral channel related to US households in the years around the GFC. For instance, Mian and Sufi (2011) show that the strong house price appreciation from 2002 to 2006 caused a sharp increase in indebtedness for existing homeowners. Indeed, greater collateral values have facilitated the access to debt through home-equity borrowing; while the authors do not observe effective economic choices by individuals in their sample, they conclude that a large fraction of home equity-based borrowing has been used for consumption and home improvement, which have potentially contributed to the economic growth in the years before the GFC (see also

Chapter 2 on how this could be conceptualized through Minsky's financial instability hypothesis). Mian et al. (2013) showed that households with greater wealth losses have witnessed larger reduction in credit limits, refinancing likelihood, and credit scores. Taken together, these results confirm the presence of a collateral channel that works through households' and firms' creditworthiness both in booms and busts, especially for borrowers that are marginally financially constrained.

3.3.2 The Real Impact of Intermediaries' Shock

According to Bernanke and Lown (1991), a "credit crunch" episode consists in a leftward shift in the supply of credit for reasons unrelated to both the safe real interest rate and the creditworthiness of borrowers in the economy. As explained in the previous sections, such a credit-related shock provides a source of FA dynamics whenever the following conditions are met: (i) financial intermediaries, once affected by the external disturbance, face constraints in increasing their liabilities, for instance due to high costs of rising equity; (ii) borrowers are unable to smooth the negative supply effect by borrowing from alternative sources, such as unaffected banks or directly from the financial market.

The GFC has provided a prolific ground to researchers aimed at investigating the mechanisms characterizing the FAF, both from a macro and a micro point of view. Regarding the former, Gertler and Kiyotaki (2010) proposed a model of financial intermediation and business fluctuations which, indeed, leverages the experience learnt from the GFC. Regarding the latter, instead, the heterogeneity in banks' balance sheets during the financial crisis has provided a source of variation in the intensity of this external shock. However, it is worth underlining that, in this context, the main identification challenge is represented by the identification of the sources of variation in the supply of credit that do not contemporaneously affect the demand of credit. Interestingly, the idea of exploiting variation in the "health" of banks which is orthogonal to the status of their borrowers is not new. Notably, Peek and Rosengren (2000) exploit the reduction in credit supplied to US borrowers from Japanese banks at the onset of the Japanese banking crisis in the early 1990s. The shock was external to the US credit market and, consequently, unrelated to the credit demand. The authors document the presence of real negative effects on the economic activity as a result of the credit crunch.

More recently, this literature has greatly benefited from the use of credit registry data owned by central banks which allow the tracking of the bank-firm credit relationships over time. Specifically, empiricists have exploited the presence of multiple banking relationships for identification purposes, that is, the evidence that firms borrow from more than one lender at each point in time. Starting from an initial group of banks, in fact, the econometrician can separate those that are affected by an external shock from those that instead are unaffected; at the same time, it is possible to identify a company that borrows from both types of lenders. In this case, one can isolate credit demand from supply effects by including firm fixed effects in a specification that aims at testing the pre-post difference in the supply of credit following a shock. The firm fixed effects, in fact, allow to control for firm-level time changes in credit demand which are arguably the same for all banks, independently of whether they are affected or not by an external disturbance. This idea has been developed by Khwaja and Mian (2008), who study the impact of external negative shocks to bank liquidity on firms' access to credit and default rate in Pakistan. The authors conclude that smaller and less business-connected firms are less able to smooth negative credit supply shocks. However, one of the limits of this strategy is that the empiricist must rely on multi-bank-firm credit relations and ignore firms borrowing from only one bank. More generally, single bank-firm relation is quite common in many countries such as the US or Belgium. Degryse et al. (2019) have suggested that, in order to control for demand, industry–location–size–time fixed effects can be alternatively included in the econometric specification; this strategy allows us to isolate bank credit supply shocks using both single- and multi-bank-firm credit relationships.

Using credit registry data, Chodorow-Reich (2014) investigates the real effects of the US credit crunch for business activities, finding that firms that experienced pre-crisis relationships with more affected banks following the Lehman bankruptcy suffered a stronger credit supply reduction, which in turn negatively affected their employment. Similarly, Cingano et al. (2016) document that, following the drop of liquidity due to the 2007 financial crisis, the credit reduction for firms previously borrowing from mostly affected banks has implied a significant drop in investment expenditure, value added, employment and input purchases. Focusing on Spain, a similar empirical strategy has been employed (with similar results) by Bentolila et al. (2017), who examined the reduction in employment due to bank-related shocks that followed the 2008 financial and economic crisis. Furthermore, Paravisini et al. (2014) study the effect of bank credit shocks on the export of Peruvian firms in the aftermath of the 2008 financial crisis; they document the presence of a transmission channel from a negative supply shock to export through an increase in the variable cost of production for affected borrowers. However, the effects of liquidity on bank lending can potentially be non-symmetric, that is, positive liquidity shocks can potentially be ineffective in increasing credit supply to firms. This evidence has been highlighted by Khwaja et al. (2010) who find that in the presence of unexpected inflows of liquidity, backward-looking credit limit constraints imposed by banks to borrowers can limit the transmission channel from liquidity to real economic activities. In this respect, it is important to highlight that banks' regulatory and institutional constraints may curb the magnitude of the FA effect.

In the wake of the sovereign debt crisis that hit several countries from the European periphery in 2010–12, empiricists have identified its negative impact on the real economy through credit supply. For instance, using European data on syndicated loans, Acharya et al. (2018) document the negative credit supply impact of the sovereign debt crisis for banks that had large sovereign exposure. By exploiting the presence of multiple lending relationship, the authors find that the negative credit supply shock has a significant impact on investment, employment and sales growth of firms that were affiliated with affected banks. More recently, using a large sample of countries and banks, Hale et al. (2020) expanded the original idea of Peek and Rosengren (2000) on the role of banks in transmitting financial sector shocks to the real economy through cross-border linkages. They highlight a significant impact of asset-side exposures to banks in countries suffering systemic banking crises on credit, and then investment and growth of borrowing firms.

All these results confirm the presence of a real effect of credit supply shocks in different settings and for different types of shocks and validate the presence of a FA mechanism originating from shocks that arise within the credit market.

3.3.3   On the Empirics of Financial Accelerator and Monetary Policy

One of the most diffused applications of the insights from the FAT in the macroeconomic literature pertains to the monetary policy environment (Bernanke and Gertler, 1995). In particular, the so-called credit view of monetary policy highlights that exogenous shocks to the interest rates may trigger two distinct acceleration effects: (i) a central bank can directly impact the amount of credit supplied either by adjusting bank reserves or by affecting banks' net worth (which in turn affects credit supply in the presence of binding capital requirements); (ii) a central bank can influence the borrowers' creditworthiness by affecting the value of their collateral or their expected default rates. These two channels are difficult to isolate empirically since the first one strictly concerns the credit supply effect, whereas the second one is intrinsically related to changes in the demand of credit by constrained firms.

In this section we review the recent contributions in the applied microeconomic literature that confirm the predictions of the theory and tackle some key identification challenges. In line with the related literature on credit supply shocks highlighted in the previous section, we also noticed an increasing use of credit registry data in studies focusing on the impact of monetary policy shocks. Notably, Jiménez et al. (2012) addressed the identification issues by using credit registry data from Spain in the period preceding the financial crisis, that is, 2002–08. They analyse the impact of monetary policy shocks on bank credit supply and verify to what extent the transmission channel acting through bank lending to firms depends on the banks' balance sheet strength (measured by banks' capitalization and liquidity ratio). More precisely, the identification hypothesis is that monetary policy shocks arising from the European Central Bank's initiative can be considered fairly exogenous for the Spanish economy during the sample period: Spain, in fact, accounts for roughly 10 per cent of the euro area output and its business cycle does not converge with those of the euro area core countries. Furthermore, in order to control for credit demand by borrowing firms, the authors focus their analysis on loan applications made in the same month by the same borrower for the same loan to different banks. This allows the inclusion of firm-month-level fixed effects in the econometric specification that keep constant the creditworthiness of potential borrowers. The results highlight a large role of monetary policy shocks: tighter monetary conditions imply a reduction in credit supply which is stronger for constrained banks (with low capital or liquidity). On the other side, the authors find that firms are not able to smooth the effect of loan supply restrictions turning to more healthy banks, and the most affected firms are those with few existing bank relationships, pointing to a FA channel to the real economy.

Using the same data, Jiménez et al. (2014) also found that an expansionary monetary policy shock lowers the credit standards of banks and increases the risk-taking behaviour of low capitalized banks that grant more loan applications to *ex ante* riskier firms with less collateral. This result points to a potential short-run positive amplification effect of monetary policy shocks to the real economy, which, however, may seed a potential collapse in the medium run. This risk-taking channel of monetary policy has also been confirmed by Ioannidou et al. (2015) who analyse the impact of monetary changes originating from the US Federal Reserve that were exogenously transmitted to Bolivia, a dollarized country.

More recently, the literature also focused on the real impact of the collateral channel of monetary policy. In particular, Bahaj et al. (2019) show that monetary policy propagates via asset prices through corporate collateralized debt, and ultimately impacts on firms' employment. The identification strategy employed by these authors is in line with the one of Bahaj et al. (2020), with the difference of exploiting changes in monetary policy; the spatial separation between firms' location and firms' collateral allows to control for confounding effects due to contemporaneous changes in demand. They find that younger and more levered firms are particularly sensitive to monetary policy and show that these firms are subject to the largest employment response, as predicted by the FAT.

In summary, the literature has detected the presence of the FA mechanism arising from interest rate shocks, thus confirming the relevance of the credit view of monetary policy also at the microeconomic level.

3.4   FINANCIAL ACCELERATOR AT WORK IN THE COVID-19 CRISIS

The worldwide contagion of the COVID-19 virus and the absence of effective cures and vaccines prompted political authorities to reduce mobility across and within countries and to impose social distancing, quarantines and, ultimately, prolonged lockdowns. All these actions are having a visible and strong impact on the economy. In this regard, the recent COVID-19 economic crisis is different from previous crisis episodes, including the GFC, since it has not originated in the financial markets. In this section, we briefly assess whether (and to which extent) the FAF provides useful insights to better understand the future dynamics of firms' investments.

As a result of the social distancing measures and lockdown, the revenues of many companies, especially those operating in non-strategical sectors, vanished for a prolonged period. At the same time, given the unexpected nature of the shock, the reduction in revenues has not been necessarily followed by a proportional reduction in production costs, especially in the fixed ones. Moreover, firms experienced a sudden liquidity crisis which, in line with the predictions of the FAT and previous empirical evidence, could produce further large effects on the real economy. On the other side, building on the experiences learnt from the GFC, several policymakers around the world have reacted to this shock by providing a lot of liquidity to the business sector, especially in the form of debt, usually supported by government guarantees.

In a recent paper, Carletti et al. (2020) analyse the Italian case and highlight that liquidity support may not be enough to ensure recovery for two main reasons. Firstly, the longer the crisis, the greater the danger that firms may find themselves not just illiquid, but insolvent in the long run, as liquidity shortfalls may turn into equity shortfalls. Secondly, if firms emerge from this crisis overloaded with debt, their investment and growth will likely slow down due to binding financial constraints. To avoid the negative consequences of over-indebtedness in the near future, the results highlight the need for policymakers to support firms through direct equity injections in addition to liquidity supports via credit guarantees.

This position is in line with recent findings by Bergman et al. (2020) who study the effect of cash injections during the 1980s Farm Debt Crisis in the US. They exploit random weather conditions to measure the effect of weather-driven cash flow shocks on the real and the financial sectors. They find that cash flow shocks significantly reduce loan delinquency rates, the probability of bank failure, employment and wages. These results point to direct cash transfers and equity injection as a policy tool to smooth the negative impact of the COVID-19 crisis and to avoid that firms and banks will be weakened by the crisis since a sound and healthy financial sector is key for a rapid recovery.

Further insights from the FAF applied to the COVID-19 economic crisis regard the banking sector. The recovery from such an unprecedented negative shock to the firms' liquidity needs requires the presence of a robust banking sector that should not be impaired by the unavoidable increase in non-performing loans. Bank lending, in fact, tends to be procyclical, and recent policy interventions by regulatory authorities aimed at dampening the tightening of lending conditions. For example, to keep a large and robust capital base, regulators and banking federations in Europe, the UK and the USA have recommended that banks should suspend dividend distributions and share buybacks until the end of 2020 (Svoronos and Vrbaski, 2020). In this regard, Gambacorta et al. (2020) estimated that, keeping fixed the balance sheet ratios of an international sample of banks, a complete suspension of banks' dividends during the COVID-19 pandemic could have increased the bank lending capacity by roughly \$0.8–1.1 trillion of loans, equivalent to 1.1–1.6 per cent of total GDP in analysed countries.

This type of policy is undoubtedly inspired by the insights from the FAT, which can be also applied to the current context. Thanks to this theory, its insights and empirical tests, in fact, we are now aware that removing financial frictions for firms in crisis periods may be largely beneficial for the recovery.

3.5 CONCLUDING REMARKS

This work provided a summary of the financial accelerator theory, focusing in particular on the most recent contributions that have provided empirical tests of the theory, especially in the wake of the GFC. The literature has found strong empirical support for the various dynamics implied by the FAF, which are centred, in particular, on the role of financial intermediaries for the origination and/or the propagation of real and monetary policy shocks. This theory, although developed in the 1980s, still provides a backbone for analysing and interpreting some of the dynamics of recent crises, such as the COVID-19 crisis. The normative aspects of the theory, and the consequent policy actions, have not been studied in this chapter and provide, in our opinion, an important ground of research in the future.

REFERENCES

Acharya, V.V., Eisert, T., Eufinger, C. and Hirsch, C. (2018). "Real Effects of the Sovereign Debt Crisis in Europe: Evidence from Syndicated Loans". *Review of Financial Studies*, vol. 31(8), pp. 2855–96.

Adelino, M., Schoar, A. and Severino, F. (2015). "House Prices, Collateral and Self- Employment". *Journal of Financial Economics*, vol. 117(2), pp. 288–306.

Bahaj, S., Foulis, A. and Pinter, G. (2020). "Home Values and Firm Behavior". *American Economic Review*, vol.110, pp. 2225–70.

Bahaj, S., Pinter, G., Foulis, A. and Surico, P. (2019). "Employment and the Collateral Channel of Monetary Policy". Bank of England working papers, no. 827.

Bentolila, S., Jansen, M., Jiménez, G. and Ruano, S. (2017). "When Credit Dries up: Job Losses in the Great Recession". *Journal of the European Economic Association*, vol. 16(3), pp. 650–95.

Bergman, N.K., Iyer, R. and Thakor, R.T. (2020). "The Effect of Cash Injections: Evidence from the 1980s Farm Debt Crisis". *The Review of Financial Studies*, vol. 33(11), pp. 5093–130.

Bernanke, B.S. (1983). "Nonmonetary Effects of the Financial Crisis in the Propagation of the Great Depression". *American Economic Review*, vol. 73(3), pp. 257–76.

Bernanke, B.S. and Blinder, A.S. (1988). "Credit, Money, and Aggregate Demand". *American Economic Review*, vol. 78, pp. 435–9.

Bernanke, B.S. and Gertler, M. (1989). "Agency Costs, Net Worth, and Business Fluctuations". *American Economic Review*, vol. 79(1), pp. 14–31.

Bernanke, B.S. and Gertler, M. (1995). "Inside the Black Box: The Credit Channel of Monetary Policy Transmission". *Journal of Economic Perspectives*, vol. 9, pp. 27–48.

Bernanke, B.S. and Lown, C.S. (1991). "The Credit Crunch". *Brookings Papers on Economic Activity*, vol. 2, pp. 205–47.

Bernanke, B.S., Gertler, M. and Gilchrist, S. (1996). "The Financial Accelerator and the Flight to Quality". *The Review of Economics and Statistics*, vol. 78(1), pp. 1–15.

Bolton, P. and Freixas, X. (2000). "Equity, Bonds, and Bank Debt: Capital Structure and Financial Market Equilibrium under Asymmetric Information". *Journal of Political Economy*, vol. 108(2), pp. 324–51.

Carletti, E., Oliviero, T., Pagano, M., Pelizzon, L. and Subrahmanyam, M.G. (2020). "The COVID-19 Shock and Equity Shortfall: Firm Level Evidence from Italy". *Review of Corporate Finance Studies*, vol. 9(3), pp. 534–68.

Chaney, T., Sraer, S. and Thesmar, D. (2012). "The Collateral Channel: How Real Estate Shocks Affect Corporate Investment". *American Economic Review*, vol. 102(6), pp. 2381–409.

Chodorow-Reich, G. (2014). "The Employment Effects of Credit Market Disruptions: Firm-level Evidence from the 2008–09 Financial Crisis". *Quarterly Journal of Economics*, vol. 129(1), pp. 1–59.

Cingano, F., Manaresi, F. and Sette, E. (2016). "Does Credit Crunch Investment Down? New Evidence on the Real Effects of the Bank-Lending Channel". *Review of Financial Studies*, vol. 29(10), pp. 2737–73.

Degryse, H., De Jonghe, O., Jakovljević, S., Mulier, K. and Schepens, G. (2019). "Identifying Credit Supply Shocks with Bank-Firm Data: Methods and Applications". *Journal of Financial Intermediation*, vol. 40, p. 100813.

Fazzari, M.S., Hubbard, R.G. and Petersen, B.C. (1988). "Financing Constraints and Corporate Investment". *Brooking Papers on Economic Activity*, vol. 1, pp. 141–95.

Fisher, I. (1933). "The Debt-Deflation Theory of Great Depressions". *Econometrica*, vol. 1, pp. 337–57.

Gambacorta, L., Oliviero, T. and Shin, H.S. (2020). "Low Price-to-Book Ratios and Bank Dividend Payout Policies". BIS working paper, no. 907.

Gan, J. (2007). "Collateral, Debt Capacity, and Corporate Investment: Evidence from a Natural Experiment". *Journal of Financial Economics*, vol. 85(3), pp. 709–34.

Gertler, M. and Kiyotaki, N. (2010). "Financial Intermediation and Credit Policy in Business Cycle Analysis". In *Handbook of Monetary Economics* (ed. B.M. Friedman and M. Woodford), vol. 3, chapter 11, pp. 547–99, North-Holland, Netherlands.

Gilchrist, S. and Himmelberg, C.P. (1995). "Evidence on the Role of Cash Flow for Investment". *Journal of Monetary Economics*, vol. 36, pp. 541–72.

Hale, G., Kapan, T. and Minoiu, C. (2020). "Shock Transmission through Cross-Border Bank Lending: Credit and Real Effects". *The Review of Financial Studies*, vol. 33(10), pp. 4839–82.

Holmstrom, B. and Tirole, J. (1997). "Financial Intermediation, Loanable Funds, and the Real Sector". *Quarterly Journal of Economics*, vol. 112(3), pp. 663–91.

Ioannidou, V., Ongena, S. and Peydró, J.-L. (2015). "Monetary Policy, Risk-Taking, and Pricing: Evidence from a Quasi-Natural Experiment". *Review of Finance*, vol. 19, pp. 95–144.

Jiménez, G., Mian, A., Peydró, J.L. and Saurina, J. (2019). "The Real Effects of the Bank Lending Channel". *Journal of Monetary Economics*, vol. 115, pp. 162–79.

Jiménez, G., Ongena, S., Peydró, J.-L. and Saurina, J. (2012). "Credit Supply and Monetary Policy: Identifying the Bank Balance-Sheet Channel with Loan Applications". *American Economic Review*, vol. 102, pp. 2301–26.

Jiménez, G., Ongena, S., Peydró, J.-L. and Saurina, J. (2014). "Hazardous Times for Monetary Policy: What Do Twenty-three Million Bank Loans Say about the Effects of Monetary Policy on Credit Risk-taking?". *Econometrica*, vol. 82, pp. 463–505.

Khwaja, A.I. and Mian, A. (2008). "Tracing the Impact of Bank Liquidity Shocks: Evidence from an Emerging Market". *American Economic Review*, vol. 98, pp. 1413–42.

Khwaja, A.I., Mian, A. and Zia, B. (2010). "Dollars Dollars Everywhere, Nor Any Dime to Lend: Credit Limit Constraints on Financial Sector Absorptive Capacity". *The Review of Financial Studies*, vol. 23(12), pp. 4281–323.

Mian, A. and Sufi, A. (2011). "House Prices, Home Equity Based Borrowing, and the U.S. Household Leverage Crisis". *American Economic Review*, vol. 101, pp. 2132–56.

Mian, A., Rao, K. and Sufi, A. (2013). "Household Balance Sheets, Consumption, and the Economic Slump". *Quarterly Journal of Economics*, vol. 128, pp. 1687–726.

Paravisini, D., Rappoport, V., Schnabl, P. and Wolfenzon, D. (2014). "Dissecting the Effect of Credit Supply on Trade: Evidence from Matched Credit-Export Data". *Review of Economic Studies*, vol. 82, pp. 333–59.

Peek, J. and Rosengren, E.S. (2000). "Collateral Damage: Effects of the Japanese Bank Crisis on Real Activity in the United States". *American Economic Review*, vol. 90(1), pp. 30–45.

Svoronos, J.P. and Vrbaski, R. (2020). "Banks Dividends in Covid-19 Times", FSI Briefs, 6.

PART II

Main channels of transmission of the financial shock

4. The role of the household balance sheets

Christophe André[1]

4.1 INTRODUCTION

Excessive household leverage, generally associated with property market booms, has often contributed to financial crises, with notable variations in the role of the household balance sheets and the associated transmission channels across countries and historical episodes. In a few cases, excessive optimism from borrowers and risk-taking by financial institutions directly led to a wave of mortgage defaults. The most notorious example is the US subprime mortgage crisis, which started in 2007 and triggered the 2008 Global Financial Crisis (GFC) (see Chapter 1), but other countries, especially where foreign currency mortgages were widely marketed, also saw a sharp rise in defaults in the wake of the GFC. In other cases, mortgage defaults were mostly the consequence of a sharp deterioration in general economic conditions, notably a fall in income and a rise in unemployment. Nevertheless, in most financial crises, mortgage arrears and foreclosures remained relatively modest. Even so, household finance played an important role in many financial meltdowns through a number of indirect channels. In some cases, rapid lending growth led banks to rely on fragile financing structures, which were vulnerable to an evaporation in liquidity. Mortgages account for the bulk of household debt in Organisation for Economic Co-operation and Development (OECD) countries. Housing markets are prone to boom-bust cycles and recessions associated with housing market meltdowns are generally deeper and more protracted than other downturns. Banks are often heavily exposed to the construction and commercial real estate sectors, which tend to be highly leveraged and vulnerable to changes in market conditions. Moreover, housing price cycles affect household consumption through wealth and collateral effects. The weakening in economic conditions associated with a sharp fall in housing prices can result in second round effects on loan performance and lead to a credit crunch, which worsens the recession. This chapter first examines risks related to excessively soft lending standards for household loans. It goes on to describe the relations between household finance and developments in the property market and their macroeconomic consequences. Finally, it looks at the policies which have been implemented to contain risks associated with excessive household indebtedness, especially since the GFC.

4.2 LENDING STANDARDS AND HOUSEHOLDS' VULNERABILITY

Household balance sheets are sizeable. Total liabilities amount to more than a year of household income in the majority of advanced economies and more than two and a half years in Denmark (Table 4.1). Mortgages account for about two-thirds of household liabilities in OECD countries on average. In most OECD countries, gross household debt is now higher than in 2000 and in several cases it has increased significantly since the GFC. However, in most countries, the debt service ratio is lower than in 2008, as interest rates have fallen. At the aggregate level, household assets are much greater than debt. For the countries in Table 4.1, both financial and non-financial assets (in large part dwellings and land) range from about two and a half to seven years of income. A large part of the debt is held by households in the upper part of the income distribution, which in addition to the asset which serves as collateral, often have financial buffers. This can be illustrated by data from the euro area and the US (Figure 4.1). In the euro area, less than a quarter of households in the bottom 20 per cent of the income distribution (first quintile) are indebted, compared to more than 60 per cent in the top quintile (Panel A). Furthermore, the amount of debt rises with income. Half of the borrowers in the bottom income quintile have debt below EUR 6,800 (Panel B). Median mortgage debt in the same income quintile is substantially higher (EUR 43,200), but less than 8 per cent of households in this quintile have mortgages. In the upper quintile, median total debt reaches EUR 75,000 and median mortgage debt exceeds EUR 100,000. Households in the bottom income quintile account for a low share of debt, but they are more vulnerable to a deterioration in economic conditions than other groups, as they have substantially higher debt-to-assets and debt service-to-income ratios, as well as much lower liquidity buffers (Panel C).[2] In the US, nearly half of total debt and 55 per cent of mortgage debt is concentrated in the top income quintile. Households in the bottom 40 per cent of the income distribution only hold about 13 per cent of outstanding debt (Panel D). The concentration of mortgage debt among households with relatively high income explains the generally low default rates on mortgages. In addition, in most countries, mortgages are full-recourse, meaning

Table 4.1 Household liabilities and assets in selected countries

| | Liabilities | | | Assets | | | | | | Debt service ratio | | |
| | | | | Financial | | | Non-financial | | | | | |
	2000	2008	2018	2000	2008	2018	2000	2008	2018	2000	2008	2018
Australia	131.3	192.5	219.2	321.0	352.2	469.6	525.3	604.6	708.3 (1)	11.4	17.1	15.7
Belgium	71.4	90.0	113.9	486.1	439.1	525.9	400.0	550.0	615.0	5.9	6.4	7.2
Canada	106.6	149.5	176.1	408.1	391.4	534.3	327.9	393.3	495.5	11.0	13.0	13.0
Denmark	227.2	334.6	277.6	453.1	510.8	629.9	n.a.	596.6	431.9	17.5	22.6	15.1
Finland	67.4	114.3	144.8	218.9	203.7	266.9	350.9	396.0	389.1 (1)	5.0	8.2	7.1
France	76.5	102.8	120.7	315.9	300.9	387.5	332.8	538.7	575.5	4.8	5.9	6.3
Germany	118.4	101.9	95.3	274.7	279.4	326.1	359.7	376.5	455.9	9.8	8.0	6.2
Ireland	110.7 (3)	228.6	140.4	333.2 (3)	303.0	356.7	n.a.	n.a.	n.a.	n.a.	n.a.	n.a.
Italy	41.5	68.6	74.0	369.3	351.3	376.2	436.7	619.3	589.5 (1)	3.5	5.2	4.3
Japan	114.5	112.9	110.9	490.0	514.9	603.9	456.5	401.2	363.9	8.9	7.7	6.8
Korea	91.3	138.5	184.2	231.4	273.3	383.8	441.2	672.9	697.6	9.0	11.6	11.7
Netherlands	192.9	261.9	235.4	528.9	542.0	706.9	444.5	571.2	540.8	14.7	17.8	15.8
Norway	135.7	209.0	240.3	212.0	275.5	316.5	357.9	448.9	504.2 (2)	11.2	16.4	15.1
Portugal	105.9	148.9	126.7	262.8	295.6	329.7	n.a.	n.a.	n.a.	7.6	10.8	6.3
Spain	84.7	146.6	107.0	252.5	265.1	310.2	494.2	855.9	704.7	5.8	11.4	6.4

Sweden	109.8	157.8	188.5	376.5	426.2	595.0	233.7	335.8	394.4 (1)	9.1	11.5	11.5
United Kingdom	105.6	162.6	141.3	456.6	433.0	487.2	263.9	380.2	421.2	9.1	12.7	9.0
United States	99.9	131.7	101.8	465.0	440.0	542.4	236.9	255.9	240.6	9.9	11.1	8.0

(1): 2017, (2): 2016, (3): 2001.

Note: Debt service includes interest payments and debt amortisation. Non-financial assets: for Belgium, Germany, fixed assets and land; For Finland,Norway and Sweden, produced assets and land; for the Netherlands, fixed assets, inventories and land; for Spain, dwellings and land.

Source: OECD, Bank for International Settlements, Statistics Denmark and ISTAT.

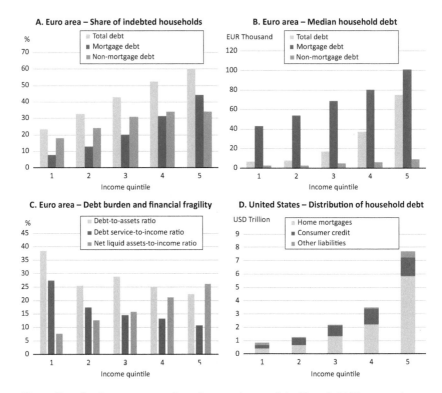

Note: Data for the euro area are from the second wave of the Household Finance and Consumption Survey, in which the reference year is 2013 or 2014 for most countries (2011 for Spain). Data for the United States refer to 2019 Q3. In panel B, median debt for households holding the relevant type of debt.

Source: European Central Bank and US Federal Reserve.

Figure 4.1   *Distribution of debt by income quintile in the euro area and the United States*

that surrendering an asset with a value below that of the loan would not eliminate the liability. This removes the opportunity for strategic default. Altogether, residential mortgage debt has historically been relatively safe in most countries. Even in severe economic crises with large drops in housing prices, residential mortgage defaults have generally been contained, with a number of exceptions examined below. Consumer debt accounts for a much smaller share of total household debt than mortgages and has so far played a limited role in financial crises, even though it is generally riskier, as it tends to be unsecured and concentrated among lower-income households. Nevertheless, concerns about rapid growth and relatively high delinquencies among US student and auto loans in recent years are compounded by the COVID-19 outbreak's impact on jobs and incomes.

While mortgage arrears have remained modest in most OECD countries in the wake of the GFC, they have soared in a few countries. Figure 4.2 shows the evolution of mortgage arrears in five countries to illustrate differences in magnitude and timing. All these countries experienced sharp falls in housing prices from 2007, ranging from 21 per cent in the UK to 52 per cent in Ireland, from peak to trough (André and Chalaux, 2018). Nevertheless, mortgage arrears vary widely across these countries. In addition, the timing of the rise in arrears points to different underlying causes. In the US, mortgage defaults jumped from early 2007, almost immediately after housing prices had started to fall in some states, reflecting the fact that many subprime mortgages were likely to be repaid only under the assumption of continuously rising housing prices, which would allow selling the dwelling or refinancing the loan. Indeed, some lender pre-crisis default projections conditional on housing price developments turned out to be strikingly accurate when housing prices fell, confirming

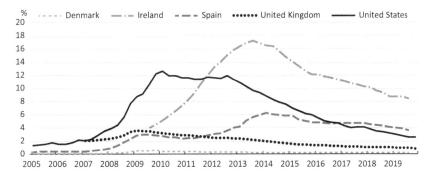

Note: The rate levels are not fully comparable across countries, as definitions of arrears differ. The purpose of this chart is to illustrate the pattern of mortgage defaults during and after the GFC. For Denmark, share of the total repayments unmet 3½ months after the latest due date for private owner-occupied homes, based on reports from the mortgage banks. For Ireland, percentage of residential mortgage loan balances in arrears for more than 90 days; for Spain, percentage of loans for house purchase more than 30 days in arrears; for the United Kingdom, percentage of residential loans to individuals with arrears amounting to 1.5 per cent or more of loan balances; for the United States, delinquency rate (30 days or more) on single-family residential mortgages, booked in domestic offices, top 100 banks ranked by assets.

Source: Finance Denmark, Central Bank of Ireland, Bank of Spain, Bank of England – Financial Conduct Authority, Federal Reserve Bank of St. Louis (FRED).

Figure 4.2   Patterns of mortgage delinquencies around the GFC in selected countries

the role of over-optimistic housing price expectations during the subprime market expansion (Foote and Willen, 2018).[3] The rapid subprime mortgage market growth from the early 2000s to its peak between 2004 and 2006, when it reached around 20 per cent of total mortgage originations, was accompanied by a marked loosening of underwriting standards. As described in Chapter 1, the subprime mortgage market caters to borrowers unable to qualify for conventional loans because of poor credit history, insufficient guarantees or both. A variety of non-standard products were used to generate more business, including mortgages with teaser rates (low interest rates for a limited period), interest-only, negative amortisation and flexible repayment loans. In the worst case, so-called NINJA (No Income, No Job, No Assets) loans were extended to households who could not certify an income or a job and had no assets to guarantee the repayment of the loan. Many borrowers were unlikely to be able to pay back their loans out of ordinary income, especially at the expiration of a teaser rate period. Hence, the viability of the mortgage depended on the rise in home equity. Once housing prices started falling, subprime defaults soared. The prevalence of non-recourse mortgages in many US states also led to some strategic defaults for mortgages in negative equity, that is, those with an amount higher than the value of the underlying asset. By 2012, nearly a third of mortgages were in negative equity.

Spain and Ireland had experienced rapid housing price increases and construction booms in the run up to the GFC. Lending standards had also been eased during this period. Nevertheless, the rise in arrears immediately after initial housing price falls was much more modest than in the US. However, defaults continued to increase for much longer. In Spain, although mortgage defaults increased rapidly after housing prices had started to fall in late 2007, their level remained moderate and stabilised towards the end of 2009. However, a greater increase followed the European sovereign debt crisis, with a peak as late as early 2014. In Ireland, where housing prices peaked in mid-2007, arrears in the third quarter of 2009, albeit relatively high, were still far from the peak they would reach in the third quarter of 2013. The timing of defaults in Spain and Ireland contrasts with the pattern observed in the US and is consistent with different underlying causes. Contrary to US households with negative equity, their Spanish and Irish counterparts had no incentive to default, as they had recourse loans. Hence, as long as they had the capacity to repay their loans, they were likely to do so. However, the Spanish and Irish economies were very dependent on construction and their financial sectors were highly exposed to property at the time of the crisis, which was followed by a deep recession and a banking crisis. The financial position of households was further weakened by austerity measures, which pushed up mortgage defaults as incomes shrank and unemployment soared. In Ireland, even though the number of foreclosures rose sharply in the wake of the GFC, it remained relatively low with respect to the number of outstanding mortgages. Personal insolvency legislation was reformed in 2012 to facilitate the orderly debt restructuring and resolution, which has yet to be completed, since 3.6 per cent of mortgages on primary dwellings remained over 720 days in arrears at end-2019. In Spain, more than 4 per cent of mortgages ended in foreclosure between 2008 and 2013, a high share by European standards, although less than a third of the US percentage (Andritzky, 2014).

Denmark and the UK stand out as countries which, despite sharp falls in housing prices during the GFC, recorded relatively few mortgage defaults. The introduction of interest-only loans in Denmark in 2004 was followed by a housing price and consumption boom, many households had no clear repayment strategy (Lunde et al., 2008) and aggregate gross household debt is the highest in the OECD. Nevertheless, household finances remained generally sound. The recession was much less severe than in Ireland or Spain. In particular, although the unemployment rate increased, it peaked at a much lower level. The strong Danish social safety net also helps households weather recessions and legal settings discourage strategic defaults. The fall in interest rates in the aftermath of the GFC alleviated the financial burden on households. Lower interest rates also contributed to resilience in the UK, where the early 2000s had seen rapid growth in household debt, boosted by declining interest rates and a loosening in credit standards. In 2007, high-risk loans, such as those lacking income verification, with a high loan-to-income value or interest-only, accounted for a significant share of underwriting (FSA, 2009). Nevertheless, UK mortgage defaults remained fairly low during the downturn. As discussed below, the UK financial system was more vulnerable through the funding strategy of some of its mortgage lenders than through household credit risk.

In some Central and Eastern European countries, mortgages denominated in foreign currencies, mainly Swiss franc and euro, were a major source of mortgage distress in the wake of the GFC. One of the worst hit countries was Hungary, where the share of foreign currency mortgages was about 70 per cent in 2008. These loans carried much lower interest rates than those labelled in the national currency, but exposed borrowers to rising repayments in case of exchange rate depreciation. Banks with funding in foreign currency offloaded the currency risk to borrowers, but at the price of higher credit risk. The large depreciation of the forint after 2008 increased the household loan repayment burden by 30 to 40 per cent on average, pushing up the share of non-performing loans to about

15 per cent in 2012 (IMF, 2012). Iceland experienced rapid lending growth, following the deregulation of its mortgage market in 2004. Mortgages were generally linked to the consumer price index (CPI) and, from 2006, increasingly linked to foreign currencies, notably the Japanese yen and the Swiss franc. Following the GFC, the krona depreciated by more than 50 per cent in effective terms, pushing the inflation rate to about 17 per cent. As a result of foreign currency or CPI-indexation, nearly a quarter of homeowners had debt service exceeding 40 per cent of their disposable income at the end of 2008 and a collapse in housing prices pushed close to 40 per cent of homeowners into negative equity by 2010. Eventually, the government and financial authorities set up a plan to allow writing off mortgage debt exceeding 110 per cent of the property value under specific conditions and household debt written off amounted to more than 12 per cent of GDP at end-2011 (Skulason, 2012).

To sum up, defaults on household debt are generally not primary causes of financial crises. A large share of this debt is generally held by households with relatively high income, most of whom generally remain able to service the debt even under adverse economic and housing market conditions. However, there are exceptions, the most notorious being the US subprime crisis, which triggered the GFC, even though it is insufficient to explain its magnitude, which was amplified by high leverage and vulnerabilities in the global financial system (Bernanke, 2010; Kamin and DeMarco, 2012). Second round effects, and notably the rise in unemployment, caused a rise in mortgage arrears in countries severely hit by the crisis, especially in some countries at the periphery of the euro area. The importance of unemployment as a determinant of mortgage defaults should be highlighted as the COVID-19 crisis takes its toll on jobs around the world (see Chapter 9). Income support from governments is decisive to allow households to continue repaying their debt, but additional measures like debt payment deferral and forbearance may be necessary in some countries, especially if the crisis lingers. The next section turns to the broader effects of housing boom-bust cycles on financial stability and the economy.

4.3   HOUSEHOLD DEBT AND HOUSING MARKET DYNAMICS

Buying dwellings is the main borrowing motive for households and increases in mortgage debt are closely related to rising housing prices, with a two-way causality (Anundsen and Jansen, 2013; Basten and Koch, 2015). Higher housing prices require bigger loans to purchase dwellings and increase the value of collateral available to secure credit. But cheaper and more accessible credit also allows households to increase their demand for housing, pushing prices up (Duca et al., 2011). The housing market is at the core of the relation between household balance sheets and financial crises. Property markets are volatile, prone to bubbles and tend to generate large spillovers to the wider economy (Goodhart and Hofmann, 2008; Iacoviello and Neri, 2010). Recessions linked with housing price busts are generally deeper and longer than other downturns (Reinhart and Rogoff, 2013; Jordá et al., 2016). Moreover, international synchronisation of housing prices has increased over time, worsening the risk of international spillovers and global recessions. According to *The Economist*, the global housing boom which preceded the GFC was the "biggest bubble in history".[4]

Housing prices are loosely anchored. While the price of structures is closely related to construction costs, at least in a competitive environment, the price of land in a particular location is essentially determined by the price buyers are willing to pay for it. This, in turn, depends on amenities (e.g. access to good schools, leisure, transports), preferences and expectations of future prices. As a consumption good, housing demand would decrease with prices. However, housing is also an investment. To the extent households expect prices to increase further and have access to credit, they may not be discouraged by high prices. Potential homebuyers are often afraid of being priced out of the market if prices continue rising. Their willingness to buy may be reinforced by the observation that the combination of rising demand and inelastic supply has led to a persistent upward long-term trend in housing prices in favoured locations (Gyourko et al., 2013). In fact, housing demand is largely driven by potential buyers' ability to pay (Damen et al., 2016). Furthermore, the financial accelerator (see Chapter 3) increases borrowing capacities during housing price upswings (Iacoviello, 2005). With rising asset prices, the value of collateral increases, allowing more borrowing, which further fuels investments in assets and lifts their prices, generating more collateral and borrowing and so on.

In the long run, housing prices are driven by household income, mortgage rates, credit availability, demographics, property taxation, including mortgage interest deductibility, as well as supply responsiveness (Meen, 2002; Muellbauer and Murphy, 2008), which is affected by both physical and regulatory constraints (Glaeser et al., 2005; Green et al., 2005; Caldera and Johansson, 2013). Small changes in fundamentals can trigger large swings in housing prices. It is also important to note that not only real, but also nominal interest rates affect households' ability to borrow, as higher nominal rates imply a higher initial repayment annuity. As banks generally set the ceiling for the repayment annuity as a percentage of the borrower's income, a higher nominal interest rate creates a tighter credit constraint, for a given level of real interest rate. Hence, falling trends in global inflation over the past decades have loosened households' financial constraint, aiding to lift housing demand. Besides, the relation between interest rates and borrowing capacity is non-linear. A given percentage point reduction in mortgage rates from a low level has a greater impact on borrowing capacity than the same reduction from a higher level. Obviously, the increase in borrowing can be contained by other constraints on borrowers, such as loan-to-value (LTV) caps and debt service-to-income limits.

However, in the run-up to the GFC, the fall in interest rates was generally accompanied by a loosening of borrowing constraints. For example, mortgage repayment periods were often extended, up to 50 years in Spain. Many countries allowed LTV ratios as high as 100 per cent and in a few cases, like the Netherlands, even higher. The share of variable rate and interest-only loans increased markedly in some countries, including the US. As noted above, some Central and Eastern European and Icelandic banks abundantly used foreign currency mortgages to take advantage of lower foreign interest rates, at the price of exposing borrowers to sizeable exchange rate risk. Low documentation loans became more common. Such loans, which have traditionally been granted to self-employed who could not document a steady stream of income, were increasingly extended to salaried workers, creating an incentive to overstate their income. For example, according to the UK Financial Services Authority, incomes were not verified in the case of 49 per cent of all UK regulated mortgage sales in 2007 (FSA, 2009). After the GFC, lending conditions generally tightened, as a result of both lenders' behaviour and stricter regulations.

Shifts in housing demand, for example related to a loosening of credit conditions, tend to generate ample cycles. Expectations of housing prices tend to be extrapolative (Muellbauer, 2012; Glaeser and Nathanson, 2015), which leads housing prices to overshoot. The combination of extrapolative expectations and delayed supply responses generates cycles, whose amplitude depends on the price elasticity of supply. This can be illustrated by the experience of some OECD countries around the GFC. In the UK, where land-use planning rules are very restrictive, the pre-crisis years were marked by a rapid increase in housing prices and a limited expansion of construction. Conversely Ireland, Spain and some US states experienced both soaring housing prices and construction booms. Following the crisis, an overhang of unsold homes pulled housing prices much further down in these places than in the UK and the collapse in residential investment had a large impact on GDP growth and employment.

Housing supply responses also have implications for financial stability, as loans to highly leveraged real estate developers and construction companies tend to generate much more defaults than residential mortgages during downturns. Following the GFC, the construction sector went into a deep crisis in Ireland and Spain, where residential investment had peaked at respectively almost 14 per cent and 12 per cent of GDP during the boom, when the typical range in OECD countries is 3 to 6 per cent. In both cases, sharp competition between lenders lowered underwriting standards and the financial accelerator was powerful during the boom, with developers borrowing increasing amounts against the rising value of real estate and land. The expansion was in great part financed by foreign capital inflows, reflected in current account deficits of more than 9 per cent of GDP in Ireland and more than 6 per cent of GDP in Spain in 2007. The GFC triggered a severe banking crisis in Ireland, where most of the banks had to be nationalised and recapitalised. A "bad bank", the National Asset Management Agency (NAMA), was established in late 2009 to manage impaired development-related loans. It acquired assets for around 46 per cent of GDP, with an average haircut of 58 per cent. By early 2020, it had disposed of most of these assets and was expected to return a surplus of EUR 4 billion. Even though the "bad bank" was ultimately a success, like earlier similar experiences in Finland, Sweden and the US, the cost of the banking sector bailout initially weighed heavily on public finances, which already suffered from the fall in revenue resulting from the collapse in economic activity. In November 2010 the government had to apply for a European Central Bank-European Union-International Monetary Fund (ECB-EU-IMF) rescue programme, which imposed tough austerity measures. Real GDP fell cumulatively more than 8 per cent in 2008–09 and the unemployment rate soared from below 5 per cent in 2007 to above 14 per cent in 2012.

While major Spanish commercial banks proved more solid than Irish banks, partly thanks to better international diversification, savings banks suffered from their exposure to the real estate sector and underwent vast restructuring, their number dropping from 45 in 2007 to just 2 at the end of 2012. As in Ireland, a "bad bank" was created in July 2012 to take over the distressed real estate assets of troubled financial institutions (SAREB, Sociedad de Gestión de Activos procedentes de la Reestructuración Bancaria). It bought assets amounting to nearly 5 per cent of GDP, of which 80 per cent were financial assets and 20 per cent property, at a discount of 46 per cent and 63 per cent respectively. Disposing of assets proved more difficult for SAREB than for NAMA, as it faced persistent difficult market conditions and competition from banks selling assets with large discounts. By end-2019, SAREB had reduced its loan portfolio and total assets by only 51 per cent and 36 per cent respectively. SAREB has been given until 2027 to dispose of its assets and its ability to achieve this in a satisfactory way will depend largely on market conditions. The financial crisis, the recession and the euro area sovereign debt crisis weighed heavily on Spanish public finances, eventually forcing the government to apply for support from the European Financial Stability Facility (EFSF) in June 2012. The collapse of the real estate sector, financial distress and contractionary fiscal policy pushed the economy into a deep recession. Real GDP contracted almost 9 per cent between 2008 and 2013 and unemployment jumped to over a quarter of the labour force in 2013.

Another source of vulnerability for financial institutions can be their funding model (see Chapter 6). Although maturity transformation is an intrinsic function of banking and not specific to property-related business, the funding of mortgages is a key issue for financial stability. Mortgages amount on average to about 60 per cent of bank lending in advanced economies, a share which has been on an upward long-term trend (Jordá et al., 2016). The rising share of mortgages in bank portfolios has increased the maturity mismatch between assets and liabilities (Goodhart and Perotti, 2015). When mortgages are funded through the issuance of short-term securities, liquidity risks can be sizeable. This is illustrated by the case of the UK during the GFC. While mortgage delinquencies increased sharply in the US, making it difficult to disentangle liquidity from solvency issues, they remained contained in the UK. However, mortgage lenders were vulnerable through their funding model. Between 2001 and 2008, the UK bank funding gap between lending and retail deposits had grown from close to zero to roughly 50 per cent of GDP, and almost half of it was financed through interbank deposits from abroad. As a result of the tensions on global money markets generated by the shockwave from the US subprime crisis, in September 2007 Northern Rock faced the first run on a British bank since 1866. The bank had relied heavily on wholesale funding to fund a rapid expansion of its loan portfolio, which grew at an average annual rate of over 30 per cent between 2001 and 2006 (Onado, 2009). When confidence in mortgage-backed securities evaporated, refinancing proved impossible and the government had to bail out the bank. Another important UK mortgage lender, Bradford and Bingley, also collapsed and in 2010 the government had to set up the UK Asset Resolution holding (UKAR) to manage and wind down the mortgage portfolios of the failed mortgage lenders. UKAR's initial assets amounted to more than 7 per cent of GDP and the holding received about 3 per cent of GDP in government loans, which were fully repaid by June 2019.

Since the GFC, prudential regulations have been reinforced, both in terms of capital requirements and liquidity buffers. Nevertheless, part of housing finance may remain vulnerable to financial market turmoil. For example, Kim et al. (2018) point to a systemic liquidity risk associated with US non-bank mortgage lenders, which tend to serve lower income households, face looser regulatory constraints than banks, and have seen their share of total originations grow rapidly, to about half of the market in 2019. The Swedish central bank has also warned about structural liquidity risks related to the funding of mortgages using covered bonds with a much shorter maturity (Sveriges Riksbank, 2016). These examples point to the need for policymakers to carefully monitor the liquidity risks taken by mortgage lenders and encourage better maturity matching between assets and liabilities.

Risks related to short-term funding are amplified when a large part comes from abroad. Sudden capital inflows, often triggered by financial deregulation accompanied by inadequate supervision of financial institutions, have fuelled numerous asset price bubbles around the world over the past decades. Foreign investors are generally quick to exit in times of crisis, which exacerbates the difficulties. Financial crises are often preceded by current account imbalances (Reinhart and Rogoff, 2008).[5] The association between current account deficits and rising housing prices can derive from two different mechanisms, which are not mutually exclusive. On the one hand, net capital inflows, which are the mirror image of the current account balance, can lift housing prices by lowering long-term mortgage rates (Sá and Wieladek, 2015; Miles, 2018). This mechanism was emphasised in a famous speech by Ben Bernanke shortly before he became Chairman of the US Federal Reserve, in which he pointed to the role of a global saving glut, mainly resulting from high saving in East Asia and oil producing countries, in explaining the US current account deficit and the low level of long-term interest rates, which in turn fuelled the housing market boom (Bernanke, 2005). However, the US is not an isolated case and many past property booms were largely financed from abroad, including those that preceded the Nordic and Asian crises of the 1990s (André and Chalaux, 2018). Looking at a more recent period, Figure 4.3 shows that, with a few exceptions, real housing prices and residential investment move in the opposite direction from the current account balance. In particular, a large deterioration of the current account coincided with the Irish and Spanish construction booms. On the other hand, higher housing prices can boost consumption through wealth and collateral effects and higher domestic demand can deteriorate the current account balance (Ferrero, 2015). The relation between housing prices and private consumption is explored in more detail in the next section.

4.4 HOUSEHOLD BALANCE SHEETS AND AGGREGATE DEMAND

Cycles in credit to households have a major impact on aggregate demand. As described above, higher housing wealth can boost consumption, especially where housing equity withdrawal is easily accessible.[6] Residential investment is a relatively small, but volatile component of GDP. Figure 4.3 provides a snapshot of developments in real housing prices, residential investment, saving ratios and the current account balance around the GFC in the same country sample as in Table 4.1. As housing prices peaked around 2007 in most of the countries covered, changes in the preceding and following five years are shown. Although this summary does not fully capture the diversity in national housing market developments, as cycles were not exactly synchronised across countries, it allows identifying broad patterns in relations between housing prices and some key macroeconomic variables.

In the majority of countries, real housing prices and the saving ratio move in opposite directions. This is consistent with the well-known impact of housing prices on private consumption through the collateral effect, whereby higher housing wealth allows households to borrow against the value of their home to finance consumption (Muellbauer and Murphy, 2008). Recent studies using sub-national or micro data show

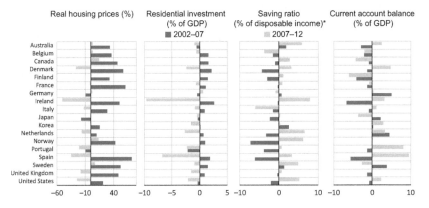

Note: * Gross saving for France, Portugal and the United Kingdom, net saving for other countries.

Source: OECD Economic Outlook database.

Figure 4.3   Change in real housing prices and selected macroeconomic indicators around the GFC

that highly indebted households reduced consumption more than others during the downturn following the GFC. Mian et al. (2013) find that the marginal propensity to consume out of housing wealth is highest in areas of the US with poorer and more leveraged households, which are facing the tightest credit constraints. Bunn (2014) shows that highly indebted households in the UK cut spending more than less leveraged ones after 2007, reversing stronger pre-crisis consumption growth, and presents survey evidence that lower spending was associated with a combination of tighter credit constraints and concerns about ability to make future debt repayments. Lau Andersen et al. (2016) find that highly leveraged Danish households reduced consumption more than less leveraged ones after 2007, correcting unsustainable pre-crisis consumption levels, and point to precautionary savings and revisions to income expectations. Van Beers et al. (2015) find a negative relation between housing price changes and savings in a large panel of Dutch households over the period 2006–11, with the strongest response for young households with negative equity, which is consistent with the presence of credit constraints.

A rise in housing prices generally triggers a supply response, albeit varying widely across places, in particular according to land availability, which is often limited by natural or regulatory constraints. In countries where construction is relatively responsive, residential investment can make a substantial contribution to the business cycle. Leamer (2007) documents weakness in residential investment prior to most US post-war recessions. Figure 4.3 shows large falls in the share of residential investment in GDP in many countries following the GFC, with the most dramatic collapses in Ireland and Spain. In 2009 alone, the contraction in residential investment shaved off 2.5 percentage points from Irish GDP and nearly 2 percentage points from Spanish GDP. In the US, where the construction boom had been more localised, the collapse of residential investment subtracted a full percentage point from GDP growth in both 2008 and 2009. Furthermore, spillovers from construction to the wider economy tend to be large, especially as it is a labour-intensive industry. Construction alone accounted for close to half of the employment fall in the wake of the GFC in Spain and the US, and about two-thirds in Ireland. To sum up, housing market crises can have a large negative impact on aggregate demand, especially in countries where construction expands massively during upswings, which in turn weakens the wider economy and can create solvency risks beyond housing-related loans.

4.5   POLICIES AIMED AT MITIGATING RISKS RELATED TO HOUSING FINANCE

As outlined above, excessive household leverage has contributed to financial and economic crises through a number of channels, calling for a range of policies to enhance households' resilience during economic downturns. Sound microprudential regulations are crucial to limit default risk on mortgages. However, they may not be sufficient to prevent systemic risk arising from correlated exposures and financial interconnections, calling for the implementation of macroprudential policies, which have been stepped-up in advanced economies since the GFC. Monetary policy can encourage excessive leverage, but is a crude tool to curb housing price bubbles and often faces conflicting challenges, notably when a weak economy and low consumer price inflation coincide with rapidly rising housing prices. Finally, addressing structural weaknesses in housing markets may facilitate financial stabilisation and reduce households' vulnerability to economic shocks.

Even though residential mortgage defaults are usually not the greatest source of financial instability, unsustainable lending practices in some countries in the run-up to the GFC point to the importance of sound microprudential regulations. In particular, the loosening of lending standards was notable in the US subprime mortgage market, which was at the epicentre of the GFC (Mian and Sufi, 2009; Dell'Ariccia et al., 2012). As a response, the 2010 Dodd-Franck legislation introduced the Ability-to-repay rule and Qualified mortgages, which provide lenders with some legal protection against borrower lawsuits. Qualified mortgages require inter alia full documentation of the borrower's income and assets, exclude negative amortisation, interest-only and balloon payments, and impose a maximum debt-to-income ratio[7] of 43 per cent, with some exceptions. However, they do not impose a LTV cap, despite the higher default risk associated with a higher LTV ratio. While the new legislation ensures better assessment of borrowers' ability to repay, it has been criticised for limiting consumer choice, increasing compliance costs and failing to address the perverse incentives imbedded in the US housing finance system, which played a key role in the subprime crisis. In addition, riskier forms of lending may re-emerge through non-bank lenders, whose share of mortgage originations has risen steadily over recent years, to more than half of the market (Lea, 2018). Many other countries have reinforced their financial and consumer protection regulations, or their mortgage underwriting guidelines, to ensure a better assessment of ability to repay and to stop or limit the expansion of high-risk products, such as loans denominated in foreign currency or without income documentation. While such products may be suited for some particular customers, they have often been used to increase borrowing capacity in periods of rising housing prices, reinforcing the boom and heightening financial risks.

Recent research sheds light on the main determinants of housing defaults. In the US context, where non-recourse loans are prevalent, defaults are generally related to a double trigger: inability to repay and negative equity. Foote and Willen (2018) and Gerardi et al. (2018) point to the prominence of inability to repay, due to a significant negative income or expenditure shock, in triggering mortgage default, even though strategic defaults are also substantial. Their results highlight the importance of the assessment of ability to repay and related risks at origination, and also suggest that during crises loan modifications reducing monthly payments may be more effective to lower defaults than measures targeting negative equity, such as principal reduction. In the European context, where recourse loans prevail, higher LTV and loan-to-income ratios at origination, longer original loan maturity, self-employment and floating interest rate increase the probability of loan default (Gaudêncio et al., 2019).

The US subprime mortgage crisis highlighted the need for caution in securitisation processes, which are subject information asymmetries, which get worse as the securities become more complex. Nevertheless, securitisation can make a valuable contribution to housing finance, provided underwriting is sound and products are transparent, allowing investors to assess risks reliably. For example, Albertazzi et al. (2011) find a low probability of default in a large sample of Italian securitised mortgages, as banks applied stringent underwriting standards to build up a reputation among investors. A requirement for issuers of mortgage-backed securities to retain a significant part of the exposure can mitigate risks related to asymmetries of information. Covered bonds, which offer dual recourse to both the mortgage pool and the issuer, are more widely used than mortgage-backed securities in several European countries and performed relatively well during the financial crisis compared to asset-backed securities and senior bank debt. There is nevertheless a need for continued vigilance to ensure that underwriting standards remain strong. In addition, lengthening the maturity of the covered bonds issued, which is often short compared to the duration of the mortgages they finance, would reduce liquidity risks.

While sound microprudential regulations are essential to prevent mortgage defaults, they may not be sufficient to address systemic vulnerabilities, when individual financial institutions underestimate the impact of their actions on the financial system as a whole and the risks related to correlated exposures and interconnectedness (De Nicolò et al., 2012). To deal with such externalities, many countries have introduced macroprudential policies. Some instruments are general, such as countercyclical capital buffers, limits on bank leverage or reserve requirements. Others target specific areas. In this chapter, the focus is on measures specifically targeting households.[8] These are particularly relevant, as mortgage lending is generally perceived as a low-risk activity by banks, but often accounts for a large share of their balance sheets and can fuel housing bubbles, whose burst can lead to deep and protracted recessions. Rapid increases in household debt or deviations from trend, often associated with housing price booms, are often strong predictors of financial crises (Borio, 2014; Mian and Sufi, 2018).[9] Moreover, the shift in bank lending from corporate credit towards mortgages in advanced economies, which accelerated since the mid-1990s (Jordà et al., 2016), is associated with weaker productivity growth, higher private debt-to-GDP ratios, rising income inequality and financial fragility (Beck et al., 2012; Bezemer et al., 2016; Bezemer and Zhang, 2019; Mian et al., 2020).

The use of macroprudential tools has increased markedly in OECD countries since the GFC, reflecting both lessons drawn from the crisis and the need to mitigate potential adverse effects from exceptionally expansionary monetary policy, notably the emergence of housing bubbles. Macroprudential measures are particularly useful when financial exuberance is not accompanied by rising inflation, when monetary policy is constrained by the exchange rate regime or when capital inflows counteract monetary policy tightening. The most common macroprudential instruments targeted at households are LTV and DTI caps.[10] In 2000, 33 out of the 37 current OECD members had no such caps. In 2017, less than a third of these countries had neither a LTV nor a DTI cap, about a third had a LTV cap only and another third had both a LTV and a DTI cap (Figure 4.4).

LTV caps limit the risk for households of falling into negative equity and can dampen credit growth and housing price appreciation, but are pro-cyclical, as rising housing prices increase borrowing capacity. This can be addressed by proactive adjustments to the maximum LTV ratio according to the housing market cycle, as some Asian countries have been doing for a long time. LTV caps can also be usefully complemented by limits on debt service relative to income. Potential adverse side-effects of macroprudential measures are that they might lower GDP growth and hamper access to homeownership for households that could afford it. The impact on economic growth is likely to be modest (Richter et al., 2019). Moreover, growth fuelled by excessive credit in the short run is generally paid back in the longer run (Mian et al., 2013). Macroprudential measures reduce the ability of young households to become homeowners, particularly those who cannot benefit from family help for a downpayment (Whitehead and Williams, 2017). The problem of restricting access to homeownership for

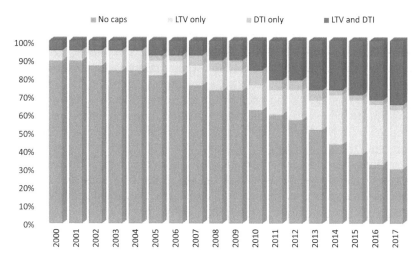

Note: LTV caps refer to strictly enforced caps on new loans, as opposed to supervisory guidelines or merely determinants of risk weights. DTI refers to instruments that constrain household indebtedness by enforcing or encouraging a limit. The 37 countries which were OECD members as of April 2020 are included.

Source: 2018 update of Cerutti, Claessens and Laeven (2017) macroprudential policy dataset.

Figure 4.4 Share of OECD countries using macroprudential instruments targeted at households

households which could likely afford repayments, but cannot make a large downpayment, can be mitigated by some flexibility in the macroprudential rules (e.g. allowing higher LTVs for a limited share of a loan portfolio) or by permitting higher LTV loans for mortgages with insurance.

Given the relatively recent introduction of macroprudential instruments in most advanced economies, it is very early to assess their effectiveness in preserving financial stability, as their use has often not even spanned a complete financial cycle. Some East Asian economies have been using macroprudential tools for a longer period, with some success. For example, Hong Kong, where monetary policy is constrained by a currency peg, has actively used LTV caps, along with other instruments, since the early 1990s. Macroprudential policy has been successful in reducing household leverage and containing delinquencies following housing price falls, but the impact on the housing cycle has been more modest. Mortgage insurance programmes allowing higher LTVs for insured mortgages have mitigated the liquidity constraint on first-time buyers (Wong et al., 2011). Korea has been using macroprudential tools actively since the early 2000s and their perimeter has been gradually extended from covering banks and insurance companies to all financial institutions, to avoid circumvention. LTV and debt-to-income caps vary with the type of area (e.g. speculative, metropolitan), the value of the housing unit and some characteristics of the loan or the borrower. They appear to have damped transaction and housing price increases, lowered housing price expectations and affected investors more than first-time buyers (Igan and Kang, 2011). Housing policies stimulating supply are likely to have facilitated the task of macroprudential policies in stabilising the Korean housing market.

Looking beyond case studies, recent research covering large country samples provides some evidence on the impact of macroprudential policies.[11] Kuttner and Shim (2016) investigate the effectiveness of non-interest rate policy tools in stabilising housing prices and credit, using a panel of 57 advanced and emerging economies, going back to the 1980s for some countries. They find some evidence of an impact of changes in the maximum debt service-to-income and LTV ratios, limits on exposure to the housing sector and housing-related taxes on housing credit growth. However, only housing-related taxes are found to significantly affect increases in housing prices. Akinci and Olmstead-Rumsey (2018), covering the same countries from 2000 to 2013, find that macroprudential tightening is associated with lower bank and housing credit growth and weaker housing price appreciation. Cerutti et al. (2017), covering 119 countries from 2000 to 2013, show that the use of macroprudential tools is generally associated with lower credit growth, especially to households. They also find some evidence of circumvention through cross-border borrowing and of asymmetry, with higher efficiency in booms than in busts. Despite evidence of the effectiveness of macroprudential policies in achieving intermediate targets, only time will tell whether they will be able to prevent new systemic crises.

Monetary policy influences the desired level of debt by affecting borrowing costs, but the policy rate is a blunt instrument to tackle credit bubbles and using it for that purpose may at times conflict with the objective of maintaining price stability and output close to its potential. However, in the wake of the GFC central banks have been using a range of instruments beyond the policy rate, which opens opportunities to influence financial stability. For example, Stein (2013) points to the possibility of flattening the yield curve to weaken incentives for maturity transformation. Some coordination between monetary and macroprudential policies is warranted, as they complement each other and interact in different ways, depending on the business cycle position, economic and financial structures and institutional settings. In theory, addressing financial stability issues through prudential tools, while allowing monetary policy to focus on its primary objectives of price and output stabilisation would seem optimal. However, in practice, macroprudential policies alone may not be powerful enough to contain excessive leverage and systemic risk, in particular due to difficulties to deliver timely adjustments and optimal targeting, and to overcome political economy and institutional constraints. Macroprudential and monetary policies can reinforce each other to rein in a credit boom and seem most successful when they move in the same direction (Bruno et al., 2017). However, when monetary policy needs to remain accommodative to prop up inflation and output, tighter macroprudential rules may be necessary to reduce the risk of asset price bubbles, albeit at the price of weakening somewhat the short-term boost to the economy.

Finally, housing policy settings also matter for financial stability. Governments often encourage homeownership and demand for housing through tax advantages and measures to facilitate access to credit, while at the same time constraining supply through tight land-use planning regulations. In some countries, stringent rent control hampers the development of a well-functioning private rental market, pushing households to take more risk to become homeowners. Such policies can generate structural imbalances, which complicate the task of monetary and financial authorities in stabilising the housing market and ensuring the sustainability of household debt.

4.6 CONCLUSION

Household balance sheets often play an important role in financial crises, of which strong credit growth and rapidly rising housing prices are generally good predictors. Mortgages account for the majority of household debt and for a large share of bank lending and housing markets are prone to boom-bust cycles. Recessions associated with housing market meltdowns are generally deeper and more protracted than other downturns. The relation between household indebtedness and financial fragility is complex and households' responses to financial shocks have varied widely across countries and historical episodes, reflecting the composition of balance sheets, as well as broader economic and financial conditions. Defaults on residential mortgages are generally relatively limited, even though a relaxation of underwriting standards or the extensive use of risky financial products, like non-documented or foreign currency denominated loans, can result in distress for households and financial institutions. Unsecured credit is more risky than mortgages, but accounts for a smaller share of debt, although it has been rising recently in the US and could generate substantial credit losses if the COVID-19 pandemic lingers. As mortgage lending accounts for a large share of bank lending and involves considerable maturity mismatch, funding structures can be fragile, as the GFC demonstrated. Financial pro-cyclicality, concentration and interconnectedness generate systemic risks. When a housing price upswing is associated with a construction boom, losses on loans to real estate developers and construction companies can be huge. Beyond direct financial risks, household debt and housing market dynamics can amplify the business cycle. During housing price booms, households often take advantage of rising collateral to increase debt-financed consumption, which subsequently falls when prices start declining and access to credit tightens. Overall, a rapid expansion of household debt creates a number of risks, which can lead to or amplify a financial crisis. Sound microprudential regulations can contain default risks. Macroprudential tools are increasingly used to contain systemic risks, but only time will tell if this will be sufficient to avoid new financial crises. Reforms to improve the functioning of housing markets would facilitate financial stabilisation. Policies aimed at reducing income inequality, which is likely to weaken aggregate demand and lower interest rates (Mian et al., 2020), could also help contain the rise in household debt and limit the risk of future financial crises.

NOTES

1. The views expressed in this chapter are those of the author and do not necessarily reflect those of the Organisation for Economic Co-operation and Development (OECD) or the governments of its member countries.
2. For more details on household finance in the euro area, see Household Finance and Consumption Network (2016).
3. Such over-optimistic expectations are typical of unsustainable financial expansions, as demonstrated by Minsky (1986). See Chapter 2 in this book.
4. *The Economist*, 16 June 2005.
5. The current account balance is the opposite of net capital inflows. In some cases gross capital inflows may also fuel asset price bubbles without showing in net flows (Borio and Disyatat, 2011). Two examples are the Japanese asset price bubble of the late 1980s, which coincided with current account surpluses and the European banks' massive investment in US asset-backed securities in the run-up to the GFC, which was masked in net flows by the use of US money market funding (André and Chalaux, 2018). On the role of international banks in the transmission of financial shocks, see Chapters 5 and 7 in this book.
6. Housing equity withdrawal refers to new borrowing secured on dwellings less investment in housing.
7. Ratio of monthly debt payment to monthly gross income.
8. Akinci and Olmstead-Rumsey (2018) note that macroprudential policies have been used far more actively after the GFC and have primarily targeted the housing sector, especially in advanced economies. One measure affecting capital requirements which

is worth mentioning here is the imposition of minimum risk weights on mortgages in a number of countries, like Norway, Sweden and Switzerland.

9. The aggregate household debt *level* is generally less relevant, as it is related to a variety of factors, such as the depth of the financial system, the level of housing prices, demographics, the pension system, social safety nets and social attitudes relative to saving and borrowing.

10. Following Cerutti et al. (2017), DTI caps refer to instruments that constrain household indebtedness by enforcing or encouraging a limit.

11. See Finocchiaro and Grodecka (2018) for a review of recent studies and Galati and Moessner (2018) for a critical review of recent progress in theoretical and empirical research on the effectiveness of macroprudential instruments.

REFERENCES

Akinci, O. and J. Olmstead-Rumsey (2018), "How effective are macroprudential policies? An empirical investigation", *Journal of Financial Intermediation*, 33, 33–57.

Albertazzi, U., G. Eramo, L. Gambacorta and C. Salleo (2011), "Securitization is not that evil after all", *BIS Working Papers* No. 341, Bank for International Settlements, Basel.

André, C. and T. Chalaux (2018), "Real estate booms, recessions and financial crises", in: Łaszek, J., K. Olszewski and R. Sobiecki (eds), *Recent Trends in the Real Estate Market and its Analysis*. Warsaw School of Economics Press, pp. 17–64.

Andritzky, J.R. (2014), "Resolving residential mortgage distress: time to modify?" *International Monetary Fund Working Papers* 14/226, Washington, DC.

Anundsen, A.K. and E.S. Jansen (2013), "Self-reinforcing effects between housing prices and credit", *Journal of Housing Economics*, 22, 192–212.

Basten, C. and C. Koch (2015), "The causal effect of house prices on mortgage demand and mortgage supply: evidence from Switzerland", *Journal of Housing Economics*, 30, 1–22.

Beck, T., B. Buyukkarabacak, F.K. Rioja and N.T. Valev (2012), "Who gets the credit? And does it matter? Household vs. firm lending across countries", *The B.E. Journal of Macroeconomics*, 12(1), Art. 2.

Bernanke, B.S. (2005), "The global saving glut and the U.S. current account deficit", Remarks by Governor Ben S. Bernanke at the Sandridge Lecture, Virginia Association of Economists, Richmond, Virginia, 10 March.

Bernanke, B.S. (2010), *Statement before the Financial Crisis Inquiry Commission*. Washington, DC, 2 September.

Bezemer, D. and L. Zhang (2019), "Credit composition and the severity of post-crisis recessions", *Journal of Financial Stability*, 42, 52–66.

Bezemer, D., M. Grydaki and L. Zhang (2016), "More mortgages, lower growth?", *Economic Inquiry*, 54, 652–74.

Borio, C. (2014), "The financial cycle and macroeconomics: what have we learnt?", *Journal of Banking & Finance*, 45, 182–98.

Borio, C. and P. Disyatat (2011), "Global imbalances and the financial crisis: link or no link?" *BIS Working Papers* No. 346, Bank for International Settlements, Basel.

Bruno, V., I. Shim and H.S. Shin (2017), "Comparative assessment of macroprudential policies", *Journal of Financial Stability*, 28, 183–202.

Bunn, P. (2014), "Household debt and spending", *Quarterly Bulletin* Q3, Bank of England, London.

Caldera, A. and Å. Johansson (2013), "The price responsiveness of housing supply in OECD countries", *Journal of Housing Economics*, 22(3), 231–49.

Cerutti, E., S. Claessens and L. Laeven (2017), "The use and effectiveness of macroprudential policies: new evidence", *Journal of Financial Stability*, 28, 203–24.

Damen, S., F. Vastmans and E. Buyst (2016), "The effect of mortgage interest deduction and mortgage characteristics on house prices", *Journal of Housing Economics*, 34, 15–29.

De Nicolò, G., G. Favara and L. Ratnovski (2012), "Externalities and macroprudential policy", *IMF Staff Discussion Note*, 12/05, International Monetary Fund, Washington, DC.

Dell'Ariccia, G., D. Igan and L. Laeven (2012), "Credit booms and lending standards: evidence from the subprime mortgage market", *Journal of Money, Credit and Banking*, 44(2–3), 367–84.

Duca, J.V., J. Muellbauer and A. Murphy (2011), "House prices and credit constraints: making sense of the US experience", *Economic Journal*, 121(552), 533–51.

Ferrero, A. (2015), "House price booms, current account deficits, and low interest rates", *Journal of Money, Credit and Banking*, 47, 261–93.

Finocchiaro, D. and A. Grodecka (2018), "Financial frictions, financial regulation and their impact on the macroeconomy", *Sveriges Riksbank Economic Review*, 2018:1, Stockholm.

Foote, C.L. and P.S. Willen (2018), "Mortgage-default research and the recent foreclosure crisis", *Annual Review of Financial Economics*, 10(1), 59–100.

FSA (2009), "Mortgage Market Review", Discussion Paper No. 09/3, Financial Services Authority, London.

Galati, G. and R. Moessner (2018), "What do we know about the effects of macroprudential policy?", *Economica*, 85, 735–70.

Gaudêncio, J., A. Mazany and C. Schwarz (2019), "The impact of lending standards on default rates of residential real estate loans", *European Central Bank Occasional Paper Series*, No. 220, Frankfurt am Main.

Gerardi, K., K.F. Herkenhoff, L.E. Ohanian and P.S. Willen (2018), "Can't pay or won't pay? Unemployment, negative equity, and strategic default", *Review of Financial Studies*, 31(3), 1098–131.

Glaeser, E.L. and C.G. Nathanson (2015), "An extrapolative model of house price dynamics", *NBER Working Paper* No. 21037, National Bureau of Economic Research, Cambridge, MA.

Glaeser, E.L., J. Gyourko and R.E. Saks (2005), "Why have housing prices gone up?", *NBER Working Paper* No. 11129, National Bureau of Economic Research, Cambridge, MA.

Goodhart, C. and B. Hofmann (2008), "House prices, money, credit, and the macroeconomy", *Oxford Review of Economic Policy*, 24(1), 180–205.

Goodhart, C. and E. Perotti (2015), "Maturity mismatch stretching: banking has taken a wrong turn", *CEPR Policy Insight*, No. 81, Centre for Economic Policy Research, London.

Green, R.K., S. Malpezzi and S.K. Mayo (2005), "Metropolitan-specific estimates of the price elasticity of supply of housing, and their sources", *American Economic Review*, 95(2), 334–9.

Gyourko, J., C. Mayer and T. Sinai (2013), "Superstar cities", *American Economic Journal: Economic Policy*, 5(4), 167–99.

Household Finance and Consumption Network (2016), "The Household Finance and Consumption Survey: results from the second wave", *ECB Statistics Paper Series*, 18, European Central Bank, Frankfurt am Main.

Iacoviello, M. (2005), "House prices, borrowing constraints, and monetary policy in the business cycle", *American Economic Review*, 95(3), 739–64.

Iacoviello, M. and S. Neri (2010), "Housing market spillovers: evidence from an estimated DSGE model", *American Economic Journal: Macroeconomics*, 2(2), 125–64.

Igan, D. and H. Kang (2011), "Do loan-to-value and debt-to-income limits work? Evidence from Korea", *International Monetary Fund Working Paper* 11/297, Washington, DC.

IMF (2012), "Dealing with household debt", Chapter 3 in: *World Economic Outlook*, April, International Monetary Fund, Washington, DC.

Jordà, Ò., M. Schularick and A.M. Taylor (2016), "The great mortgaging: housing finance, crises and business cycles", *Economic Policy*, 31(85), 107–52.

Kamin, S.B. and L.P. DeMarco (2012), "How did a domestic housing slump turn into a global financial crisis?", *Journal of International Money and Finance*, 31, 10–41.

Kim, Y.S., S.M. Laufer, K. Pence, R. Stanton and N. Wallace (2018), "Liquidity crises in the mortgage market", *Brookings Papers on Economic Activity*, Economic Studies Program, The Brookings Institution, 49(1), 347–428.

Kuttner, K.N. and I. Shim (2016), "Can non-interest rate policies stabilise housing markets? Evidence from a panel of 57 economies", *Journal of Financial Stability*, 26, 31–44.

Lau Andersen, A., C. Duus and T.L. Jensen (2016), "Household debt and spending during the financial crisis: evidence from Danish micro data", *European Economic Review*, 89, 96–115.

Lea, M. (2018), "US housing finance policy in the aftermath of the crisis", in: Łaszek, J., K. Olszewski and R. Sobiecki (eds), *Recent Trends in the Real Estate Market and Its Analysis*, Warsaw School of Economics Press, pp. 207–38.

Leamer, E.E. (2007), "Housing is the business cycle", *Proceedings, Economic Policy Symposium, Jackson Hole*, Federal Reserve Bank of Kansas City, 149–233.

Lunde, J., K. Scanlon and C. Whitehead (2008), "Interest-only and longer-term mortgages: easier access, more risk", in: *Hypostat 2007*, European Mortgage Federation.

Meen, G. (2002), "The time-series behavior of house prices: a transatlantic divide?", *Journal of Housing Economics*, 11, 1–23.

Mian, A. and A. Sufi (2009), "The consequences of mortgage credit expansion: evidence from the U.S. mortgage default crisis", *Quarterly Journal of Economics*, 124, 1449–96.

Mian, A. and A. Sufi (2018), "Finance and business cycles: the credit-driven household demand channel", *Journal of Economic Perspectives*, 32(3), 31–58.

Mian, A., K. Rao and A. Sufi (2013), "Household balance sheets, consumption, and the economic slump", *The Quarterly Journal of Economics*, 128(4), 1687–726.

Mian, A., L. Straub and A. Sufi (2020), "Indebted demand", *NBER Working Papers* No. 26940, National Bureau of Economic Research, Cambridge, MA.

Miles, W. (2018), "Home prices and global imbalances: which drives which?", *Kyklos*, 72, 55–75.

Minsky, H.P. (1986), *Stabilizing an Unstable Economy.* Yale University Press, New Haven, CT and London.

Muellbauer, J. (2012), "When is a housing market overheated enough to threaten stability?", in: Heath, A., F. Packer and C. Windsor (eds), *Property Markets and Financial Stability, Proceedings of a Conference Held in Sydney on 20–21 August*, Reserve Bank of Australia, Sydney.

Muellbauer, J. and A. Murphy (2008), "Housing markets and the economy: the assessment", *Oxford Review of Economic Policy*, 24(1), 1–33.

Onado, M. (2009), "Northern Rock: just the tip of the iceberg", in: Bruni, F. and D.T. Llewellyn (eds), *The Failure of Northern Rock: A Multi-dimensional Case Study. SUERF Studies*, 2009/1, Vienna, pp. 99–113.

Reinhart, C.M. and K.S. Rogoff (2008), "Is the 2007 U.S. subprime crisis so different? An international historical comparison", *American Economic Review*, 98(2), 339–44.

Reinhart, C.M. and K.S. Rogoff (2013), "Banking crises: an equal opportunity menace", *Journal of Banking and Finance*, 37, 4557–73.

Richter, B., M. Schularick and I. Shim (2019), "The costs of macroprudential policy", *Journal of International Economics*, 118, 263–82.

Sá, F. and T. Wieladek (2015), "Capital inflows and the U.S. housing boom", *Journal of Money, Credit and Banking*, 47, 221–56.

Skulason, M.A. (2012), "Housing debt crisis in light of a major banking crisis in Iceland: restructuring of household debt in Iceland – an example for other indebted countries?", in: *Hypostat 2011*, European Mortgage Federation, Brussels.

Stein, J.C. (2013), "Overheating in Credit Markets: Origins, Measurement, and Policy Responses", Speech at the Restoring Household Financial Stability after the Great Recession: Why Household Balance Sheets Matter research symposium, Federal Reserve Bank of St. Louis, Missouri, 7 February.

Sveriges Riksbank (2016), "The major Swedish banks' structural liquidity risks", *Riksbank studies*, November, Stockholm.

Van Beers, N., M. Bijlsma and R. Mocking (2015), "House price shocks and household savings: evidence from Dutch administrative data", *CPB Discussion Paper* No. 299, CPB Netherlands Bureau for Economic Policy Analysis, The Hague.

Whitehead, C. and P. Williams (2017), "Changes in the regulation and control of mortgage markets and access to owner-occupation among younger households", *OECD Social, Employment and Migration Working Papers* No. 196, OECD Publishing, Paris.

Wong, E., T. Fong, K. Li and H. Choi (2011), "Loan-to-value ratio as a macroprudential tool – Hong Kong's experience and cross-country evidence", *Hong Kong Monetary Authority Working Paper* 01/2011.

5. The European network of cross-border lending

Ornella Ricci and Francesco Saverio Stentella Lopes

5.1 INTRODUCTION

The Global Financial Crisis has been widely viewed as unprecedented, at least since the Great Depression of the 1930s. As detailed in Chapter 1, initially originated from the mortgage market in the US, the crisis quickly spread across the globe and rapidly moved from the financial markets to the real economy. In January 2008, foreclosures in the US were growing at an unprecedented pace, causing large losses in many investment funds across the globe. In February, the British Treasury took state ownership of Northern Rock, the UK's fifth-largest mortgage lender because of its large exposure in the real estate market. The peak of the crisis was reached in September when Fannie Mae and Freddie Mac were nationalized and Lehman Brothers, one of the largest investment banks in the world, filed for Chapter 11 of the Bankruptcy Code. The financial hurricane rapidly escalated to a global level. In October, Central Banks in the US, Europe, Canada, the UK, Sweden and Switzerland cut their interest rates roughly at the same time by half a point to lower Libor and the cost of bank borrowing. Despite this global effort, the financial hurricane eventually moved to the real economy. In November 2008, the largest automobile companies in the US requested $50 billion in bailout funds to the Treasury. Moreover, the US unemployment rate kept growing for two years from 2008 until 2010. This chain of events tragically emphasizes how financial distress can rapidly move across the globe and from the financial markets to the real economy. It is then critical to study how the financial system connects different countries and to investigate whether these connections generate systemic risk.

Existing studies have outlined several different sources of systemic risk in banking. For instance, bank runs, engendered by depositors' partial information about their bank's solvency, have been widely indicated as a major source of instability in banking (Diamond and Dybvig, 1983; Temzelides, 1997; Goldstein and Pauzner, 2004). Liquidity shortages in the interbank market (Rochet and Tirole, 1996; Aghion et al., 2000; Brunnermeier and Pedersen, 2009) and equity cross-holdings (Blavarg and Nimander, 2002; Elliott et al., 2014) have also been outlined as a potential source of systemic risk in banking. Bruno and Shin (2015) argue that international banking could facilitate the transmission of economic shocks across the border. This result agrees with the empirical findings of Peek and Rosengren (2000) and Huber (2018), showing how economic crises can spill over from their source countries globally through the international branches of banks headquartered in the country where the crisis originated. Hence, examining the connections generated by banks' international activities is crucial as these connections may facilitate the diffusion of financial shocks with severe consequences for the real economy (Lin and Paravisini, 2013; Chodorow-Reich, 2014; Benmelech et al., 2015).

In this chapter, we examine the features of the networks generated by cross-border lending activities of European banks. Hence, our contribution is complementary to that of Chapter 7, considering international banks from a global perspective. More specifically, we analyse the characteristics and features of the networks engendered by cross-border corporate and retail lending in Europe. We also present a focus on small and medium-sized enterprises (SMEs). We take advantage of the results from the transparency exercise published by the European Banking Authority (EBA) in the second quarter of 2019. The data on cross-border exposures disclosed by the EBA are aggregated at the country level. We focus on the European countries for which data for both the credit inflow and outflow are available. Moreover, we aggregate the original exposures in the standardized approach and internal rating-based (IRB) portfolios.

Our results show that lending exposures represent a significant source of connection in Europe. We show that several countries have high centrality in our networks and are connected with up to 75 percent of the countries in our sample. This is crucial because the high centrality of some countries may underline a high potential for contagion in the European banking system.

The chapter is organized as follows. In the next section, we review the contagion literature in banking with a focus on lending. In the third and fourth sections, we present our data and findings, respectively. Finally, in the fifth section, we conclude the chapter.

5.2 LITERATURE REVIEW

Foundation banking activities such as the management of different sources of risk and asset transformation make the banking system inherently fragile. Liquidity and solvency problems may quickly spread in the banking system because of the existing connections among financial institutions. To manage and prevent contagion among banks, understanding the exact structure of the interbank connections is crucial.

The seminal works of Allen and Gale (2000) and Freixas et al. (2000) suggest that more interconnected and complete structures improve the soundness of the banking system and its resilience to the default of individual banks. The underpinning intuition in the model presented by Allen and Gale (2000) is that in a dense financial network, where each bank is connected to many other institutions, the losses generated by the default of a single bank are divided among many creditors, thereby reducing the impact of negative shocks to individual institutions on the rest of the system. Studies that modeled contagion across banks as an epidemic (Blume et al., 2011, 2013) challenged the view that a dense network would increase financial stability.

In a more recent study, Acemoglu et al. (2015) reconcile these two contrasting views showing that the resilience of a financial network crucially depends on the size of the aggregate shock that the network must absorb. If the shock is relatively small, a more complete network would be more desirable because the losses will be shared among many counterparties. However, when the magnitude or the number of the shocks increases, contagion is more likely to occur in complete financial networks. The intuition behind this important result is clear: each entity or node in a network can absorb shocks up to a specific threshold. If the shock has a magnitude below this critical level, it will be absorbed by the network, and contagion will not exist. By contrast, if the magnitude of the shock becomes large enough, single nodes in the financial network cannot absorb their portion of the shock, which may become a default cascade. Thus, the study of Acemoglu et al. (2015) sheds light on an important additional layer of complexity in defining the optimality of the financial network structure. Understanding the features that make a financial system more resilient is crucial in banking because contagion could occur through many channels. The seminal model of Diamond and Dybvig (1983) first highlighted how bank runs could increase systemic risk. This phenomenon has been later examined by Temzelides (1997), and Goldstein and Pauzner (2004). Aghion et al. (2000) and Brunnermeier and Pedersen (2009) outline that contagion in banking could also arise from liquidity shortage, whereas

Rochet and Tirole (1996) emphasized the interbank market. Meanwhile, Blavarg and Nimander (2002) and Elliott et al. (2014) emphasized the role of cross-holdings.

Several studies have also argued that contagion in banking may be generated through common exposures of bank assets to similar risk factors (Acharya and Yorulmazer, 2008). This theoretical result agrees with the empirical findings of Peek and Rosengren (2000), who showed how the Japanese economic crisis spilled over to US companies through American branches of Japanese banks that cut their lending during the crisis. Huber (2018) also outlines a similar result in a recent study showing how the financial crisis was initially transmitted from the US to Germany through the lending cuts operated by a large German bank in response to the losses generated by the bank's international exposures.

In the remainder of the chapter, we focus on the potential diffusion of country-specific shocks through the international lending activities of banks, since several studies suggested the relevance of this channel and its ability to directly affect the real economy. For instance, Campello et al. (2010) show that credit constraints may have severe consequences on the ability of companies to operate properly. Robb and Robinson (2014) also outline that companies of all sizes, in particular SMEs, heavily rely on bank lending to satisfy their credit needs. The economic consequences of lending cuts (Chodorow-Reich, 2014; Benmelech et al., 2015) may not be limited to employment and investment, but they may also affect consumption behavior. The findings of recent studies by Jensen and Johannesen (2017) and Ramcharan et al. (2016) show that the transmission of economic shocks through the banking system has important economic implications on consumption and household borrowing. Hence, studying the structure of the network generated by international credit exposure of European banks is critical as the transmission of economic shocks across the border in Europe may have severe consequences on many economies that struggled to recover from the last financial crisis.

Surprisingly, still only a few empirical studies have used network analysis to examine the potential impact of cross-border banking on financial stability. One notable exception is Tonzer (2015), who adopted a spatial model to study the effect of cross-border banking on the stability for 15 European countries, Canada, Japan and the US over the sample period 1994–2012. Results confirm the importance of cross-border banking as a channel of contagion, finding a direct relationship between a country's financial stability and the soundness of the banking systems to which it is exposed. Furthermore, the characteristics of the network matter:

diversification lowers risk, whereas large cross-border exposure fosters contagion, especially during bad times. Using pre-crisis data and outlining the role played by some central countries in shock propagation, previous studies also suggested the importance of measuring centrality in the network (e.g., Degryse et al., 2010).

We contribute to this small literature by considering the most updated information on cross-border banking in Europe and giving a focus on SMEs, which represent a fundamental portion of the economic system and are strongly dependent on bank lending.

5.3   DATA

Our data on cross-border exposures are obtained from the EBA transparency exercise in June 2019. The transparency exercise, which has been conducted annually since 2011, provides stakeholders with detailed data on capital positions, risk exposure amounts, leverage exposures and asset quality for 131 European banks. The data are based on supervisory reporting and published at the highest level of consolidation for the reference dates. Our focus is on credit risk as depicted by the exercise conducted on 30 June 2019. More specifically, we aggregate the data at the country level and examine the networks generated by the original credit exposure in the corporate and retail portfolios of banks involved in the transparency exercise. We also present a focus on SMEs and report the portion of the retail and corporate portfolios used for SMEs. In the resulting graphs, countries denote the nodes, and the flows of credit generate the edges among different nodes.

5.4   EUROPEAN NETWORKS OF CROSS-BORDER EXPOSURES

The precise structure of a financial network is essential in the analysis of systemic risk. In their study, Allen and Gale (2000) present a simple example with four financial institutions holding financial claims to each other to show that the same shock may engender a contagion in some structures, but not in other networks. More specifically, a complete structure, where every bank has symmetric exposures to all other banks would be more stable than an incomplete structure where nodes are linked only to one neighbor. Incomplete structure may prevent large shocks affecting all the nodes in a network even though it is less stable and more prone to contagion (Acemoglu et al., 2015). An essential ingredient of any network is the definition of edges or links along which contagion across nodes should occur. In this chapter, the edges are defined as the credit granted by banks to counterparties located across the border of their home country. As an example, the outflow of credit from France to Germany in this chapter is defined as the total number of credit exposures granted by French banks to counterparties located in Germany. This network can be represented either in graphical or in matrix form.

5.4.1   Corporate and Corporate SMEs

Figure 5.1 depicts the graphical form of the network generated by cross-border corporate exposures granted by the European banks in the EBA sample to corporate counterparties in different countries. The network represented in Figure 5.1 is incomplete because no country is connected to all the other nodes in the network. However, a strong heterogeneity exists in the number of connections of each node: some nodes have a small number of connections, such as Hungary and Iceland, and other

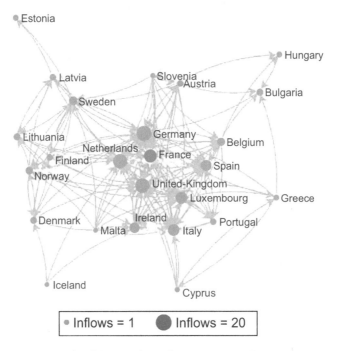

Figure 5.1   Network of Original Credit Exposures: Corporate

nodes, such as Germany and the UK, are connected to a high number of nodes. Thus, financial shocks in different countries can generate different outcomes. When hit severely by financial shocks, countries with a small number of connections may easily transmit the shock to their neighbors, but those shocks would rarely spread to all countries in Europe. When financial shocks hit more harshly in countries with a high number of connections, those shocks would less easily spread to other countries, but could affect a higher number of countries.

The first two tables present the details of the network generated by cross-border corporate exposures. In Table 5.1, the first two columns show the number of connections and the amount of credit (in € billion) flowing among countries in the network generated by corporate cross-border exposures.

Table 5.1　Centrality in the network of original credit exposures – corporate

| | Corporate | | | | of which: SME | | | |
| | Outflows | | Inflows | | Outflows | | Inflows | |
	(1)	(2)	(3)	(4)	(5)	(6)	(7)	(8)
Austria	12	121.32	4	141.21	9	29.71	3	32.84
Belgium	12	149.37	7	236.95	9	37.58	7	59.83
Bulgaria	2	1.24	5	9.79	1	0.04	5	3.09
Cyprus	6	6.97	2	7.75	4	3.96	2	4.01
Denmark	7	295.85	5	260.71	7	129.12	4	119.88
Estonia	1	0.87	3	7.91	1	0.79	3	2.36
Finland	10	220.41	4	130.86	10	75.76	3	41.93
France	9	1439.06	17	1167.80	9	276.77	12	238.14
Germany	14	1002.58	20	1035.69	13	138.97	16	153.05
Greece	6	54.94	3	52.22	5	17.34	3	16.88
Hungary	2	8.92	3	18.70	2	3.56	3	6.38
Iceland	4	11.65	1	11.64	2	5.06	1	5.05
Ireland	9	119.67	11	62.75	8	22.84	6	18.61
Italy	8	873.64	13	803.44	8	265.79	7	252.51
Latvia	6	0.90	4	5.11	3	0.51	3	1.79
Lithuania	6	0.44	5	9.73	1	0.01	5	3.60
Luxembourg	9	25.90	14	193.70	7	5.47	9	16.22
Malta	10	5.01	1	3.02	1	2.45	1	2.45
Netherlands	7	520.00	18	441.19	7	112.71	14	98.41
Norway	8	96.21	6	175.25	7	26.28	5	60.76
Portugal	9	60.72	4	84.03	9	24.88	3	29.68
Slovenia	10	4.57	2	4.92	3	1.10	2	1.35

Table 5.1 *(continued)*

	Corporate				of which: SME			
	Outflows		Inflows		Outflows		Inflows	
	(1)	(2)	(3)	(4)	(5)	(6)	(7)	(8)
Spain	6	512.82	12	458.90	6	118.54	10	112.88
Sweden	10	329.90	8	295.95	10	120.20	6	105.15
UK	8	809.71	19	1053.49	8	70.47	17	103.04

Note: This table lists the number of linkages for each country (Columns 1, 3, 5 and 7) and the amount of credit inflows and outflows in € billion (Columns 2, 4, 6 and 8). Figures include the country itself (e.g., Belgian banks provide credit to corporate clients located in Belgium and in other 11 countries, for a total amount of €149.37 billion). Credit exposures are considered in original values under both the standardized and the IRB approaches.

Source: European Banking Authority, 2019 EU-wide Transparency Exercise.

The first column shows the number of credit outflows from each country in the sample, in particular, the number of countries to which banks located in a given geographical area are granting credit to (including the country itself). For example, saying that Belgian banks grant credit to corporate clients located in 12 countries means that they provide loans to firms located in Belgium and in 11 other countries. The third row shows the inflows of credit and highlights that Belgian corporations receive credit from banks located in six countries in addition to Belgian banks. The number of connections is an important measure of centrality that suggests the importance of a country in spreading large economic shocks. However, the amount of credit granted to banks in a given country is also highly significant to appreciate the exposure of banks in each European country to companies located abroad.

In Table 5.2, we present a focus on the first ten countries in our sample, with the largest number of total credit exposures. Credit inflows are reported in rows and credit outflows in columns. Table 5.2 shows that the largest amount of credit in each node is granted to companies located in the country where the banks are headquartered. As an example, the amount of credit granted by German banks to German companies is substantially higher than that to companies operating outside Germany. Table 5.2 displays this strong domestic concentration for all countries presented in the sample. The values on the diagonal of the matrix presented in Table 5.2 are the highest value of each column. However, other entries in Table 5.2 are of large magnitude. As an example, British companies receive more than 80

Table 5.2 *Network of original credit exposures: ten countries with largest amount of credit outflows – corporate*

Panel A: Corporate (IRB and SA)

	Belgium	Denmark	Finland	France	Germany	Italy	Netherlands	Spain	Sweden	UK
Belgium	103.73			70.86	1.34		59.37			
Denmark		198.60	45.69						14.28	
Finland		15.15	91.07		0.41				24.23	
France	11.01		0.60	941.09	51.87	21.33	29.51	24.66		64.74
Germany	2.17	2.94	1.81	83.33	692.35	122.65	28.97	17.66	10.03	41.68
Italy	1.67			110.51	29.01	647.25		7.20		2.73
Netherlands	6.92		0.19	15.12	52.21	1.45	338.84		0.64	15.53
Spain	1.90			28.79	23.49	7.94	7.95	372.57		3.65
Sweden		44.15	40.17		3.40				196.29	
UK	15.29	9.14	2.56	108.45	82.95	19.76	39.01	62.72	25.44	644.95

Table 5.2 (continued)

Panel B: Corporate SME (IRB and SA)

	Belgium	Denmark	Finland	France	Germany	Italy	Netherlands	Spain	Sweden	UK
Belgium	34.24			11.42	0.00		14.14			
Denmark		99.06	18.00						2.82	
Finland		4.42	31.02						6.48	
France	0.26	0.15	0.15	227.13	3.93	0.42	4.56	1.03		0.09
Germany	0.15	0.15	0.12	7.67	111.82	26.27	1.07	2.01	0.61	0.02
Italy				17.58	5.72	229.09		0.10		0.01
Netherlands	0.30		0.04	0.27	5.77	0.04	91.61		0.09	0.13
Spain	0.01			3.85	2.97	0.24	0.00	104.01		0.00
Sweden		13.89	13.31		0.13				77.82	
UK	0.00	3.69	0.09	3.96	2.90	0.42	1.27	4.19	11.66	67.95

Note: Credit inflows are reported in rows, and credit outflows in columns (e.g., Italian banks provide €21.33 billion to corporate clients located in France and French banks provide €110.51 billion to corporate clients located in Italy).

Source: European Banking Authority, 2019 EU-wide Transparency Exercise.

billion euro in credit from German banks, French and Dutch companies more than 50 billion, and Italian companies more than 29 billion.

This evidence outlines that countries such as Germany, France, the Netherlands and Italy have a large number of connections within Europe in terms of magnitude.

In some cases, these connections also show a high level of concentration, which is potentially a driver of contagion in case of crisis (Tonzer, 2015). For example, Italian corporate clients receive a significant amount of credit from both German and French banks, but the latter provide almost four times the credit granted by German banks (€110.51 billion vs 29.01).

When we focus on SMEs, our data show that the number of connections across countries is lower than that for general corporations. This suggests that some nodes only grant credit to large corporations in some other European countries. Although this difference in the number of connections is spread in our network, it does not capture the difference in magnitude in terms of credit granted to companies abroad by banks in a given country. Panel B of Table 5.2 presents a focus on the countries with the largest amount of credit granted to SMEs. Our data suggest that approximately one-third of credit granted by banks located in the countries in our sample goes to SMEs located in the same country. However, there are some important exceptions, such as Denmark, where almost half of the corporate credit goes to SMEs, and the UK, where slightly more than 10 percent of corporate credit is granted to SMEs. When we look at credit granted to SMEs abroad, our data show that each country in our sample has a small number of important connections to SMEs located abroad. As an example, 31 percent of Danish banks' corporate credit exposures in Sweden was granted to Swedish SMEs. Similarly, the French banking system has about 16 percent of their corporate credit exposure in Italy granted to Italian SMEs. Although corporate exposures represent a large portion of credit granted to SMEs, lines of credit issued to small companies are often classified by banks as retail. In the next section, we then focus on retail exposures and present a focus on SMEs.

5.4.2 Retail and Retail SMEs

Figure 5.2 presents a graph similar to the one presented in Figure 5.1 and shows the network generated by cross-border exposures granted by banks in the EBA sample to retail counterparties located in countries within Europe for which we have both outflows and inflows of credit. Even though the nodes in Figure 5.2 have a lower number of connections compared with that in Figure 5.1, the evidence reported in Figure 5.2 also suggests a strong

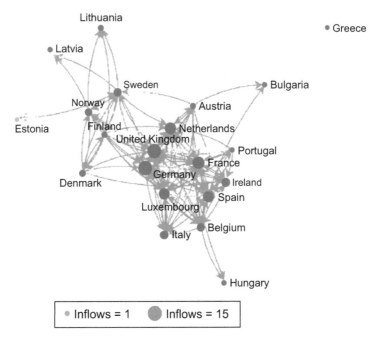

Figure 5.2   Network of Original Credit Exposures: Retail

heterogeneity across nodes where some countries only have a small number of edges and other countries are more central in the network.

Tables 5.3 and 5.4 shed some light on the network generated by cross-border retail exposures in Europe. The first two columns of Table 5.3 show the number of connections and the amount of credit flowing among countries in our sample. The first column in Table 5.3 outlines the number of outflows in each country. Our data show that countries in our sample, on average, are connected to six other countries by retail credit exposure. However, several countries such as Austria, Belgium and Germany have more than ten connections generated by retail credit. We focus on SMEs in the last two columns of Table 5.3 where we present the connections generated by retail credit exposures granted to SMEs and secured by a real estate property.[1]

On average, countries in our sample are connected only to four other countries; when we look at the connections generated by retail exposures granted to SMEs, the size of this connection is also relatively small, measuring slightly more than 13 billion euros.

In Table 5.4, we examine the amount of credit granted to retail counterparties and focus on the ten countries in our sample, with the largest

Table 5.3   Centrality in the network of original credit exposures – retail

| | Retail | | | | of which: Retail SME secured by Real Estate Properties | | | |
| | Outflows | | Inflows | | Outflows | | Inflows | |
	(1)	(2)	(3)	(4)	(5)	(6)	(7)	(8)
Austria	11	64.36	3	81.19	7	7.07	3	8.48
Belgium	11	168.73	6	265.37	8	18.73	4	33.42
Bulgaria	0	0	2	1.57	0	0.00	2	0.21
Denmark	7	283.63	4	291.27	7	14.34	3	13.90
Estonia	0	0	1	7.59	0	0.00	1	0.18
Finland	10	245.15	3	120.89	4	2.35	3	2.23
France	8	1750.29	12	1582.89	8	113.12	10	103.25
Germany	11	485.17	15	628.56	8	14.64	10	15.37
Greece	1	19.96	1	19.96	1	4.04	1	4.04
Hungary	0	0	2	5.56	0	0.00	1	0.01
Ireland	6	70.48	7	76.38	0	0.00	2	0.00
Italy	8	441.16	7	489.94	6	26.97	5	28.14
Latvia	0	0	2	3.41	0	0.00	1	0.11
Lithuania	0	0	3	6.53	0	0.00	1	0.08
Luxembourg	8	27.05	10	37.17	7	0.82	4	1.20
Netherlands	7	754.9	11	616.75	7	36.02	7	27.70
Norway	8	90.77	5	161.98	0	0.00	3	0.30
Portugal	8	32.81	2	55.36	3	1.64	2	1.68
Spain	6	723.83	11	472.6	6	22.47	9	22.51
Sweden	10	320.73	6	347.46	8	16.09	3	15.98
UK	8	1142.12	15	1348.71	6	13.74	11	13.27

Note: This table lists the number of linkages for each country (Columns 1, 3, 5 and 7) and the amount of credit inflows and outflows in € billion (Columns 2, 4, 6 and 8). Figures include the country itself. Credit exposures are considered in original values under the IRB approach ("0" means that the country does not have any credit exposure in the IRB approach).

Source: European Banking Authority, 2019 EU-wide Transparency Exercise.

amount of retail credit exposure. Similar to corporate credit exposure, Table 5.4 shows that the largest amount of credit granted by a given banking system to retail counterparties stays in countries where banks are headquartered. The values on the diagonal of the matrix are the highest values in each column. Interestingly, the difference between the amount of credit granted to retail counterparties in the country where banks are headquartered and the number of credit exposures granted to retail counterparties abroad is larger than the difference for corporate exposures.

Table 5.4 Network of original credit exposures: ten countries with largest amount of credit outflows – retail

Panel A: Retail (IRB)

	Belgium	Denmark	Finland	France	Germany	Italy	Netherlands	Spain	Sweden	UK
Belgium	138.51			76.67	0.00		49.55			
Denmark		231.72	51.86						7.66	23.00
Finland		13.56	102.48						4.85	
France	0.37		0.08	1547.25	0.43	0.06	2.05	8.13		6.88
Germany	0.21	0.11	0.17	13.96	455.34	36.62	91.97	22.19	0.03	8.77
Italy	0.00			82.62	16.92	381.55		0.07		8.81
Netherlands	17.25		0.01	0.10	0.32	0.00	590.22		0.02	0.07
Spain	0.01			14.06	11.22	0.01	16.27	430.87		
Sweden		16.26	53.29		0.00				277.85	
UK	0.01	0.20	0.25	6.54	0.75	0.26	1.74	239.34	0.17	1076.92

Panel B: Retail (IRB) SME secured by Real Estate Properties

	Austria	Belgium	Denmark	France	Germany	Italy	Netherlands	Spain	Sweden	UK
Austria	6.68				0.00	1.79				
Belgium		18.71		6.58			8.12		0.11	
Denmark			13.68							
France	0.00	0.01	0.00	102.67	0.00	0.00	0.02	0.02		0.52
Germany	0.16	0.01	0.00	0.01	14.29	0.88	0.01	0.00		0.00
Italy		0.00		3.63	0.22	24.30		0.00		
Netherlands	0.00	0.01		0.00	0.01		27.69			0.00
Spain		0.00		0.00	0.11	0.00	0.00	22.39		0.00
Sweden			0.32						15.55	
UK	0.01	0.00	0.00	0.01	0.00	0.00	0.01	0.02	0.00	13.22

Note: Credit inflows are reported in rows, and credit outflows in columns (e.g., Italian banks provide €0.06 billion to corporate clients located in France and French banks provide €82.6 billion to corporate clients located in Italy).

Source: European Banking Authority, 2019 EU-wide Transparency Exercise.

This evidence outlines that banks are more willing to grant credit to distant companies than to distant retail counterparties.

Panel B of Table 5.4 focuses on the countries with the largest retail credit exposure granted to SMEs and secured by real estate properties. Our data suggest that only a small portion of retail credit exposure goes to SMEs. In our sample, approximately 5.8 percent of retail exposures granted by banks in a given country go to SMEs in the same country and are secured by a real estate property. However, countries like Belgium go well beyond this level with approximately 13 percent. Meanwhile, countries like the UK only have 1.2 percent.

5.5 CONCLUSIONS

In this chapter, we have examined the structure of the networks generated by cross-border credit exposures granted by banks to counterparties in other European countries. The structure of financial networks is essential because it may be informative in predicting the diffusion of economic shocks across countries. As outlined by Acemoglu et al. (2015), a complete network may be desirable when the financial network must absorb small shocks, whereas an incomplete network may avoid the diffusion of the shock to all the nodes in the system when the system is hit by a very large shock. We use data made available by the EBA to show that the financial networks generated by banks' credit exposures are incomplete as no countries are connected to all the other nodes in our sample. Nevertheless, the networks we presented are characterized by very central countries that display a large number of connections in our sample. This evidence may suggest that the European network of credit exposures could be exposed to large economic shocks that may spread to many countries in Europe. Further research is then needed to explore the potential economic consequences of international credit exposure of European banks.

NOTE

1. This classification is identical to the one presented in the data published by the EBA. We only consider internal rating-based (IRB) portfolios since their amount is more significant than standardized approach (SA) portfolios and the classification offered by the EBA is different. When referring to SMEs, we consider the portion of loans granted by real estate properties consistently with the important role of the real estate market in spreading the Global Financial Crisis.

REFERENCES

Acemoglu, D., Ozdaglar, A., and Tahbaz-Salehi, A. 2015. Systemic Risk and Stability in Financial Networks. *American Economic Review*, 105 (2), 564–608.

Acharya, V.V. and Yorulmazer, T. 2008. Cash-in-the-Market Pricing and Optimal Resolution of Bank Failures. *Review of Financial Studies*, 21 (6), 2705–42.

Aghion, P., Bolton, P., and Dewatripont, M. 2000. Contagious Bank Failures in a Free Banking System. *European Economic Review*, 44 (4–6), 713–18.

Allen, F. and Gale, D. 2000. Financial Contagion. *Journal of Political Economy*, 108 (1), 1–33.

Benmelech, E., Bergman, N., and Seru, A. 2015. Financing Labor. SSRN Electronic Journal.

Blavarg, M. and Nimander, P. 2002. Inter-Bank Exposures and Systemic Risk. *Sveriges Riksbank Economic Review*, 2, 19–45.

Blume, L., Easley, D., Kleinberg, J., Kleinberg, R., and Tardos, E., 2011. Which Networks Are Least Susceptible to Cascading Failures? In *Proceedings of the 2011 52nd IEEE annual symposium on Foundations of Computer Science*, 393–402. Washington, DC: IEEE Computer Society, 39.

Blume, L., Easley, D., Kleinberg, J., Kleinberg, R., and Tardos, E., 2013. Network Formation in the Presence of Contagious Risk. *ACM Transactions on Economics and Computation*, 1 (2), 1–20.

Brunnermeier, M.K. and Pedersen, L.H. 2009. Market Liquidity and Funding Liquidity. *Review of Financial Studies*, 22 (6), 2201–38.

Bruno, V. and Shin, H.S. 2015. Cross-Border Banking and Global Liquidity. *The Review of Economic Studies*, 82 (2, April), 535–64.

Campello, M., Graham, J.R., and Harvey, C.R. 2010. The Real Effects of Financial Constraints: Evidence from a Financial Crisis. *Journal of Financial Economics*, 97 (3), 470–87, ISSN 0304-405X.

Chodorow-Reich, G. 2014. The Employment Effects of Credit Market Disruptions: Firm-Level Evidence from the 2008–9 Financial Crisis. *Quarterly Journal of Economics*, 129 (1), 1–59.

Degryse, H., Elahi, M.A., and Penas, M.F. 2010. Cross-Border Exposures and Financial Contagion. *International Review of Finance*, 10 (2), 209–40.

Diamond, D.W. and Dybvig, P.H. 1983. Bank Runs, Deposit Insurance, and Liquidity. *Journal of Political Economy*, 91 (3), 401–19.

Elliott, M., Golub, B., and Jackson, M.O. 2014. Financial Networks and Contagion. *American Economic Review*, 104 (10), 3115–53.

Freixas, X., Parigi, B.M., and Rochet, J.C. 2000. Systemic Risk, Interbank Relations, and Liquidity Provision by the Central Bank. *Journal of Money, Credit and Banking*, 32 (3 Pt 2), 611–38.

Goldstein, I. and Pauzner, A. 2004. Contagion of Self-Fulfilling Financial Crises Due to Diversification of Investment Portfolios. *Journal of Economic Theory*, 119 (1), 151–83.

Huber, K. 2018. Disentangling the Effects of a Banking Crisis: Evidence from German Firms and Counties. *American Economic Review*, 108 (3), 868–98.

Jensen, T.L. and Johannesen, N. 2017. The Consumption Effects of the 2007–2008 Financial Crisis: Evidence from Households in Denmark. *American Economic Review*, 107 (11), 3386–414.

Lin, Huidan and Paravisini, D. 2013. The Effect of Financing Constraints on Risk. *Review of Finance*, 17 (1), 229–59.

Peek, J. and Rosengren, E.S. 2000. Collateral Damage: Effects of the Japanese Bank Crisis on Real Activity in the United States. *American Economic Review*, 90 (1), 30–45.

Ramcharan, R., Verani, S., and Van den Heuvel, S.J. 2016. From Wall Street to Main Street: The Impact of the Financial Crisis on Consumer Credit Supply. *The Journal of Finance*, 71 (3), 1323–56.

Robb, A.M. and Robinson, D.T. 2014. The Capital Structure Decisions of New Firms. *Review of Financial Studies*, 27 (1, January), 153–79.

Rochet, J.C. and Tirole, J. 1996. Interbank Lending and Systemic Risk. *Journal of Money, Credit and Banking*, 28 (4), 733–62.

Temzelides, T. 1997. Evolution, Coordination, and Banking Panics. *Journal of Monetary Economics*, 40 (1), 163–83.

Tonzer, L. 2015. Cross-Border Interbank Networks, Banking Risk and Contagion. *Journal of Financial Stability*, 18, 19–32.

6. International banks and the transmission of financial shocks[1]

Eugenio Cerutti and Haonan Zhou[2]

6.1 INTRODUCTION

The sweeping development of international banking is one of the key features of international financial integration. Before the Global Financial Crisis (GFC), barriers to foreign bank entry were progressively eased, and the scale of cross-border lending was on the rise: globally, the number of foreign-owned banks increased by 70 percent, from 788 in 1995 to 1,330 in 2009 (Figure 6.1a; Claessens and van Horen, 2014). Meanwhile, at its pre-GFC peak, the outstanding amount of global direct cross-border lending was in the order of 30 trillion US dollars (Figure 6.1b).

Opening up to global banking has obvious benefits, including, but not limited to, access to large and stable sources of funding of global banks, alleviation of domestic financing constraints, and efficiency gains from more intensive competition in the domestic banking sector (Clarke et al., 2003). On the other hand, being incorporated into the interconnected global banking network comes with risks of sudden stops and unhedged

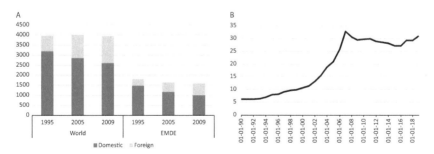

Source: (a) Claessens and van Horen (2014); (b) Bank for International Settlements (BIS).

Figure 6.1 Development of global banking (a) Number of domestic and foreign banks; (b) Global direct cross-border bank claims (trillions USD)

currency mismatch. As Laeven and Valencia (2012) demonstrate, banking crises are very likely to transform into systemic events. With the help of global banks' wide reach, financial shocks originating in core banking systems, mostly from advanced economies, may quickly transmit to peripheral countries' banking systems. Domestic financial turmoil and spillover to the real economy in the form of credit crunch, cascading effects along firms' balance sheets and disruption to trade finance, among other channels, may well follow. Dissecting the role of international banks in the transmission of financial shocks, therefore, is and will remain a crucial topic of interest to academia, domestic regulators and international policymakers alike.

Much progress has been made in understanding the costs and benefits of global banking. But as this chapter will show, it was not until the GFC that academic research began to actively scrutinize the role of global banks as key conduits for the transmission and amplification of financial shocks, possibly due to the systemic and global nature of the GFC (see also Chapter 1). Despite this, several events prior to the GFC provided an environment to study shock propagation through banks' global operations, and this chapter will offer an overview. After 2009, the GFC's lasting impact on the structure of global banking network and the new global regulatory landscape introduced new issues while from time to time highlighting old ones, spurring a large literature on related topics, including the cross-border spillover of macroprudential regulations, the implications of dollar dominance, the role of China as a systemically important lender, and the global retreat of correspondent banking.

It is thus appropriate to use the GFC as a milestone event to guide the organization of this chapter, in which we offer a "helicopter tour" of the academic literature on the relationship between financial shocks and international banks before, during and after the GFC. The complex scope, function and structure of the global banking network warrants a definition of the term "international banking." This chapter considers various forms of international banking, from direct cross-border lending to domestic lending of foreign-owned bank affiliates (either in the form of branches or subsidiaries).[3] We focus mostly on empirical works, but also draw on key theoretical underpinnings. By offering a broader view, our approach can thus be regarded as complementary to Chapter 5, which focuses on cross-border credit exposures in the European Union.

This chapter considers various forms of global banking, including direct lending cross-border and foreign bank entry as branches and subsidiaries. Throughout the chapter, we stress the important linkage between financial shocks and the real economy. An adverse financial shock loses much of its policy relevance if it does not spill over to affect output, investment and other real economic variables, possibly due to sufficient adjustment in general equilibrium. To illustrate this point, in a frictionless environment, firms facing international funding freezes may be able to easily switch to alternative funding sources, so that the disruption to their production and investment decision is minimized. The literature, however, often finds very weak general equilibrium forces that counter the direct impact of financial shocks. International banks may well serve as the key intermediaries that transform fluctuations of foreign financial sectors into domestic recession. Therefore, we also include some discussion on empirical studies related to domestic banking activities with a clear global focus, such as trade finance and lending to multinational companies.

The end of this chapter briefly touches upon two crucial contemporaneous issues. The recent global pandemic and subsequent global lockdown brought challenge to the stability of global banking networks, even though the shock did not stem from the financial system. We also briefly discuss global banks' sustainable and green finance commitment, or the lack thereof, to address climate change.

6.2   BEFORE THE GFC

The rising trend of global financial integration before the GFC attracted the attention of academic literature. Consistent with influential work by Rajan and Zingales (1998), who establish a positive relationship between growth and improved credit access and allocation, a number of empirical studies that focus on pre-GFC periods find positive effects of global banking on domestic financial sectors and the real economy. Foreign entrants tend to be more efficient, as noted by Claessens et al. (2001), who find a negative correlation between foreign bank presence and profitability of the domestic banking system, possibly driven by competitive pressure.[4] Bruno and Hauswald (2014) study the role of foreign bank entry in alleviating the financial constraints of local borrowers. Foreign bank entry does not seem to crowd out local and cross-border credit. Rather, it serves as an additional source of stable funding that improves the growth prospect of local industries. By comparing between different modes of bank entry, Bruno and Hauswald further highlight the ability of foreign banks to overcome informational and legal barriers. Foreign entry via acquiring local institutions and assets, due to its information advantage that enables them to better compete with local incumbents relative to greenfield investment, has a stronger association with industry growth, especially in developing countries.[5] Foreign banks may favor large firms due to the relative availability of "hard" versus "soft" information, but their presence could also address misallocation problems plaguing developing economies by directing resources to productive projects. The literature tends to doubt the existence of global banks' bias towards large, established and multinational firms. De Haas and Naaborg (2006) find that foreign affiliates in Eastern Europe participate in the loan markets for small and medium enterprises as competition and technology improve. Shen (2020) finds evidence from a large cross-country panel of firm-bank relationships that global banks also extend loans to firms of all sizes and ages. Meanwhile, Giannetti and Ongena (2009) show that while smaller firms do grow more slowly relative to large firms as foreign banks enter, young firms grow faster, and politically connected firms tend to face higher funding costs. Recent studies exploiting the capital inflow episode of southern Europe following Eurozone integration, such as Cingano and Hassan (2020), also find a positive match between banks more dependent on foreign funding and high productivity firms.

A natural question to consider against these findings is whether foreign banks also have a potentially destabilizing impact on the business cycles of host economies. On this front, the academic literature paints a more mixed picture. Morgan et al.'s (2004) thought experiment demonstrates that whether banking integration is stabilizing or amplifying business cycle movement depends on the source of shocks. Credit supply shocks that arise from domestic banks may be well absorbed by foreign banks through general equilibrium adjustment (and vice versa) while credit demand shocks due to worsening firm collateral quality or wealth may well result in increased volatility and the retrenchment of both domestic and foreign banks. This ambivalent role of banking integration is empirically reaffirmed in Morgan and Strahan (2004), who find that while relaxation of inter-state branch restrictions in the US has a dampening effect on local bank capital shocks, in the international context, foreign bank entry has a zero to positive contribution to the volatility of firms' investment spending. Clarke et al. (2003), on the other hand, find no clear evidence that foreign banks could substantially threaten domestic financial stability.[6] In some cases, foreign banks are even considered as lenders of last resort, given their access to stable internal capital markets from their parent banks or the possibility that domestic depositors considered them safer than domestic.[7] Regulatory arbitrage may be a key margin driving foreign banks' international lending decision, as shown by Houston et al. (2012) using cross-country regressions. Nevertheless, these cross-border banking flows that seem to exploit differences in banking regulations are typically channeled to countries with a stronger institutional environment, partly alleviating the concern on financial stability.

Despite the seeming lack of clear-cut pre-GFC empirical evidence, the role of international banks in transmitting financial shocks globally into the domestic financial sector and the real economy should not be ignored. Relying on cross-country observational data, rarely do the studies reviewed above estimate the *causal* impact of global banking. Recent advances in empirical techniques that emphasize causal inference achieve more credible identification, by focusing on historical events and exploiting plausibly exogenous variations in the data. Xu (2021) studies the international spread of the 1866 British banking crisis. Financial panic and bank runs triggered by the unexpected bankruptcy of discounting house Overend, Gurney & Company led to massive failure of British multinational banks chartered to intermediate trade activities. As an immediate consequence, foreign subsidiaries closed, trade finance collapsed, and exporting activity contracted. While access to trade finance was restored shortly after the banking crisis as the banking sector recovered, Xu finds permanent loss of exports for countries exposed to the banking crisis. General equilibrium adjustment is key to alleviating the negative impact: the long-term loss in exports is mostly driven by exporters that could not access trade financing from alternative partners.

Originating from the global financial centre (London) and spreading to the periphery, the Panic of 1866 might be regarded as the first systemic financial crisis with a far-reaching impact, both spatially and temporally. Going down the path of history, as global financial linkages became stronger among leading economies at the time of the Great Depression, one may expect international banks to play a similar role. Yet there is, perhaps surprisingly, little empirical work on this topic, possibly due to difficulties in achieving identification. Explanation for the global spread of financial crises relies on sentiment factors and central banks' policy response to preserve the gold standard (Temin, 1993; Eichengreen and Temin, 2000). It is not until the late 20th century that a series of balance-of-payments and banking crises around the world generated renewed academic interest in the international propagation of financial shocks.

In a series of papers, Joe Peek and Eric Rosengren provide causal evidence on the transmission of financial shocks during Japan's stock and property market crash in the early 1990s. The decline in equity and real estate prices put heavy pressure on Japanese banks' capital. With a market share close to 20 percent in the commercial and industrial loan business in the US, Japanese banks shrank their overseas lending substantially to preserve domestic lending relationships, as shown by Peek and Rosengren (1997). The real effect of Japanese banks' retreat is large: following the loan supply shock, construction activities declined significantly (Peek and Rosengren, 2000), again suggesting that general equilibrium adjustment to alternative funding sources seems weak, if not absent.

For emerging market (EM) economies, global financial conditions are also a key determinant of domestic loan activities. In Bruno and Shin's (2015) "double decker" model of international banking, global banks attract wholesale funds and channel them into local banks, which subsequently lend to local borrowers. The economic impact of foreign financial shocks thus critically depends on the exposure of local bank-firm relationships to global factors due to difference in ownership and funding structure. In this spirit, Schnabl (2012) studies the transmission of Russia's debt default shock to the Peruvian economy exploiting heterogeneous exposure of firms and banks. The 1998 default of Russia triggered a large drop in equity prices of international banks. The spillover of this liquidity shock to recipient banks in Peru, however, was heterogeneous across bank types. Compared to foreign-owned banks, domestically owned banks received substantially less loans from international lenders. With little means to offset this funding shock by switching to alternative lenders, domestically owned banks reduced lending to Peruvian firms by 8 percent relative to foreign-owned banks, and 13 percent compared to locally funded banks. Hit by a more difficult financing condition, firms with more exposure to affected domestically owned banks were more likely to default and exit.

To summarize, despite a large part of the literature prior to the GFC highlighting net benefits to international banking, there were already some cases of crises being transmitted to local economies through international bank linkages. Nonetheless, most crises before the GFC (the 1994 Tequila crisis of Mexico, the Asian financial crises of 1997 and the 2001 Argentine crisis, for instance) were related to individual or a small group of EMs, not at the core of the banking network. The global banking system proved able to diversify idiosyncratic risks and prevent these risks becoming sufficiently systemic to affect the real economy of most core countries in the network. That said, international banks' exposure to individual cases of banking crises, once cumulated into a regional systemic phenomenon and transmitted to financial centers, may have non-negligible economic implications on credit allocation and funding condition of countries not directly affected by the crises, as demonstrated in the Mexican and Asian crisis episodes (Van Rijckeghem and Weder, 2003; Kaminsky and Reinhart, 2008; Hale et al., 2020).

6.3   THE GFC AND INTERNATIONAL BANKS

The GFC started as a shot to the very center of the global financial system – US and European banks, and quickly transmitted to the entire world. Instead of fully diversifying risks, dense interconnections led to cascading failures and contagion, highlighting the nonlinear nature of an integrated banking system's resilience to adverse shocks according to post-GFC theoretical advances (Elliott et al., 2014; Acemoglu et al., 2015). As global banks dealt with financial turmoil by shedding their international presence, the impact of the GFC was felt in the periphery of the global banking network through balance sheet linkages. Credit supply in EMs responded to the GFC in ways much like the just reviewed pre-GFC crises. The bank lending channel (see also Chapter 3) worked through the contraction in direct cross-border borrowing, the retreat of foreign banks' affiliates, as well as domestic banks' reduction in loan supply as funding shocks hit their balance sheets (Cetorelli and Goldberg, 2011). Owing to the GFC's outsized impact on the core of the banking network, and the joint action of these channels, however, the scale of shrinkage in global banks' overseas exposure and thus the worsening of financial conditions of peripheral countries dwarfed any of the previous crises. Globally, direct cross-border lending experienced a sharp trend reversal (Figure 6.1b) with sluggish recovery. In addition, foreign affiliates' status as stable funding sources, shielded by parent banks, was no longer solid. During the GFC, parent banks' default risks were positively correlated with their foreign subsidiaries' default risks (Anginer et al., 2017), and foreign subsidiaries of international banks reduced growth of credit nearly three times faster than domestically owned banks (De Haas and van Lelyveld, 2014). Aiyar (2011, 2012) uses detailed data on banks in the UK to show that domestic lending dropped by around 0.6 percent for each 1 percent loss of foreign funding, with foreign subsidiaries and branches reducing lending by a larger amount relative to domestically owned banks. As highlighted in Cerutti and Schmieder (2014) and Cerutti and Claessens (2017), limitations or even ring fencing by host/home regulators of the liquidity and capital buffers across locations within the same baking group did not allow for the full use of multinational banks' international geographical diversification, amplifying the cross-border lending adjustments during the GFC. A larger amount of indirect asset-side exposure to crises due to increasing interbank linkages since the Asian financial crises further contributed to shock transmission through heightened counterparty risks that may lead to balance sheet contagion (Hale et al., 2020).

By merely focusing on the aggregate responses of global banks during the GFC, we run the risk of missing interesting details. Influential studies by Giannetti and Laeven (2012a, 2012b) attribute the sharp contraction of global syndicated lending to a "flight-home" effect, as international lenders rebalanced their portfolio towards domestic borrowers. They argue that this time-varying home bias in portfolio allocation is better characterized as a disorderly "running for the exit" rather than the conventional notion of flight to liquidity, safety and quality. Lenders in countries experiencing banking crises originated fewer loans to foreign borrowers, regardless of borrowers' quality, exposure to domestic crises or the institutional environment of recipient countries. This home bias was stronger for banks relying on wholesale (non-deposit) funding (De Haas and van Lelyveld, 2014) and could possibly be explained by higher cost of monitoring and expectation of bailout (Giannetti and Laeven, 2012a). Aiyar (2011) also finds that foreign-owned banks' deleveraging did not correlate with the actual size of external funding shocks, while the scale of locally owned banks' cut to their lending was aligned with shocks to their foreign liabilities.

In turn, a number of studies attempt to qualify the findings of Giannetti and Laeven by digging into the nuanced mechanism of retrenchment and highlighting the importance of liquidity management and strategic motives in shaping the geographical pattern of shock transmission. Employing loan-level data on global syndicated lending, De Haas and van Horen (2013) argue that various measures of "closeness" – geographical proximity, incorporation into the domestic banking network and country-specific lending history, among others – helped stabilize cross-border lending to destinations satisfying these criteria. The same authors also show that relatively smaller borrowers, in particular, lost funding from banks with large exposure to subprime mortgage write-downs (De Haas and van Horen, 2012). Cetorelli and Goldberg (2012b) focus on the important interaction between parent banks and foreign affiliates. Instead of utilizing internal capital markets to make one-way transfers from headquarters to all subsidiaries to support lending to foreign counterparties, global banks acted strategically to protect important affiliates that generate more revenues, while channeling resources from more peripheral affiliates.

Is the deleveraging driven by some specific characteristics of global banks? Empirical literature overwhelmingly supports the role of *ex ante* vulnerabilities. Large pre-crisis exposure to markets that collapsed during the GFC, including asset-backed commercial papers and subprime mortgages, led to worsened market perception of a weak balance sheet and reduced the ability for exposed banks to raise external funding (Cetorelli and Goldberg, 2012a). Creditors' excessive *ex ante* dependence on short-term dollar funding subject to runs is another good predictor of the extent to which shocks propagate (Cetorelli and Goldberg, 2011). Cerutti and Claessens (2017) find that market-based systemic risk indicators, such as Brownlees and Engle's (2017) SRISK measure of capital shortfall, can explain much of the cross-sectional variation in the contraction of banks' direct cross-border lending. Substantial heterogeneity in the relationship between balance sheet characteristics and the response of cross-border banking activities to financial shocks exists across countries, as shown by the International Banking Research Network (IBRN) from analysing individual countries' experience with a consistent econometric framework (see the meta-analysis by Buch and Goldberg, 2015). These findings highlight the importance of both macroprudential regulation and well-suited microprudential supervision and monitoring of international banks, as their global externality is non-negligible.

We close this section by exploring the real consequences of the contraction of global banking during the GFC. For advanced economies, the GFC represents another episode in which real output comoves closely. Kalemli-Ozcan et al. (2013) show that while in normal times banking activity among advanced countries is related to a more differentiated economic outcome, with global banks benefiting from diversification, the GFC stood out among banking crises, in that countries linked closely with the US through cross-border banking also share more synchronized output dynamics with the US. For EM economies, Popov and Udell (2012) show a significant tightening of financial constraints for small and medium enterprises in Eastern Europe. Hale et al. (2020) use a matched firm-loan sample from 1997 to 2012 to further demonstrate that firms whose lenders are directly exposed to banking crises tend to have lower growth and investment. This negative relationship between crisis exposure and real outcomes is especially pronounced during 2007–09. Morelli et al. (2019) offer a theory of interaction between global banks and EM economies' borrowing cost and the real economy. In their model, a shock to the quality of global banks' portfolio holdings of advanced economy assets has a negative impact on net worth and transmits into lending to EMs, leading to higher costs of borrowing and lower output. Endogenously heightened default risks and second-round effects due to further reduction of global banks' net worth depress asset prices even more. Empirically, the authors find a positive relationship between the price of EM debt and debt holders' exposure to the GFC.

Firm-bank linkage is not the only channel through which banks transmitted financial shocks internationally in the GFC period. Just like the Panic of 1866, trade finance was again severely disrupted, contributing to the global trade collapse. Amiti and Weinstein (2009) associate one-quarter of the contraction in Japanese exports in the two years between March 2007 and 2009 to financial shocks. Ahn et al. (2011) exploit the relationship between trade finance dependence and shipping methods and find that US seaborne imports, more price-sensitive to shocks to trade credit than shipments through air or land, saw an increase in relative prices. The rise of foreign direct investment further amplified the transmission of financial shocks from the lenders of multinational corporations to firms' global affiliates through internal capital markets. Using the deleveraging of

Commerzbank – the second-largest bank in Germany – during the GFC, Biermann and Huber (2019) show that despite not directly exposed to the Commerzbank shock, affiliates whose German parents were funded by Commerzbank experienced lower growth, falling sales and smaller equity injection from the headquarters, and, on a net basis, made positive internal transfers in order to alleviate external funding pressure faced by the parents. General equilibrium adjustment was again at work here: for firms that could overcome credit market friction and address funding shortfalls via other banking relationships, the real impact on affiliates was weakened.

6.4   POST-GFC: STRUCTURAL CHANGE AND NEW ISSUES

The GFC is unique among all modern banking crises in that its global impact remains persistent, even more than a decade after its onset. The post-crisis "new normal" of monetary policy and financial regulation have led to a number of significant new developments in financial globalization and the structure of international banking. From a broad perspective, the solid image of financial integration as an irreversible global trend is challenged directly by the contraction in direct cross-border banking activities. Even after the crisis, the heightened portfolio home bias observed during the GFC has not returned to its pre-crisis level (Bremus and Fratzscher, 2015). The concept of "financial deglobalization" was first proposed by Broda et al. back in 2009, and is still receiving fresh academic and policy debate.

The near consensus of studies analysing recent trends in international banking nonetheless offers a qualification to the degree of retreat from globalization by pointing out interesting structural shifts in the global financial network. Cerutti and Zhou (2017, 2018a) use a gravity model and draw tools from network analysis to highlight the increasing regional interconnectedness of banking after the GFC. An indicator of intra-regional banking connection in the form of direct cross-border lending as well as lending via local affiliates is increasing and highly significant in a gravity model saturated with traditional indicators of proximity among countries, such as distance, common language and historical ties (Cerutti and Zhou, 2018a). Using network analysis, Cerutti and Zhou (2017) also find evidence in favor of a clearer partition of the global banking network into distinct regional clusters after the GFC, with denser connection within each cluster. The regionalization process is nevertheless highly unbalanced: as measured by a number of network importance metrics, large EM economies with a heavy regional presence gain most connections, while small and peripheral recipient countries do not. This echoes the finding of Claessens and van Horen (2015) that European banks strategically preserve their presence in important trading partners while exiting from new ventures and smaller deals. The fact that large banking conglomerates headquartered in Europe and North America spun off some of their foreign operations in distant markets is not necessarily consistent with a full-fledged "financial deglobalization." Instead, regionalization of global banking is primarily driven by the takeover of regional banks, as in the case of Latin America, as well as European banks' recalibration of operating focus towards their own regional market (Claessens and van Horen, 2015; McCauley et al., 2019).

Furthermore, even the aggregate decline in direct cross-border lending cannot speak much to the extent of "deglobalization," since it can be mostly explained by the deleveraging of European banks. In fact, following the implementation of unconventional monetary policies in advanced economies, non-European international banks led by Japanese institutions have been expanding their footprint by extending a large sum of cross-border loans in search of better yields outside the "low-for-long" interest rate environment at home (Bremus and Fratzscher, 2015; McCauley et al., 2019; Cerutti and Zhou, 2018a). One may still point to the overall shrinkage of cross-border lending as a worrying sign of declining credit intermediation activities across the globe, but this argument ignores the fast growth of international capital market for EM bonds – the "second phase of global liquidity" as put by Shin (2013). In this sense, as countries find themselves in an increasingly easier position to tap alternative sources and forms of financing, financial constraints may actually loosen rather than tighten, so as to smooth out the real impact when financial shocks hit. From a structural point of view, if the systemic transmission of the GFC is regarded as a sign of excessive interconnectedness within the global banking network, then these post-crisis developments may, in fact, indicate a gradual return to a globally optimal degree of arrangement that mitigates concerns over financial stability.

The GFC's lasting impact is not limited to structural changes in the global banking network, however. Coordinated efforts after the GFC to enhance bank capital and step up macroprudential policy have created a new regulatory landscape. Figure 6.2 plots, on a global level, the total number of macroprudential regulations from 2000 to 2018, with an acceleration after the GFC. While these policy innovations seek to safeguard the resilience of the global banking system and deter the unduly transmission of adverse shocks (and recent literature indeed finds that macroprudential toolkit as a whole seems successful in achieving these goals[8]), the implementation of regulation may entail unintended spillovers through the scaling of banks' cross-border operations. The macroprudential toolkit was also expanded

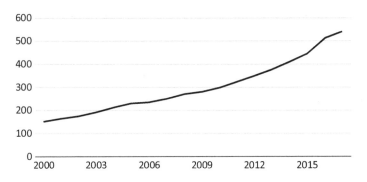

Source: Cerutti et al. (2017, 2018a).

Figure 6.2   Global use of prudential instruments

in the context of Basel III, which included some of the key reforms such as the Net Stable Funded Ratio (NSFR) and the liquidity coverage ratio (LCR). These measures were envisaged to control and measure liquidity risk exposures and funding needs both at the consolidated banking group level as well as individual foreign branches and subsidiaries (BIS, 2014) We focus on two types of spillovers analysed in recent empirical literature. First, regulatory arbitrage activities may undo some of the benefits of a strengthened macroprudential framework. Restrictions on one group of banks may "leak" by implicitly encouraging other unregulated financial intermediaries to fill in the void created by the restrictions. Focusing on the years leading up to the GFC, Ongena et al. (2013) provide early evidence that more stringent home regulation, by fostering greater competition and restricting risk-taking activities in the domestic market, encouraged global banks to shift lending to riskier borrowers in Eastern Europe. Aiyar et al. (2014) study the impact of the UK's capital requirement before the GFC and find that unaffected foreign branches increased their lending when the capital ratio was raised on locally owned banks and foreign subsidiaries. On the other hand, Reinhardt and Sowerbutts (2015) do not find evidence that a tightening of lending standards, such as loan-to-value ratios, led to increased borrowing from foreign branches, as these types of regulations do not discriminate between foreign and domestic banks. More recently, using a dataset of global macroprudential policy and capital control measures and accounting for multidimensional lender-borrower relationship, Cerutti and Zhou (2018b) find a higher level of direct cross-border banking inflows following borrowers' macroprudential policy tightening, and an increase in local affiliates' lending associated with motives to circumvent lender countries' capital outflow restrictions.

In addition to spillovers through regulation leakages, country-level financial and monetary policies are financial shocks themselves, as they directly impose additional constraints on the balance sheet of global banks and affect the relative margins of investment across different countries. As banks manage liquidity at a global level and adjust their overseas operations in response, financial conditions in recipient countries may worsen. Tripathy (2020) uses the implementation of additional loan-loss provisions requirement on real estate assets in Spain as a quasi-natural experiment and studies the change in Spanish banks' lending to Mexico. He finds that household credit in municipalities with a higher presence of Spanish subsidiaries, such as those of BBVA and Santander, experienced a larger contraction following the regulation. The cross-country initiative of IBRN using loan-level data finds that, in general, the spillovers of prudential instruments depend on a number of factors, including the strength of affiliates' balance sheets, types of funding, as well as access to internal capital markets, and heterogeneity across countries suggest that country-specific characteristics also play a role (Buch and Goldberg, 2017). The interaction between post-crisis monetary and macroprudential policy has equally important implications for cross-border lending. Bräuning and Ivashina (2020) build a stylized model in which global banks, facing capital constraints and limited amount of equity, optimally choose lending in different currencies by equating their marginal returns. In this way, monetary policy tightening in one country affects lending decision globally.

A large fraction of international investment positions, especially vis-à-vis EM economies, are denominated in US dollars. US and European banks transform wholesale dollar funding to support their lending activities to both the US and the world. Despite potential currency mismatch on their balance sheets, borrowers across the globe are willing to take on dollar liabilities, as the dollar-dominated international capital market is deep and liquid, whereas local-currency markets in EM economies remain underdeveloped. For exporters with foreign income as natural hedges or expenditures in foreign intermediate inputs, borrowing in dollars is often the natural (and optimal) choice. While the Euro, following its launch at the end of the 20th century, had gained some traction as an international currency before the onset of the GFC, events during and after 2008 further strengthened the dominance of the dollar (Maggiori et al., 2019). Figure 6.3 shows that the US dollar consistently accounts for around half of total cross-border banking claims, with its share slightly increasing and Euro's share diminishing after the GFC. As a result, the financial market becomes highly sensitive to movements in the price of the dollar – the exchange rate – that signals global risk aversion, and the relative shortage of US dollar induced by flight to safety. Again, drawing from

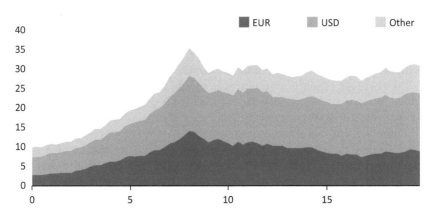

Source: Bank for International Settlements (BIS).

Figure 6.3   Currency composition of direct cross-border bank claims

the "double-decker" model of Bruno and Shin (2015), an appreciation of the dollar not only raises the real value of debt for dollar borrowers, it also leads to a rise in the riskiness of global banks' portfolio that prompts banks to swiftly curtail their exposure to overseas borrowers.

Since the GFC, episodes of dollar funding strain have plagued financial institutions on a global level. While the establishment of dollar swap lines between advanced economies' central banks temporarily eased dollar funding condition during the GFC (Baba and Packer, 2009), funding shortfall continues to have a detrimental impact on cross-border dollar lending to both advanced and emerging economies since then. During the Eurozone debt crisis, the perceived worsening creditworthiness of European banks led to the spike of direct and synthetic dollar funding cost (through the use of foreign exchange swaps) and the withdrawal of US money market funds – the primary wholesale dollar funding source for European banks. As a consequence, these banks shrank lending in dollars relative to Euros (Ivashina et al., 2015). This funding shock was further transmitted to US firms borrowing from European banks, as they responded by reducing investment and increasing cash holdings as a precautionary safeguard measure (Correa et al., 2018). Outflows from EM economies during the 2013 Fed Taper Tantrum are also systemically associated with dollar borrowing, as shown by Avdjiev and Takáts (2019): dollar share of cross-border lending right before the Taper Tantrum (the first quarter of 2013) is a significant predictor of the scale of cross-border lending retrenchment during this episode. Post-GFC strengthening of the US dollar's central role in the international monetary system is intimately related to macroprudential policy innovations that seek to preserve global financial stability, as well as countries' asymmetric recovery from the GFC, as both the regulation-induced global search for safety and the global quest for higher returns primarily reflect international investors' appetite for dollar-denominated assets.[9] Taking stock, dollar dominance and prudential instruments are parts of the key building blocks of post-GFC international financial architecture, and their impact on global banking is expected to continue.

We close this section by discussing two novel and understudied developments after the GFC with implications for financial stability, with particular relevance for developing countries. Within two decades, China's share in international investment has grown substantially (Figure 6.4a), particularly in the form of bank lending (counted as "other investment" in balance of payments terms.) Official statistics do not provide a detailed picture of China's overseas lending until 2016, despite China's outsized share of claims on EM and low-income countries. Aggregate figures suggest that Chinese banks lent out around 600 billion dollars to external borrowers, both to banks and non-banks (Figure 6.4b). With accurate numbers on China's bilateral exposure still not publicly available at the time of this writing, researchers have come up with various estimates.[10] Cerutti and Zhou (2018c) exploit the statistical breaks introduced after the incorporation of Chinese banks' international claims into BIS banking statistics. In a number of cases such as Djibouti and Laos, low-income economies overwhelmingly depend on Chinese banks for external funding, with China claiming over 80 percent of these countries' total liabilities to all international banks. While the size of such claims amounts to a

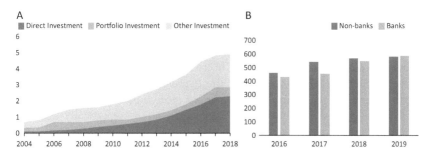

Source: (a)   CEIC; (b) Bank for International Settlements (BIS).

Figure 6.4   Rising importance of China in international finance (a) International investment position, by type (percent world GDP); (b) China's cross-border claims, by counterparty sector (billions USD)

tiny fraction relative to Chinese banks' total assets, they plant the seed for abrupt retrenchment of capital should financial institutions in China encounter large shocks to their operation, through the usual bank lending channel reviewed in this chapter. Improving our knowledge on the global reach of the opaque yet systemically important Chinese banking system is among the key objectives on the agenda for future work.

Receiving similarly little attention is the decline of correspondent banking relationship since the GFC. As one of the key functions of global banking networks, correspondent banking is an arrangement to reduce the cost of making cross-border transactions, by maintaining banking relationship among banks in multiple countries to send and receive payments on behalf of the end customers. As pointed out by Rice et al. (2020), however, in the recent decade, global correspondent banking has scaled back on a broad basis. Several factors contribute to this decline, but similar to the reason for the retreat of cross-border lending, stringent regulations and banks' recalibration of business model appear to be the leading explanation. The dissolution of correspondent banking relationship raises concern not only over the rising cost of cross-border payment, particularly relevant for exporters and migrants, but also over the possible switch to unregulated, risky payment services offered by shadow banks (Rice et al., 2020). More efforts are needed to better understand the role of banks in facilitating cross-border payment and the persistence of correspondent banking's decline, in order to inform the design of a more efficient international payments scheme that minimizes downside risks to financial stability.

6.5   POLICY IMPLICATIONS AND OUTLOOK

Banking globalization is a vivid example of a "double-edged sword": cross-border lending and foreign entry relax financial constraints, provide market access for small firms and households, and impose market discipline and competition to improve the overall efficiency of the domestic banking system. Conversely, increasingly interconnected balance sheets mean that global banks could propagate and systematically amplify adverse shocks arising from (or coming through) the core to the rest of the banking network. A collapse in financial intermediation has grave effects on the real economy, and even countries not directly exposed to banking crises could feel the heat.

Global banking has undergone substantial structural changes in the aftermath of the GFC. With a non-negligible number of prudential instruments having large cross-border externalities set at the discretion of national authorities facing political-economy frictions,[11] a regionalized global banking system may shift parts of the burden (and the duty) of regulation to countries with less well-established institutions. Despite a safer banking system compared to pre-GFC periods, regulatory arbitrage activities could still be destabilizing especially for emerging and developing economies, calling for more efforts to overcome national barriers and step up international coordination in policymaking and stress testing at the global level.[12] Already equipped with ample knowledge on the major channels of shock transmission through global banks, policymakers need to actively evaluate new sources of risks in the economy that might be passed on to global banks and improve the understanding of important new players in global financial intermediation, such as China, as well as the unintended spillovers of the new macroprudential regulatory landscape.

With rising capital and liquidity buffers under Basel III, as well as the advance of well-calibrated prudential policy framework, it remains to be seen if the international banking system could withstand financial shocks of a calibre similar to the GFC. The recent pandemic, albeit not a financial shock in itself, led financial markets into a temporary tailspin while dealing a severe blow to the real economy. When market turmoil peaked in late March 2020, funding costs overshot and bank stocks underperformed, with equity prices and default risk mimicking the level seen during the Lehman collapse (Aldasoro et al., 2020). Cross-border syndicated loans contracted by 15 percent in the first four months of 2020 relative to 2019 (Martinez et al., 2020). Market functioning was largely restored and market sentiment recovered, thanks to extraordinary coordinated actions from central banks around the world. International banking claims record a high annual growth rate of 4.8 percent through mid-2020, indicating the overall resilience of the global banking network to the pandemic shock (Hardy and Takáts, 2020). Nevertheless, under an uncertain prospect of new waves of cases, the pressure of the pandemic on the stability of the global banking system is expected to persist.

The central role of banks in the global financial system comes with great responsibility, especially in an era when the risk of catastrophic climate change has plausibly raised global concern. As more resources are needed to develop sustainable and climate-friendly projects, international banks could and should play a more active role by leveraging complementarity and competition. For now, however, little can be said about major banking groups' appetite for green finance. Pinchot and Christianson (2019) show that only half of the 50 largest banks have committed to tilt their portfolio towards sustainable projects, sometimes under the guideline of the United Nations Sustainable and Development Goals. Uncertainty over the prospect of sustainable investment, and the reluctance to lose market shares in traditional energy sectors are among the major impediments for global banks to deepen their interest in green finance. It is, however, imperative for banks to fully incorporate climate risk into their business model and risk management practices, as substantial progress can be made to deal with the challenges posed by climate change with the participation of banks at the global level.

Increasing availability of micro-data and the close connection between global banks and the real sectors invite researchers to go beyond observational studies in order to draw a more accurate picture of global banking and better identify the causal impact of international banking flows. Do tax havens and offshore financial centers complicate the geography of international banking? What is the relationship between foreign banks and factor misallocation? Is there an optimal level of dollar dependence that works best in trading off between financial access and unwanted currency mismatch? These interesting questions in international macro-finance are waiting to be addressed in depth by future research.

NOTES

1. The views expressed in this article are those of the author and do not necessarily represent the views of the IMF, its Executive Board, or IMF management.
2. For helpful comments, the authors thank the editors, Giovanni Ferri and Vicenzo D'Apice, as well as Ralph Chami, Vikram Haksar, Jan Strasky and Mindaugas Leika. Zhou acknowledges financial support from the International Economics Section at Princeton University.
3. While subsidiaries are separate entities from their parent banks (so exposure is limited), under most circumstances, parent banks are responsible for the liabilities of their branches. Cerutti et al. (2007) find that branches are preferred in countries that have higher taxes and lower regulatory restrictions on bank entry and on foreign branches. Instead, subsidiary operations are favored by international banks seeking to penetrate host markets by establishing large retail operations or when they prefer to limit the risk exposure to the host economic crisis.
4. Cull and Martínez Pería's (2010) literature review also finds strong evidence on the efficiency of foreign banks in Eastern Europe and Latin America.
5. As part of international banks' access to large and stable sources of funding, large multinational banks can not only fund their domestically incorporated subsidiaries, but they can also book large exposures as direct cross-border credit from their headquarters or other affiliates within the banking group.
6. Similar empirical findings in the literature are summarized in Goldberg (2009).
7. Foreign banks could play a stabilizing role in host countries during domestic crises if depositors perceive them as a "safe haven" (i.e., for "flying to quality" within the country's banking system). See Adler and Cerutti (2015).
8. For a recent review on the stabilizing role of macroprudential regulation, see Bergant et al. (2020). At the same time, as highlighted by Cerutti et al. (2018a), it is too early to know how much macroprudential polices can deliver in terms of overall financial stability. The implementation of many macroprudential instruments is still recent and the literature has not been able to perform a full analysis since most countries had not gone through a full economic and financial cycle before the COVID-19 shock hit.

9. Dollar funding shortage is most pronounced during period-end financial reporting dates as financial institutions window-dress their balance sheets and is reflected in significant deviations from covered interest parity, a no-arbitrage relationship between forward, spot exchange rates and interest rates that breaks down only after the global financial crisis. Du et al. (2018) and Cerutti et al. (2021) discuss the various macrofinancial determinants of this barometer of global dollar shortfall. Committee on the Global Financial System (2020) offers a detailed picture on the structure of global dollar funding.

10. A comprehensive database on China's overseas lending is provided by Horn et al. (2020) using various estimates on official lending. Using confidential BIS data, Cerutti et al. (2018b, 2020) show how important banks from emerging countries, especially China, have become in recent years. As of 2018Q2, not only do Chinese banks have a higher share (about 45 percent) of their global cross-border claims on emerging market and developing economies (EMDE) borrowers than other banking systems, but their claims (about USD 919 billion) are also more than half that of other banking systems (e.g., Japanese banks' cross-border claims on EMDEs are about USD 488 billion). Moreover, 63 EMDEs already borrow more from Chinese banks than from any other bank nationality.

11. Müller (2020) uses a cross-country dataset with wide coverage and documents the loosening of macroprudential policies in the run-up to elections.

12. Clayton and Schaab (2020) provide a theoretical treatment of globally inefficient quantity-based macroprudential regulation implemented nationwide.

REFERENCES

Acemoglu, Daron, Asuman Ozdaglar, and Alireza Tahbaz-Salehi. 2015. "Systemic Risk and Stability in Financial Networks." *American Economic Review* 105 (2): 564–608.

Adler, Gustavo, and Eugenio Cerutti. 2015. "Are Foreign Banks a 'Safe Haven'? Evidence from Past Banking Crises." IMF Working Paper 15/43.

Ahn, JaeBin, Mary Amiti, and David E. Weinstein. 2011. "Trade Finance and the Great Trade Collapse." *American Economic Review: Papers and Proceedings* 101 (3): 298–302.

Aiyar, Shekhar. 2011. "How Did the Crisis in International Funding Markets Affect Bank Lending? Balance Sheet Evidence from the United Kingdom." Bank of England Working Paper No. 424.

Aiyar, Shekhar. 2012. "From Financial Crisis to Great Recession: The Role of Globalized Banks." *American Economic Review: Papers and Proceedings* 102 (3): 225–30.

Aiyar, Shekhar, Charles W. Calomiris, and Tomasz Wieladek. 2014. "Does Macro-Prudential Regulation Leak? Evidence from a UK Policy Experiment." *Journal of Money, Credit and Banking* 46 (1): 181–214.

Aldasoro, Iñaki, Ingo Fender, Bryan Hardy, and Nikola Tarashev. 2020. "Effects of Covid-19 on the Banking Sector: The Market's Assessment." *BIS Bulletin*, No. 12.

Amiti, Mary, and David E. Weinstein. 2009. "Exports and Financial Shocks." *Quarterly Journal of Economics* 126 (4): 1841–77.

Anginer, Deniz, Eugenio Cerutti, and María Soledad Martínez Pería. 2017. "Foreign Bank Subsidiaries' Default Risk during the Global Crisis: What Factors Help Insulate Affiliates from Their Parents?" *Journal of Financial Intermediation* 29 (January): 19–31. https://doi.org/10.1016/j.jfi.2016.05.004.

Avdjiev, Stefan, and Elöd Takáts. 2019. "Monetary Policy Spillovers and Currency Networks in Cross-Border Bank Lending: Lessons from the 2013 Fed Taper Tantrum." *Review of Finance* 23 (5): 993–1029.

Baba, Naohiko, and Frank Packer. 2009. "Interpreting Deviations from Covered Interest Parity during the Financial Market Turmoil of 2007–08." *Journal of Banking and Finance* 33 (11): 1953–62.

BIS (Bank for International Settlements). 2014. "Basel III: The Net Stable Funding Ratio." Basel Committee on Banking Supervision. Available at https://www.bis.org/bcbs/publ/d295.pdf (accessed October 25, 2020).

Bergant, Katharina, Francesco Grigoli, Niels-Jakob H. Hansen, and Damiano Sandri. 2020. "Dampening Global Financial Shocks: Can Macroprudential Regulation Help (More Than Capital Controls)?" IMF Working Paper 20/106.

Biermann, Marcus, and Kilian Huber. 2019. "Tracing the International Transmission of a Crisis through Multinational Firms." Working Paper.

Bräuning, Falk, and Victoria Ivashina. 2020. "Monetary Policy and Global Banking." Working Paper.

Bremus, Franziska, and Marcel Fratzscher. 2015. "Drivers of Structural Change in Cross-Border Banking since the Global Financial Crisis." *Journal of International Money and Finance* 52: 32–59.

Broda, Christian, Piero Ghezzi, and Eduardo Levy-Yeyati. 2009. "The New Global Balance: Financial De-globalisation, Savings Drain, and the US Dollar." VoxEU. Available at https://voxeu.org/article/financial-de-globalisation-savings-drain-and-us-dollar (accessed August 25, 2021).

Brownlees, Christian T., and Robert Engle. 2017. "SRISK: A Conditional Capital Shortfall Measure of Systemic Risk." *Review of Financial Studies* 30 (1): 48–79.

Bruno, Valentina, and Robert Hauswald. 2014. "The Real Effect of Foreign Banks." *Review of Finance* 18 (5): 1683–716.

Bruno, Valentina, and Hyun Song Shin. 2015. "Cross-Border Banking and Global Liquidity." *Review of Economic Studies* 82 (2): 535–64.

Buch, Claudia M., and Linda S. Goldberg. 2015. "International Banking and Liquidity Risk Transmission: Lessons from across Countries." *IMF Economic Review* 63 (3): 377–410.

Buch, Claudia M., and Linda S. Goldberg. 2017. "Cross-Border Prudential Policy Spillovers: How Much? How Important? Evidence from the International Banking Research Network." *International Journal of Central Banking* 13: 505–58.

Cerutti, Eugenio, and Stijn Claessens. 2017. "The Great Cross-Border Bank Deleveraging: Supply Constraints and Intra-Group Frictions." *Review of Finance* 21 (1): 201–36.

Cerutti, Eugenio, and Christian Schmieder. 2014. "Ring Fencing and Consolidated Banks' Stress Tests." *Journal of Financial Stability* 11: 1–12.

Cerutti, Eugenio, and Haonan Zhou. 2017. "The Global Banking Network in the Aftermath of the Crisis: Is There Evidence of De-globalization?" IMF Working Paper 17/232.

Cerutti, Eugenio, and Haonan Zhou. 2018a. "The Global Banking Network: What Is behind the Increasing Regionalization Trend?" IMF Working Paper 18/46.

Cerutti, Eugenio, and Haonan Zhou. 2018b. "Cross-Border Banking and the Circumvention of Macroprudential and Capital Control Measures." IMF Working Paper 18/217.

Cerutti, Eugenio, and Haonan Zhou. 2018c. "The Chinese Banking System: Much More than a Domestic Giant." VoxEU. Available at https://voxeu.org/article/chinese-banking-system (accessed October 25, 2020).

Cerutti, Eugenio, Giovanni Dell'Ariccia, and Maria Soledad Martínez Pería. 2007. "How Banks Go Abroad: Branches or Subsidiaries?" *Journal of Banking and Finance* 31 (6): 1669–92.

Cerutti, Eugenio, Stijn Claessens, and Luc Laeven. 2017. "The Use and Effectiveness of Macroprudential Policies: New Evidence." *Journal of Financial Stability* 28: 203–24.

Cerutti, Eugenio, Stijn Claessens, and Luc Laeven. 2018a. "The Increasing Faith in Macroprudential Policies." VoxEU. Available at https://voxeu.org/article/increasing-faith-macroprudential-policies (accessed October 25, 2020).

Cerutti, Eugenio, Catherine Koch, and Swapan-Kumar Pradhan. 2018b. "The Growing Footprint of EME Banks in the International Banking System." *BIS Quarterly Review* (December): 27–37.

Cerutti, Eugenio, Catherine Koch, and Swapan-Kumar Pradhan. 2020. "Banking across Borders: Are Chinese Banks Different?" BIS Working Paper No. 892.

Cerutti, Eugenio, Maurice Obstfeld, and Haonan Zhou. 2021. "Covered Interest Parity Deviations: Macrofinancial Determinants." *Journal of International Economics* 130, May: 103447. https://www.sciencedirect.com/science/article/pii/S0022199621000246.

Cetorelli, Nicola, and Linda S. Goldberg. 2011. "Global Banks and International Shock Transmission: Evidence from the Crisis." *IMF Economic Review* 59 (1): 41–76.

Cetorelli, Nicola, and Linda S. Goldberg. 2012a. "Follow the Money: Quantifying Domestic Effects of Foreign Bank Shocks in the Great Recession." *American Economic Review: Papers and Proceedings* 102 (3): 213–18.

Cetorelli, Nicola, and Linda S. Goldberg. 2012b. "Liquidity Management of U.S. Global Banks: Internal Capital Markets in the Great Recession." *Journal of International Economics* 88 (2): 299–311.

Cingano, Federico, and Fadi Hassan. 2020. "International Financial Flows and Misallocation." Working Paper.

Claessens, Stijn, and Neeltje van Horen. 2014. "Foreign Banks: Trends and Impact." *Journal of Money, Credit and Banking* 46 (s1): 295–326.

Claessens, Stijn, and Neeltje Van Horen. 2015. "The Impact of the Global Financial Crisis on Banking Globalization." *IMF Economic Review* 63 (4): 868–918.

Claessens, Stijn, Asli Demirgüç-Kunt, and Harry Huizinga. 2001. "How Does Foreign Entry Affect Domestic Banking Markets?" *Journal of Banking and Finance* 25 (5): 891–911.

Clarke, G., Robert Cull, Maria Soledad Martinez Peria, and Susana M. Sanchez. 2003. "Foreign Bank Entry: Experience, Implications for Developing Economies, and Agenda for Further Research." *The World Bank Research Observer* 18 (1): 25–59.

Clayton, Christopher, and Andreas Schaab. 2020. "Multinational Banks and Financial Stability." Working Paper.

Committee on the Global Financial System. 2020. "US Dollar Funding: An International Perspective." CGFS Papers No. 65.

Correa, Ricardo, Horacio Sapriza, and Andrei Zlate. 2018. "Wholesale Funding Runs, Global Banks' Supply of Liquidity Insurance, and Corporate Investment." Working Paper.

Cull, Robert, and María Soledad Martínez Pería. 2010. "Foreign Bank Participation in Developing Countries: What Do We Know about the Drivers and Consequences of This Phenomenon?" World Bank Policy Research Working Paper No. 5398.

Du, Wenxin, Alexander Tepper, and Adrien Verdelhan. 2018. "Deviations from Covered Interest Rate Parity." *Journal of Finance* 73 (3): 915–57.

Eichengreen, Barry, and Peter Temin. 2000. "The Gold Standard and the Great Depression." *Contemporary European History* 9 (2): 183–207.

Elliott, Matthew, Benjamin Golub, and Matthew O. Jackson. 2014. "Financial Networks and Contagion." *American Economic Review* 104 (10): 3115–53.

Giannetti, Mariassunta, and Luc Laeven. 2012a. "Flight Home, Flight Abroad, and International Credit Cycles." *American Economic Review: Papers and Proceedings* 102 (3): 219–24.

Giannetti, Mariassunta, and Luc Laeven. 2012b. "The Flight Home Effect: Evidence from the Syndicated Loan Market during Financial Crises." *Journal of Financial Economics* 104 (1): 23–43.

Giannetti, Mariassunta, and Steven Ongena. 2009. "Financial Integration and Firm Performance: Evidence from Foreign Bank Entry in Emerging Markets." *Review of Finance* 13: 181–223.

Goldberg, Linda S. 2009. "Understanding Banking Sector Globalization." *IMF Staff Papers* 56 (1): 171–97.

Haas, Ralph De, and Ilko Naaborg. 2006. "Foreign Banks in Transition Countries: To Whom Do They Lend and How Are They Financed?" *Financial Markets, Institutions and Instruments* 15 (4): 159–99.

Haas, Ralph De, and Neeltje Van Horen. 2012. "International Shock Transmission after the Lehman Brothers Collapse: Evidence from Syndicated Lending." *American Economic Review: Papers and Proceedings* 102 (3): 231–7.

Haas, Ralph De, and Neeltje Van Horen. 2013. "Running for the Exit? International Bank Lending during a Financial Crisis." *Review of Financial Studies* 26 (1): 244–85.

Haas, Ralph De, and Iman Van Lelyveld. 2014. "Multinational Banks and the Global Financial Crisis: Weathering the Perfect Storm?" *Journal of Money, Credit and Banking* 46 (S1): 333–64.

Hale, Galina, Tümer Kapan, and Camelia Minoiu. 2020. "Shock Transmission through Cross-Border Bank Lending: Credit and Real Effects." *Review of Financial Studies* 33 (10): 4839–82.

Hardy, Bryan, and Előd Takáts. 2020. "International Banking amidst Covid-19: Resilience and Drivers." *BIS Quarterly Review* (December): 89–99.

Horn, Sebastian, Carmen Reinhart, and Christoph Trebesch. 2020. "China's Overseas Lending." NBER Working Paper No. 26050.

Houston, Joel F., Chen Lin, and Yue Ma. 2012. "Regulatory Arbitrage and International Bank Flows." *Journal of Finance* 67 (5): 1845–95.

Ivashina, Victoria, David S. Scharfstein, and Jeremy C. Stein. 2015. "Dollar Funding and the Lending Behavior of Global Banks." *Quarterly Journal of Economics* 130 (3): 1241–81.

Kalemli-Ozcan, Sebnem, Elias Papaioannou, and Fabrizio Perri. 2013. "Global Banks and Crisis Transmission." *Journal of International Economics* 89 (2): 495–510.

Kaminsky, Graciela, and Carmen Reinhart. 2008. "The Center and the Periphery: The Globalization of Financial Turmoil." In *Money, Crises, and Transition: Essays in Honor of Guillermo Calvo*, 171–216. Cambridge, MA: MIT Pres.

Laeven, Luc, and Fabian Valencia. 2012. "Systemic Banking Crises Database: An Update." IMF Working Paper 12/163.

Maggiori, Matteo, Brent Neiman, and Jesse Schreger. 2019. "The Rise of the Dollar and Fall of the Euro as International Currencies." *American Economic Review: Papers and Proceedings* 109 (3): 521–6.

Martinez, Marina Conesa, Giulia Lotti, and Andrew Powell. 2020. "Covid-19 and the Deglobalization of Banking." IDB Blogs. https://blogs.iadb.org/ideas-matter/en/covid-19-and-the-deglobalization-of-banking/.

McCauley, Robert N., Agustín S. Bénétrix, Patrick M. McGuire, and Goetz von Peter. 2019. "Financial Deglobalisation in Banking?" *Journal of International Money and Finance* 94 (June): 116–31.

Morelli, Juan M., Pablo Ottonello, and Diego J. Perez. 2019. "Global Banks and Systemic Debt Crises." Working Paper.

Morgan, Donald P., and Philip Strahan. 2004. "Foreign Bank Entry and Business Volatility: Evidence from U.S. States and Other Countries." In *Banking Market Structure and Monetary Policy*, ed. Luis Antonio Ahumada, J. Rodrigo Fuentes, Norman Loayza, and Klaus Schmidt-Hebbel, 1st edn, 241–70. Central Bank of Chile.

Morgan, Donald P., Bertrand Rime, and Philip Strahan. 2004. "Bank Integration and State Business Cycles." *Quarterly Journal of Economics* 119 (4): 1555–84.

Müller, Karsten. 2020. "Electoral Cycles in Macroprudential Regulation." Working Paper.

Ongena, Steven, Alexander Popov, and Gregory F. Udell. 2013. "'When the Cat's Away the Mice Will Play': Does Regulation at Home Affect Bank Risk-Taking Abroad?" *Journal of Financial Economics* 108 (3): 727–50.

Peek, Joe, and Eric S. Rosengren. 1997. "The International Transmission of Financial Shocks: The Case of Japan." *American Economic Review* 87 (4): 495–505.

Peek, Joe, and Eric S. Rosengren. 2000. "Collateral Damage: Effects of the Japanese Real Estate Collapse on Credit Availability and Real Activity in the United States." *American Economic Review* 90 (1): 30–45.

Pinchot, Ariel, and Giulia Christianson. 2019. "How Are Banks Doing on Sustainable Finance Commitments? Not Good Enough." World Resources Institute.

Popov, Alexander, and Gregory F. Udell. 2012. "Cross-Border Banking, Credit Access, and the Financial Crisis." *Journal of International Economics* 87 (1): 147–61.

Rajan, Raghuram, and Luigi Zingales. 1998. "Financial Dependence and Growth." *American Economic Review* 88 (3): 559–86.

Reinhardt, Dennis, and Rhiannon Sowerbutts. 2015. "Regulatory Arbitrage in Action: Evidence from Banking Flows and Macroprudential Policy." Bank of England Working Paper No. 546.

Rice, Tara, Goetz von Peter, and Codruta Boar. 2020. "On the Global Retreat of Correspondent Banks." *BIS Quarterly Review* (March): 37–52.

Rijckeghem, Caroline Van, and Beatrice Weder. 2003. "Spillovers through Banking Centers: A Panel Data Analysis of Bank Flows." *Journal of International Money and Finance* 22: 483–509.

Schnabl, Philipp. 2012. "Financial Globalization and the Transmission of Bank Liquidity Shocks: Evidence from an Emerging Market." *Journal of Finance* 67 (3): 897–932.

Shen, Leslie Sheng. 2020. "Global vs. Local Banking: Firm Financing in a Globalized Financial System." Working Paper.

Shin, Hyun Song. 2013. "The Second Phase of Global Liquidity and Its Impact on Emerging Economies." In *Prospects for Asia and the Global Economy*, ed. Reuven Glick and Mark Spiegel, 215–24. Federal Reserve Bank of San Francisco.

Temin, Peter. 1993. "Transmission of the Great Depression." *Journal of Economic Perspectives* 7 (2): 87–102.

Tripathy, Jagdish. 2020. "Cross-Border Effects of Regulatory Spillovers: Evidence from Mexico." *Journal of International Economics*, 103350.

Xu, Chenzi. 2021. "Reshaping Global Trade: The Immediate and Long-Term Effects of Bank Failures." Working Paper.

7. The role of bank ownership types and business models

Giorgio Caselli

7.1 INTRODUCTION

The Global Financial Crisis (GFC) that broke out in 2007 has unveiled the key role played by the financial sector as a source of business cycle fluctuations (see Chapters 1, 2 and 3). In the years prior to the outbreak of the crisis, many banks endeavoured to maximise equity returns by venturing beyond their core business and assuming high-risk strategies. In many cases, this shift in business models (BMs) occurred through a greater reliance on wholesale capital markets for funding and an increased focus on non-interest income as a source of revenue. The impact that banks' strategic choices had on the real economy has been unprecedented and has paved the way for what is now referred to as the 'great crash' (Hodgson, 2009).

While the macroeconomic literature abounds with efforts to study the influence of the financial sector on the propagation of shocks originating elsewhere in the economy, financial shocks – that is, perturbations originating from within the financial sector – have not yet been fully explored. Insofar as the COVID-19 pandemic that has been spreading around the world since the start of 2020 will trigger further research on the effects that shocks external to the financial system might have for financial stability and the real economy, this gap is likely to become even wider. This chapter addresses the issue of whether a diversity of ownership types and BMs in the banking industry has a bearing on the origination of financial shocks.

The academic literature on the extent to which a diversity of players in banking has an influence on financial stability has increased significantly over the past decade, partly as a result of the observation that a number of banking systems in Western Europe – where financial intermediaries with different ownership structures and BMs compete with one another – were less upset by the GFC than those that tend to rely on banks of a similar nature. This is the case for countries such as Germany and Austria, where customer-owned financial cooperatives and not-for-profit savings banks exceed commercial banks in both number and total assets.

The chapter is organised as follows. Section 7.2 describes the key differences across bank ownership types and presents the main approaches that have been proposed by the literature to measure ownership diversity in the banking system. The second part of the section surveys the empirical literature on the link between bank ownership and risk taking, together with the impact that the co-existence of different bank ownership types has on monetary policy transmission. Section 7.3 provides a typology of bank BMs as recently developed by the literature and reviews the empirical evidence on the financial stability implications of different BMs in the banking sector. Specific attention is devoted to assessing the contribution that various BMs make to systemic risk and the origination of financial shocks. Section 7.4 discusses the policy implications of the findings and suggests some avenues for future research.

7.2   BANK OWNERSHIP TYPES AND FINANCIAL SHOCKS

7.2.1   Characterising Bank Ownership Types

In the aftermath of the global financial downturn, there has been renewed interest on the part of researchers and economic commentators in the ownership structure of banks and its implications for financial intermediation (e.g. Shiwakoti et al., 2018). Figure 7.1 shows the number of peer-reviewed journal articles on the topic of bank ownership that have been published since the 1990s, together with the sub-set of these that address bank ownership (and bank BMs) in relation to financial stability issues.[1] The significantly upward trend in the data confirms the growing interest in the ownership structure of banks over time, particularly from 2009 onwards.

The focus of this chapter is on three bank ownership types that have drawn considerable attention from the academic literature in recent times, that is, commercial, cooperative and savings banks. Although important differences exist across countries and over time, it is possible to establish a number of key features that embody the nature of each of these bank ownership types.

Commercial banks are owned by their shareholders, who expect a certain rate of return on the equity capital they have invested in the bank. It follows that profit maximisation tends to represent the primary objective of this type of financial intermediaries. While commercial banks may be

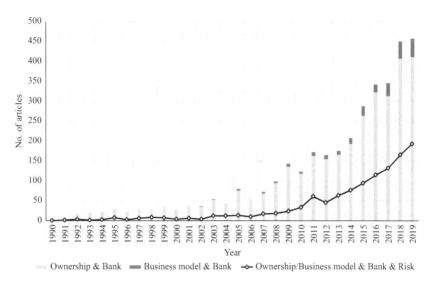

Source: Web of Science (Clarivate Analytics).

Figure 7.1 *Number of articles on bank ownership, business models and risk by year of publication*

regarded as shareholder-oriented institutions, cooperative and savings banks strive to create value for a wider range of stakeholders (Groeneveld and Llewellyn, 2012).

A distinguishing feature of cooperative banks is that they are owned by their members, who are individuals and entrepreneurs whose aim is not the maximisation of their ownership stake in the bank (Ayadi et al., 2010). Although cooperative banks need to generate profit in order to survive and expand, profit maximisation is neither their sole nor their primary bottom-line objective (Llewellyn, 2017). Cooperative banks also differ from their commercial counterparts in that members are entitled to only one vote at general meetings (i.e. 'one member, one vote' principle) and generally they cannot sell their ownership stakes in a secondary market. Furthermore, profit distribution tends to be limited at cooperative banks, since retained profits constitute the almost exclusive source of capital for this type of financial intermediaries as well as an 'intergenerational endowment' that is held for the benefit of present and future members (Ayadi et al., 2010).

Similar to cooperative banks, savings banks are not strictly profit-oriented institutions and pursue a dual financial and social mission (i.e. 'double bottom line') to contribute to the communities within which they operate (Ayadi et al., 2009). At the same time, savings banks differ from their cooperative counterparts as they are not owned by their members but by a private foundation or an organisation that belongs to the government. For this reason, customers of savings banks are likely to have fewer ownership rights compared with customers of cooperative banks (Ferri et al., 2013).

Taking this categorisation of bank ownership types as the point of departure, the next sub-section illustrates the main approaches that have been put forward by the literature to quantify ownership diversity in the banking system.

7.2.2 Quantifying Ownership Diversity in the Banking System

One of the seminal studies to acknowledge the importance of measuring, monitoring and reporting the degree of diversity in banking is Michie (2011, p. 318), who addresses this topic within the context of the UK financial services sector and argues the following:

> The first and most urgent step for Government to take is to develop an effective set of metrics, to measure the degree of diversity – and to then actually undertake this measurement exercise at regular intervals, making the information publicly available.

The introduction of a measure of diversity in financial services was made by Michie and Oughton in 2013, who constructed an indicator – the 'D-Index' – that brings together four sub-indicators across the following dimensions:

- Corporate diversity: the first sub-indicator proposed by Michie and Oughton (2013) is based on the Gini-Simpson Index of biodiversity and captures heterogeneity across corporate types as opposed to biological species. It is computed by examining the number of corporate forms in the banking sector and their respective market shares in terms of either mortgages or retail deposits. To this end, Michie and Oughton (2013) distinguish between three corporate forms, namely private banks limited by shares, mutual building societies and government-owned National Savings and Investments (NS&Is).
- Market competition: this sub-indicator aims to quantify the degree of competition in the banking industry. It is calculated as the inverse of the Herfindahl-Hirschman Index, a widely used measure of market concentration, for the mortgage and retail deposit markets. For comparative purposes, the five-firm concentration ratio, which measures the aggregate market share of the five largest financial institutions in relation to the industry as a whole, is also considered by Michie and Oughton (2013).

- Balance sheet structure and resilience: the third sub-indicator is designed to capture risk on the funding side of financial institutions' balance sheets and corresponds to the funding gap, that is, the difference between loans and deposits expressed as a proportion of total loans. Michie and Oughton (2013) combine the funding gap with a Herfindahl-Hirschman Index of funding model concentration to arrive at an overall index of funding model diversity, which is used to assess the degree of resilience of the banking sector to external shocks.
- Geographic spread: starting from the observation that the geographic concentration of financial services can have significant effects on the performance of an economy, Michie and Oughton (2013) include the geographical dispersion of the financial services sector as a fourth dimension to their D-Index for the UK. This sub-indicator measures the distance, weighted by market share, of each financial institution's head office from the City of London – where most of the UK financial services sector tends to be concentrated.

The four sub-indicators summarised above are combined into a single index and used by the authors to study the evolution of diversity in the UK financial services sector over the period 2000–11. Irrespective of whether the mortgage or retail deposit market is considered, the key finding obtained by Michie and Oughton (2013) is that the D-Index has witnessed a fall since the early 2000s. Although diversity in the UK financial services sector has remained somewhat unchanged during most recent years, there is evidence of a drop in the run-up to the GFC – with diversity touching its lowest point in 2009.[2]

Building on the pioneering work by Michie and Oughton (2013), Caselli et al. (2020) treat bank ownership types as analogous to species in an ecosystem and develop indices of ownership diversity for 17 Western European countries covering the period 1999–2011. The findings by Caselli et al. (2020) are broadly consistent with Michie and Oughton (2013), in that they suggest a considerable decline in ownership diversity in Western European banking systems during the last decade. This decline was particularly marked in the UK, which is found to exhibit a degree of ownership diversity that is almost half the equivalent figure for Switzerland. Conversely, countries such as Germany and Austria appear to show higher levels of ownership diversity on both the loan and deposit sides of financial intermediaries' balance sheets, pointing to substantial heterogeneity across countries with respect to the ownership composition of their banking systems.

The approach that is proposed by Caselli et al. (2020) to derive indices of ownership diversity for the banking sector is described in more detail in Box 7.1.

BOX 7.1   QUANTIFYING OWNERSHIP DIVERSITY IN THE BANKING SYSTEM

The starting point of Caselli et al. (2020) is the observation that banks and other types of financial institutions, like living organisms, interact with one another and with their surrounding environment. These interactions may have important implications for the way they behave and may ultimately affect their probability of survival. For this reason, it is possible to make an analogy between financial and natural ecosystems, implying that some of the concepts that were originally devised in the field of ecology may provide useful insights for finance and banking research.

Among the most widely subscribed tenets in ecology is the view that the functioning of an ecosystem largely depends on the degree of diversity (or heterogeneity) of its species (e.g. Jizhong et al., 1991; Tilman and Downing, 1994). It comes as no surprise that ecologists have suggested a number of measures directed at quantifying the diversity of ecosystems. A common practice is to think of biological diversity, also known as 'alpha diversity' (Whittaker, 1972), as consisting of two components – richness and evenness (Tuomisto, 2012). While richness captures 'the relative wealth of species in a community' (Peet, 1974, p. 288), evenness 'expresses how evenly the individuals in the community are distributed over the different species' (Heip et al., 1998, p. 63).

A definition of diversity that has found widespread support in the literature corresponds to the effective number of types (or 'true diversity'), which considers diversity (D) of species (S) as the inverse of the weighted generalised mean of their proportional abundances (p_i). This definition of diversity was provided for the first time by Hill (1973) and can be written in the following terms:

$$
{}^q_i D = \left({}^q_i \bar{P}_i \right)^{-1} = {}^{q-1}\!\!\sqrt{\sum_{i=1}^{S} p_i p_i^{q-1}}^{\,-1} = \left(\sum_{i=1}^{S} p_i^q \right)^{\frac{1}{(1-q)}}
\tag{7.1}
$$

where the order of diversity is given by q and determines the weight assigned to rare vis-à-vis abundant species. Large values of this parameter (i.e. $q > 1$) increase the sensitivity to abundant species, whereas low values (i.e. $q < 1$) put more weight on rare species. In the case where $q = 0$, all species are taken to be equally abundant and diversity corresponds to species richness (Tuomisto, 2010).

The overwhelming majority of the diversity indicators that are used in the ecological literature represent a set of 'diversity numbers' of different order q (Heip et al., 1998). The first of these indicators is the Simpson Index (Simpson, 1949), which measures the probability that two individuals selected randomly and independently from the community will belong to the same species. Hill (1973) shows that the Simpson Index is a special case of the true diversity index (Equation 7.1) with $q = 2$. The reciprocal of the Simpson Index (D') is generally adopted when the degree of diversity (rather than the degree of concentration) is of concern (Magurran, 2004). This is calculated as follows:

$$D' = \sum_{i=1}^{S} p_i^2 \quad^{-1} \tag{7.2}$$

Some of the most popular diversity indices are those derived from information theory, among which is the Shannon–Wiener Index (Shannon and Weaver, 1949). This index, which was originally developed by Shannon (1948) to quantify the entropy (i.e. information content) in strings of text, measures the average degree of uncertainty in predicting the species of an individual who is chosen at random from a community. Compared with the Simpson Index, the Shannon–Wiener Index has an order $q = 1$ and is sensitive to changes in rare species. To simplify interpretation, this indicator tends to be formulated in terms of the antilogarithm of H' (Peet, 1974) and can be expressed as follows:

$$e^{H'} = \exp\left(-\sum_{i=1}^{S} p_i \ln(p_i)\right) \tag{7.3}$$

Alongside heterogeneity indices such as the Simpson Index and the Shannon–Wiener Index, the ecological literature has put forward several indicators focusing on the evenness component of biological diversity. It is argued that evenness should also be assessed separately, since the effects of species richness and evenness may be confounded if only diversity is reported (Kwak and Peterson, 2007). An evenness indicator that possesses the desirable properties of being independent of species richness and taking lower values in communities with more unequal abundance across species is proposed by Heip (1974). This index is given by:

$$E' = \frac{\left(e^{H'} - 1\right)}{\left(S - 1\right)} \tag{7.4}$$

Drawing on the concepts presented above, Caselli et al. (2020) estimate the shares of loans and deposits held by commercial, cooperative and savings banks in the markets of 17 Western European countries between 1999 and 2011 and construct measures of ownership diversity à la Simpson (1949), Shannon and Weaver (1949) and Heip (1974). These measures are used to study the implications of ownership diversity for the transmission of monetary policy to bank risk. The results of this research are reviewed in the next sub-section.

7.2.3 Ownership Diversity and Financial Stability

Bank ownership and risk taking

The academic literature suggests that the fundamental differences in ownership structure that exist between commercial, cooperative and savings banks – as outlined in Section 7.2.1 above – have a bearing on their behaviour (e.g. Fama and Jensen, 1983; O'Hara, 1981). One of the areas that has attracted considerable attention on the part of researchers relates to the risk-taking incentives of stakeholder-oriented banks, and financial cooperatives in particular, vis-à-vis shareholder-oriented banks. A number of reasons have been put forward by the literature to explain why banks that aim to generate value for a broader array of stakeholders may adopt a different risk profile than banks that are owned by their shareholders.

According to Ayadi et al. (2010), risk-taking incentives are likely to be higher for commercial banks due to the potential conflict of interest between owners (i.e. equity shareholders) and customers (i.e. depositors). While equity shareholders may exert pressure on bank managers to boost the rate of return on their investment via an increase in leverage, depositors tend to prefer a lower risk profile as they receive hardly any upside gain from risk taking and have to bear the downside potential because of the limited scope of deposit insurance. Since they are owned by their customers, who have no direct claim on profits, this agency problem – commonly referred to as the 'asset substitution problem' (Jensen and Meckling, 1976) – is virtually absent at cooperative banks (Groeneveld and Llewellyn, 2012). Combined with the greater barriers to raise external capital, in that retained earnings often represent their only source of capital, these aspects underlying the property right structure of stakeholder-oriented banks are unlikely to lead to risk-taking behaviour (Llewellyn, 2017).

Consistent with these theoretical arguments, evidence is found in the literature for significant differences in the behaviour of shareholder-oriented banks alongside their stakeholder-oriented counterparts. Building a sample of over 950 German banks during the period between 1987 and 2005, Foos (2009) shows that cooperative and savings banks adjust their loan rates over the business cycle to a lesser extent than commercial banks. Support is also found for the impact of GDP growth on loan growth being less pronounced for public sector savings banks, which is interpreted by Foos (2009) as a direct consequence of savings banks' social mission to support their local community.

Similar findings are presented by Bolton et al. (2013), who examine how relationship lending and transaction lending vary over the business cycle using detailed information from the Italian Credit Register before and after the bankruptcy of Lehman Brothers in September 2008. Their empirical analysis reveals that relationship banks – such as many cooperative and savings banks, which tend to reduce informational asymmetries through a dense branch network – are likely to charge higher spreads in normal times and provide more stable lending during periods of financial turmoil compared with transaction banks.

More recently, evidence from a panel of 18 Western European countries offered by Meriläinen (2016) points to important differences in lending growth between shareholder- and stakeholder-oriented banks over the period 2004–13. While both the GFC and the subsequent European sovereign debt crisis triggered a negative shock in lending growth, stakeholder banks acted as shock absorbers by not curtailing their lending supply to the non-financial sector. In addition, the results by Meriläinen (2016) indicate that cooperative and publicly owned savings banks did not contribute to excessive credit growth in the run-up to the two crises.

Alongside the above evidence on the link between bank ownership and lending behaviour, a growing number of empirical studies have endeavoured to cast light on the implications of financial intermediaries' ownership structure for their approach to risk taking. Some of the seminal studies in the area originated from the US, where a strand of research set out to examine differences in the risk profile of stock associations vis-à-vis mutuals. Drawing on data from individual associations' regulatory reports submitted to the Federal Home Loan Bank Board (FHLBB) for the period 1973–76, Verbrugge and Goldstein (1981) find that mutuals have a preference towards less risky loan portfolios (as measured by the ratio of scheduled items to total loans) compared with stock associations. Similarly, O'Hara (1981) shows that stock associations tend to rely more on borrowed funds and to hold higher amounts of Real-Estate-Owned (REO) property than mutual associations.

These early findings are confirmed by Esty (1997), who tests for the hypothesis that risk taking is greater at stock thrifts than at mutual thrifts because the fixed and residual claims are separable. Using data from the FHLBB's thrift financial reports over the period 1982–88, Esty (1997) establishes that stock thrifts exhibit greater profit variability than their mutual counterparts and that conversion from mutual to stock ownership leads to increased investment in risky assets and greater profit variability. Lamm-Tennant and Starks (1993) collect data, accounting for over 95 per cent of the total assets of all US property-liability insurance companies between 1980 and 1987, to test for risk differences between stock and mutual insurers. After controlling for the relative size of the insurer, they present evidence consistent with stock insurers taking on average more risk (as proxied for by the variance of firm loss ratios) than mutual insurers – while having more concentration in the lines of business and geographic areas that bear the greatest level of risk.

The negative effect of stakeholder orientation on bank risk taking finds additional support in a more recent study by Leung et al. (2019), who exploit the staggered enactment of constituency statutes across US states as a unique empirical setting. Based on a Difference-In-Differences

(DID) model estimated with data on 939 publicly traded Bank Holding Companies (BHCs) from 1986 to 2012, their findings suggest that banks with directors whose legal duties are expanded to include stakeholder interests significantly reduce risk via an increase in capital and a shift to safer borrowers.

Further insights into the different appetite for risk between shareholder- and stakeholder-oriented banks are provided for European countries, where commercial banks operate alongside large – in certain cases predominant – cooperative and savings bank sectors (Ferri et al., 2013). Among the first studies to address the link between ownership type and bank risk within the European context is Hesse and Cihák (2007), who build a sample of commercial, cooperative and savings banks from 29 Organisation for Economic Co-operation and Development (OECD) countries during the period 1994–2004. By quantifying the riskiness of banks with the Z-score, which captures the number of standard deviations by which bank returns have to drop before equity is depleted and the bank becomes insolvent (e.g. Boyd et al., 1993; Hannan and Hanweck, 1988), Hesse and Cihák (2007) find that cooperative banks tend to be more stable than commercial banks and (to a lesser extent) savings banks. This finding is shown to stem from the lower volatility of returns for cooperative banks compared with their commercial and savings counterparts, which appears to offset their relatively low profitability and capitalisation.

Similar results are reported by Ayadi et al. (2009, 2010), who calculate Z-scores for banks in some of the major European economies and lend support to the view that cooperative and savings banks have a lower insolvency risk than commercial banks. Evidence also exists for mutuals in 15 Western European countries exhibiting better loan quality and lower asset risk relative to both private and public sector banks, which is interpreted primarily as the consequence of more favourable relationships with their customers (Iannotta et al., 2007). This evidence is corroborated by findings from a handful of single-country studies, including Spain (García-Marco and Robles-Fernández, 2008), Germany (Beck et al., 2009) and the UK (Casu and Gall, 2016).

A more recent contribution by Caselli (2018) compares bank stability across commercial, cooperative and savings banks located in 15 European Union (EU) countries from 1999 to 2013, distinguishing between the periods before and after the outbreak of the GFC. Whereas cooperative banks' stability is shown to have increased in the aftermath of the crisis, the evidence suggests that the Z-score for commercial banks has declined from 2.75 in the years prior to the crisis to 2.65 in the post-crisis period. According to Caselli (2018), this result is due to the fact that the standard deviation of returns has fallen in the period since the onset of the crisis only for cooperative banks, while it has increased somewhat significantly for commercial banks.

Collectively, the findings from the empirical literature on the link between bank ownership and risk taking suggest that diversity of bank ownership types might favour financial stability. The co-existence of a critical mass of financial intermediaries with different ownership structures and risk-taking incentives tends to reduce systemic risk through enhanced competition in the banking industry (Llewellyn, 2012). This point is summarised by Michie (2011, p. 310):

> [Diversity of ownership types] creates a corresponding diversity in forms of corporate governance; risk appetite and management; incentive structures; policies and practices; and behaviours and outcomes. It also offers wider choice for consumers through enhanced competition that derives in part from the juxtaposition of different business models.

One of the factors that lie behind the GFC is the existence of herding behaviour on the part of bank managers, which is likely to have moved asset prices away from fundamentals and added to the build-up of risks in the financial system (Rajan, 2006). Among the consequences of this herding behaviour has been a higher degree of homogeneity in the financial system, with key implications for its ability to withstand periods of financial distress as examined further in Chapter 13. Andy Haldane, Chief Economist at the Bank of England and Chair of the Government's Industrial Strategy Council, describes the effects that homogeneity of behaviour in the banking sector might have on financial stability as follows (Haldane and May, 2011, p. 353):

> [E]xcessive homogeneity within a financial system – all the banks doing the same thing – can minimize risk for each individual bank, but maximize the probability of the entire system collapsing.

In light of the important role that diversity of ownership types in banking might have for the stability of the financial system and the origination of financial shocks, a recent strand of literature has started to explore the extent to which the presence of stakeholder-oriented banks has a bearing on the behaviour of their shareholder-oriented counterparts (Smolders et al., 2012). Early evidence on this topic is presented by Hesse and Cihák (2007), who show that a larger share of cooperative banks (measured in terms of total assets) tends to be associated with greater stability of an average bank in the system. While this finding appears to be driven by the impact that cooperative banks' behaviour exerts on the stability of other non-profit maximising banks, the soundness of weaker commercial banks – that is, commercial banks with a relatively low level of stability to start with – is negatively affected by a larger share of cooperative banks. According to Hesse and Cihák (2007), these results – which have been confirmed by a recent study using balance sheet data for Italian banks from 2001 to 2014 (Barra and Zotti, 2019) – support the view that cooperative banks may take advantage of their lower average cost of capital to pursue expansion plans that leave less space for weaker commercial banks in the retail market.

The question of whether cooperative banks affect the soundness of an average bank in the system is also addressed by Chiaramonte et al. (2015). By constructing a panel of commercial, cooperative and savings banks from 26 OECD countries over the period 2001–10, they conclude that financial cooperatives played a stabilising role in the financial system during the years of the GFC (yet only after reaching a certain market share threshold). A key finding reported by Chiaramonte et al. (2015) is that, in an adverse macroeconomic scenario such as the period in the aftermath of the crisis, a greater presence of cooperative banks has a positive influence on the stability of large commercial banks in the system. Chiaramonte et al. (2015) explain these results by positing that banking instability phenomena are likely to be less acute and to propagate more slowly in banking systems with a critical mass of stakeholder-oriented banks, given that interconnections between cooperative and large commercial banks tend to be weaker than those among large commercial banks.

Similar evidence is put forward by Caselli et al. (2020), who use the ownership diversity measures à la Simpson (1949), Shannon and Weaver (1949) and Heip (1974) as illustrated in Box 7.1 to examine how the ownership composition of the banking system affects the stability of an average bank in the system. The results, based on a sample of approximately 5,700 commercial, cooperative and savings banks from 17 Western European economies between 1999 and 2011, reveal that – *ceteris paribus* – shareholder- and stakeholder-oriented banks competing in loan and deposit markets with greater diversity of ownership types are likely to be more stable than their counterparts from less diverse markets. As Caselli et al. (2020) postulate, these results might be due to the effects that diversity of ownership types has on the nature and degree of competition in the banking industry, for example by encouraging greater disciplining efforts on the part of customers and/or depositors.

Bank ownership and monetary policy transmission
The 'great crash' and the ensuing economic contraction that followed the Lehman bankruptcy have intrigued researchers and other observers for over a decade. Among the factors that might have amplified the severity

of the GFC, as discussed in Chapter 1, considerable attention has been devoted to monetary policy and the effects it might have had on financial intermediaries' incentives (Rajan, 2006).

In the years following the dot-com bubble, central banks in various Western economies tried to counteract the potential for an economic downturn by way of a more accommodative monetary policy. For example, the US saw nominal interest rates falling from 6.26 per cent at the beginning of the 2000s to 3.22 per cent in 2005, while the euro area witnessed a drop in money market rates from 4.12 to 2.09 per cent over the same period. According to a growing line of research (e.g. Borio and Zhu, 2012; Jiménez et al., 2014), the relatively low interest rate environment that prevailed during the mid-2000s increased the procyclicality of the financial system through the impact it had on the loan supply of banks. The outcome was eventually a financial system with higher aggregate credit and riskier bank portfolios (Dell'Ariccia and Marquez, 2006).

Motivated by an initial lack of attention to the moderating role of bank ownership in monetary policy transmission, several studies have set out to establish whether financial intermediaries with different ownership structures react differently to changes in monetary policy. Most of these studies have focused on the 'bank lending channel' of monetary transmission, that is, the mechanism that links monetary policy to banks' loan supply via policy-induced changes in bank deposits as described in Chapter 3 (Bernanke and Blinder, 1988, 1992).

Andries and Billon (2010) offer a seminal contribution within this context and examine the implications of bank ownership as well as deposit insurance for monetary policy transmission. By developing a model of a competitive banking sector with an explicit deposit insurance scheme, they show that the credit supply of state-owned banks responds less to monetary policy impulses compared with private banks. This result, arguably due to the greater ease with which government-owned banks can collect additional deposits relative to private banks, implies that monetary authorities in countries with a higher state participation in banks' capital will have to be more reactive over their policy instruments than monetary authorities elsewhere.

Turning to the empirical literature, Bhaumik et al. (2011) draw on balance sheet data for the Indian banking sector over the period 2001–07 and find support for banks of different ownership types reacting differently to monetary policy initiatives. During periods of monetary tightening, state-owned, old private – that is, banks that have been in operation since before the financial sector reforms that were initiated by the Reserve Bank of India in 1992 – and foreign banks tend to curtail their lending in response to an increase in interest rates. By contrast, there is evidence that only the loan supply of old private banks is affected by higher interest rates when periods of monetary easing are considered.

Support for a statistically and economically significant impact of bank ownership on the bank lending channel is also available for Europe. A ground-breaking contribution in this area is provided by Ferri et al. (2014), who explore whether there are differences between shareholder- and stakeholder-oriented banks with respect to the reaction of their loan supply to changes in monetary policy. Using micro-level data for over 4,300 commercial, cooperative and savings banks operating in 12 eurozone countries between 1999 and 2011, they show that cooperative and savings banks cut back on lending to a lesser extent compared with their shareholder-oriented counterparts following an increase in interest rates. Their results also reveal that, during the years of the GFC, cooperative banks continued to smooth the effects of tighter monetary policy on their loan supply. As Ferri et al. (2014) point out, this evidence suggests that stakeholder banks are likely to adopt less procyclical lending policies than shareholder banks in order to smooth financial conditions for their customers and maintain borrower-lender relationships in the longer term.

Besides the bank lending channel, a few studies have investigated the extent to which bank ownership has a bearing on the transmission of monetary policy to bank risk. In its standard formulation (Borio and Zhu, 2012), the 'risk-taking channel' of monetary transmission originates from the impact that changes in policy rates have on either risk perception or tolerance by banks, for example, by inducing financial intermediaries to search for yield by making riskier assets more attractive than safe bonds (Cociuba et al., 2016).

The first study to explicitly take into account the ownership structure of banks when studying the interest rates-bank risk nexus is put forward by Drakos et al. (2016), who present evidence on the functioning of the risk-taking channel in ten Central and Eastern European (CEE) economies and in the Russian Federation during the period 1997–2011. By constructing an unbalanced panel of commercial, cooperative and savings banks split into domestic and foreign owned, they find that risk taking by foreign banks increased in all countries as long-term interest rates gradually declined during the 2000s. This effect was particularly strong for foreign banks in the ten CEE economies, whose risk decisions responded more aggressively than those of Russian banks and were sensitive even to the decline of short-term interest rates.

Building on the work by Ferri et al. (2014), Caselli and Figueira (2020) address the question of whether the risk-taking behaviours of shareholder- and stakeholder-oriented banks react differently to variations in the monetary environment. The results, based on banks' balance sheet data for 17 Western European countries for a period covering both the GFC and the eurozone sovereign debt crisis, indicate that the effects of lower interest rates on bank risk are dampened by cooperative and savings banks. A closer look at the results before and after the outbreak of the GFC suggests that these results are driven by the years prior to the Lehman bankruptcy, when shareholder-oriented banks are found to adjust the riskiness of their portfolios more actively relative to their stakeholder-oriented counterparts.

Caselli et al. (2020) also test for the hypothesis that the ownership composition of the banking system moderates monetary policy transmission via the risk-taking channel. Using the ownership diversity measures à la Simpson (1949), Shannon and Weaver (1949) and Heip (1974) as presented in Box 7.1, Caselli et al. (2020) show that the impact of exogenous monetary policy shocks on banks' probability of default is reduced in countries with greater ownership diversity. These results, which hold across several econometric specifications and are not affected by the proxy for monetary policy used, emphasise the stabilising influence that ownership diversity might play in modern financial systems.

7.3 BANK BUSINESS MODELS AND FINANCIAL SHOCKS

7.3.1 Identifying Bank Business Models

In parallel with the research on bank ownership types and financial shocks reviewed in the previous section, another strand of literature has studied the implications of bank BMs for bank risk and financial stability (e.g. Ayadi et al., 2019; Köhler, 2015; Mergaerts and Vander Vennet, 2016). A useful starting point for our discussion is Ayadi et al. (2019), who identify a discrete set of BMs that co-exist in the banking sector and track their data over time as part of a Global Monitor of bank BMs.

This analysis was first introduced in 2011 (Ayadi et al., 2011), with the aim of discerning the BMs of 26 major European banking groups before and after the GFC. Since then, a number of further screening exercises were conducted, resulting in a database of bank BMs that now covers financial intermediaries operating in Europe, the US and Canada. For example, the latest Bank Business Models (BBM) Monitor for Europe (Ayadi et al., 2019) provides an up to date assessment of BMs for more than 3,200 banking groups and subsidiaries located in the European Economic Area (EEA) and Switzerland over the period 2005–17.

To identify bank BMs, Ayadi et al. (2019) use cluster analysis and distinguish between the banking activities (i.e. retail versus market or mixed) and the funding strategies (i.e. retail versus market or mixed).[3] Specifically, five main instruments – all expressed as a percentage of assets – are used to form the clusters:

- Loans to banks: this indicator, which quantifies the scale of wholesale and interbank activities, captures exposure to risks originating from the interconnectedness with other banks.
- Customer loans: this is a proxy for the extent to which banks engage in traditional banking activities and is measured by the proportion of loans to non-bank customers.
- Trading assets: these assets include non-cash assets other than loans, with a higher value of this indicator denoting greater engagement in investment activities that are prone to market and liquidity risks.
- Debt liabilities: calculated as the share of non-equity liabilities other than deposits and derivatives to total assets, this indicator seizes banks' reliance on market funding.
- Derivative exposure: this indicator captures the extent to which banks engage in investment and trading activities by measuring the carrying value of all negative derivative exposures.

Based on this method, Ayadi et al. (2019) identify five distinct BMs in the banking sector:

- 'Focused retail': this category includes banks that are retail oriented on both the asset and liability sides of their balance sheets. These banks tend to be active in standard deposit-loan intermediation and to be relatively small in size.
- 'Diversified retail (type 1)': these are banks that are diversified on the asset side and have a relatively large share of retail deposits on the liability side. They have more trading assets and bank loans compared with 'Focused retail' banks.
- 'Diversified retail (type 2)': these banks are diversified on the asset side with high reliance on wholesale funding. On average, banks included in this category make the greatest use of market funding across all sample banks.
- 'Wholesale': this group comprises banks that are by and large wholesale on both the asset and liability sides. These banks, which form the smallest group among the five business models, are active primarily in intermediation between banks and rely heavily on interbank lending and funding.

- 'Investment': banks included in this category are predominantly investment oriented with diversified sources of funding. They are characterised by substantial trading activities and are the largest banks in the sample.

Departing from the above categorisation, Ayadi et al. (2019) explore the contribution of different BMs to systemic risk and financial stability, together with their interaction with banks' ownership structures. Their results are summarised in the next sub-section.

7.3.2 Bank Business Models and Financial Stability

Among their main contributions, Ayadi et al. (2019) assess the risk attributes that are associated with each of the five BMs summarised in the previous sub-section. By considering eight risk indicators, including the Z-score and the share of non-performing loans to total loans, they uncover significant differences in risk across bank BMs. While 'Focused retail' and 'Diversified retail (type 1)' banks appear to show the greatest distance to default, banks with any of the other three BMs have a higher insolvency risk. There is also evidence that the contribution to systemic risk varies across BMs, with 'Diversified retail (type 2)' banks contributing the most to the accumulation of risk in the financial system.[4]

Another issue addressed by Ayadi et al. (2019) is the relationship between the business model of a bank and its ownership structure. Their results suggest that the 'Focused retail' and 'Diversified retail (type 1)' models tend to be skewed towards stakeholder-oriented banks, whereas the 'Wholesale' and 'Investment' models are found primarily among shareholder-oriented banks. The 'Diversified retail (type 2)' group includes nationalised, cooperative and public banks and has the highest share of listed financial institutions in the sample.

Alongside Ayadi et al. (2019), the link between bank BMs and financial stability has been the subject of investigation by several empirical studies. One of the first works in this area is Demirgüç-Kunt and Huizinga (2010), who study the implications of a bank's activity mix and funding strategy for its risk and rate of return. Based on a sample of 1,334 listed banks from 101 countries over the period 1995–2007, their results reveal that banking strategies that rely heavily on non-interest income or wholesale funding tend to be associated with significant levels of risk. Thus, Demirgüç-Kunt and Huizinga (2010) contend that traditional banks – that is, banks that focus primarily on interest income and deposit funding – are generally less risky than banks with greater reliance on fee income and wholesale funding.

Similar evidence is provided by Altunbas et al. (2011) using data for listed banks in 15 EU countries and the US for the pre-crisis and crisis periods. They compute various measures of realised bank risk, namely the likelihood of a bank rescue, systematic risk and the intensity of recourse to central bank liquidity, to examine whether differences between bank BMs explain the materialisation of risk during the years of the crisis. Consistent with Demirgüç-Kunt and Huizinga (2010), Altunbas et al. (2011) find that BMs characterised by greater income diversification and a large deposit base in the run-up to the crisis accounted for lower *ex post* levels of distress. Conversely, lower capitalisation, larger size and aggressive credit growth are all features that tend to translate into higher risk exposure.

In contrast to Demirgüç-Kunt and Huizinga (2010) and Altunbas et al. (2011), who focus their analyses on listed banks, Köhler (2015) compiles a panel of 3,362 listed and unlisted banks operating in 15 EU countries between 2002 and 2011 to assess the impact of BMs on bank stability, where extending the analysis to unlisted banks is important as they account for the majority of banks in the EU and have a more retail-oriented business model. Using the Z-score as the main proxy for bank risk, the results by Köhler (2015) suggest that the effects of diversification in terms of income and funding sources vary depending on the bank type. While cooperative and savings banks are likely to be more stable if they increase their share of non-interest income, investment banks will become riskier. Similarly, diversifying into non-deposit funding is shown to have a positive impact on stability only for investment banks.

One of the limitations of the three studies reviewed above is that they fail to typify bank business models that can be adopted by regulators and other policymakers alike. Alongside earlier research by Ayadi and colleagues (e.g. Ayadi et al., 2011; Ayadi and De Groen, 2014), among the first contributions to address this limitation is the work by Roengpitya et al. (2014). Using a statistical clustering algorithm on data for 222 banks from 34 countries over the period 2005–13, Roengpitya et al. (2014) identify three distinct BMs that co-exist in the banking sector: a retail-funded commercial bank, a wholesale-funded commercial bank and a capital market-oriented bank. Their results point to significant differences in stability and performance across these BMs, with retail-funded commercial banks exhibiting the lowest volatility of earnings. Evidence is also found of a shift by banks towards this more traditional business model in the wake of the GFC.

In an attempt to reduce the influence of the researcher's priors on the results, Farnè and Vouldis (2017) employ a statistical clustering algorithm enhanced by a procedure to detect 'outlier' banks – that is, banks with idiosyncratic BMs – in order to arrive at a categorisation of bank BMs in the euro area. Utilising a cross-sectional dataset for the last quarter of 2014, they classify banks into four different BMs: traditional commercial, complex commercial, wholesale funded and securities holding. Using this classification, they assess risk and performance indicators of each BM and show that they follow different statistical distributions. A key finding is that the two models that depart the most from the standard approach to financial intermediation – namely wholesale funded and securities holding – lie at the upper end of a risk-return space.

An alternative method to identifying bank BMs is followed by Mergaerts and Vander Vennet (2016), who use factor analysis rather than a statistical clustering algorithm to account for the existence of mixed BMs. Drawing on balance sheet and income statement data for 505 banks in 30 European countries between 1998 and 2013, they identify two main BM strategies in banking, labelled as 'retail' and 'diversification'. They find that stronger reliance on retail activities tends to be associated with higher bank stability, while greater diversification does not seem to cause financial distress. In light of this evidence, they call for banking supervisors to account for the heterogeneity of bank BM decisions in applying prudential regulation.

7.4 CONCLUSIONS

This chapter set out to shed light on the implications that a diversity of ownership types and business models in the financial sector has for the origination of financial shocks. A survey of the academic literature available to date shows that differences in ownership types and BMs across banks have a bearing on their risk taking. Evidence is found for banks that strive to create value for a larger set of stakeholders being generally more stable and less prone to engaging in risk behaviour compared with banks that aim primarily at maximising shareholder returns. Stakeholder-oriented banks also appear to be less exposed to fluctuations in monetary policy than shareholder-oriented banks, while support exists for financial intermediaries competing in more ownership diverse industries having a lower insolvency risk than their counterparts from industries where any single type dominates – irrespective of their ownership structure. In addition, the literature review points to BMs that are closest to the standard, retail-oriented approach to financial intermediation as those contributing the least to systemic risk.

Taken together, these results suggest that the co-existence of different ownership types and BMs in the banking sector might reduce the probability of a financial shock occurring, or at least its severity in the event it materialises. Hence, a key policy implication of the findings presented in this chapter is that a more stable and resilient financial system is likely to be one where banks with different ownership types, BMs and corporate objectives are each properly represented. It is ultimately competition across (rather than within) different ownership types and BMs that appears to be conducive to financial stability. The extent to which banking regulators and other policymakers alike are on track to accomplishing this objective could be established using diversity measures such as the ones illustrated in this chapter.

Notwithstanding the growing evidence on the role that bank ownership types and BMs play in the origination of financial shocks, more research remains to be done. A line of enquiry that seems to demand further investigation relates to the interactions between financial intermediaries of a different nature and their implications for financial stability. It has not yet been fully examined how the co-existence of banks with different ownership structures and BMs shapes their risk decisions and, as a result, the aggregate level of risk in the financial system. For instance, future research could include spatial information into the analysis of ownership and BM diversity to study how geographical proximity affects bank risk taking. This work has the potential to generate novel insights into the extent to which the spatial configuration of banks within and between bank types matters for the origination of financial shocks. At the same time, there appears to be scope for additional research into the interplay between the ownership structure of banks and the BM they adopt, leading to a better understanding of how these bank features might reduce both the frequency and magnitude of perturbations originating from within the financial sector. To this end, it might be particularly fruitful if future research extends the work on measuring ownership diversity presented in this chapter so as to include information capturing the degree of BM diversity in the banking system. Greater knowledge about the implications of different bank ownership types and BMs for the origination of financial shocks is bound to become increasingly important in light of climate change, which has the potential to undermine the stability of the financial system by increasing the financial risks faced by banks and other financial institutions. It is the responsibility of future research to study financial shocks within the context of a changing climate and a post-COVID-19 world rather than in isolation.

NOTES

1. Figures include Early Access articles that, despite being peer-reviewed, published and citable, have not yet been assigned a volume or issue number. The results were retrieved from Web of Science (Clarivate Analytics) by searching for the following keywords in

the article's topic: (i) Ownership & Bank: '(ownership AND bank*)'; (ii) Business model & Bank: '("business model" AND bank*)'; (iii) Ownership/Business model & Bank & Risk: '((ownership OR "business model") AND bank* AND ("financial stability" OR "financial shock" OR risk*))'.

2. Further analysis of the UK financial services sector using the D-Index proposed by Michie and Oughton is reported in Casu and Gall (2016).

3. The methodology used by Ayadi and colleagues is described in more detail in Ayadi (2019).

4. The measure of systemic risk used by Ayadi et al. (2019) is an estimate of the amount of capital that a bank would need to raise in order to function properly should a financial crisis occur.

REFERENCES

Altunbas, Y., Manganelli, S., and Marques-Ibanez, D. (2011). Bank risk during the financial crisis: Do business models matter? *ECB Working Paper Series*, 1394.

Andries, N. and Billon, S. (2010). The effect of bank ownership and deposit insurance on monetary policy transmission. *Journal of Banking and Finance*, 34(12): 3050–4.

Ayadi, R. (2019). *Banking business models: Definition, analytical framework and financial stability assessment*. Palgrave Macmillan, Cham, Switzerland.

Ayadi, R. and De Groen, W.P. (2014). *Banking Business Models Monitor 2014 Europe*. Centre for European Policy Studies, Brussels.

Ayadi, R., Arbak, E., and De Groen, W.P. (2011). *Business models in European banking: A pre- and post-crisis screening*. Centre for European Policy Studies, Brussels.

Ayadi, R., Cucinelli, D., and De Groen, W.P. (2019). *Banking Business Models Monitor: Europe*. Centre for European Policy Studies, Brussels.

Ayadi, R., Schmidt, R.H., and Carbó Valverde, S. (2009). *Investigating diversity in the banking sector in Europe: The performance and role of savings banks*. Centre for European Policy Studies, Brussels.

Ayadi, R., Llewellyn, D.T., Schmidt, R.H., Arbak, E., and De Groen, W.P. (2010). *Investigating diversity in the banking sector in Europe: Key developments, performance and role of cooperative banks*. Centre for European Policy Studies, Brussels.

Barra, C. and Zotti, R. (2019). Bank performance, financial stability and market concentration: Evidence from cooperative and non-cooperative banks. *Annals of Public and Cooperative Economics*, 90(1): 103–39.

Beck, T., Hesse, H., Kick, T., and von Westernhagen, N. (2009). Bank ownership and stability: Evidence from Germany. Unpublished manuscript.

Bernanke, B.S. and Blinder, A.S. (1988). Credit, money, and aggregate demand. *American Economic Review*, 78(2): 435–9.

Bernanke, B.S. and Blinder, A.S. (1992). The Federal funds rate and the channels of monetary transmission. *American Economic Review*, 82(4): 901–21.

Bhaumik, S.K., Dang, V., and Kutan, A.M. (2011). Implications of bank ownership for the credit channel of monetary policy transmission: Evidence from India. *Journal of Banking and Finance*, 35(9): 2418–28.

Bolton, P., Freixas, X., Gambacorta, L., and Mistrulli, P.E. (2013). Relationship and transaction lending in a crisis. *BIS Working Papers*, 417.

Borio, C. and Zhu, H. (2012). Capital regulation, risk-taking and monetary policy: A missing link in the transmission mechanism? *Journal of Financial Stability*, 8(4): 236–51.

Boyd, J.H., Graham, S.L., and Hewitt, R.S. (1993). Bank holding company mergers with nonbank financial firms: Effects on the risk of failure. *Journal of Banking and Finance*, 17(1): 43–63.

Caselli, G. (2018). The cooperative banks today in the EU perspective. In Migliorelli, M. (ed.), *New cooperative banking in Europe: Strategies for adapting the business model post crisis*, pp. 201–29. Palgrave Macmillan, Cham, Switzerland.

Caselli, G. and Figueira, C. (2020). Monetary policy, ownership structure and risk taking at financial intermediaries. Unpublished manuscript.

Caselli, G., Figueira, C., and Nellis, J.G. (2020). Ownership structure and the risk-taking channel of monetary policy transmission. *Cambridge Journal of Economics*, 44(6): 1329–64.

Casu, B. and Gall, A. (2016). *Building societies in the financial services industry*. Palgrave Macmillan, London.

Chiaramonte, L., Poli, F., and Oriani, M.E. (2015). Are cooperative banks a lever for promoting bank stability? Evidence from the recent financial crisis in OECD countries. *European Financial Management*, 21(3): 491–523.

Cociuba, S.E., Shukayev, M., and Ueberfeldt, A. (2016). Collateralized borrowing and risk taking at low interest rates. *European Economic Review*, 85: 62–83.

Dell'Ariccia, G. and Marquez, R. (2006). Lending booms and lending standards. *Journal of Finance*, 61(5): 2511–46.

Demirgüç-Kunt, A. and Huizinga, H. (2010). Bank activity and funding strategies: The impact on risk and returns. *Journal of Financial Economics*, 98(3): 626–50.

Drakos, A.A., Kouretas, G.P., and Tsoumas, C. (2016). Ownership, interest rates and bank risk-taking in Central and Eastern European countries. *International Review of Financial Analysis*, 45: 308–19.

Esty, B.C. (1997). Organizational form and risk taking in the savings and loan industry. *Journal of Financial Economics*, 44(1): 25–55.

Fama, E.F. and Jensen, M.C. (1983). Agency problems and residual claims. *Journal of Law and Economics*, 26(2): 327–49.

Farnè, M. and Vouldis, A. (2017). Business models of the banks in the euro area. *ECB Working Paper Series*, 2070.

Ferri, G., Kalmi, P., and Kerola, E. (2013). Governance and performance: Reassessing the pre-crisis situation of European banks. In Goglio, S. and Alexopoulos, Y. (eds), *Financial cooperatives and local development*, pp. 37–54. Routledge, New York.

Ferri, G., Kalmi, P., and Kerola, E. (2014). Does bank ownership affect lending behavior? Evidence from the euro area. *Journal of Banking and Finance*, 48: 194–209.

Foos, D. (2009). Lending conditions, macroeconomic fluctuations, and the impact of bank ownership. Unpublished manuscript.

García-Marco, T. and Robles-Fernández, M.D. (2008). Risk-taking behaviour and ownership in the banking industry: The Spanish evidence. *Journal of Economics and Business*, 60(4): 332–54.

Groeneveld, H. and Llewellyn, D.T. (2012). Corporate governance in cooperative banks. In Mooij, J. and Boonstra, W.W. (eds), *Raiffeisen's footprint: The cooperative way of banking*, pp. 19–35. VU University Press, Amsterdam.

Haldane, A.G. and May, R.M. (2011). Systemic risk in banking ecosystems. *Nature*, 469(7330): 351–5.

Hannan, T.H. and Hanweck, G.A. (1988). Bank insolvency risk and the market for large certificates of deposit. *Journal of Money, Credit, and Banking*, 20(2): 203–11.

Heip, C.H.R. (1974). A new index measuring evenness. *Journal of the Marine Biological Association of the United Kingdom*, 54(3): 555–7.

Heip, C.H.R., Herman, P.M.J., and Soetaert, K. (1998). Indices of diversity and evenness. *Océanis*, 24(4): 61–87.

Hesse, H. and Cihák, M. (2007). Cooperative banks and financial stability. *IMF Working Papers*, 2.

Hill, M.O. (1973). Diversity and evenness: A unifying notation and its consequences. *Ecology*, 54(2): 427–32.

Hodgson, G.M. (2009). The great crash of 2008 and the reform of economics. *Cambridge Journal of Economics*, 33(6): 1205–21.

Iannotta, G., Nocera, G., and Sironi, A. (2007). Ownership structure, risk and performance in the European banking industry. *Journal of Banking and Finance*, 31(7): 2127–49.

Jensen, M.C. and Meckling, W.H. (1976). Theory of the firm: Managerial behavior, agency costs and ownership structure. *Journal of Financial Economics*, 3(4): 305–60.

Jiménez, G., Ongena, S., Peydró, J.-L., and Saurina, J. (2014). Hazardous times for monetary policy: What do twenty-three million bank loans say about the effects of monetary policy on credit risk-taking? *Econometrica*, 82(2): 463–505.

Jizhong, Z., Shijun, M., and Changming, C. (1991). An index of ecosystem diversity. *Ecological Modelling*, 59(3–4): 151–63.

Köhler, M. (2015). Which banks are more risky? The impact of business models on bank stability. *Journal of Financial Stability*, 16: 195–212.

Kwak, T.J. and Peterson, J.T. (2007). Community indices, parameters, and comparisons. In Guy, C.S. and Brown, M.L. (eds), *Analysis and interpretation of freshwater fisheries data*, pp. 677–763. American Fisheries Society, Bethesda, MD.

Lamm-Tennant, J. and Starks, L.T. (1993). Stock versus mutual ownership structures: The risk implications. *Journal of Business*, 66(1): 29–46.

Leung, W.S., Song, W., and Chen, J. (2019). Does bank stakeholder orientation enhance financial stability? *Journal of Corporate Finance*, 56: 38–63.

Llewellyn, D.T. (2012). UK building societies: The strengths of mutuality. In Mooij, J. and Boonstra, W.W. (eds), *Raiffeisen's footprint: The cooperative way of banking*, pp. 231–46. VU University Press, Amsterdam.

Llewellyn, D.T. (2017). Conversion from stakeholder value to shareholder value banks: The case of UK building societies. In Michie, J., Blasi, J.R., and Borzaga, C. (eds), *The Oxford handbook of mutual, co-operative, and co-owned business*, pp. 550–69. Oxford University Press, Oxford.

Magurran, A.E. (2004). *Measuring biological diversity*. Blackwell Publishing, Oxford.

Mergaerts, F. and Vander Vennet, R. (2016). Business models and bank performance: A long-term perspective. *Journal of Financial Stability*, 22: 57–75.

Meriläinen, J.-M. (2016). Lending growth during the financial crisis and the sovereign debt crisis: The role of bank ownership type. *Journal of International Financial Markets, Institutions and Money*, 41: 168–82.

Michie, J. (2011). Promoting corporate diversity in the financial services sector. *Policy Studies*, 32(4): 309–23.

Michie, J. and Oughton, C. (2013). Measuring diversity in financial services markets: A diversity index. *Centre for Financial and Management Studies Discussion Papers*, 113.

O'Hara, M. (1981). Property rights and the financial firm. *Journal of Law and Economics*, 24(2): 317–32.

Peet, R.K. (1974). The measurement of species diversity. *Annual Review of Ecology and Systematics*, 5: 285–307.

Rajan, R.G. (2006). Has finance made the world riskier? *European Financial Management*, 12(4): 499–533.

Roengpitya, R., Tarashev, N., and Tsatsaronis, K. (2014). Bank business models. *BIS Quarterly Review*, December.

Shannon, C.E. (1948). A mathematical theory of communication. *The Bell System Technical Journal*, 27(3): 379–423.

Shannon, C.E. and Weaver, W. (1949). *The mathematical theory of communication*. University of Illinois Press, Urbana, IL.

Shiwakoti, R.K., Iqbal, A., and Funnell, W. (2018). Organizational form, business strategies and the demise of demutualized building societies in the UK. *Journal of Banking and Finance*, 94: 337–50.

Simpson, E.H. (1949). Measurement of diversity. *Nature*, 163(4148): 688.

Smolders, N., Koetsier, I., and de Vries, B. (2012). Performance of European cooperative banks in the recent financial and economic crisis. In Mooij, J. and Boonstra, W.W. (eds), *Raiffeisen's footprint: The cooperative way of banking*, pp. 67–86. VU University Press, Amsterdam.

Tilman, D. and Downing, J.A. (1994). Biodiversity and stability in grasslands. *Nature*, 367(6461): 363–5.

Tuomisto, H. (2010). A consistent terminology for quantifying species diversity? Yes, it does exist. *Oecologia*, 164(4): 853–60.

Tuomisto, H. (2012). An updated consumer's guide to evenness and related indices. *Oikos*, 121(8): 1203–18.

Verbrugge, J.A. and Goldstein, S.J. (1981). Risk return, and managerial objectives: Some evidence from the savings and loan industry. *Journal of Financial Research*, 4(1): 45–58.

Whittaker, R.H. (1972). Evolution and measurement of species diversity. *Taxon*, 21(2–3): 213–51.

8. The role of market valuation in financial crises

Paola Bongini and Emanuele Rossi

8.1 INTRODUCTION

This chapter focuses on market valuation and its role during financial shocks. We adopt a long-term perspective, that is, not confined to the 2008 Global Financial Crisis (GFC) and concentrate on the theoretical and empirical literature on asset mispricing and market bubbles and their links to the financial crisis (Section 8.2).

Subsequently, the chapter takes into consideration the potential contribution of the new accounting rules (i.e., fair value accounting), introduced right before the burst of the 2008 subprime crisis, to the excessive leverage in boom periods and excessive write-downs in busts (Section 8.3).

Section 8.4 focuses on market valuation of banks during and after financial shocks. This topic is critical as banking is central to the orderly functioning and stability of the overall economy. This section also deals with the opacity puzzle of bank equity valuation, which is hotly debated by an emerging strand of finance literature.

The final section concludes with policy implications.

8.2 MARKET EFFICIENCY, ASSET (MIS)PRICING AND FINANCIAL CRISES

One of the pillars of Modern Financial Theory – and probably the most famous one – is the well-known Efficient Market Hypothesis (EMH – Fama, 1965), according to which asset prices reflect all available information and, consequently, they are the correct valuation of an asset. Prices have a rational basis in terms of fundamentals like the optimal forecast of earnings or assessments of the standard deviation of risk factors facing corporations (Shiller, 2014 Nobel lecture). Being rationally determined, only genuine, unforecastable news can lead to price movements and changes. Depending on the scope of the notion of "all available information", it is common to distinguish between a *weak-form EMH* (all information contained in the history of past trading); a *semi-strong-form EMH* (all publicly available information) and *strong-form of EMH* (all relevant information, including inside information). Empirical tests for the presence of weak-form EMH abound (for a review, see Lim and Brooks, 2011); on the contrary, there is a long list of patterns of returns that seem to contradict the semi-strong form EMH: the presence of anomalies, such as the so-called *size effect*[1] or *January and weekend effects*[2] are considered direct or indirect evidence that semi-strong-form EMH does not hold.[3]

As admitted by its main proponent (Fama, 2013, Nobel Prize Lecture), the difficulty was and still is making the hypothesis testable: a joint hypothesis problem arises as long as to test the EMH we need an asset pricing model, that is, a model that specifies the characteristics of rational expected returns in a market equilibrium. If the test rejects the hypothesis that actual returns follow the properties of expected returns as implied by the asset pricing model, we don't know whether the problem resides in the inefficiency of the market or in a bad model of market equilibrium.

Notwithstanding this relevant issue, modern financial theory assumes that markets (at least those of advanced economies) are informationally efficient and bubbles do not exist. In fact, if prices are not predictable and are good signals for the fundamental value of assets, the very notion of asset bubbles is non-existent. Where a bubble can be defined as a deviation of the market price from the asset's fundamental value or an "irrational strong price increase that implies a predictable – and by definition implausible – strong decline" (Fama, 2013, Nobel Prize Lecture).

However, after so many market crashes, with boom periods followed by bust periods, can this be considered the dominant paradigm in finance?

As a matter of fact, the EMH had its opponents since the 1980s and the fundamental questions in the literature have become: (i) why prices deviate so much and for so long from their fundamental value? (ii) why do investors not exploit arbitrage opportunities when they arise?

One of the most serious criticisms of EMH came from Grossman (1976), Grossman and Stiglitz (1980), and Greenwald and Stiglitz (1986): their studies pointed out that because information is costly, information-ally efficient markets are impossible. Prices cannot perfectly reflect all the available information since if they did, those who spent resources to gather information would receive no compensation. Besides, if prices reflect all available information, there are no incentives to collect information; if information collection stops short of the point where full information is gathered, markets are less than fully efficient.

Taking another (sociological) perspective, Zuckerman (2012) argues that if we all believe that EMH holds, it would be irrational for investors to engage in arbitrage; however, if no one is engaged in arbitrage, prices have no anchor in intrinsic, fundamental value. At that point, there should be great arbitrage profits to be made but no one there to exploit them (as investors believe in the EMH)!

In sum, in the last 40 years the fundamental questions in the literature have become: (i) are asset prices unduly volatile and often (or sometimes) detached from their fundamentals? (ii) when arbitrage opportunities arise (Internet or housing bubble), why do investors not exploit them?

As for the first research question, the answer is a new and flourishing stream of literature on bubbles that in fact seem to exist, either as rational or irrational deviations of asset prices from fundamental asset value. As the analysis of this rich literature is beyond the scope of this chapter, we refer the interested reader to Vogel (2010), Scherbina (2013) or to the paper by Brunnermeier et al. (2020). Scherbina (2013) is an overview of recent literature on bubbles, with a specific focus on behavioural models and rational models with frictions that can model the common characteristics of historical bubble episodes while offering insight for how bubbles are ignited and sustained, the reason why they burst and why arbitrage forces are unable to defeat them. Brunnermeier et al. (2020) take an interesting insight linking bubbles to the banking industry. In particular, they show that asset price bubbles are associated with higher systemic risk at bank level and that the relationship is not limited to the turmoil following the burst of the bubble, but it exists already during its emergence. Their results emphasize the importance of bank-level factors in the build-up of financial fragility during bubble episodes and push us to investigate the issue of market valuation of bank equity (see Section 8.4).

As for the second research question – that is, why there is no arbitrage or at least not as much as there should be when prices deviate from their fundamental value – the answer can be found in a statement attributed to Lord J.M. Keynes: "markets can stay irrational longer than you can stay solvent". Short selling is indeed highly limited, even when short-selling constraints are not binding, due to the need for a critical mass and positions held for an extended period to bring prices down (Shleifer and Vishny, 1997; Abreu and Brunnermeier, 2003; Brunnermeier and Nagel, 2004). When investors believe in a particular theory of value, there is little that an arbitrageur can do to profit taking a position against a widely held, though folly, belief. Besides, what is interesting, in our point of view, is in which markets bubbles are generated. In fact, in the subprime crisis (see Chapter 1), bubbles emerged in primary markets (those of Real Estate Mortgage-Backed Securities (REMBS) and markets for Collateral

Debt Obligations (CDO) and associated derivatives) where information costs are high and effective arbitrage is severely constrained (Gilson and Kraakman, 2014). In such markets, prices cannot be good signals for the fundamental value of assets.

In sum, prices can and do deviate from fundamental value, which is commonly defined as the present discounted value of future cash flows, and it is an unobservable variable that can be influenced by accounting rules and depend on the level of transparency/opacity of a firm's activities. For these reasons, the next two sections address the two following issues: (i) are prices influenced by the accounting rules that shape the quantity and quality of information about fundamental value available to investors? (ii) are prices affected by the opacity in the kind of activities performed by a firm/bank?

8.3 FAIR-VALUE ACCOUNTING AND FINANCIAL CRISES

Studying the role and the consequences of how financial markets value assets on instigating and/or hastening financial crises cannot rule out a critical discussion of the accounting rules through which relevant information reaches market participants.

There are two relevant reasons for considering the relationship between accounting standards and financial crises. First, accounting data released in firms' financial reports provide the raw information set that market participants use in shaping their expectations on firms' fundamentals that are discounted into equity market prices. If this information is somehow distorted or ambiguous at the origin, market prices turn out to be less reliable as signals to guide market participants' choices. For instance, given the complexity of establishing the fair value of illiquid assets, it could be debatable whether, during a financial crisis, fair-value accounting of those illiquid assets deteriorates the interpretation, by market participants, of the underlying firms' financial conditions behind the accounting data. In theory, the market could react differently according to the set of accounting rules in force. Second, some scholars and practitioners claim that fair-value accounting intensified the severity of the GFC. Indeed, fair-value accounting (FVA) and its application across business cycles have been subject to considerable dispute – see, for example, ECB (2004), Banque de France (2008), IMF (2008), and Panetta et al. (2009). The main concerns are that FVA contributes to excessive leverage in boom periods and leads to excessive write-downs in downturns (Allen and Carletti, 2008).

Box 8.1 briefly recalls the differences across alternative accounting rules and their likely impact on asset values, while the rest of the section focuses on the potential contribution of the new accounting rules (i.e., FVA) introduced in the mid-2000s to the development of the GFC. It is important to underline that FVA is not equivalent to a strict (or pure) mark to market accounting, and this is particularly true for banks' key assets as the practical application of FVA allows banks to deviate from market prices under certain circumstances. Besides, not all fair-value changes enter the computation of banks' regulatory capital. These provisions should act as

---

BOX 8.1   FAIR-VALUE ACCOUNTING: HOW FAIR VALUE IS APPLIED IN PRACTICE

Financial statements provide standardized information to various parties that use it for investment and credit decisions, to monitor the value of their claims, for private contracting, and for regulatory purposes. Therefore, it is critical that accounting data are relevant and reliable.[4] However, relevance and reliability can be in conflict; thereby accounting standards setters often face trade-offs.

IFRS and US GAAPs (in particular FAS 157) outline a hierarchy of inputs to derive the fair value of an asset or liability. Level 1 inputs are quoted prices in active markets for identical assets. If such prices are available from orderly transactions, they must be used to determine fair value, which means that the asset is "marked to market". If Level 1 inputs are not available, models are used to determine fair value, known as "marking to model". Fair-value accounting standards require that these models use observable inputs which include quoted prices for similar assets or other relevant market data. Level 3 inputs are unobservable inputs, typically model assumptions, and can be used if observable inputs are not available.

The alternative to fair-value accounting is "historical-cost accounting". In this case, assets are booked at historical cost, which generally equals the fair value when the assets are originally acquired. Subsequently, historical costs are adjusted for amortization and impairments, but not for increases in asset values. When asset values decline, and impairment is unrestricted, fair-value accounting and historical-cost accounting are conceptually the same.

If Level 1 inputs – prices from active markets for the same asset – are available, fair-value accounting provides little room for manipulation and generally provides reliable information. When Level 2 inputs are used, fair-value accounting offers some discretion to management. With Level 3 inputs, management has considerable discretion. On the contrary, historical-cost accounting offers little room for discretion if original purchase prices or amortized costs are used; however, this accounting standard is often criticized for not delivering relevant or timely information. Moreover, because historical-cost accounting does not recognize gains unless the asset is sold, it may provide incentives to firms to selectively sell (and repurchase) assets that trade in liquid markets and have appreciated in value.

safeguards, making downward spirals and contagion less likely to occur compared to a regime of pure mark to market accounting.

The literature on accounting standards and their linkages to financial shocks and crises presents mixed voices (Landsman, 2007; Penman, 2007; Allen and Carletti, 2008; Benston, 2008; Plantin et al., 2008; Ryan, 2008; Laux and Leuz, 2009, 2010; Huizinga and Laeven, 2012).

On one side we find those studies whose major concern is that FVA is procyclical in nature as it can exacerbate swings of market prices and may even cause a downward spiral in financial markets. This can occur both during boom-and-bust periods for two main reasons. First, FVA and asset write-ups allow banks to increase leverage during booms, which in turn makes the financial system more vulnerable and subsequent financial crises more severe (Persaud, 2008; Platin et al., 2008). Second, FVA can provoke contagion in financial markets (Allen and Carletti, 2008; Wallison, 2008; Whalen, 2008). The most likely mechanism through which FVA could contribute to a financial crisis involves the link between accounting and bank capital regulation.[5] During a financial shock, market prices can deviate rapidly from their fundamental value since markets become less informationally efficient because the typical "flight-to-quality" towards safe (low risk) assets creates a sudden lack of demand for risky assets. Thus, risky assets trade at a heavy discount with respect to their fundamental value. If FVA leads a bank to recognize losses, to write-down the value of these assets and, as result, bank capital is reduced, then the bank can be forced to sell the assets at fire-sale prices, setting off a downward spiral. In addition, if fire-sale prices from a distressed bank become a relevant yardstick for other banks, mark-to-market accounting can cause write-downs and regulatory capital adequacy problems for otherwise sound banks (Allen and Carletti, 2008). This channel of contagion also implies a worrying vicious loop from an EMH perspective. Since fundamental value is mainly shaped on the accounting information publicly available to investors, an evident issue arises if mark-to-market accounting information is based on distorted prices. Under these circumstances, the fundamental value could rapidly become more uncertain and elusive, and it can no longer provide the non-observable anchor through which market participants' expectations are discounted in the (observable) market prices. Thus, the unavailability of a reliable fundamental value may hasten the downward spiral during a liquidity crisis or in the presence of limits to arbitrage as discussed in Shleifer and Vishny (1997).

On the other side, opposite voices substantially defend the role of FVA even during crises (Veron, 2008; Laux and Leuz, 2009, 2010). According to these studies, there is not enough evidence to conclude that FVA contributed to banks' problems in the GFC in a critical way. Fair values played only a limited role in impacting banks' income statements and regulatory capital ratios, except for a few banks with large trading positions. For these banks, investors would have taken notice of exposures to subprime mortgages and made their own judgements even in the absence of fair-value disclosures. Second, prevailing FVA rules present various safeguards and offer substantial discretion to banks, which allows them to avoid marking to distorted market prices; besides there is enough evidence that banks used this flexibility during the GFC. Moreover, a critical aspect put forward by the advocates of FVA is the well-known trade-off between relevance and reliability of accounting information. Despite the fact that FVA could lose many of its desirable properties when prices from active markets are no longer available or become inefficient and hence models (rather than actual prices) are to be used,[6] relaxing accounting rules or giving management more flexibility to avoid potential problems of FVA in times of crisis creates the opportunity for manipulation and can decrease the reliability of accounting information at a critical time.[7] In an asymmetric information setting, if investors believe that banks may use more accounting discretion to overstate the value of their assets substantially, the resulting lack of transparency on banks' solvency could result in a bigger problem, during crises times, than the potential contagion effects from a stricter implementation of FVA. Finally, some sponsors of FVA argue that even if stricter FVA were to contribute to contagion and downward spirals, these negative effects in times of crisis must be weighed against the positive effects of a timely loss recognition (Laux and Leuz, 2010). More timely recognition of losses on non-performing loans and a faster application of write-downs as losses occur should incentivize banks to take prompt corrective actions and limit imprudent lending in the first place, which ultimately reduces the severity of a crisis. According to this line of reasoning, if policy makers' goal is to dampen procyclicality, it may be more appropriate to loosen regulatory bank capital constraints in a crisis than modifying accounting standards in force, as the latter venue could hurt transparency and market discipline.

8.4   MARKET VALUATION OF BANK EQUITY

We now focus on market valuation of bank equity for three main reasons. First, the banking industry is central in the smooth functioning and stability of the overall economy due to its role in the financial intermediation process in sustaining the real sector. Second, the market capitalization of large banks explains a large portion of stock market indexes and, thus, can have a key role in the transmission of contagion to other industries during financial shocks. Third, the opacity of bank assets provides additional uncertainty to investors about the inherent risks of banks (Campbell and Kracaw, 1980; Berlin and Loeys, 1988; Diamond, 1989, 1999). Under these conditions, bank stocks become hard-to-value assets. This results in greater exposure to contagion and higher systemic risk, impeding the efficient transmission of information to stock prices. The implications of this last issue are somehow less familiar and warrant a deeper discussion.

8.4.1   Bank Opacity, Stock Price Efficiency, and Financial Shocks

A major concern discussed by scholars is bank opacity: are bank assets more opaque than those of similar-sized non-banking firms? As the theory of efficient markets posits that asset prices reflect all publicly available information (Fama, 1991; Fama and French, 1992), what happens if information about the risks associated to bank assets is relatively opaque?

In the last 20 years a new strand of finance literature has aimed at shedding new light on whether the relative opacity in the intermediation process creates additional obstacles to the valuation of banks' intrinsic risks, particularly during periods of financial distress.

Jin and Myers (2006) and Veldkamp (2006) are among the first studies to provide a general framework that attain a compelling definition of firm opacity from the perspective of financial market investors. Specifically, Jin and Myers (2006) define firm opacity or opaqueness as a "reduced firm information set" available to outside investors, in particular firm-specific information, and claim that opacity shapes information asymmetry between firm insiders and outside equity holders. Outside investors, in the presence of limited firm-specific information, replace unknown firm-specific information with its expected value, conditioned on the information available to them. Thus, the authors claim that the stock returns of opaque firms are less likely to reflect firm-specific information and more likely to reflect market and industry-wide information. Veldkamp (2006) concurs on the impact of firm opacity on the information content of stock returns. Investors rely mainly on common information signals in the presence of incomplete firm-specific information. The author notices that information is associated with a high fixed cost of production and a low marginal cost of replication. As a result, it will be economically feasible to produce only the information that allows to price multiple assets as such information can be sold to many different investors. Conversely, firm-specific information that is only valuable for pricing the stock of one firm is less likely to be produced due to the high fixed costs and smaller base of potential customers for such information. Thus, investors are more likely to use common information than firm-specific information to value opaque firms, resulting in the returns of such firms reflecting more market and, eventually, industry information and less firm-specific information.

Howe and Haggard (2012) show empirically that banks have less firm-specific information than industrial matching firms following the seminal framework by Jin and Myers (2006). Such opacity exposes banks and the financial system to contagion, in which even healthy banks are harmed because opacity prevents outsiders from being able to distinguish sound from unsound banks. To support their conclusion, they use coefficients of determination from asset pricing model regressions (as a measure of stock co-movements) and find a higher price synchronicity among bank stocks. They conclude that bank stocks returns contain less firm-specific information than matching industrial firm returns.

These findings have been extended and supported by other studies (Huizinga and Laeven, 2012; Jones et al., 2012, 2013; Blau et al., 2017). Using price delay referred to a broad sample of banks and non-bank stocks as a proxy for informational (in)efficiency, Blau et al. (2017) identify stocks that have difficulty incorporating market-wide information into their share prices. If bank opacity creates informational uncertainty, then bank stocks are likely to have greater difficulty incorporating (or interpreting) market-wide information. Consistent with their hypothesis, the authors show that price delay is markedly higher for bank stocks than for non-bank stocks. After controlling for other factors that may influence the level of price delay, listed banks experience price delay that is between 5.6 and 8.2 per cent higher than matched non-banks. The differences are not only statistically significant but are also economically meaningful, indicating that stock prices of banks are indeed less efficient than those of non-banks. Besides, banks that are most opaque – using either microstructure proxies for informational opacity or opaque asset composition – have significantly higher delay than other banks. Furthermore, these results are stronger during the GFC period but persist during other periods. The authors conclude that bank opacity results in greater exposure to contagion and higher systemic risk, hindering the efficient transmission of information to stock prices.

Jones et al. (2013) specifically address the systemic risk consequences of bank opacity. In the absence of a deposit insurance, the opaque nature of banks' assets makes these institutions vulnerable to depositors' runs because depositors cannot easily distinguish healthy from unhealthy banks (Diamond and Dybvig, 1983). Credible deposit insurance deters depositor bank runs and yet incentivizes banks' moral hazard (Grossman, 1992; Wheelock and Kumbhakar, 1995), which regulation and supervision aim to mitigate. For this reason, opaqueness is an important reason for regulating banks as discussed in Flannery (1998). The relevant contribution of Jones et al. (2013) is that even in the presence of a credible deposit insurance, bank opacity still matters because it makes it difficult for even the most sophisticated investor to accurately assess fundamental value and weakens the effectiveness of market discipline on banks. The authors also discuss the implications of their framework on the expected returns of opaque assets. Because of their higher risks, opaque assets should yield higher returns than non-opaque (transparent) assets and investors should apply a higher valuation discount to opaque assets. But when the discount is insufficient to offset the higher marginal risk, banks are rewarded for their investments in opaque assets with higher share prices, which can create a feedback effect that encourages banks to increase their investments in opaque assets. The resulting overinvestment is a consequence of a market that underestimates the true risks of opaque investments. Prior literature also shows that opacity, which limits investors' ability to discriminate across firms, creates price synchronicity or co-movement (Morck et al., 2000). Markets use idiosyncratic, firm-specific information on a firm to update the valuation of other opaque but seemingly similar firms. The absence of reliable firm-specific information (as depicted by Jin and Myers, 2006; Veldkamp, 2006; Howe and Haggard, 2012) fosters price contagion that contributes to financial instability. Financial crises resulting from indiscriminate declines in equity values exacerbate cycles of speculative bubbles and subsequent crashes.

In contrast to this stream of literature, Flannery et al. (2004), using stock market microstructure features such as bid-ask spread, trading activity, and return volatility, provide evidence that bank stocks are no more opaque than those of non-financial firms trading in the same market (either NASDAQ or NYSE/AMEX). Additionally, the authors show that, on average, I/B/E/S research equity analysts predict bank earnings rather accurately, with forecast errors statistically similar to those for non-bank firms. However, when the study was updated in 2013, to consider the GFC, the authors found that during crisis times the opacity of banks increases indeed, consistently with the presumption that a fall in a bank's asset value will increase the opacity of its equity.

The next section analyses the effect of the GFC on the market valuation of bank assets.

8.4.2   The Effect of the Great Financial Crisis on Market Valuation of Banks

Beyond the empirical literature on bank opacity and its consequences on the formation of market prices, a new strand of literature has emerged since the GFC, focusing on potential discontinuities in banks' market valuation around major financial shocks.

The hypothesis under test is that the GFC was a watershed in the market valuation of bank equity. Indeed, market to book value of US and European banks have dropped dramatically since the GFC and in some cases never reached the pre-crisis levels, due to higher credit losses, poor profitability in a low interest rate environment coupled with increased capital requirements. If banks trade below their tangible book value, is the market valuing bank characteristics (assets, liabilities, business models, etc.) different than before the crisis, leading to a detachment from account-ing (book) values, which in fact have greater coherence to fundamental value while the market is myopic?

The answer is negative: the market is not myopic and is indeed cor-rectly discounting investors' true expectations of how much shareholder value the bank will be able to create from a given stock of assets and liabilities.

Bogdanova et al. (2018) provide evidence that there was no major break in the factors driving bank valuations after the GFC. Indeed, even though post-crisis price-to-book ratios (PBRs) were compressed relative to their pre-crisis levels, they were not generally out of line with estimates based on the full pre- and post-crisis sample: neither for the aggregate, nor at the country level. As a matter of fact, the authors demonstrate that bank analysts did not change their pre-crisis methods of valuation after the GFC. Hence, one should be careful not to overemphasize the effect of the crisis and of crisis-related policies for how banks are valued in the post-crisis environment.

In a similar vein, Bertsatos et al. (2017), examining the stock market valuation of large and systemic US banks, prove that the financial crisis has not altered investors' attitudes towards bank characteristics. In par-ticular, before, during, and after the crisis, investors in large and systemic US banks seemed to penalize leverage, albeit temporarily. Both before and after the crisis, they rewarded size in the short run. In addition, they find evidence that stress testing has been informative to the market and that those banks that failed at the post-crisis stress tests were not subsequently valued differently by the market.

With a different view, Huizinga and Laeven (2012) reach similar conclusions. The authors, in fact, provide a comprehensive picture of accounting discretion by banks during the financial crisis and that banks' balance sheets offered a distorted view of the financial health of the banks. According to the authors, the discrepancy between market and book values suggests that banks have been slow to adjust book values to reflect market expectations about future asset losses. The slowness of book values to reflect changes in market expectations does not merely reveal the rigidity of financial reporting rules, but in part shows the active use by banks of accounting discretion to prevent book value deterioration. Specifically, banks with large mortage-backed security (MBS) exposures systematically reported lower loan loss provisioning rates in 2008 to inflate asset values and book capital. At the same time, banks with large real estate exposures tended to classify more of their MBS as held-to-maturity, to be able to carry these assets at higher amortized cost. Therefore, it was not the market that exaggeratedly discounted banks' asset values but the problem was a distorted use of accounting discretion by banks in order not to recognize looming losses.

Notwithstanding the importance of the delayed recognition of losses on banks' financial instruments, Calomiris and Nissim (2014) claim that much of the persisting decline in banks' PBRs can be explained by a change in the fundamentals, specifically in the value of intangible assets and liabilities, which in turn may be affected by market developments and the competitive environment. For example, if interest rates are low for an extended period, having a stable base of core deposits may be less valuable to banks, to the extent that they are unable to reprice deposit rates in line with rates earned on the asset side of their balance sheets (Bank for International Settlements, 2016). Similarly, loan relationships may lose value if the economic environment implies a lower ability for banks to benefit from the cross-selling of services (Bogdanova et al., 2018).

On balance, this strand of literature tends to confirm that in the aftermath of the GFC the market valuation of bank equity has been hugely affected by the changed economic environment rather than by a myopic view of the market itself. The open question is still how investors can assess banks' equity if they happen to use distorted or inefficient market prices. This topic is addressed in the next section.

8.4.3   Bank Valuation in Practice: Use and Misuse of Multiples

Another debated topic concerns how market participants value bank equity when relying on potentially distorted market information. This is a non-trivial issue since the methods employed by practitioners in assessing the fundamental value of banks can influence the efficient transmission of information into stock prices.

Among these valuation methods, stock market multiples is considered the core valuation approach that makes an extensive use of market prices in order to reach an informed and balanced opinion on the fundamental value of a stock. Analysts' recommendations based on this approach are found everywhere in business and equity research reports.[8]

A vast body of empirical studies in finance and accounting have largely evaluated the efficiency of stock market multiples as a tool for equity valuation of non-financial firms (e.g. Alford, 1992; Cheng and McNamara, 2000; Bhojraj and Lee, 2002; Lie and Lie, 2002; Liu et al., 2002; Bhojraj et al., 2003; An et al., 2010). Fewer investigations and evidence are available on financial firms (Nissim, 2013; Forte et al., 2020).

In particular, Nissim (2013) deals with the accuracy of relative valuation methods in the insurance industry, while Forte et al. (2020) discuss multiples' ability to evaluate bank market prices. Nissim assesses the accuracy of multiples in the US insurance industry across ten years up to 2011, finding that book value multiples perform relatively well in valuing insurance companies and are not dominated by earnings multiples, a result that passes the test of the GFC.

Forte et al. (2020) analyse a sample of around 1,700 listed banks in the US and in the Eurozone and find that the potential stock mispricing arising from higher banks' opaqueness during financial shocks brings two consequences for bank multiples. On one hand, it blurs the valuation of banks through multiples, as observed depressed market prices are not a reliable measure of the equity value. In this case, the "valuation or pricing error" – that is, the distance between the equity value estimated through a banking multiple approach and the observed market price – defined by the standard empirical literature on multiples' accuracy (Liu et al., 2002; Nissim, 2013) is biased, as the market price is not fully efficient. Second, the ability (or accuracy) of bank multiples to assess current market prices declines markedly during financial crises (Figures 8.1 and 8.2). In Figure 8.1, which considers large US commercial banks, the performances of a set of different forward-looking and historical bank multiple metrics are displayed.

The patterns of forward and historical P/Es, P/revenue, P/BV, and P/customer deposits are correlated. Multiples' valuation (particularly using the forward P/E multiples) is severely affected at the start of the GFC, but a recovery is visible later on. Multiple valuation accuracy also worsened rapidly during the collapse of the dot-com bubble at the start of the 2000s owing to weak links between prices and fundamentals. Similar findings can be observed in the sample of US small commercial banks shown in Figure 8.2.

The burst of the dot-com bubble impairs the accuracy of multiples, as happened for the sample of large retail banks. During the GFC, the accuracy performance of forward and trailing P/E recovered more slowly for smaller banks than for large banks. Moreover, the accuracy decline is stronger in the case of small banks, which are clearly the banks' size class less visible to investors and with higher information asymmetries even in normal times.

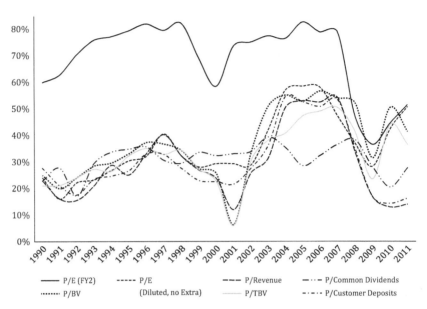

Note: The Y-axis represents the percentage of banks valued within 25 per cent of their actual price. Valuation errors are computed as the difference between the fundamental price and the actual price of the stock at the end of April, divided by the actual price. The fundamental price is estimated with an out-of-sample approach, calculating for each multiple a peer-group measure and multiplying it by each relevant value driver.

Source: Forte et al. (2020).

Figure 8.1   *Bank multiples' accuracy performance across financial crises: large US commercial banks*

Forte et al. (2020) conclude that bank multiples rapidly lose predictive accuracy throughout phases of uncertainty triggered by financial crises. These results are consistent with the main findings in the literature on bank opacity (see Section 8.4.1), which show that during financial crises increased bank opacity turns bank equity into a hard-to-value asset. These circumstances, in turn, may generate further uncertainty on the fundamental value of banks inducing market participants to portfolio choices that prefer less hard-to-value stocks and industries, according to a "flight-to-quality" behaviour in which investors with lower risk tolerance look for more visible (or less opaque) and less risky assets. For these reasons, we can expect that financial crises have a noteworthy impact on multiples' ability to assess banks' fundamental value.

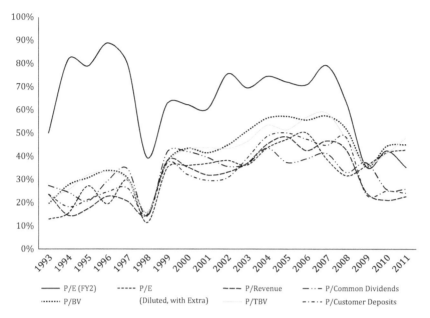

Figure 8.2 *Bank multiples' accuracy performance across financial crises: small US commercial banks*

8.5 CONCLUSIONS

This chapter dealt with the issue of market valuation during financial crises. According to the dominant paradigm in finance (i.e. EMH), market prices are the best estimate of a firm's fundamental value and they move as long as new, unpredictable information is revealed. However, recent theoretical and empirical literature in finance highlights that market prices can be influenced by the accounting rules in force and by the level of transparency/opacity of the firms' activities.

Such problems are more acute in the case of bank equity valuation for two main reasons:

1. fair-value accounting applied to banks' assets leaves significant margins of discretion to managers in valuing Level 3 assets (the most opaque ones) and this can have a distorting effect on market prices;
2. by definition, banks invest in opaque projects and by doing so they perform a valuable economic and societal function. However, market discipline is sometimes insufficient to restrain banks' risk-taking because markets do not always correctly price the risks imbedded in opaque assets.

Bank opacity also adversely affects the efficient transmission of information to stock prices. As a matter of fact, stock price inefficiency due to opacity is higher for banks (Blau et al., 2017); bank opacity increases prices co-movements and weakens market discipline on banks' investment (Jones et al., 2013; Blau et al., 2017); bank opacity is a relevant factor of higher (and concentrated) systemic risk and reduced firm-specific (idiosyncratic) risk even in the presence of a credible deposit insurance (Howe and Haggard, 2012; Jones et al., 2013); bank opacity increases and becomes more acute during financial shocks or crises (Flannery et al., 2013); finally, during financial shocks investors face substantial information risk that has also to do with the investors' inability to estimate bank fundamental value (Nissim, 2013; Forte et al., 2020).

These findings have important policy and regulatory implications. While a well-functioning banking sector is vital to improvements in several economic outcomes, research findings on the opacity created by the intermediation process may potentially guide regulators on how to create an environment where the risks associated with intermediation can be made more transparent, recognizable, and measurable to outsiders. Regulation aimed specifically at disclosing more information on financial institutions' opaque assets or, in the extreme case, limiting investments in opaque assets altogether will be necessary in order to address concerns of systemic risk.

NOTES

1. Banz (1981) was the first to document that presence of a consistent premium for portfolios investing in smaller-sized firms.
2. Reinganum (1983) showed that abnormal returns earned by small firms occur primarily in the month of January and over weekends.
3. Less empirically studied is the strong-form EMH as it is the most difficult hypothesis to test requiring the use of non-public information.
4. Relevance requires that accounting information is capable of affecting decisions made by its users. This relates to timeliness, comparability, and understandability. Reliability refers to undistorted complete information that is free from errors. Verifiability and credibility are the key features of reliability.

5. A second channel of contagion could be behavioural driven. When managers are focused on short-term accounting performances such as earnings due to bonuses, stock options plans and private benefits reasons, they could be inclined to sell relatively illiquid assets at prices below their fundamental value in order to pre-empt the anticipated behaviour on the sell-side of other firms (Plantin et al., 2008). Through this policy, managers avoid having to mark the asset to an even lower market price that could worsen the impact on future short-term earnings but, in turn, create contagion effects for other banks.
6. This, in turn, makes it more difficult to determine and verify fair values.
7. On this subject a new document regarding the application of IFRS 9 *Financial Instruments* during the period of enhanced economic uncertainty arising from the COVID-19 pandemic has been released in March 2020. The document highlights requirements within the Standard that are relevant considering how the pandemic could affect accounting for expected credit losses (ECL). It does not change, remove, or add to the requirements in IFRS 9 *Financial Instruments*. It is intended to support the consistent and robust application of IFRS 9. IFRS 9 was developed in response to requests by the G20 and others to provide more forward-looking information about loan losses than the predecessor Standard and to give transparent and timely information about changes in credit risk. The document acknowledges that estimating ECL on financial instruments is challenging in the current circumstances and highlights the importance of companies using all reasonable and supportable information available – historic, current, and forward-looking to the extent possible – when determining whether lifetime losses should be recognized on loans and in measuring ECL. The document reinforces that IFRS 9 does not provide bright lines nor a mechanistic approach in accounting for ECLs. Accordingly, firms may need to adjust their approaches to forecasting and determining when lifetime losses should be recognized to reflect the current environment.
8. Asquith et al. (2005), analysing a sample of 1,126 sell-side analyst reports diffused from 1997 to 1999, showed that a very huge percentage (99.1 per cent) of equity analysts declared in their reports that they employed multiple metrics.

REFERENCES

Abreu, D., and Brunnermeier, M.K. (2003). Bubbles and crashes. *Econometrica*, 71, 173–204.

Alford, A. (1992). The effect of the set of comparable firms on the accuracy of the price-earnings valuation method. *Journal of Accounting Research*, 30(1), 94–108.

Allen, F., and Carletti E. (2008). Mark-to-market accounting and liquidity pricing. *Journal of Accounting and Economics*, 45(2–3), 358–78.

An, J., Bhojraj, S., and Ng, D. (2010). Warranted multiples and stock returns. *Journal of Accounting, Auditing and Finance*, 25, 143–70.

Asquith, P., Mikhail, M., and Au, A. (2005). Information content of equity analyst reports. *Journal of Financial Economics*, 75, 245–82.

Bank for International Settlements (2016). 86th Annual Report, Chapter VI, June.

Banque de France (2008). Valuation and financial stability. *Financial Stability Review*, no. 12 October.

Banz, R.W. (1981). The relationship between return and market value of common stocks. *Journal of Financial Economics*, 9(1), 3–18.

Benston, G.J. (2008). The shortcomings of fair-value accounting described in SFAS 157. *Journal of Accounting and Public Policy*, 27(2), 101–14.

Berlin, M., and Loeys, J. (1988). Bond covenants and delegated monitoring. *Journal of Finance*, 43, 397–412.

Bertsatos, G., Sakellaris, P., and Tsionas, M. (2017). Did the financial crisis affect the market valuation of large, systemic US banks? *Journal of Financial Stability*, 32, 115–23.

Bhojraj, S., and Lee, C. (2002). Who is my peer? A valuation based approach to the selection of comparable firms. *Journal of Accounting Research*, 40(2), 407–39.

Bhojraj, S., Lee, C., and Oler, D. (2003). What's my line? A comparison of industry classification schemes for capital market research. *Journal of Accounting Research*, 41, 745–74.

Blau, B., Brough, T., and Griffith, T. (2017). Bank opacity and the efficiency of stock prices. *Journal of Banking and Finance*, 76, 32–47.

Bogdanova B., Fender I., and Takats E. (2018). The ABC's of bank PBRs. *BIS Quarterly Review*, March, 81–95.

Brunnermeier, K.M., and Nagel, S. (2004). Hedge funds and the technology bubble. *The Journal of Finance*, 59, 2013–40.

Brunnermeier, M., Rother, S., and Schnabel, I. (2020). Asset price bubbles and systemic risk. *The Review of Financial Studies*, https://doi.org/10.1093/rfs/hhaa011.

Calomiris, C.W., and Nissim, D. (2014). Crisis-related shifts in the market valuation of banking activities. *Journal of Financial Intermediation*, 23, 400–35.

Campbell, T., and Kracaw, W. (1980). Information production, market signalling, and the theory of intermediation. *Journal of Finance*, 35, 863–82.

Cheng, C., and McNamara, R. (2000). The valuation accuracy of the price-earnings and price-book benchmark valuation methods. *Review of Quantitative Finance and Accounting*, 15(4), 349–70.

Diamond, D.W. (1989). Reputation acquisition in debt markets. *Journal of Political Economy*, 97(4), 828–62.

Diamond, D.W. (1999). Liquidity, banks and markets: effects of financial development on banks and the maturity of financial claims. Policy research working papers, World Bank.

Diamond, D.W., and Dybvig, P.H., (1983). Bank runs, deposit insurance, and liquidity. *Journal of Political Economy*, 91(3), 401–19.

ECB (European Central Bank) (2004). Fair value accounting and financial stability. *Occasional Paper Series*, no. 13, April.

Fama, E. (1965). The behavior of stock market prices. *Journal of Business*, 38(1), 34–105.

Fama, E. (1991). Efficient capital markets: II. *Journal of Finance*, 46, 1575–617.

Fama, E. (2013). Two Pillars of Asset Pricing, Nobel Prize Lecture.

Fama, E., and French, K. (1992). The cross-section of expected stock returns. *Journal of Finance*, 47, 427–66.

Flannery, M. (1998). Using market information in prudential bank supervision: a review of the US empirical evidence. *Journal of Money, Credit and Banking*, 30, 273–305.

Flannery, M.J., Kwan, S.H., and Nimalendran, M. (2004). Market evidence on the opaqueness of banking firms' assets. *Journal of Financial Economics*, 71, 419–60.

Flannery, M.J., Kwan, S.H., and Nimalendran, M. (2013). The 2007–2009 financial crisis and bank opaqueness. *Journal of Financial Intermediation*, 22, 55–84.

Forte, G., Gianfrate, G., and Rossi, E. (2020). Does relative valuation work for banks? *Global Finance Journal*, 44, 1–25.

Gilson, R.J., and Kraakman, R.H. (2014). Market efficiency after the financial crisis: it's still a matter of information costs. Stanford Law and Economics Olin Working Paper no. 458, European Corporate Governance Institute

(ECGI) – Law Working Paper No. 242/2014, Columbia Law and Economics Working Paper no. 470.

Greenwald, B.C., and Stiglitz, J.E. (1986). Externalities in economies with imperfect information and incomplete markets. *The Quarterly Journal of Economics*, 101(2), 229–64.

Grossman, S.J. (1976). On the efficiency of competitive stock markets where traders have diverse information. *The Journal of Finance*, 31/2(573), 85.

Grossman, R. (1992). Deposit insurance, regulation, and moral hazard in the thrift industry: evidence from the 1930's. *American Economic Review*, 82, 800–21.

Grossman, S.J., and Stiglitz J.E. (1980). On the impossibility of informationally efficient markets. *American Economic Review*, 70(3), 393–407.

Howe, J.S., and Haggard, K.S. (2012). Are banks opaque? *International Review of Accounting, Banking and Finance*, 4(1), 51–72.

Huizinga, H., and Laeven, L. (2012). Bank valuation and accounting discretion during a financial crisis. *Journal of Financial Economics*, 106, 614–34.

IMF (International Monetary Fund) (2008). Chapter 3: Fair value accounting and procyclicality. *Global financial stability report*, October.

Jin, L., and Myers, S. (2006). R2 around the world: new theory and tests. *Journal of Financial Economics*, 79, 257–92.

Jones, J., Lee, W., and Yeager, T. (2012). Opaque banks, price discovery, and financial instability. *Journal of Financial Intermediation*, 21, 383–408.

Jones, J., Lee, W., and Yeager, T. (2013). Valuation and systemic risk consequences of bank opacity. *Journal of Banking and Finance*, 37, 693–706.

Landsman, W.R. (2007). Is fair value accounting information relevant and reliable? Evidence from capital market research. *Accounting and Business Research*, Special Issue: International Accounting Policy Forum, 19–30.

Laux, C., and Leuz, C. (2009). The crisis of fair-value accounting: making sense of the recent debate. *Accounting, Organizations and Society*, 34(6–7), 826–34.

Laux, C., and Leuz, C. (2010). Did fair-value accounting contribute to the financial crisis? *Journal of Economic Perspectives*, 24, 93–118.

Lie, E., and Lie, H. (2002). Multiples used to estimate corporate value. *Financial Analysts Journal*, 58(2), 44–54.

Lim, K.P., and Brooks, R. (2011). The evolution of stock market efficiency over time: a survey of the empirical literature. *Journal of Economic Surveys*, 25(1), 69–108.

Liu, J., Nissim, D., and Thomas, J. (2002). Equity valuation using multiples. *Journal of Accounting Research*, 40(1), 135–72.

Morck, Randall, Yeung, Bernard, and Wu, Wayne (2000). The information content of stock markets: why do emerging markets have synchronous stock price movements? *Journal of Financial Economics* 58 (1), 215–60.

Nissim, D. (2013). Relative valuation of U.S. insurance companies. *Review of Accounting Studies*, 18(2), 324–59.

Panetta, F., Angelini, P. et al. (2009). Financial sector pro-cyclicality: lessons from the crisis. Occasional Paper 44, Bank of Italy.

Penman, Stephen, H. (2007). Financial reporting quality: is fair value a plus or minus? *Accounting and Business Research Special Issue: International Accounting Policy Forum*, 33–44.

Persaud, A. (2008). Regulation, valuation and systemic liquidity. Banque de France, Financial stability review – Special issue on valuation, no. 12, October.

Plantin, Guillame, Sapara, Haresh, and Song Shin, Hyun (2008). Marking-to-market: panacea or Pandora's Box? *Journal of Accounting Research*, 46(2).

Reinganum, M.R. (1983). The anomalous stock market behavior of small firms in January: empirical tests for tax-loss selling effects. *Journal of Financial Economics*, 12(1), 89–104.

Ryan, S.G. (2008). Accounting in and for the subprime crisis. *The Accounting Review*, 83(6), 1605–38.

Scherbina, A. (2013). Asset price bubbles: a selective survey, IMF Working Paper 13/45.

Shiller, R.J. (2014). Speculative Asset Prices (Nobel Prize Lecture). Cowles Foundation Discussion Paper no. 1936.

Shleifer, A., and Vishny R.W. (1997). The limits of arbitrage. *Journal of Finance*, 52(1), 35–55.

Veldkamp, L. (2006). Information markets and the comovement of asset prices. *Review of Economic Studies*, 73, 823–45.

Veron, N. (2008). Fair value accounting is the wrong scapegoat for this crisis. *European Accounting Review*, 5(2), 63–9.

Vogel, H.L. (2010). *Financial Markets Bubbles and Crashes*. New York: Cambridge University Press.

Wallison, P.J. (2008). Fair value accounting: a critique. American Enterprise Institute for Public Policy Research Outlook Series, July.

Whalen, R.C. (2008). The subprime crisis – cause, effect and consequences. Networks Financial Institute Policy Brief no. 2008-PB-04, March.

Wheelock, D., and Kumbhakar, S. (1995). Which banks choose deposit insurance? Evidence of adverse selection and moral hazard in a voluntary insurance system. *Journal of Money, Credit, and Banking*, 27, 186–201.

Zuckerman, E.W. (2012). Market efficiency: a sociological perspective, in *The Oxford Handbook of the Sociology of Finance*, Karin K. Cetina and Alex Preda (eds), Oxford: Oxford University Press, pp. 223–49.

PART III

The role of public policies

9. Reflections on the shifting consensus about monetary and fiscal policies following the GFC and the COVID-19 crises

Alex Cukierman

9.1 INTRODUCTION

The twenty first century witnessed two major crises that forced policymakers to revise their thinking about desirable codes of conduct for monetary and fiscal policies. The establishments of price stability by means of central bank (CB) independence and inflation targets during the last decade of the twentieth century managed to establish an era of great moderation which solidified the view that CBs should focus on long-run price stability and stabilization of the business cycle in between. The budget should be balanced over the business cycle and fiscal policy should be subject to strict limits on the deficits and national debt.

The large financial shock associated with the global financial crisis (GFC) forcefully reminded CBs that they also are expected to deliver financial stability. The short-run policy rate was reduced to zero and replaced by large quantitative easing operations (see Chapter 1 for more details). Large fiscal packages were deployed and the coordination between fiscal and monetary authorities increased (for a broader view on the role of fiscal policies see Chapter 10). A new consensus charged CBs to handle the previously neglected macro-prudential regulation.

Unlike the GFC that originated in the financial sector, the COVID-19 crisis originated in a medical shock whose large effects on the economy and the financial sector are due to full or partial lockdowns designed to moderate the spread of the virus. To date monetary and fiscal policies responded to the economic and financial challenges by using instruments developed during the GFC on a scale never seen before. The limits on deficits and debts were quickly forgotten and the world's debt/GDP ratios swelled to levels previously seen only during major wars.

This chapter describes those policy responses against the background of those two major crises. It then discusses their impact on the shifting consensus about current and future monetary and fiscal policies.

The chapter is organized as follows. Section 9.2 describes the consensus about recommended monetary and fiscal policies in the pre-GFC era. The consensus that emerged following the GFC including regulatory reforms and the low interest rate phenomenon are discussed in Section 9.3. The evolution of the COVID-19 crisis and the responses of fiscal and monetary policies during the first half of 2020 is discussed in Section 9.4. Section 9.5 describes the changes in the consensus about aggregate demand policies caused by the crisis and Section 9.6 discusses the wider implications of the coronavirus crisis for the future. This is followed by concluding remarks.

9.2   THE PRE-GLOBAL FINANCIAL CRISIS CONSENSUS

Prior to the GFC the common view about the division of labour between fiscal and monetary policies was that, due to its longer decision-making lag and political nature, the role of fiscal policy (FP) in short-run stabilization policy should be limited to the operation of automatic stabilizers. In parallel, stabilization of the cycle should be left mainly to monetary policy implemented by a politically independent CB.

Fiscal policy should be conducted subject to appropriate limits on the GDP shares of deficits and of the national debt. When those limits are binding government's budget should be balanced over the business cycle. When those limits are not binding full employment deficits may be allowed temporarily. The stability and growth pact in the European Union (EU) required that the debt/GDP ratio not exceed 60 per cent and the deficit to GDP ratio not exceed 3 per cent. Although many countries in the EU did not always abide by those limits they became a standard for responsible government behaviour within and outside the EU. Obviously, a country with initial debt substantially above the limit cannot achieve the limit in one year or two. But it can decide to commit to a path of deficits/GDP ratios that will eventually reduce the debt/GDP ratio to 60 per cent.[1]

During the two decades preceding the GFC the following consensus on monetary policy and institutions emerged: The main objective of monetary policy is to maintain price stability in the medium and long terms. This objective is operationalized in terms of an inflation target (usually 2 per cent). As long as inflation does not deviate too much and/or too long from the target, monetary policy can and should be used to reduce the output gap.[2] The conduct of monetary policy should be delegated to an independent CB with full authority to set policy interest rates and to conduct open market operations. The interest rate is the main instrument of monetary policy and open market operations should be devised so as to support decisions about this instrument. Lending to government and interference with the instruments of monetary policy is prohibited. It bears repeating that since it can react more swiftly than fiscal authorities to changing circumstances most of the burden of short stabilization of the inflation and output gaps was expected to be borne by the independent CB.

In parallel, the New-Keynesian framework provided a micro-founded sticky prices conceptual framework that recognized explicitly the central role of forward-looking expectations for the conduct of monetary policy within an inflation targeting (IT) framework.[3] In this micro-founded version of IT, an independent CB picks the short-term interest rate (taking the structure of the economy and inflationary expectations as given), so as to minimize a weighted linear combination of the social costs of the inflation and output gaps. Here the first gap is the deviation of inflation from the IT and the second gap is the deviation of actual from potential output.

Prior to the 1990s most CBs were largely dominated by treasuries and governments. Under the Bretton-Woods (BW) regime that operated between 1945 and 1971 price stability in many countries was achieved by a system of fixed, but periodically adjustable, pegs with respect to the US dollar backed by limited capital mobility implemented through exchange controls. During this period the role of CBs was limited to maintaining the fixed pegs and they had little independence. The post-BW period witnessed a period of experimentation with alternative nominal anchors that would permanently stabilize the high inflations of the 1970s and the 1980s. This process culminated during the 1990s to a wholesale process of upgrading's in CB independence.[4]

9.3   CONSENSUS FOLLOWING THE GLOBAL FINANCIAL CRISIS

The GFC eroded the pre-crisis consensus along several dimensions. Policymakers and the economics profession realized the central role of financial stability (see Chapter 2) and of systemic risks that had taken second seat prior to the crisis. This led to widespread regulatory reforms as well as to the emergence of, at the time, unconventional monetary policy instruments. The emergence of the zero lower bound (ZLB) constraint led to the widespread use of quantitative easing (QE) as a substitute for interest rate policy. In the US, to prevent potential inflationary consequences of widespread QE operations the Fed supplemented this policy by paying interest on bank reserves.[5] The Fed and other CBs bought long-term bonds in order to directly affect interest rates over the entire yield curve. Other instruments like forward guidance became standard instruments of monetary policy and a number of economies engaged in direct forex intervention.

During the early stages of the crisis large fiscal packages were deployed to lift the equity capital and the liquidity of both financial and non-financial institutions. Two examples from the US are the 2008 TARP bill designed to help the financial sector and the 2009 ARRA designed to stimulate investments and the real economy. Governments in the EU, China and elsewhere also deployed fiscal packages, albeit of relatively smaller magnitudes than the US. Thus, in the face of large financial shocks that spread to the real economy policymakers responded by substantial expansionary fiscal policies.

9.3.1 Unconventional (at the Time) Monetary Policy Instruments[6]

This subsection contains a somewhat more detailed discussion of the unconventional monetary instrument deployed during the GFC.

Quantitative easing (QE): (also known as Large Scale Asset Purchases) are not new. Buying or selling assets by the CB is a normal by-product of conventional interest rate policy even during normal times since mainte-nance of the policy rate at the level desired by the CB has to be supported by the injection or removal of liquidity through the buying or selling of assets. There are several factors that distinguish asset purchases during the crisis from their normal times counterparts. First, such purchases increased dramatically only once the policy rate reached the ZLB. Second, particularly in the US, the range of assets purchased was much wider than during normal times. Rather than limiting itself to government debt, the Fed bought mortgage-backed securities and other types of commercial debt. During the immediate aftermath of Lehman's fall the Fed also bought banking stocks in an attempt to strengthen the capital position of the banking system. Finally, the exceptionally large magnitude of US QE operations distinguishes it from asset purchases during normal times. In reaction to the panic that engulfed financial markets in the immediate aftermath of Lehman's collapse QE was used mainly to inject liquidity into the capital market. But, as the recession caused by the financial crisis persisted, QE gradually became a device for circumventing the ZLB by directly lowering long-term interest rates in order to stimulate the economy. Between August 2008 and October 2014, the monetary base in the US increased by a factor of five. Although it receded somewhat since then it was still about four times larger at the eve of the coronavirus crisis than in August 2008. This reflected the Fed's decision to reduce the monetary base gradually by attrition.

Although it engaged in some limited asset purchases already in 2008–09 the ECB started to engage in large-scale asset purchases only at the beginning of 2015.[7] From that time and on the ECB intensified the use of this instrument. A partial reason for this later adoption of QE is the strong focus of the ECB charter on price stability.

Forex market interventions are not new. They have been used by CBs of emerging markets as a device for ironing out "excessive fluctuations" in exchange rates long before the GFC. For several decades prior to the crisis China pegged its currency to the US dollar in order to maintain the competitiveness of its exports. But the sustained zero interest rate policy of the Fed and the negative European Central Bank (ECB) policy rate since 2015 added a new dimension to such interventions. To preserve their competitiveness small open economies such as Switzerland, Israel, the Czech Republic and others reacted to the expansionary monetary policies of the big blocs by lowering their policy rates, often in conjunction with forex interventions designed to stem the appreciation of their currencies. The potential importance of such interventions gradually increased as their policy rates approached the ZLB. In small open economies an important transmission channel of monetary policy operates through the exchange rate. Once the ZLB is reached, the relative importance of foreign exchange purchases as a device for moderation of appreciation rises. Some countries such as Israel have initially used this instrument to build up forex reserves and occasionally to iron out excessive appreciation tendencies.

As of September 2011, the Swiss National Bank (SNB) introduced a one-sided peg on the Euro/SF exchange rate at 1.2 and effectively defended it until January 2015 when the ECB announced a large QE programme. This policy led to a substantial increase in Switzerland's forex reserves which, as of late 2015, were at a level similar to that of the country's GDP. The SNB's extreme reliance on forex interventions is directly related to the GFC. Being a safe haven currency the Swiss franc tended to appreciate in reaction to frequent panics experienced during the GFC eroding the competitiveness of Swiss exports. Having reached the ZLB relatively early the SNB found it expedient to rely relatively heavily on forex interventions. It is notable that, once the ZLB is reached, there is no need to sterilize such interventions implying that they become similar to the QE operations practised by the Fed and the ECB.

Negative interest rates and long-term asset purchases: recent negative inflation rates along with economic activity below potential induced a number of CBs to experiment with negative policy rates. Sweden, Denmark and Switzerland set their deposit rates at negative levels to preserve competitiveness and to induce banks to lend. During the first quarter of 2015 the ECB adopted a negative deposit rate mainly in order to stimulate banks' lending. A similar policy was enacted in early 2016 by the Bank of Japan.

Negative rates on banking reserves mean that banks have to pay for keeping deposits at the CB. Most banks did not initially pass this cost to small and medium-size deposits but did charge large depositors. Those developments suggested that the bound on the policy rate may be reduced somewhat below zero. Nonetheless, as long as the returns on cash and on deposits differ, it will not be possible for institutional reasons to reduce the policy rate substantially below zero.

This may be a serious problem if the short-term Wicksellian natural rate of interest is expected to remain below zero for an extended period of time. Cúrdia et al. (2015) and Cúrdia (2015) estimate that this rate reached a minimum of –4 per cent in the US over the GFC and remained below zero for several years. However, long-term risky rates whose impact on economic activity is more important than the direct impact of the short-term policy rate remained in the positive range. Recognizing this the Fed directed a large part of its QE operations to the purchase of long-term risky bonds. The accepted view prior to the GFC was that the CB should influence long-term rates through the short end of the yield curve. Once this became infeasible due to the ZLB the Fed aimed at directly reducing long-term risky rates through targeted QE operations. In chapter 22 of his memoirs Bernanke (2015, p. 521) recounts that this policy was initially criticized by the political establishment in Congress on the grounds that the Fed should "resist further extraordinary interventions in the US economy".

Forward guidance: like QE and forex interventions forward guidance is not a new monetary policy instrument. However, the ZLB constraint along with widespread use of QE in the US and more recently in the Euro area made it an effective complementary policy tool. Obviously, to be effective, preannouncements of future policy plans have to be subsequently delivered. This may be a problem if unexpected future developments call for deviations from previously announced policies.

Following experimentation with date-based statements about the target policy rate through 2012 the Fed started to handle this difficulty by using contingent forward guidance. In 2013 the Fed announced numerical thresholds for the rate of unemployment and inflation. In particular, it stated that the target policy rate will stay low as long as unemployment is above 6.5 per cent and inflation remained at or below 2.5 per cent. In his memoirs Bernanke (2015, p. 532) stresses that the figure for unemployment was a threshold rather than a trigger in the sense that the FOMC would not even consider lifting the policy rate as long as unemployment was above 6.5 per cent. This numerical statement had repeatedly been backed up by the more general statement that the Fed would do "whatever it takes" to reduce the rate of unemployment. In the face of mounting doubts about the viability of the Eurozone (EZ) President Draghi of the ECB used similar language to signal that the ECB will do whatever it can to assure the viability of the EZ.

9.3.2 Is the Low Rates Phenomenon a Consequence of Monetary Policies during the Global Financial Crisis?

Shortly after the collapse of Lehman brothers in September 2008 the Fed reduced the policy rate to practically zero and maintained it there until the last quarter of 2015. CBs of most developed and emerging economies followed similar paths shortly after.[8] Along with QE operations over the entire yield curve monetary policies contributed to the creation of an era of low short- and long-term interest rates. In addition, by depressing real economic activity and growth the GFC reduced the natural rate of interest.

On the other hand, Bean et al. (2015) document a downward trend in long-term riskless rates much before the GFC. They attribute it mainly to a world saving glut that preceded the GFC and to a lesser extent to a decrease in the demand for investment. A large part of the increase in savings was due to a very high Chinese saving rate out of which a high fraction was directed at the purchase of long-term high-quality bonds. In parallel there was an increase in the fraction of individuals in the middle-aged cohort in other economies. Since those individuals are responsible for the bulk of savings this also contributed to the increase in savings. Caballero et al. (2016) argue that the demise of mortgage-backed securities that were considered as safe assets prior to the GFC also contributed to reduce long-term safe interest rates by reducing the supply of safe assets.

In summary, it appears that, although large liquidity injections through QE operations and maturity extension programmes were not the only cause of low safe long-term rates, it contributed to their persistence and solidification.

9.3.3 Increasing Awareness of Financial Stability Considerations and Regulatory Reform

Although, prior to the GFC, financial stability was not as visible as IT CBs kept an eye on the segments of this objective that were under their regulatory authority. As is well known, the allocation of regulatory functions between different regulators varies across countries. Pre-crisis regulation, whether within or outside the CB, focused mainly on micro-economic regulation and paid relatively less attention to the risks posed by systemic crises and "too big to fail" institutions. The confluence of large-scale failures of systemic institutions and the associated financial panics that combined to start the GFC gave monetary policymakers and other regulators a dramatic wake up call. This triggered a wholesale process of regulatory reform with a strong focus on macro-prudential regulation, substantial increases in banks' capital requirements, stress tests for systemically important financial institutions and the closing of loopholes. Major pieces of legislation in this context are the July 2010 Dodd-Frank Act in the US and the creation of a European banking union by the heads of state and government of the EU in June 2012. In both cases, the respective CBs (the Fed in the US and the ECB in the EZ) were charged with the supervision and regulation of systemic risks and, in parallel, given more authority in comparison to the pre-crisis era. Similarly, in the UK, an independent Financial Policy Committee charged with monitoring and reducing systemic risks was created in April 2013 within the Bank of England.[9]

Regulatory reforms in all three areas are based on the notion that the CB is the choice institution for macro-prudential supervision and regulation. This consensus is supported by two main considerations. First, the CB is the public sector's institution that is likely to have the widest view of the overall state of the financial system. Second, the CB is also the institution that acts as lender of last resort in case of crisis. It therefore makes sense to charge the CB with systemic stability and to endow it with the additional policy instruments needed to perform this task. Consequently, the CB is well positioned to evaluate the trade-offs involved in taking preventive measures against a systemic crisis and the injection of public funds to limit the adverse effects of such a crisis if it materializes (see Chapter 13).

9.4 EVOLUTION OF THE COVID-19 CRISIS AND AGGREGATE DEMAND POLICY RESPONSES

Unlike the GFC and the Great Depression the coronavirus crisis originated in the real economy and was totally unanticipated. The initial absence of vaccine against the COVID-19 virus and its speedy contagiousness prompted medical and political authorities to curtail mobility by imposing lockdowns, quarantines, social distancing and an almost complete standstill of international air travel. By forcing large portions of the work force into segregation and closing down businesses this inevitable policy reaction transformed the impact of the virus from a pure medical emergency into a major real negative supply shock.

Mobility restrictions led to a substantial shut down of the economy, reduced production, layoffs, income losses, disruption of supply chains, and elevated personal and aggregate uncertainty. Those effects were amplified by the universality of the medical cum economic crisis and the associated reduction in world trade. The actual and expected GDP shrinkages quickly spilled over to financial markets leading to credit restrictions and capital outflows from developing economies. Sectors relying on social interactions such as travel, entertainment, restaurants and tourism took a particularly heavy toll. In parallel, international demand for producers of medical supplies soared. The drastic reduction in air and car travel along with production stoppages led to the collapse of the price of crude oil creating serious problems for government finances in some oil producing countries like Russia and Saudi Arabia. Unlike the GFC the COVID-19 crisis is characterized by a sharp decrease in aggregate consumption.

Table 9.1 shows actual rates of growth by major country groups and selected countries as well as projections for 2020 and 2021 from the April and June issues of the World Economic Outlook. As of June 2020, world output was expected to shrink by 4.9 per cent, advanced economies by 8.0 per cent and emerging markets and developing economies by 3.0 per cent. Except for China, all the countries in the table were predicted to experience negative rates of growth in 2020 reflecting the global reach of the virus and its economic ramifications.

Rates of growth were more negative in advanced economies than in emerging markets and developing countries. Within developed economies there were substantial differences in the adverse growth effects on GDP ranging from a minimum of –4.8 per cent for other advanced economies to a maximum of –12.8 per cent for Italy and Spain. Due to initially overoptimistic assumptions, the projections for 2020 growth as of June were uniformly more pessimistic than those made in April 2020. In particular, in economies with declining infection rates, the slower recovery path in the updated forecast reflected persistent social distancing into the second half of 2020; more persistent damage to supply potential from the larger-than-anticipated hit to activity during the lockdown in the first and second quarters of 2020; and a hit to productivity as surviving businesses incorporate workplace safety and hygiene practices. For economies still struggling to control infection rates, a lengthier lockdown would inflict an additional toll on activity. The June forecast assumed that financial conditions, which had eased following the release of the

Table 9.1 *World yearly growth projections for 2020 and 2021 from the April 2020 IMF World Economic Outlook and the June 2020 update*

	2019 (actual)	2020 projection (as of April)	2020 projection (as of June)	2021 projection (as of April)	2021 projection (as of June)
World Output	**2.9**	**−3.0**	**−4.9**	**5.8**	**5.4**
Advanced Economies	**1.7**	**−6.1**	**−8.0**	**4.5**	**4.8**
US	2.3	−5.9	−8.0	4.7	4.5
Euro Area	1.2	−7.5	−10.2	4.7	6.0
Germany	0.6	−7.0	−7.8	5.2	5.4
France	1.3	−7.2	−12.5	4.5	7.3
Italy	0.3	−9.1	−12.8	4.8	6.3
Spain	2.0	−8.0	−12.8	4.3	6.3
Japan	0.7	−5.2	−5.8	3.0	2.4
UK	1.4	−6.5	−10.2	4.0	6.3
Canada	1.6	−6.2	−8.4	4.2	4.9
Other Advanced	1.7	−4.6	−4.8	4.5	4.2
Emerging Markets and Developing Economies	**3.7**	**−1.0**	**−3.0**	**6.6**	**5.9**
China	**6.1**	**1.2**	**1.0**	**9.2**	**8.2**
India	**4.2**	**1.9**	**−4.5**	**7.4**	**6.0**
ASEAN-5	4.8	−0.6	−2.0	7.8	6.2
Russia	**1.3**	**−5.5**	**−6.6**	**3.5**	**4.1**
Latin America and the Caribbean	0.1	−5.2	−9.4	3.4	3.7
Saudi Arabia	0.3	−2.3	−6.8	2.9	3.1
Nigeria	2.2	−3.4	−5.4	2.4	2.6
South Africa	0.2	−5.8	−8.0	4.0	3.5
Low Income Developing Countries	5.1	0.4	−1.0	5.6	5.2

April 2020 IMF World Economic Outlook, would remain at current levels. Those forecasts as well as the general outlook were subject to an unusually high degree of uncertainty whose sources and implications are discussed later.

9.4.1   Fiscal and Monetary Policy Responses

The deep decreases in economic activity, employment and incomes triggered by lockdowns quickly led to a wide consensus that extraordinarily expansionary fiscal policies should come to the rescue even at the cost of large budget deficits and substantial increases in debt/GDP ratios. This consensus was quickly put into action through fiscal packages that often were substantially larger than their counterparts at the beginning of the GFC. Thus, at the end of March 2020 President Trump signed into law a historic 2.2 trillion-dollar stimulus package marking the biggest rescue deal ever in US history. In parallel, the Fed expanded its QE operations in both size and scope buying, for the first time, corporate bonds below investment grade. As a consequence, by the last quarter of June, the bloated balance sheet it cumulated during the GFC increased further by about 75 per cent. Similar policies, although not always as extreme, were deployed by the majority of governments and CBs the world over.

Fiscal responses
As of June 2020, the IMF estimated that global public debt would reach an all-time high; exceeding 101 per cent of GDP in 2020/21 and the average overall fiscal deficit would soar to 14 per cent of GDP in 2020. Figure 9.1 shows the yearly changes in the global public debt and the global fiscal deficit in comparison to their counterparts in 2009 – a year that marks the peak of the response to the GFC. Those changes are larger by an order of magnitude during the COVID-19 pandemic than during the GFC. In particular, the debt/GDP ratio was expected to rise by almost 19 per cent during the pandemic in comparison to an increase of "only" 10.5 per cent in 2009 and the increase in the overall fiscal deficit in 2020 was expected to be about two times larger than in 2009.

Beyond discretionary fiscal measures, automatic stabilizers from taxes and social protection were expected to help cushion the fall in household incomes during the recession, but also to contribute to one-third of the rise in deficits on average. In particular, government revenues were expected to fall more than output and projected to be 2½ percentage points of GDP lower, on average, than in 2019, reflecting lower personal and corporate incomes and hard-hit private consumption. Figure 9.2 shows the magnitudes of fiscal stimulus for selected countries and country groups through additional spending and foregone revenues as well as through loan and equity guarantees measured in percentages of GDP. The fiscal stimulus was uniformly positive but was substantially larger for advanced economies and the G20 than in the rest of the world. The combined stimulus package was largest in advanced economies (about 20 per cent), second

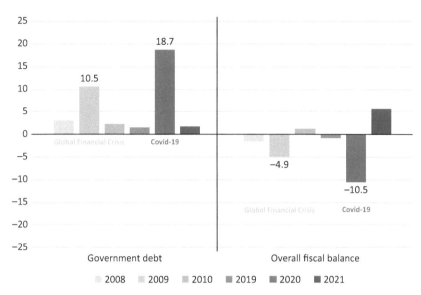

Source: Author elaborations on IMF data (World Economic Outlook Update, June 2020, IMF).

Figure 9.1 *Change in global government debt and overall fiscal balance (per cent of GDP)*

largest in the G20 (about 12 per cent), 5 per cent in emerging markets and about 1 per cent in low income developing countries.

Monetary policy responses[10]

Policy rates in a number of countries have been cut further and investors expect interest rates to remain at very low levels for several years. Balance sheets of advanced economies' CBs have swelled following new rounds of asset purchases, liquidity support for the banking system, US dollar swap lines, and other facilities intended to sustain the flow of credit to the economy. Aggregate assets of the Group of Ten (G10) CBs have increased by about $6 trillion since mid-January, more than double the increase seen during the two years of the GFC from December 2007, with the rise in assets accounting for almost 15 per cent of G10 GDP.

A number of emerging markets CBs have embarked on unconventional policy measures for the first time. In some countries, these asset purchase programmes were started to support the economy; in other countries, the motivation was to support market liquidity. These programmes have included purchases of a range of assets, including government bonds, state-guaranteed bonds, corporate debt and mortgage-backed securities.

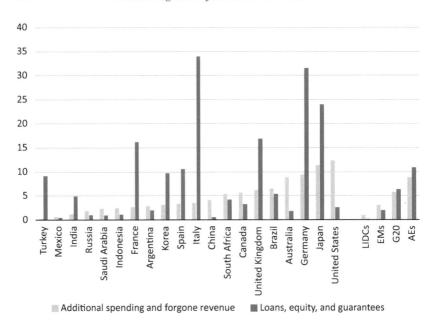

Note: AEs, advanced economies; G20, Group of Twenty economies; EMs, emerging markets; LIDCs, low income developing countries.

Source: Author elaborations on IMF data (World Economic Outlook Update, June 2020, IMF).

Figure 9.2   Fiscal measures in response to the COVID-19 pandemic (per cent of GDP)

Fiscal and financial policy measures have also helped support investor sentiment. Financial policies by both fiscal and monetary authorities have bolstered market confidence through government credit guarantees, support for the restructuring of loans, and encouraged banks to use available capital and liquidity buffers to support lending. This combination of unprecedented policy support appears to have been successful in maintaining credit flows. The lift to investor risk appetite has helped raise bond issuance in markets, and banks have also continued to lend in most major economies.

9.5   POLICY CONSENSUS EMERGING IN THE WAKE OF THE COVID-19 CRISIS

The consensus emerging from those actions is that, in the face of emergencies such as the COVID-19 crisis, restrictions on budget deficits and debt/GDP ratios should be suspended. This consensus is reinforced by the very low cost of government debt in advanced economies (see for example Blanchard, 2019) and by the argument that fiscal policy is particularly effective at the ZLB. On the monetary policy front, large and risky QE operations designed to safeguard the stability of the financial system and to revive the economy are increasingly becoming accepted practice even in CBs with initially large balance sheets. Although the GFC and its aftermath paved the way for such instruments the COVID-19 pandemic raised their scope to previously unseen levels.

The extraordinary increases in debt/GDP ratio prompted some economists to recommend a temporary lifting of the taboo on monetary financing of deficits (Galí, 2020a; Yashiv, 2020). Using a New-Keynesian framework Galí (2020b) finds that a fiscal stimulus is more effective when it is money financed than when it is financed by debt – and particularly so when the ZLB is not binding. In the UK, the government even borrowed directly from the Bank of England in April 2020 for a limited period of time in order not to flood the bond market with the extraordinary financial requirements imposed by the large fiscal responses to the crisis. Although most countries did not have recourse to direct monetary finance, large QE operations with minimal limits on maturities and risk classes purchased by the CB provide a non-negligible substitute to monetary financing by maintaining the market for government and corporate bonds (Cukierman, 2020).

9.6 POLICY AND WIDER IMPLICATIONS FOR THE FUTURE

During the first years of the GFC there was a deep and persistent drop in the provision of credit to the economy (Cukierman, 2019, figure 3). By contrast, following a brief financial panic in March 2020 the massive responses of monetary and fiscal authorities quickly restored a reasonable flow of credit to the economy and facilitated the financing of budgetary deficits. Looking into the future, this success is likely to increase the coordination between fiscal and monetary authorities. Although the CBs of advanced economies are likely to remain responsible for price and financial stability they will become more sensitive to the large financing needs of their governments.

The massive expansion of aggregate demand management policies also lifted asset markets from their initially depressed levels in March 2020 and created a disconnect between expectations about the future of the real economy and stock market values. In particular, the S&P 500 index became overly high in comparison to the US Conference Board index of consumer confidence.

It is likely that the ZLB will become binding more frequently than in the past. Partly in response to this, large QE operation and accumulation of huge balance sheets by western CBs will become a norm. In spite of opposition of economists that believe in established standards of pre-crisis good behaviour, some countries may temporarily lift the taboo on monetary financing of deficits. In the foreseeable future this tendency is likely to be reinforced by the absence of inflation and even deflation in some countries.

9.6.1 The Impact of Uncertainty

The COVID-19 pandemic created an unusually high level of uncertainty for everybody in the economy including businesses, consumers and policymakers. The initial absence of a vaccine and of sufficient knowledge about the virus opened the door for experimentation with a wide array of methods for addressing the medical/economic trade-offs of the crisis. It also injected politics into the decision-making processes of governments. The drop in consumption and investment is likely to persist as long as unemployment is large and there is substantial uncertainty about future levels and duration of governmental income relief and other forms of help.[11]

The pandemic demonstrated once again that in the face of a worldwide shock such as the COVID-19 pandemic the only insurer of last resort is government. Looking into the future this implies that governments should prepare in advance sufficient financial and medical resources to be able to provide a minimal safety net in case similarly disruptive shocks realize in the future. If left with no response a real shock like the pandemic endangers the stability of the financial system and the flow of credit reinforcing reductions in economic activity. Luckily, the massive responses of fiscal and monetary policies in advanced economies stopped such a scenario but introduced new distortions some of which are discussed later.

Uncertainty about the length of the lag between partial or full lockdowns and their sanitary outcomes also complicates communications with the public and may dent the process of building trust between policymakers and the public. Needless to say, that trust is essential since, in its absence, part of the public will not abide by the lockdowns reducing their effectiveness and pushing the economy into longer than necessary lockdowns in the future.

An example may clarify the mental process involved. Suppose that following a period of a tight lockdown the contagion curve flattens and the lockdown is lifted. After a while indicators of contagion resume a modest upward trend which convinces medical experts that, in the absence of targeted lockdowns, this trend will intensify within several weeks. Even if this information is honestly conveyed to the public some individuals who observe the current low contagion levels will not take the medical recommendation seriously, particularly if an economic or other personal cost is involved. In retrospect, they might realize their error when the contagion rises but this is too late.

9.6.2 Impact on Inequality

The distribution of financial wealth in many advanced economies is highly skewed. In the US the top 1 per cent of the wealthiest families holds 40 per cent of all wealth and the bottom 90 per cent owns less than a quarter of total wealth. Furthermore, the financial wealth of individuals below the median is practically nil. A by-product of the large fiscal packages and extraordinarily expansionary monetary policies deployed since the start of the pandemic is that financial assets have flourished while large numbers of employees and small businesses experienced unemployment and income losses. The trend in financial markets is likely to permanently raise the value of financial assets. Since individuals with incomes below the median hold only a small share of those assets this will tend to permanently increase inequality in the distribution of wealth and (after various temporary social policies subside) also to an increase in income inequality.

The income of workers in occupations that make it possible to work from home are largely immune to income losses due to lockdowns. By contrast, employees in occupations in which this is not feasible lose their jobs and are subject to substantial cuts in their income. Since on average the income of the second group of workers tends to be lower lockdowns raise inequality in the distribution of income.

At the global level low income countries that have less fiscal and monetary space and relatively underdeveloped medical facilities are less prepared to meet the challenges of the pandemic. Interestingly, evidence from previous pandemics shows that the loss of employment and income makes the uneducated poor even poorer (Furceri et al., 2020).

9.6.3 Will the Pandemic Reinforce International Cooperation in the Struggle against the Virus?

The high contagiousness of the coronavirus within and across countries implies that success in moderating its spread in any given country produces a positive spillover effect for the rest of the world. Looking forward, this factor should reinforce international cooperation in fighting the virus. But another factor is likely to operate in the opposite direction. Countries may compete to be the first in line to obtain the effective vaccines. Since, in the early post-vaccine phase world demand will exceed the available supply by an order of magnitude this will, at least temporarily, reduce cooperation between countries. Strong and reasonably equitable international leadership is needed to help the long-run basic common interest dominate the short-run scramble to acquire the vaccine.

9.7   CONCLUDING REMARKS

Major crises trigger substantial adjustments, and at times even revolutions in accepted views about the role of the public sector and the structure of its institutions. In particular, this statement applies to monetary and fiscal policies. Ninety years ago, the Great Depression led to the birth of Keynesian economics, to the creation of the US social security system and to the discovery of the potency of fiscal policy. With a lag of about 30 years the Friedman-Schwartz (1960s) counter-revolution recognized the potency of monetary policy. The inflation of the 1970s and the breakdown of the Bretton-Woods system led with a lag of about ten years to the CB independence revolution and to the establishment of inflation targeting. For almost 20 years this system helped maintain the great moderation in which CBs delivered price stability in the long run and stabilization of the cycle in the short and medium term while, subject to limits on debts and deficits, stabilization by fiscal means was expected to operate through automatic stabilizers and discretionary actions.

The GFC drove monetary policies to the zero lower bound, leading to the emergence of large-scale asset purchases by CBs, triggered large fiscal packages and generally increased cooperation between fiscal and monetary authorities. At times this cooperation dented CB independence. Monetary policy tools such as forward guidance and forex intervention became more popular and the realization that prior to the crisis regulation was inadequate and that systemic factors were neglected led to regulatory reforms and the creation of macro-prudential authorities, often within the CB.

The COVID-19 crisis led to expansionary monetary and fiscal policies at levels observed only during major wars. Conventional limits on debts and deficits were set aside and global government debt was forecasted to rise by almost 19 per cent over 2020 (Figure 9.1). Some economists and policymakers even advocate temporary lifting of the taboo on monetary financing of deficits. The overblown balance sheets of CBs in developed economies inherited from the GFC have almost doubled. In spite of those measures, as of June 2020 world output for 2021 was forecasted to shrink by almost 5 per cent (Table 9.1). This economic cost is directly traceable to the full and temporary lockdowns and to an unusually high degree of uncertainty about the future. Unfortunately, although many countries have recently exited from total lockdowns, partial lockdowns uncertainty will persist due to virus variants.

NOTES

1. Using such a strategy Israel reduced the debt/GDP ratio from over 90 per cent in 2003 to around 60 per cent in 2019.
2. Although most CBs were sensitive to financial stability considerations this objective did not take centre stage until the arrival of the GFC.
3. Woodford (2003) and Galí (2008) are prominent examples.
4. Further details appear in Cukierman (2008) and Cukierman (2018).
5. Those inflation risks did not materialize. Instead sustained periods of below target and even negative inflation followed during the second half of the GFC and its aftermath.
6. The following discussion draws on parts of section 2 in Cukierman (2019).
7. Prior to that the bulk of its liquidity injections operations were done through limited term advances to the banking system.
8. An important exception is the ECB whose deposit facility rate reached the ZLB only during the last quarter of 2013.
9. Further details appear in section 5 of Cukierman (2019).
10. This subsection draws on the Global Financial Stability Report Update (June 2020).
11. Forecasting at currently high levels of uncertainty is obviously difficult. In the June 2020 WEO update the IMF presents forecast under several alternative scenarios in order to capture some of the dimensions of this uncertainty.

REFERENCES

Bean, C., C. Broda, I. Takatoshi and R. Krozner (2015), *Low for Long? Causes and Consequences of Persistently Low Interest Rates*, Geneva Report on the World Economy 17, ICMB and CEPR, September. https://voxeu.org/sites/default/files/file/Geneva17_28sept.pdf.

Bernanke, B. (2015), *The Courage to Act: A Memoir of a Crisis and Its Aftermath*, W.W. Norton, New York.

Blanchard, O. (2019), "Public Debt and Low Interest Rates", *American Economic Review*, 109(4), 1197–229. April. https://www.aeaweb.org/articles?id=10.1257/aer.109.4.1197.

Caballero, R., E. Farhi and P.O. Gourinchas (2016), "Safe Asset Scarcity and Aggregate Demand", *American Economic Review, Papers and Proceedings* 106(5), 513–18.

Cukierman, A. (2008), "Central bank independence and monetary policymaking institutions – past, present and future", *European Journal of Political Economy*, 24, 722–36. https://www.tau.ac.il/~alexcuk/pdf/Published%20Version-POLECO 1087.pdf.

Cukierman, A. (2018), "Central banks", in W. Thompson (ed.), *Oxford Research Encyclopedia of Politics*, Oxford University Press. https://www.tau.ac.il/~alexcuk/pdf/Published%20version%20Feb%202018%20(acrefore-9780190228637-e-64). pdf.

Cukierman, A. (2019), "The Impact of the Global Financial Crisis on Central Banking", in David G. Mayes, Pierre L. Siklos and Jan-Egbert Sturm (eds), *The Oxford Handbook of the Economics of Central Banking*, Oxford University Press. https://www.tau.ac.il/~alexcuk/pdf/Published%20online%20version%20 oxfordhb-9780190626198-e-6.pdf.

Cukierman, A. (2020), "COVID-19, Helicopter Money & the Fiscal-Monetary Nexus", CEPR DP 14734, May.

Cúrdia, V. (2015), "Why So Slow? A Gradual Return for Interest Rates", Federal Reserve Bank of San Francisco Economic Letter, 2015–32, October.

Cúrdia, V., A. Ferrero, G. Ng and A. Tambalotti (2015), "Has U.S. Monetary Policy Tracked the Efficient Interest Rate?" *Journal of Monetary Economics*, 70, 72–83.

Friedman, M. and A. Schwartz (1963), *A Monetary History of the US: 1867–1960*, Princeton University Press, Princeton, NJ.

Furceri, D., P. Loungani and J. Ostry (2020), "How Pandemic Leave the Poor Even Farther Behind", IMF blog, 11 May. https://blogs.imf.org/2020/05/11/ how-pandemics-leave-the-poor-even-farther-behind/.

Galí, J. (2008), *Monetary Policy, Inflation and the Business Cycle: An Introduction to the New-Keynesian Framework*, Princeton University Press, Princeton, NJ and Oxford.

Galí, J. (2020a), "Helicopter Money: The Time Is Now", VoxEU, March, https:// voxeu.org/article/helicopter-money-time-now.

Galí, J. (2020b), "The Effects of a Money-Financed Fiscal Stimulus", *Journal of Monetary Economics*, 115, November, 1–19. https://www.sciencedirect.com/ science/article/pii/S0304393219301357.

Global Financial Stability Report Update, June 2020, IMF.

History of the Stability and Growth Pact, European Union. https://ec.europa.eu/info/ business-economy-euro/economic-and-fiscal-policy-coordination/eu-economic-governance-monitoring-prevention-correction/stability-and-growth-pact/history-stability-and-growth-pact_en.

Woodford, M. (2003), *Interest and Prices: Foundation of a Theory of Monetary Policy*, Princeton University Press, Princeton, NJ.

World Economic Outlook Update, June 2020, IMF.

Yashiv, E. (2020), "Breaking the Taboo: The Political Economy of COVID-Motivated Helicopter Drops", VoxEU, March. https://voxeu.org/article/politi cal-economy-covid-motivated-helicopter-drops.

10. Fiscal policy lessons since the Global Financial Crisis

Jérémie Cohen-Setton

10.1 INTRODUCTION

The view that fiscal policy is an important tool to fight recessions had for the most part receded during the Great Moderation (1984–2007).[1] By 1997, the leading macroeconomist Martin Eichenbaum (1997) even wrote that "there is now widespread agreement that countercyclical discretionary fiscal policy is neither desirable nor politically feasible."

Monetary policy was simply a better tool than fiscal policy to provide countercyclical support. Increases in government spending and tax cuts came with long implementation lags whereas swift interest cuts were possible. Because recessions are typically short-lived, the effects of fiscal stimulus typically came too late. Fiscal multipliers – the size of real output changes following fiscal policy impulses – were in any case low, with public spending crowding out rather than crowding in private demand. And with financial innovations, which allowed consumers to diversify their financial holdings and improved access to credit made public, public risk-sharing arrangements had altogether become less necessary.

Or so was the conventional wisdom until the Global Financial Crisis (GFC) (see also Chapter 9). With interest rate cuts rapidly reaching their limits, policymakers had little choice but to rely on fiscal policy. Early on, the scale of the disruptions induced by the GFC cast doubts on the possibility of a V-shape recovery. Lasting damage was instead likely, which provided fiscal policy ample time to yield a beneficial impact. In the meantime, new empirical methods that relied on more convincing identification strategies challenged the view that fiscal multipliers were always and everywhere small. At least in some circumstances – especially when unemployment was high and when monetary policy was constrained by the effective lower bound (ELB) on nominal interest rates – fiscal multipliers were, in fact, likely to be large. In addition, private risk-sharing arrangements proved less resilient than expected under stress.

This chapter argues that the rethinking of fiscal policy was not only the result of a new macroeconomic environment that puts limits on monetary policy and lowers the fiscal costs of debt, but also reflected new research findings on the overall effectiveness of fiscal policy as a countercyclical tool.

The chapter is organized as follows. Section 10.2 argues that the secular decline in interest rates compelled policymakers to broaden their policy toolkit beyond conventional monetary policy. Forward guidance and quantitative easing played an important role in increasing monetary ammunition during the Great Recession following the GFC. But these relatively new instruments did not substitute for the need of fiscal policy support.

Section 10.3 argues that the renewed interest in fiscal policy as a counter-cyclical tool also reflects a new consensus on fiscal multipliers. Part of that new consensus arises from methodological advances, which allow calculating the impact of fiscal policy for different macroeconomic environments. As surprising as it may sound, empirical guidance could not until then differentiate the impact of fiscal policy in good and bad times. But this renewed support for fiscal policy activism also reflects the finding that previous estimates of low multipliers were often due to basic identification and measurement problems. When these problems were corrected, fiscal multipliers were larger.

Section 10.4 argues that the renewed interest for a central fiscal capacity inside the euro area also reflects new empirical evidence, which suggests that private risk-sharing arrangements cannot fully substitute for government-led risk-sharing arrangements, especially when the entire monetary union is in recession. Finally, Section 10.5 concludes.

10.2   THE STRENGTHENED ROLE OF FISCAL POLICY IN A LOW INTEREST RATES ENVIRONMENT

Short-term interest rates have been near zero in advanced economies since the GFC, making it difficult for central banks to provide appropriate economic stimulus and increasing the need for fiscal policy support. The difficulty associated with nominal interest rates that cannot go much into negative territory is painfully obvious today when dealing with the COVID-19 economic shock (see also Chapter 9). In advanced economies, interest rates were reduced by only 100 basis points in 2020 compared to declines of 500 basis points in previous recessions (Reifschneider, 2016).

It would, however, be wrong to interpret the current difficulty as reflecting the mere product of an unfortunate series of events that are likely to reverse soon. First, because the decline in r-star – the real short-term interest rate expected to prevail when the economy is at full employment and inflation is stable – did not start with the GFC (Figure 10.1). It is estimated that r-star had already declined from 3.5 percent in the early 1970s to 1 percent by the mid-2000s.

Second, because with 10-year rates and 30-year rates still below 2 percent, the yield curve suggests that low rates will persist.[2] Option prices indicate that investors put the implicit probability that the short rate will exceed 4 percent in five years at less than 10 percent (Blanchard, 2019).

This is not surprising. While many factors have been identified as potential causes for the decline in r-star – population aging, the rise in inequality, higher precautionary saving in emerging economies, higher demand for safe assets, and the low price of capital – none of these appears likely to reverse any time soon.

The implication for stabilization policy is straightforward. With inflation expectations anchored at 2 percent and a real neutral interest rate as low as 1 percent, the Federal Reserve can only combat small recessions with interest rate cuts. Any recession that pushes the unemployment rate more than 1.1 percentage points above the natural rate would either bring the central bank against the effective lower bound or require a less aggressive response than was historically the case (Ball et al., 2016).

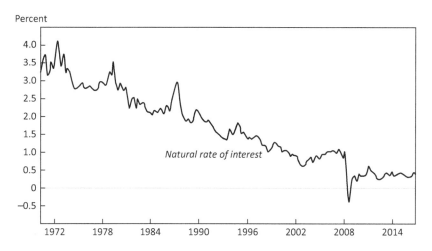

Source: Rachel and Summers (2019).

Figure 10.1   Changes in advanced economies' r-star, 1971–2016

True, monetary policy is not limited to modifying the policy interest rate. As explained in Chapter 9, it can shift expectations about future rates (forward guidance) or buy assets with different maturities and riskiness to reduce the interest rate faced by borrowers. But without drastic changes to frameworks, monetary policy space remains limited to fight recessions (Cohen-Setton et al., 2019a).

With the effective lower bound preventing monetary policy from decreasing the interest rate as much as required, large deficits can reduce output gaps and help provide the required policy support. It is thus natural that fiscal policy has regained importance as a countercyclical tool. In addition, low interest rates reduce the fiscal costs of debt. When the interest rate is less than the growth rate, an increase in the deficit today does not need to be offset by higher taxes or lower spending in the future. While debt will increase at the rate of interest, the economy will increase at the rate of growth, leading to a decrease in the ratio of debt to GDP over time (Blanchard, 2019).

10.3   FISCAL MULTIPLIERS: THE "GREAT" REASSESSMENT

Limits on monetary policy and the lower costs of debt have made fiscal policy an important instrument of output stabilization. But shifting views on the importance of fiscal policy have also been driven by a reassessment of the effectiveness of fiscal policy as a countercyclical tool. Ten years after the GFC, a renaissance of empirical fiscal research (Ramey, 2019) suggests that fiscal policy is also more effective at stimulating economic activity than was previously believed.

When the GFC hit and interest rates fell to zero, policymakers turned to fiscal policy to stimulate a weak economy. Trying to predict the effects of the stimulus, they were however surprised to learn that there was a lack of consensus among economists. In fact, not only did economists disagree about the size of the effects. They also disagreed on the sign of the effects, with some economists arguing that austerity could lead to economic expansion rather than contraction (International Monetary Fund, 2013).

To see the methodological issues associated with traditional studies that found small and even negative fiscal multipliers, it is useful to consider a simple linear model where output growth, expressed by ΔY_t (where Y_t is the natural logarithm of real GDP), is assumed to be a function of fiscal policy changes ΔFP_t and other factors u_t. Under these assumptions, the data-generating process can be written as:

$$\Delta Y_t = \alpha + \beta \, \Delta FP_t + u_t. \tag{10.1}$$

The key challenge in estimating the causal effects of fiscal policy, that is, the coefficient β in equation 10.1, is identification: it requires movements in fiscal policy that are uncorrelated with other factors affecting GDP growth contemporaneously, and captured by vector u_t in equation 10.1. Changes in fiscal deficits clearly do not fulfill this condition because of reverse causality, with changes in economic growth affecting the size of fiscal deficits rather than the other way around. Indicators of the fiscal stance that are calculated by removing the endogenous movements in the fiscal deficit associated with changes in economic activity help address this problem.

And yet, even indicators like the cyclically adjusted budget balance have been shown to bias fiscal multipliers downward (see International Monetary Fund, 2010 for fiscal contractions and Cohen-Setton et al., 2019b for fiscal expansions). This happens not only because standard cyclical adjustment procedures often fail to properly capture the impact of large fluctuations in output and movements in asset prices on government revenues, but also because the bulk of changes in fiscal policy are actually implemented to respond to economic conditions. With fiscal stimulus generally implemented to counter economic recessions, a naive regression of economic growth on changes in the cyclically adjusted budget balance would still suffer from reverse causality and generate downward-biased estimates of the true effect of fiscal policy.

Fortunately, new empirical methods have allowed for a more convincing identification strategy. Several papers have, for example, used narrative evidence to determine the underlying motivations behind individual tax and spending changes. Doing so allows researchers to isolate changes in fiscal policy that were not driven by changes in economic activity and address the reverse causality problem previously described. Other researchers have relied on quasi-experimental designs or forecast errors to isolate movements in fiscal policy unrelated to economic conditions. While the exact size of fiscal multipliers remains open for debate, the results emanating from this recent literature suggest that fiscal multipliers are positive and typically higher than what was believed before the GFC.

The more recent literature also emphasizes that the size of fiscal multipliers may vary greatly depending on the amount of slack in the economy and on monetary conditions. Using forecast errors to identify fiscal shocks for a panel of Organisation for Economic Co-operation and Development (OECD) countries, Figure 10.2 shows that fiscal multipliers tend to be bigger when unemployment is high, when interest rates are at the effective lower bound, and under fixed exchange rate regimes. The size of multipliers also varies by fiscal instrument, with empirical evidence, for example,

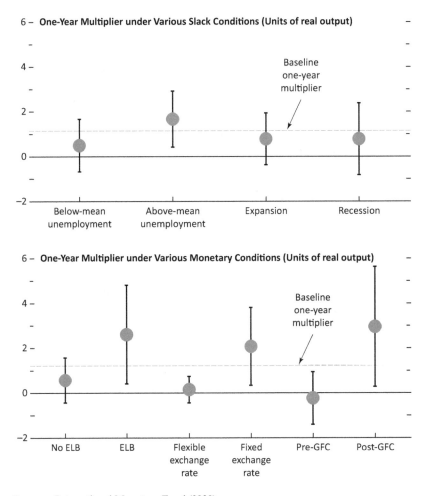

Source: International Monetary Fund (2020).

Figure 10.2   Fiscal multipliers under various conditions

suggesting that government investment is less stimulative than government consumption (Ramey, 2020) and that tax-based fiscal consolidations have a larger drag on economic activity than those based on expenditure cuts (Alesina et al., 2019).

In 1956, E. Cary Brown (1956) famously wrote that fiscal policy "seems to have been an unsuccessful recovery device in the thirties – not because it did not work, but because it was not tried." In fact, despite the size of the shock, the full-employment deficit was never significantly above 2 percent of GDP (De Long, 1998). If anything, the COVID-19 will in contrast be remembered as the one crisis when the fiscal device was extensively used. Whether it will work as well as in the past at limiting severe aftermaths after crises (Romer and Romer, 2019) remains an open question. But on the fiscal front, the policy mistakes associated with the Great Depression and the 2010 turn to austerity have at least been avoided.

10.4   REASSESSING FISCAL POLICIES IN MONETARY UNIONS

The importance of fiscal policy as a counter-cyclical tool inside a monetary union is anything but new. With one policy interest rate for all countries, the early literature on monetary unions quickly elevated fiscal policy as the main macroeconomic tool to deal with asymmetric shocks.

Despite this, it was commonplace for academics and policymakers to argue that the need for fiscal stabilization in the eurozone had been greatly reduced in practice. According to this view, the need for government transfers to deal with asymmetric shocks inside the eurozone was lower for at least two reasons. First, because the euro had improved access to cross-country borrowing and lending, thus allowing firms and households to smooth their expenditure levels in the face of temporary income shocks. And second, because the integration of European capital markets allowed for a reduction in the link between national production and income. By creating private-sector buffers, the completion of the capital market and banking unions reduced the urgency of completing the monetary union with a fiscal union and made government-sector buffers unnecessary (De Grauwe, 2007).

A critical piece of evidence in support of this view was that, even in well-functioning monetary unions like the United States, fiscal transfers played a relatively small role in stabilizing against asymmetric shocks in the data. According to Heijdra et al. (2018), "fiscal transfers across [US] states absorb [only] 9% of asymmetric shocks … while capital markets … absorb 48% and credit provision to the private sector absorbs another 17%."

Given the importance of this finding in shaping views about the needs for fiscal buffers inside a monetary union, this section reviews the empirical framework underlying this result. After outlining several limits in interpretating empirical results obtained using that framework, the section presents new empirical results on the relative role of private-sector and government-sector buffers. Rather than being substitutes, our results suggest that these channels to share risks are, in fact, complements when the entire monetary union is in recession.

In their seminal paper, Asdrubali et al. (1996) propose to quantify the size of different risk-sharing channels in the United States by investigating co-movements between the growth rates of production, income, disposable income and consumption of each US state. More specifically, the smoothing provided by the cross-state ownership of productive assets (capital market channel) is measured by the extent to which a state's income growth is disconnected from the growth of its production. The smoothing provided by a central fiscal capacity (Federal Government channel) is measured by the extent to which state disposable income growth is disconnected from state income growth. And the smoothing provided by cross-border savings and borrowings (credit market channel) is measured by how much state consumption growth is disconnected from state disposable income growth.

Box 10.1 shows the mathematical formulas associated with this empirical approach. While intuitive, the approach underestimates the role of the Federal Government in smoothing regional consumption. First, because the stabilization provided by the Federal Government is not limited to actions that create a wedge between state income growth and state disposable income growth (Dullien, 2019). An increase in Federal Government expenditures in states suffering from a negative production shock would, for instance, limit the decline in a state's consumption without creating a wedge between state income and disposable income growth. Instead, state consumption would be stabilized by sustaining state production (and thus state income) rather than through a stabilization of state disposable income against a decline in state income.

Second, because the framework puts little emphasis on whether and how the strength of these channels depend on the macroeconomic conditions of the monetary union as a whole. If, as emphasized by the former President of the European Central Bank, private risk-sharing arrangements "break down [when] large common shocks ... affect the whole monetary union" (Draghi, 2018), more fiscal risk-sharing remains necessary. Consistent with this idea, Furceri and Zdzienicka (2015) show that the portion of shocks that remains unsmoothed is significantly larger during recession in the euro area.

Using data from Nikolov (2016), which extends the sample of Asdrubali et al. (1996) to 2014, I show that this pattern is not specific to the European sovereign debt crisis. In fact, even in the United States, the importance of fiscal risk-sharing arrangements is greater during recessions than in normal times.

In Table 10.1 Column (1), the regressions presented in Box 10.1 are estimated by pooling all years together as in the original analysis of Asdrubali et al. (1996). With this specification, capital markets and credit markets

---

BOX 10.1   THE ASDRUBALI, SORENSEN AND YOSHA (1996) FRAMEWORK

Asdrubali et al. (1996) start by noting that it is possible to rewrite the per capita gross state product (*gsp*) of state *j* at time *t* as

$$gsp^j_t = \frac{gsp^j_t}{si^j_t} \frac{si^j_t}{dsi^j_t} \frac{dsi^j_t}{c^j_t} c^j_t,$$

where *si*, *dsi*, *c* respectively denote per capita state income, disposable state income and state consumption. Suppressing the time and state indexes for simplicity, it follows that one can write the decomposition of the cross-sectional variance in *gsp* as:

$$var\{\Delta log\ gsp\} = cov\{\Delta log\ gsp, \Delta log\ gsp - \Delta log\ si\}$$
$$+ cov\{\Delta log\ gsp, \Delta log\ si - \Delta log\ dsi\}$$
$$+ cov\{\Delta log\ gsp, \Delta log\ dsi - \Delta log\ c\}$$
$$+ cov\{\Delta log\ gsp, \Delta log\ c\}.$$

Dividing both sides by *var* {Δ*log gsp*}, one gets $1 = \beta_K + \beta_F + \beta_C + \beta_U$, where β_K is the ordinary least squares (OLS) estimate of the slope in the regression of Δ*log gsp* – Δ*log si* on Δ*log gsp*, β_F is the slope in the regression of Δ*log si* – Δ*log dsi* on Δ*log gsp*, β_C is the slope in the regression of Δ*log dsi* – Δ*log c* on Δ*log gsp*, β_U is the slope in the regression of Δ*log c* on Δ*log gsp*.

The empirical approach consists of running the following set of panel regressions:

$$\Delta log\ gsp^j_t - \Delta log\ si^j_t = v_{k,t} + \beta_K \Delta log\ gsp^j_t + u^j_{k,t}$$
$$\Delta log\ si^j_t - \Delta log\ dsi^j_t = v_{F,t} + \beta_F \Delta log\ gsp^j_t + u^j_{F,t}$$
$$\Delta log\ dsi^j_t - \Delta log\ c^j_t = v_{C,t} + \beta_C \Delta log\ gsp^j_t + u^j_{C,t}$$
$$\Delta log\ c^j_t = v_{U,t} + \beta_U \Delta log\ gsp^j_t + u^j_{U,t}$$

where $v_{u,t}$ are time fixed effects.

---

smooth more than two-thirds of asymmetric shocks in the United States, while the Federal Government only absorbs less than 10 percent of asymmetric shocks. Columns (2) and (3), however, divide the samples according to whether the United States was in a recession. This simple extension reveals that the contribution of the Federal Government is, in fact, twice higher during recessions than in normal times. Rather than absorbing a mere 6.5 percent of asymmetric shocks, the Federal Government absorbs up to 13 percent of asymmetric shocks during recessions.

Altogether, these results suggest that rather than being substitutes, the risk-sharing channels provided by the banking union, the capital market union and the fiscal union are complements and are all needed to strengthen the resiliency of the monetary union. The immediate

Table 10.1　Channels of risk-sharing in the United States

	(1)	(2)	(3)
	All years	Expansion	Recession
Capital markets	0.457	0.490	0.380
Federal Government	**0.084**	**0.067**	**0.128**
Credit markets	0.263	0.216	0.317
Not smoothed	0.196	0.227	0.175
Year-FE	Yes	Yes	Yes
Observations	2550	1850	700
Number of states	50	50	50

Note:　All results are statistically significant at the 1 percent level using robust standard errors clustered at the level of US states. Recession years are defined as years that include at least one NBER recession quarter.

Source:　Author's calculations using Nikolov (2016) data.

consequence of this observation is that fiscal stabilization in the form of more flexible fiscal rules or through the establishment of a central fiscal capacity is more important than what the pre-crisis policy consensus on the architecture of the euro area suggested. This finding also challenges the view that progress towards a fiscal union can wait as long as progress towards a banking and capital markets union is made. If anything, the underwriting of some fiscal risk-sharing is necessary for the private-sector risk-sharing channels to operate.

10.5　CONCLUSION

The financial and macroeconomic crisis that began in 2007 has shattered some of the core tenets of macroeconomic policymaking. Large macro-economic fluctuations came back with a vengeance. Rather than being an intellectual curiosity, the awkward condition in which monetary policy loses its grip has become a defining feature of our current macroeconomic environment.

A major rethinking of the role of fiscal policy as a countercyclical tool has taken place against this backdrop. New research findings on fiscal multipliers, the role of fiscal policy in the aftermath of financial crises, and the role of fiscal risk-sharing in monetary unions have also been instrumental in shaping a new consensus where fiscal policy no longer takes the backseat to monetary policy in providing macroeconomic support.

This new consensus has already shaped the current policy response to the COVID-19 pandemic, with exceptional level of fiscal support at the national level (see Chapter 9) and with the European Union issuing, for the first time, common debt to foster economic recovery. Whether this experience will consolidate the new consensus on the fiscal policy as a major tool to support the economy or reveal new fault lines is too early to say. But there is no doubt that COVID-19 constitutes a first major test for the new orthodoxy.

NOTES

1. The views expressed herein are those of the author only and should not be attributed to the IMF's IEO, the IMF, its Executive Board, or its management. The author thanks Plamen Nikolov for sharing data.
2. See https://fred.stlouisfed.org/series/IRLTLT01USM156N and https://fred.stlouisfed.org/series/DGS30. Last accessed on 09/13/2021.

REFERENCES

Alesina, Alberto, Carlo Favero, and Francesco Giavazzi. 2019. *Austerity: When It Works and When It Doesn't*. Princeton, NJ: Princeton University Press.

Asdrubali, Pierfederico, Bent E. Sørensen, and Oved Yosha. 1996. Channels of Interstate Risk Sharing: United States 1963–1990. *The Quarterly Journal of Economics*, 111(4), November, 1081–110. https://doi.org/10.2307/2946708.

Ball, L., J. Gagnon, P. Honohan, and S. Krogstrup. 2016. What Else Can Central Banks Do? Geneva Reports on the World Economy No. 18, ICMB and CEPR. Available at https://cepr.org/sites/default/files/geneva_reports/GenevaP285.pdf.

Blanchard, Olivier J. 2019. Prepared remarks submitted to the US House of Representatives Committee on the Budget hearing on "Reexamining the Economic Costs of Debt." Available at https://www.piie.com/commentary/testimonies/reexamining-economic-costs-debt.

Brown, E. Cary. 1956. Fiscal Policy in the Thirties: A Reappraisal. *The American Economic Review*, 46(5), 857–79. Available at https://www.jstor.org/stable/1811908?seq=1.

Cohen-Setton, Jérémie, Chris G. Collins, and Joseph E. Gagnon. 2019a. Priorities for Review of the ECB's Monetary Policy Strategy. Study for the Committee on Economic and Monetary Affairs, Policy Department for Economic, Scientific and Quality of Life Policies, European Parliament, December. Available at https://www.piie.com/commentary/speeches-papers/priorities-review-ecbs-monetary-policy-strategy.

Cohen-Setton, Jérémie, Egor Gornostay, and Colombe Ladrei. 2019b. Aggregate Effects of Budget Stimulus: Evidence from the Large Fiscal Expansions Database, No. WP19-12, Working Paper Series, Peterson Institute for International Economics. Available at https://www.piie.com/publications/working-papers/aggregate-effects-budget-stimulus-evidence-large-fiscal-expansions.

De Grauwe, Paul. 2007. *Economics of Monetary Union*. 7th edn. Oxford: Oxford University Press.

De Long, Bradford. 1998. Fiscal Policy in the Shadow of the Great Depression. In *The Defining Moment: The Great Depression and the American Economy in the Twentieth Century*, ed. Michael D. Bordo, Claudia Goldin, and Eugene N. White. National Bureau of Economic Research Project Report. Chicago, IL and London: University of Chicago Press. Available at https://www.nber.org/chapters/c6888.pdf.

Draghi, Mario. 2018. Risk-reducing and Risk-sharing in Our Monetary Union. Speech at the European University Institute, Florence. May 11. Available at https://www.ecb.europa.eu/press/key/date/2018/html/ecb.sp180511.en.html#7.

Dullien, Sebastian. 2019. Risk-sharing by Financial Markets in Federal Systems: A Critique of Existing Empirical Assessments. *Review of Keynesian Economics*, Edward Elgar Publishing, 7(3), July, 361–8.

Eichenbaum, Martin. 1997. Some Thoughts on Practical Stabilization Policy. *American Economic Review*, 87(2), 236–39. Available at https://www.jstor.org/stable/2950923?seq=1.

Furceri, Davide, and Aleksandra Zdzienicka. 2015. The Euro Area Crisis: Need for a Supranational Fiscal Risk Sharing Mechanism? *Open Economies Review*, 26, 683–710. Available at https://link.springer.com/article/10.1007/s11079-015-9347-y#citeas.

Heijdra, Michel, Tjalle Aarden, Jesper Hanson, and Toep van Dijk. 2018. A More Stable EMU Does Not Require a Central Fiscal Capacity. VoxEU, November 30. Available at https://voxeu.org/article/more-stable-emu-does-not-require-central-fiscal-capacity.

International Monetary Fund. 2010. Will It Hurt? Macroeconomic Effects of Fiscal Consolidation. Washington, DC: International Monetary Fund. Available at https://www.imf.org/external/pubs/ft/weo/2010/02/.

International Monetary Fund. 2013. Reassessing the Role and Modalities of Fiscal Policy in Advanced Economies. IMF Policy Paper. Washington, DC: International Monetary Fund. Available at https://www.imf.org/en/Publications/Policy-Papers/Issues/2016/12/31/Reassessing-the-Role-and-Modalities-of-Fiscal-Policy-in-Advanced-Economies-PP4801.

International Monetary Fund. 2020. Countering Future Recessions in Advanced Economies: Cyclical Policies in an Era of Low Rates and High Debt. Washington, DC: International Monetary Fund. Available at https://www.imf.org/en/Publications/WEO/Issues/2020/04/14/weo-april-2020.

Nikolov, Plamen. 2016. Cross-border Risk Sharing after Asymmetric Shocks: Evidence from the Euro Area and the United States. Quarterly Report on the Euro Area (QREA), Directorate General Economic and Financial Affairs (DG ECFIN), European Commission, vol. 15(2), July, pp. 7–18. Available at https://ec.europa.eu/info/sites/info/files/ip030_en_1.pdf.

Rachel, Łukasz, and Lawrence H. Summers. 2019. On Secular Stagnation in the Industrialized World. NBER Working Papers 26198, National Bureau of Economic Research. Available at nber.org/papers/w26198.

Ramey, Valerie A. 2019. Ten Years after the Financial Crisis: What Have We Learned from the Renaissance in Fiscal Research? *Journal of Economic Perspectives*, 33 (2): 89–114.

Ramey, Valerie A. 2020. The Macroeconomic Consequences of Infrastructure Investment, NBER Chapters. In *Economics of Infrastructure Investment*.

National Bureau of Economic Research. Available at https://www.nber.org/chapters/c14366.

Reifschneider, David. 2016. Gauging the Ability of the FOMC to Respond to Future Recessions, Finance and Economics Discussion Series 2016-068. Washington, DC: Board of Governors of the Federal Reserve System. Available at https://www.federalreserve.gov/econresdata/feds/2016/files/2016068pap.pdf.

Romer, Christina D., and David H. Romer. 2019. Fiscal Space and the Aftermath of Financial Crises: How It Matters and Why. Brookings Papers on Economic Activity, Spring. Available at https://www.brookings.edu/wp-content/uploads/2019/03/Fiscal-Space-and-the-Aftermath-of-Financial-Crises.pdf.

11. The government as lender of last resort and temporary owner

Aneta Hryckiewicz

11.1 INTRODUCTION

Financial crises can cause substantial destruction in financial systems if they are not timeously and correctly managed. Homar and van Wijnbergen (2017) document that early and timely government intervention is extremely important for limiting both the contagion effects of a crisis and its costs. Although recent regulations have placed several restrictions on future government actions by requiring bank stakeholders to cover losses (European Parliament and Council, 2014), it cannot be ruled out that in the case of an extreme systemic crisis, the government will have to intervene (see Chapter 12). Moreover, some banking sector problems can be managed with the resolution mechanisms available, while others will require government help. For example, Ben Bernanke, chairman of the Federal Reserve at the time, stated that the collapse of Bear Stearns in mid-March 2008 was so severe that creditors lost confidence they could recoup their loans by selling the collateral, forcing the government to intervene (Bernanke, 2008). Thus, though the recent regulatory trend toward a "bail-in" policy is an important step in reducing the risk of moral hazard (see Chapter 13), governments cannot rule out bailouts during the next systemic crisis.

Government interventions, and especially nationalizations, cause a great deal of controversy among society, policymakers, and shareholders. On the one hand, such actions incur strong and widespread opposition. In general, taxpayers do not agree with using public money to rescue bankers who have behaved irresponsibly. In addition, they are concerned that the government will overpay for rescued banks' equity, and waste the public's money (Congressional Oversight Panel, 2009). Shareholders are also skeptical about the bailout process, fearing that government will effectively jeopardize the equity interests of incumbent shareholders in these banks and realize the banks' political agendas. All of these might lead to the destruction of shareholders' economic value. On the other hand, some academic studies stress the government's beneficial role in restoring banking sector stability and stimulating economic activity (Berger and Roman, 2015; Berger et al., 2019).

All these concerns lead to the question of what role governments should play in rescuing distressed banking sectors. More specifically, should governments bail out distressed institutions, and if so, how should this rescue occur? Should governments take stakes in the institutions, and if so, should they take a minority or majority position? Alternatively, regulators could achieve banking stability avoiding government ownership by just financially recapitalizing the distressed banking sector.

The answers to these questions are not clear. The mainstream view suggests governments abuse their role as shareholder and thus jeopardize the institution's shareholder value. For example, an important stream of literature shows that state-owned bank lending is partially driven by political motives, which include enhancing re-election chances or avoiding political unrest. Such results are found by Sapienza (2004) for a sample of Italian banks, Dinç (2005) for emerging countries, Khwaja and Mian (2005) for Pakistani banks, and Jackowicz et al. (2013) for Eastern European economies. Political motives might also be dictated by social purposes or by providing subsidized lending or directing credit to special industries identified by the government. For example, during the global financial crisis (GFC), the US President and Congress pressed government-owned banks, including Bank of America and Citigroup, to increase lending to small businesses, restrain actions against struggling homeowners, and maintain specific mortgage loan modification programs (Kahan and Rock, 2011; Yang, 2019). Moreover, government majority stakeholding at banks might lead to a "free rider" problem, as the government is both an owner of the distressed institution and a market regulator (Barnes, 2010). As a result, government-owned banks tend to exhibit a larger accumulated portfolio of non-performing loans (NPLs), lower profitability, and lower capital ratios, depressing economic growth (Peek and Rosengren, 2005; Caballero et al., 2008). For these reasons government ownership as a result of rescue actions is not desirable.

There is also a view that, under certain conditions, the government might also play a beneficial role as a "lender of last resort" and owner of troubled institutions. First, government capital injections are the most efficient way to reduce the social costs of bank bankruptcies, stimulate bank lending activities, and as a result, spur economic growth (Wilson and Wu, 2012; Giannetti and Simonov, 2013; Philippon and Schnabl, 2013; Berger and Roman, 2015; Homar, 2016). An institutional constraint on exercising government ownership (like, for example, in the form of voting right restrictions) might address many problems related to the government's power as a major stakeholder. At the same time, such ownership might still give a government control over the injected taxpayer money, act as a tool to prevent mismanagement by business directors, or facilitate the necessary restructuring changes (Landier and Ueda, 2009; Kahan and Rock, 2011). Furthermore, it will be more difficult to induce governmental political decisions, as its role is more restricted to corporate governance than active management. Consequently, this literature stresses that government intervention might be inevitable to restore banking sector stability, and above all, stimulate bank lending activities.

The inconsistency in the existing literature raises the question of whether the government should actively intervene during a financial crisis by rescuing distressed banks, and if so, what role should it play. We raise these questions in this chapter by analysing the existing empirical literature and different countries' experiences, as well as by conducting our own empirical investigation into the government's role during a financial crisis. To this end, we use a sample of 215 distressed banks that were rescued by governments in 39 systemic banking crises in both developed and developing countries between 1992 and 2017. We consider three scenarios. The first and second scenarios assume that the government actively helps distressed institutions by taking ownership, either minority (i.e., partial nationalization) or majority (i.e., full nationalization). However, the third scenario assumes the government injects money into the banking sector without taking any stake in the distressed institutions (e.g., by acting as a creditor). Using the Abadie (2005) semi-parametric DID approach, we compare the lending activity of intervened banks with: (a) 708 non-intervened banks as well as (b) the lending activities of the same banks in periods before the intervention. The analysis considers six years before and six years after the intervention.

Our results are interesting. They document that the government role might be beneficial in restoring banking sector activity during a systemic banking crisis by stimulating lending to the economy. Our regression results suggest that intervened banks with government ownership grant more credit in the six-year period after the government intervention than do non-intervened banks. Importantly, we also see that these banks do not contract their offerings of credit, as compared to the period before the crisis. However, our regression results indicate that this effect is stronger when government's participation is restricted. We claim that government can play an important role in simulating banks to lend by facilitating the necessary changes, while at the same time influencing their behavior with regard to lending. Partial nationalization aimed at restricting government voting rights seems to be the most appropriate role for government to achieve such tasks, as it eliminates the possibility that government will exercise its political influence. However, full nationalization might increase such a risk. Thus, controlling for other factors, such as banks' NPLs, profitability, or capital ratios, we notice that the effect of "full nationalization" on bank lending is barely statistically significant.

Interestingly, we can, however, find no positive result for a government acting as a creditor to a distressed bank. This result seems to suggest that pure cash injections without stimulating role of government, in an environment of high uncertainty with regard to future losses, might incentivize banks to store their capital instead of granting it for future loans (Brei et al., 2020). Therefore, this result might indeed prove that the government as a shareholder may play a beneficial role in inducing improvements in distressed banks, and consequently support lending activity.

Our empirical findings have important policy implications. We claim that the recent regulatory shift from bailout to bail-in might pose a significant risk to the recovery path. Though recent studies document that bail-ins will help reduce the fiscal cost of rescuing banking sectors without creating any contagion effects (Klimek et al., 2015; Schäfer et al., 2016), we argue that economic recovery might take longer. Moreover, we also provide guidance on how governments should intervene in distressed banking sectors when bank bailouts occur inevitably. Our results seem to be especially important nowadays, when the banking sectors might cope with significant distress related to the COVID-19 pandemic.

11.2   RATIONALE FOR AND DIFFERENT FORMS OF INTERVENTION DURING FINANCIAL CRISES

11.2.1   Government Role in Financial Crises

In the initial stage of a crisis, when there is a loss of confidence in the financial system with great uncertainty prevailing, the government's role generally refers to ensuring the repayment of deposits. During this time, governments generally extend the limits for deposit protection (sometimes even lifting any limit) and may extend protection to corporate deposits. In addition, governments may decide to offer non-deposit guarantees to third parties on some or all liabilities. Finally, the government might also guarantee to the bank (in whole or in part) the value of certain bank (often doubtful) assets. More specifically, the government may promise to pay the beneficiary bank an amount equivalent to future losses on certain assets owned by the bank and identified by the guarantee (Laprévote and Coupé,

2017, p. 137). The role of government guarantees is important for avoiding potential bank runs in the banking system and to restore confidence in it. The latter is especially extremely important for the recovery of the inter-bank market and, consequently, of bank liquidity; it can protect banks against more severe solvency problems. This government role, however, is more passive than active, as it is generally limited to the announcement of guarantees. Importantly, fiscal costs do not occur unless the guarantees become callable.

When the banking sector is confronted with capital problems more than liquidity problems, governments should become more active, either stepping into the troubled institutions as shareholders or debtholders, or actively playing a part in the restructuring process of such banks.

One of the most used instruments for rescuing distressed institutions is bank recapitalization by governments. Recapitalizations can take the form of subscriptions by the government of various capital instruments issued by the bank, such as core equity (voting or not), alternative Tier1 (such as hybrid securities like preference shares, contingent convertible bonds, or non-cumulative preference shares) or Tier2 instruments, such as cumulative preference shares or deeply subordinated debt instruments (Laprévote and Coupé, 2017, p. 44).

Certainly, recapitalizations aim to restore bank capital positions, fulfill solvency criteria, and consequently rebuild confidence in the banks. This, in turn, might also help them raise private capital in the later stages of a crisis. In the end, the banking sector should return to its credit activity and long-term sustainability. Different forms of recapitalization may serve different purposes, as well as generate distinct results for the banking sector. Injecting equity with voting rights gives the government the potential to act as a shareholder with a voice.[1] In turn, the bank receives cash, the main purpose of which is to restore its solvency ratios and fulfill regulatory requirements. In addition, this form of recapitalization does not place any financial burden on a weak bank as the government primarily expects to benefit from its stake's increase in value. However, it is important to note that giving the government a voice has both pros and cons. The latter are mainly related to using bank resources for political purposes—the problem explored more deeply in the next section. It may also make it more difficult for a bank to raise additional capital from the private sector, as potential private shareholders might fear conflicts of interest with the public sector (Jensen and Meckling, 1976).

Governments may also inject funds using preferred equity or hybrid instruments. These instruments allow banks to strengthen their capital, but generally do not give the government the right to influence managerial decisions, except in specific cases. For example, during the GFC, the US

Treasury invested in preferred stock with warrants, which, although involving no voting power, gave the Treasury the chance to exercise its voice in specific situations.

However, a government subscription of convertible contingent bonds makes it possible for a government to convert the bonds into ordinary shares if certain trigger events occur (e.g., if a coupon payment is missed or the bank falls below a certain CET1 ratio) (Laprévote and Coupé, 2017, p. 144). Importantly, these securities, as compared to common equity, allow the government to profit from higher dividends and/or coupons as well as increases in equity value, thereby curbing the fiscal cost of those interventions. In the GFC, banks provided the US Treasury with holdings of non-voting preferred stock, paying quarterly dividends at an annual yield of 5 percent for the first five years and 9 percent thereafter and ten-year life warrants for common stock, giving taxpayers the opportunity to benefit from the banks' future growth.[2]

Governments can also inject cash into distressed banks in the form of subordinated debt. This kind of involvement may restrict government's role. Hoelscher and Quintyn (2003) argue that Tier2 recapitalization, especially through subordinated debt, is desirable when the government wishes to avoid ownership stakes in banks. However, it is important to notice that cash injections without appropriate control might create opportunities for managers to increase their own private benefits (Landier and Ueda, 2009).

Moreover, the experiences of many countries have shown that a government role is inevitable in making restructuring changes in the banking sector. In the initial phase of a crisis, that role might already be crucial to limit the spread of the crisis. For example, the government can actively clean up bank assets and help the institution find a buyer. In such a government-assisted merger, government support is often associated with offering financial help to the acquirer through either tax incentives or guarantees on potential losses of the acquired institution. The benefit of such a solution is avoiding the potential failure of weaker institutions and the associated negative consequences for the banking sector. Sheng (1996) claims that government-assisted M&As are particularly popular when the government has limited funds for handling closure of insolvent institutions, and the financial industry as a whole has sufficient resources to absorb the failing bank. In addition, Hryckiewicz et al. (2020) document that mergers should be used at the early stage of the crisis when the banking sector is not deeply impaired by the NPLs problem. Otherwise, this resolution method might severely depress the acquirer's financial position.

Governments may also play an important role in clearing banks' NPLs. They can help banks remove distressed assets, and consequently clean up their balance sheet. In practice, government separates the distressed assets from the healthy (often called the "good bank") and transfers them into a Special Purpose Vehicle (SPV) (sometimes called asset management companies or AMCs), a fund, or an agency (often called the "bad bank"). The role of the "bad bank" is to maximize recovery of the assets through active restructuring. Such asset relief programs offer several advantages for banks. First, they allow removal of uncertainty with regard to bank asset valuation and thus improve bank asset quality. Moreover, separating the bad assets provides transparency regarding a bank's core performance. Consequently, such actions can restore confidence in the banking sector and lower the cost of bank financing (Aït-Sahalia et al., 2012). Furthermore, they improve bank solvency and profitability, as buyers inject cash into the bank by purchasing the impaired assets (Hryckiewicz et al., 2020). Finally, as banks are not required to establish higher reserves for future losses, they might be willing to lend more to the real sector. Moreover, separating bad assets from a "good bank" allows managers to focus on regular bank operations, without spending their time managing bad assets. Last but not least, government officials may require distressed institutions (especially those participating in a recapitalization program) to conduct appropriate balance sheet restructuring. If the program appears to be voluntary, banks might not be willing to participate in it. This is mainly because under information asymmetry and high uncertainty regarding asset quality, potential buyers of distressed assets might estimate asset market values below their real economic values. Consequently, bank managers might be unwilling to sell them (Tanaka and Hoggarth, 2006). Even more, banks may not want to disclose the true value of their NPLs due to reputational fear (Corbett and Mitchell, 2000). Alternatively, assuming banks want to voluntarily participate in such a program, it might be difficult to find private buyers for these assets. The problem might be even worse if a distressed institution is already state-owned. A German example during the GFC clearly demonstrates this problem. German politicians intended to create privately owned "bad banks" for some public banks; however, they failed due to private investors' fear of sharing AMC ownership with the public sector (Gandrud and Hallerberg, 2014). Thus, government participation in the initial stage might help more efficiently coordinate the whole process. Figure 11.1(a–d) presents the popularity of resolution methods in the 39 different systemic banking crises analysed between 1992 and 2017.

As can be seen, the most common intervention method involved asset relief measures in the form of "bad banks" or "AMCs." Nationalization strategies were primarily used in developing countries, excluding the GFC.

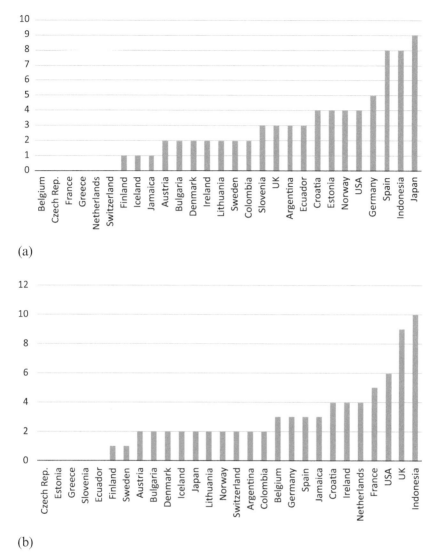

(a)

(b)

Source: Own calculations.

Figure 11.1   Number of banks exposed to different government intervention measures during 39 systemic banking crises between 1992 and 2017: (a) asset relief measures; (b) nationalizations; (c) recapitalizations; (d) government-assisted mergers

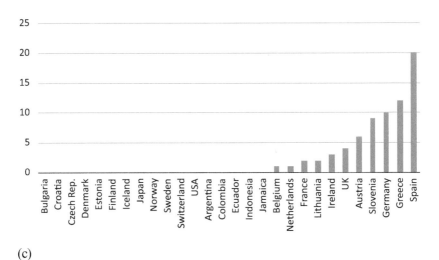

(c)

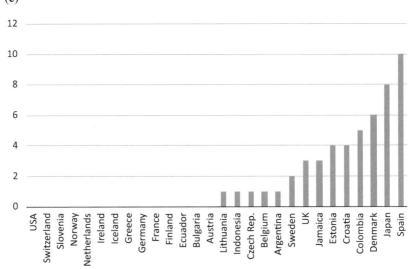

(d)

Figure 11.1   (continued)

However, recapitalizations without government ownership were mainly used in the GFC in a selected number of developed countries. The least frequent form of distressed bank resolution was mergers, which were mainly used in developed countries.

11.2.2 Rationale for Bank Nationalizations

There are several arguments for governments to hold stakes in distressed institutions. When the government takes ownership in troubled institutions, it can restore confidence in the financial sector better than by any other means (Berger et al., 2019). This is especially important in systemic crises where the potential contagion effects not only spill over to other banks but also might negatively affect banks in other countries. Moreover, by acting as a trustworthy counterparty to all current and ongoing transactions, the government is able to restore confidence in the interbank market and decrease the cost of bank financing (Aït-Sahalia et al., 2012). The lack of such confidence has, as shown by the Lehman Brothers example in 2008, been clearly documented as destructive for the whole market and has led to bankruptcies of many institutions. Government ownership can avoid this kind of risk, thus limiting the cost of crises.

Moreover, government holdings may facilitate the restructuring of distressed institutions. Through the mechanism of separating "good" and "bad" banks, the government can quickly make the necessary decisions and take the required measures to achieve the "good bank—bad bank" solution and then sell the good bank. For example, in 1991, the Swedish government went from a majority holding to a 100 percent holding in Nordbanken. It was much easier to conduct the restructuring process by transferring the toxic assets and corresponding collateral from the bank to an independent AMC. However, it was not possible to transfer bad bank assets of private institutions to government AMCs because the owners did not agree on the transfer price (Ingves et al., 2009). A good bank, generally well capitalized by the government and retaining the government's explicit guarantees for future liabilities, should not suffer bank runs. Such a bank can then operate on a stand-alone basis, including raising capital from the private sector. However, given distinct bank manager incentives as well as high market uncertainty, it would be difficult to achieve those goals with private shareholders.

The government may also play an important role in bank corporate governance, which might supplement the deficiencies in existing regulations and decrease the information asymmetry between bank management and regulators. More importantly, by having ownership, a government has the legal right to change bank management and influence executive compensation. For example, Barney Frank, chairman of the House Financial Services Committee, pushed the idea of suing AIG to get bonus money returned, claiming that the government owned an 80 percent stake in the company and invested $170 billion in aid (Liddy, 2009). Moreover, the government as majority shareholder obtained the right to appoint new independent non-executive directors, and limited executive compensation and dividend payouts (Landier and Ueda, 2009).

Government ownership might also induce banks to lend to the real sector instead of storing money as a capital buffer. As governments use taxpayer money, they might have an incentive to prove that this money was used for the right purpose and revitalized the economy. For example, President Obama said he would "hold banks 'fully accountable' for the assistance they receive" and that they "will have to demonstrate how taxpayer dollars result in more lending for the American taxpayers" (Parsons and Nicholas, 2009). Other committee members "sought promises from the bank executives that they would use the government funds they received to make loans and stimulate the economy, rather than hold funds to bolster their balance sheet" (Kerber, 2009).

It is clear that nationalization, in certain cases, might lead to some problems for the banking sector. First, governments might have different motivations that are not necessarily financial, to take a stake in banks. These include subsidies to politically connected firms or industries, funding fiscal deficits, or creating national conglomerates to counteract the potential competition from private banks. Such institutions might then be packed with political appointees "who will serve as civil servants, becoming political tools in the government's hands" (Herring, 2009). Such a board structure often leads to weak bank performance, high NPLs, and then insolvency. For example, in Indonesia during the 1997 crisis, most banks, despite government recapitalizations, became insolvent. Many of them had to be steadily recapitalized: the state-owned Bank BNI "had been recapitalized repeatedly for more than 20 years" (Enoch et al., 2001).

Moreover, nationalization might make the banking sector more vulnerable to government problems. For example, economic climate deterioration in Argentina in 2001 led to bank runs, devastating the banking sector, although only 20 percent of the whole banking sector belonged to the government. Recently, a similar situation has occurred in the Euro sovereign crisis (see Chapter 12). Greece is a good example of government's bad debt leading to bank runs (Yeyati et al., 2011).

Moreover, it has been widely shown that nationalizations spread the moral hazard problem throughout the system. An extensive literature supports the position that generous safety-net policies and deposit insurance lead to banks engaging in more risky behavior due to unlimited profits with downside protection (Demirgüç-Kunt and Kane, 2002; Demirgüç-Kunt et al., 2008).

Last but not least, nationalizations face major opposition by some political parties and society since they use taxpayer money. Although voters want financial stability, most of them are also taxpayers and hesitate to support bailouts (Keefer, 2007; Rosas, 2009), fearing that increased spending might imperil the sustainability of public finances, which could then lead to tax hikes. Other voters fear that costly bailouts might crowd out government spending on welfare programs. However, in the US, the main critics have targeted that in rescuing "too big to fail" banks, the government may overpay their equity and thus waste taxpayer money (Congressional Oversight Panel, 2009).

11.2.3   Nationalization—Different Experiences

Historically, governments have played an important role in managing banks, especially in emerging countries. However, the GFC has changed this landscape resulting in government ownership in many banking sectors of developed countries.

Nationalization before the 2008 global financial crisis
To assess the performance of nationalizations, it is crucial to identify whether the government was a temporary or permanent investor in these banks. With regard to the latter, the experiences of most countries are rather negative. Starting with Europe, where socialist governments decided to nationalize banks following World War II, nationalizations led to the dramatic failure of these banks. For many years after World War II, the emerging countries of India, China, Africa, and Latin America had banking sectors that were predominantly state-owned. These countries' experiences have also documented the negative performance of banks with the government as a long-term investor. For example, in India, where the government owned 92 percent of the banking sector, the government used banks to serve farmers and other poor groups though direct lending. Ministers organized loan *melas* (or fairs) at which money was distributed without the necessary security or expectations of repayment. Similarly, in Latin America, concerns on long-term and agricultural credit led to establish state-owned agriculture and development banks. All these experiences failed, resulting in high bank NPLs and the need to rescue banking sectors. In China, bank NPL ratios were above 40 percent by the end of 2003. Argentina's state-owned banks reported NPLs of around 50 percent, five times more than at large private banks. In India, the World Bank has been asked for a loan of $4.2 billion to support state-owned banks. Government recapitalizations of their banks did not succeed. Most of these banks had to be privatized.

In turn, there are a few positive results where the government stepped in to rescue banks as a temporary owner. A good example is Sweden, whose government decided to nationalize some of the country's banks during its crisis in the early 1990s. It decided to invest in non-voting preferred shares, with the condition that if these were not redeemed within a certain number of years, they would be converted to normal shares with strong voting rights and a high capital dilution factor. In this way, the government created a strong incentive for banks to quickly restore their activity and thus minimize this option (Ingves et al., 2009). The actions of a governmental organization, the Deposit Guarantee Fund (DGF), during the Spanish crisis in the 1970s produced another positive result. The DGF took control of failing banks, assuming temporary ownership and management. It was also responsible for restructuring troubled banks, recovering the toxic assets, and finally, finding acquirers for the banks. Interestingly, regulations required that the banks be restructured and ready for sale in one year. In reality, it took 14 months for the DGF to purchase the banks, recapitalize them, clean their assets, and sell them off (Ingves et al., 2009). The temporary ownership of the US Credit Illinois bank also appears as a success story. By providing guarantees and restructuring bad debt, the government restored confidence in the banking sector and stopped the bank run. A few years later, the government sold its stake and Bank of America purchased the bank. Similarly, Mexico managed a successful temporary nationalization of its banking system after the peso crisis in the 1990s. Although Japan does not provide a success story, the disappointment relates to the delayed government reaction and insufficient recapitalizations rather than the political motives of bank management (Caballero et al., 2008; Ingves et al., 2009).

US versus European experience with nationalization
Until the GFC, government ownership of banks was mostly associated with significant control rights and voting power. That was especially true in the mid-1990s in developing countries such as Latin America, Eastern Europe, China, and other Asian countries. By 2000, in developed countries, minority government ownership ranged instead from 0 percent in Denmark, Austria, and Norway to 11 percent in Italy, 14 percent in Finland, and 15 percent in Switzerland (Cull et al., 2017). The only exception was the German government controlling 42 percent of banking assets. The GFC changed this landscape. In many developed countries, especially in Europe, governments began to control major banks, taking over a significant part of the banking sector. While initially, most European governments were minority owners, they could not escape turning majority shareholders when the crisis worsened.

Figure 11.2 shows the cumulative direct public interventions into banks from 2007 to 2017, expressed as a percent of 2017 GDP.

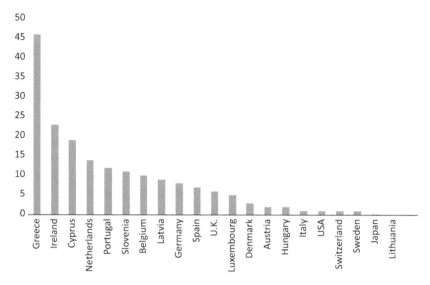

Source: National authorities; European Commission.

Figure 11.2   Cumulative direct interventions by country (2007–17; in percent of 2017 GDP)

It can easily be seen that the recapitalization of European banks cost governments more than it did in the US. It is also important to notice that the scale of recapitalization was also very different across European countries. The largest amounts were spent in Greece, Ireland, Cyprus, and the Netherlands, exceeding well above 10 percent of these countries' GDP. The smallest were in Lithuania and the Nordic countries. Interestingly, there were also significant variations in these countries in the government's role in rescuing the distressed banking sector.

Due to major taxpayer opposition, the US Treasury tried to assure that its role would be limited to only recapitalizing banks via minority stakes at distressed banks. As such, the Treasury declared that it would act as a passive shareholder and try to minimize its interventions in banks' corporate decisions. Moreover, it also promised to only keep the equities on a short-term basis (Yang, 2019).

The US Treasury invested mostly either in preferred stock with warrants, which did not involve voting power except in certain specified situations, or retained the voting rights with significant restrictions. For instance, it could not interfere in day-to-day management decisions and should dispose of its investment as soon as practicable. In addition, it could exercise its voting rights as a common shareholder only in respect of core shareholder matters, such as board membership, amendments to corporate charters or bylaws, mergers, liquidations, substantial asset sales, and significant common stock issuances (Yang, 2019). The US Treasury followed three models during the crisis. The first model was pursued with the Bank of America, where the Treasury held a low non-voting position via preferred stock with warrants. Even with further capital injections, the Treasury held only 0.04 percent of Bank of America's total outstanding shares and held no voting rights (Barnes, 2010). If the Treasury had exercised the warrants, it would still have held only 5.2 percent of Bank of America's shares. In the second model, the Treasury assumed a minority position through major ownership of shares. This model was followed with Citigroup, where the Treasury held 34 percent of Citigroup's outstanding common stock. The Treasury, however, reduced its voting power to the same proportions as other common stockholders, except regarding major corporate matters. AIG was the only institution where the government had majority ownership and could exercise its voting rights. However, it decided to manage its shares via a special trust vehicle. Instead of holding the shares directly, it established the AIG Credit Facility Trust to hold the AIG shares for the sole benefit of the Federal Reserve Bank of New York (FRBNY).[3] This design was intended to prevent potential conflicts between the government's roles as both a regulator and an investor. Although the government could not influence the voting rights vested in the stocks, it decided to use its rights to appoint two directors to AIG's board. The Trust then left the daily management of AIG to its management without any interference from the Treasury (Kahan and Rock, 2011).

European countries have only partially followed an approach similar to that in the US. In the beginning, following the US model, governments aimed at restricting their bank ownership; however, the need for large-scale recapitalizations and, often, a lack of interest from the private sector in supporting the European banks led to majority participation in many European banks.

As a result of this bailout framework, many countries ended up with nationalized banks, where governments had the controlling stake and significant voting power. For example, in Ireland, in the beginning, the government injected capital into the Allied Irish Bank through ordinary non-voting shares, which, after conversion into ordinary stock and additional injections, reached 92.8 percent government ownership. However, the Anglo Irish Bank was nationalized on January 15, 2009 and recapitalized later in 2009 with €4 billion in ordinary stock (Igan et al., 2019). In Cyprus, the government recapitalized the Cyprus Popular Bank and the Cooperative Central Bank by taking ordinary stakes of 84 percent and 99 percent, respectively. However, in the UK, the Bank of England and Financial Services Authority decided to inject £500 billion ($750 billion) in the country's eight largest banks and building societies. In 2008, the government invested £107.6 billion to acquire a controlling equity stake (84 percent of shares but only 68 percent of voting rights) in the Royal Bank of Scotland (RBS) and a 43 percent stake in Lloyds Banking Group (Lloyds). In 2010, it acquired all of Northern Rock and Bradford & Bingley (NAO Report, 2015). However, Germany nationalized its Hypo Real Estate Holding (HRE) through SoFFin (Sonderfonds Finanzmarktstabilisierung, ang. *Special Financial Market Stabilization Fund*),[4] which owned 90 percent in 2009 via capital injections.

Government divestment is another factor that distinguishes European bailouts from those in the US. The severity of the European crisis, as well as the later sovereign crisis, slowed the recovery of the European banking sector. As a result, government stakes have been almost entirely unwound by the fourth or fifth year (Igan et al., 2019). In turn, in the US, nearly all funds for banks' recapitalization provided through TARP were repaid as early as 2013.

11.3   SAMPLE AND METHODOLOGY

11.3.1   Sample

In this study, we examine different forms of government participation when rescuing distressed banks. To this end, we select a sample of institutions subject to government interventions during the systemic banking crises. The information about systemic events comes from Laeven and Valencia's (2018) database. However, the information of intervened banks comes from Hryckiewicz's (2014) sample base, which has been extended to consider banks rescued during the global crises from 2008 to 2017. Consequently, we cover government interventions that occurred during systemic events between 1992 and 2017 in both developing and developed countries. The structure of the sample has been shown in Figure 11.1(a–d). The names of the rescued institutions were manually collected from central bank reports and European Commission websites.

As discussed, there are many ways for governments to support troubled institutions. However, we consider only direct interventions of distressed banks. We are interested in the effect of different forms of government ownership on the distressed banks. To this extent, we consider the following state participation: government ownership (i.e., recapitalizations), full nationalization, and partial nationalization on bank lending activities. We argue that the government's role might be inevitable in restructuring distressed banks and incentivizing them to restore lending activities (Landier and Ueda, 2009; Kahan and Rock, 2011). In turn, pure recapitalizations might not lead to this effect, as banks might want to maintain higher capital buffers (Brei et al., 2020). Moreover, bank mangers might not have incentives to make restructuring changes for reputational reasons as well as a lack of financial incentives (Corbett and Mitchell, 2000; Tanaka and Hoggarth, 2006).

Our main interest is whether government ownership can stimulate lending activities at distressed banks. To this end, we define recapitalizations as government capital injections through debt and hybrid instruments (not converted into equities); full nationalization occurs when the government holds a controlling stake in a bank, while in partial nationalization, a government holds a minority stake (generally up to 30–40 percent).[5] However, lending activity, as our main dependent variable, is defined as a change in lending between year *t* and *t-1*, as compared to the previous year (*t-1*), expressed as a percentage.

As lending activity has been shown to respond to bank capital, liquidity, bank size, and profitability expressed as return on equity (ROE) (Berger and Roman, 2015), we use these variables in our regressions to control for differences across banks. The information on bank financials, as our control variables, were obtained from the S&P Global Market Intelligence database, which includes the bank financial information required for our analysis. We also supplement the data with a secondary bank-level source, the Bureau van Dijk/BankFocus database, which is used if financial information is missing from the primary source. However, the country-level data included in our regression, such as inflation and GDP growth, are primarily sourced from the World Bank and International Monetary Fund (IMF).

11.3.2   Methodology

In our research, we want to analyse whether and which form of government support stimulates bank activities in distressed banking sectors. More specifically, we are interested in how different government actions affect bank lending. To this end, we use the Abadie difference-in-differences (Abadie, 2005) estimation, which allows us to evaluate the casual effect of a treatment on a variable of interest *y* at some point *t*. We consider two groups of banks, those that were subject to interventions and those that did not receive government support. Consequently, we expect two potential outcomes, $y_{1,t}$ and $y_{0,t}$, where $y_{1,t}$ is the value of *y* if a bank received the treatment by time *t*, $y_{0,t}$ is the value of *y* for those banks that did not receive the treatment at time t, d is the indicator of whether or not a participant is treated by time t. At time $t = 0$—the baseline—no one is treated. At time $t \neq 0$, d equals 1 if the banks receive the treatment and 0 otherwise. We want to estimate the average treatment effect of the treatment on treated (ATT):

$$ATT = E(y_{1,t} - y_{0,t} | d = 1) \qquad (11.1)$$

The estimator is a weighted average of the difference in the trend, Δy_t, across treatment groups. It reweights the trend for untreated participants based on the propensity score $\pi(x_b)$. Abadie (2005) suggests approximating the propensity score $\pi(x_b)$ semi-parametrically using a polynomial series of the predictors of order k.[6]

In our analysis, we strive to estimate the treatment effect with respect to three groups: (1) we compare the treatment group, that is, banks that received government intervention, to the non-intervened peers, as well as to the intervened banks from the period prior to interventions; (2) we compare the intervened banks to their non-intervened peers; (3) we compare the intervened banks to their lending activity from the period before the intervention occurred; the treatment effect is then based on a comparison to the same group of banks. However, for periods before the intervention we assign the value 0 to these banks. We argue that these three approaches allow us to enrich our analysis by comparing the lending activity of intervened banks from different perspectives.

11.4   EMPIRICAL RESULTS

We next present the preliminary results of the *t-tests* for differences between means for the intervened group of banks and non-intervened control group of banks. We group the results depending on the form of government intervention. This analysis enables us to establish the differences between two groups of banks, which further allows us to assess how successful were the government interventions in stimulating banks' lending activity. Table 11.1 presents the results for different intervention measures.

The data show that there are statistically significant differences between the intervened and non-intervened banks. These differences appear for almost all financial variables. More importantly, the results suggest that the difference in financial performance between two groups of banks mainly depends on the intervention measure. We can also apply the same conclusion to the lending activity. Interestingly, the data suggest

Table 11.1 Summary statistics

Variables	Mean for intervened banks	No. of banks	Mean for intervened banks	No. of banks	Mean difference	t-stat.
Full Nationalization						
Capital ratio	16.384	6376	10.902	514	5.482	8.804***
Loan to total asset	59.239	6091	52.558	468	6.682	8.807***
Loan growth	2.031	5726	32.481	416	−30.450	−3.516***
Profitability (ROA)	5.402	7475	4.356	631	1.046	0.442
Size (ln)	8.085	7867	10.580	684	−2.495	−24.357***
Liquidity	35.590	6517	41.398	589	−5.808	−5.543***
Partial nationalization						
Capital ratio	16.356	6533	8.997	357	7.360	9.986***
Loan to total asset	58.894	6262	55.999	297	2.894	3.065***
Loan growth	2.022	5877	50.034	265	−48.012	−4.486***
Profitability (ROA)	5.368	7635	4.549	471	0.8191	0.302
Size (ln)	8.197	8047	9.680	504	−1.482	−12.255***
Liquidity	122.724	6066	96.290	266	26.433	2.895***
Recapitalization						
Capital ratio	16.105	6611	12.88771	279	3.218	3.859***
Loan to total asset	58.522	6024	61.467	535	−2.944	−4.107***
Loan growth	3.5553	5663	10.459	479	−6.904	−0.850
Profitability (ROA)	7.204	7556	−20.550	550	27.754	11.092***
Size (ln)	8.121	7928	10.367	623	−2.246	−20.825***
Liquidity	127.006	5871	52.930	461	74.076	10.5941***

Note: The results have been estimated based on the mean difference between the intervened and non-intervened banks over six-year period before and after government interventions. ***, **, * denote statistical significance at 1%, 5%, and 10%, respectively.

Table 11.2   The effect of different form of government interventions on lending activity using total sample

VARIABLES	PANEL A			PANEL B			PANEL C		
	(1) Loan growth NAT	(2) Loan growth PAR-NAT	(3) Loan growth RECAP	(4) Loan growth NAT	(5) Loan growth PAR-NAT	(6) Loan growth RECAP	(7) Loan growth NAT	(8) Loan growth PAR-NAT	(9) Loan growth RECAP
Loan reserves	-1.845	-1.496	-0.247	4.005*	-2.502*	-0.333	-1.255	6.627*	3.561
	(1.451)	(1.088)	(0.929)	(2.305)	(1.335)	(1.340)	(1.555)	(3.488)	(4.839)
Loan to asset	-0.241***	-0.340**	0.131	-0.239**	-0.472***	0.0222	-0.192	-0.220	0.257
	(0.0902)	(0.170)	(0.121)	(0.121)	(0.177)	(0.121)	(0.128)	(0.181)	(0.167)
ROE	0.0294***	0.0339***	0.0536***	0.00592	0.0247**	0.0626**	-0.00128	-0.0826	0.0616***
	(0.0114)	(0.00635)	(0.0193)	(0.0280)	(0.0113)	(0.0249)	(0.0583)	(0.107)	(0.0137)
Size (ln)	-0.110	-0.324	0.0253	-0.0789	0.194	1.745**	-0.234	0.122	2.262*
	(0.565)	(0.639)	(0.557)	(0.599)	(0.541)	(0.823)	(0.477)	(1.649)	(1.223)
Liquidity	-0.0793	-0.217*	0.118	-0.0893	-0.251*	0.0173	-0.107*	-0.304***	0.158
	(0.0582)	(0.121)	(0.0813)	(0.0713)	(0.136)	(0.0695)	(0.0634)	(0.108)	(0.161)
Capital ratio	0.0293	-0.0373	0.241	-0.140	0.208	0.312	0.303	0.397*	-0.280
	(0.149)	(0.237)	(0.228)	(0.230)	(0.208)	(0.238)	(0.210)	(0.216)	(0.195)
Constant	24.50*	36.88**	-15.25	36.39*	39.43**	-25.34	17.64	-8.905	-56.04*

Table 11.2 (continued)

VARIABLES	PANEL A			PANEL B			PANEL C		
	(1) Loan growth NAT	(2) Loan growth PAR-NAT	(3) Loan growth RECAP	(4) Loan growth NAT	(5) Loan growth PAR-NAT	(6) Loan growth RECAP	(7) Loan growth NAT	(8) Loan growth PAR-NAT	(9) Loan growth RECAP
	(14.48)	(16.82)	(13.17)	(19.54)	(18.42)	(17.73)	(18.81)	(27.85)	(31.93)
Observations	1040	883	881	787	704	654	89	16	60
Country dummy	YES	YES	YES	YES	YES	YES	YES	YES	YES
Time dummy	YES	YES	YES	YES	YES	YES	YES	YES	YES

Note: The regression is estimated on the whole sample and it is based on semi-parametric DID, as indicated by Abadie (2005). The treatment effect is indicated by constant. In Panel A we compare the treatment group, that is, banks that received government intervention, to the non-intervened peers, as well as to the intervened banks from the period prior to interventions; in Panel B we compare the intervened banks to their non-intervened peers; and in Panel C we compare the intervened banks to their lending activity from the period before the intervention occurred. All estimations have been calculated on a six-year period. All estimations include country and time dummies as well as bank and country-control variables not reported here. The reported coefficients relate to the differences between the intervened banks. ***, **, * denote the statistical significance at 1, 5, and 10% significance level, respectively.

232

that nationalized banks (both under full and partial nationalization) report much higher loan growth than their non-intervened peers. These differences also seem to be highly significant in both economic and statistical terms. We cannot, however, confirm this effect for banks, which were recapitalized without government ownership. These banks seem to keep similar lending activity as the non-intervened banks. The result might confirm our previous considerations on the stimulating role of government-owned banks during the crisis (Wilson and Wu, 2012; Philippon and Schnabl, 2013).

Table 11.2 presents the regression results using the Abadie (2005) DID on the whole sample for three different treatment effects. Since the US accounts for almost 30 percent of our observations, we also provide the results with the US excluded from the sample. Table 11.3 presents the regression results.

In both tables, Panel A shows the results of estimating the treatment effect compared to the panel of non-intervened as well as pre-intervened banks. Panel B shows the treatment effect estimations using only non-intervened banks, constituting our baseline regression. Panel C documents the results of comparing the treatment effect to the situation of the same group of banks, comparing their lending activity to that in a period prior to intervention. The latter analysis allows us to estimate whether interventions were able to recover bank activity from the pre-intervention period. The constant indicates the treatment effect.

The empirical results clearly document that government ownership matters; that is, we can see that banks where the government holds stakes lend more than other banks. The result seems to hold for both nationalization as well as partial nationalization, although the effect is stronger for the latter (Panels A and B). This is in line with the broad empirical literature documenting that government ownership may provide several benefits to banks. These benefits start with social role of banks, through the restructuring process to better corporate governance.

Interestingly, we find no such effect in Panel C, where we compare the treatment effect to the pre-crisis period. This might suggest that nationalized banks indeed did not contract their lending behavior. This is in line with studies showing that state-owned banks can play a useful role in stabilizing credit over business cycles and during financial crises (Bertay et al., 2015). More importantly, we see that partial nationalization has a stronger effect on bank lending than full nationalization. This suggests that government ownership may play an important governance role. These banks seem to extend more credit than banks controlled by government, probably due to some government's role in corporate governance structure. The latter have been shown to extend credit, though the effect is barely

Table 11.3 The effect of different form of government interventions on lending activity excluding the US

VARIABLES	PANEL A			PANEL B			PANEL C		
	(1) Loan growth NAT	(2) Loan growth PAR-NAT	(3) Loan growth RECAP	(4) Loan growth NAT	(5) Loan growth PAR-NAT	(6) Loan growth RECAP	(7) Loan growth NAT	(8) Loan growth PAR-NAT	(9) Loan growth RECAP
Loan reserves	0.249	0.0741	1.674	0.0407	-1.891	1.369	-4.789	-1.734	3.561
	(1.181)	(1.719)	(1.834)	(2.176)	(1.988)	(1.773)	(3.047)	(1.172)	(4.839)
Loan to asset	-0.364***	-0.723***	0.248*	-0.400**	-0.783***	0.166	0.0564	-0.164	0.257
	(0.103)	(0.189)	(0.143)	(0.160)	(0.239)	(0.147)	(0.158)	(0.300)	(0.167)
ROE	0.0353***	0.0461***	0.0534**	0.0160	0.0410***	0.0412***	0.0363***	0.823***	0.0616***
	(0.0128)	(0.00712)	(0.0209)	(0.0280)	(0.0119)	(0.0145)	(0.00444)	(0.209)	(0.0137)
Size (ln)	-0.250	-1.150	-0.286	0.125	0.119	2.577***	-0.467	7.837***	2.262*
	(0.667)	(1.200)	(0.681)	(0.699)	(1.104)	(0.803)	(0.803)	(1.920)	(1.223)
Liquidity	-0.147**	-0.443***	0.179**	-0.183**	-0.516**	0.109	-0.0301	-1.981***	0.158
	(0.0635)	(0.157)	(0.0862)	(0.0877)	(0.212)	(0.0825)	(0.0767)	(0.383)	(0.161)
Capital ratio	-0.00267	-0.128	0.311	-0.123	0.0236	0.288	-0.462	2.205***	-0.280
	(0.150)	(0.234)	(0.221)	(0.226)	(0.243)	(0.230)	(0.301)	(0.247)	(0.195)
Constant	29.00**	75.09***	-29.16*	31.74*	71.91***	-53.35***	31.12	-53.35	-56.04*
	(14.01)	(25.16)	(15.52)	(17.81)	(26.13)	(18.77)	(26.82)	(37.69)	(31.93)

Observations	805	563	719	551	377	495	91	9	60
Country dummy	YES	YES	YES	YES	YES	YES	YES	YES	YES
Time dummy	YES	YES	YES	YES	YES	YES	YES	YES	YES

Note: The regression is estimated on the sample excluding the US and it is based on semi-parametric DID, as indicated by Abadie (2005). In Panel A we compare the treatment group, that is, banks that received government intervention, to the non-intervened peers, as well as to the intervened banks from the period prior to interventions; in Panel B we compare the intervened banks to their non-intervened peers; and in Panel C we compare the intervened banks to their lending activity from the period before the intervention occurred. All estimations have been calculated on a six-year period. All estimations include country and time dummies as well as bank and country-control variables not reported here. The reported coefficients relate to the differences between the intervened banks. ***, **, * denote the statistical significance at 1, 5, and 10% significance level, respectively.

statistically significant. Controlling for the effects of bank profitability, capital, and liquidity, inter alia, we see full nationalization has a weaker effect than partial nationalization.

Interestingly, the regression results indicate that the results become even stronger when the US is excluded. This suggests that government interventions might especially stimulate lending activity in the countries heavily relying on banks' funding. Interestingly, the regression result of the impact of recapitalization on bank lending is negative and highly statistically significant for all three panels in Table 11.3. This result clearly shows that capital injections are not sufficient for restoring bank activity; instead, banks might tend to use capital injections to fulfill solvency criteria (Tanaka and Hoggarth, 2006). Moreover, if they are not incentivized, they will keep the funds as an additional capital buffer (Brei et al., 2020). Consequently, the results seem to confirm a positive role of government ownership in spurring lending activity in the economy, assuming government does hold control over the intervened bank.

11.5 CONCLUSIONS

In this chapter, we raise three questions on government's role during the financial crises: Is it inevitable that the government will rescue troubled institutions? What role should it play in bank ownership? What should be its role in bank restructuring? These are the questions that have not been fully answered by the academic literature so far.

By reviewing the existing literature and analysing the experiences with nationalization of different countries, we empirically investigate different scenarios of government participation in rescuing distressed banking sectors. We distinguish three possible government roles: as a controlling shareholder, as a minority owner, and in a passive role purely as a capital provider.

To answer our questions, we select a sample consisting of 215 intervened and 708 non-intervened banks and their lending behavior six years before and six years after the interventions. Using the Abadie (2005) semi-parametric DID approach, we test whether intervened banks granted more loans than non-intervened banks, as well as whether they changed their behavior as compared to before the crisis.

Our results seem to be promising. They document that governments can play a stimulating role during a crisis in the economy by spurring bank lending activity. However, the largest effect is found when government holds a minority stake, that is, have restrictions with respect to exercise of its voting rights. This demonstrates a beneficial role of government as a facilitator of the necessary restrictive changes at distressed banks, without exerting its excessive political power.

NOTES

1. A bank can issue equity without voting rights. However, first, it is more costly than preferred equity, which also does not involve voting rights; second, it might lower the return on taxpayers' money as dividend payments are not required (Landier and Ueda, 2009).
2. The Department of Treasury: http://www.treasury.gov/initiatives/financial-stability/reports/Pages/Monthly-Report-to-Congress.aspx.
3. The Department of Treasury: http://www.treasury.gov/initiatives/financial-stability/TARP-Programs/aig/Pages /status.aspx.
4. The Agency of the Bundesbank was placed under the supervision of the Federal Ministry of Finance, and later, the newly minted Federal Agency for Financial Market Stabilization, whose purpose was to help distressed banks by equipping them with liquidity and strengthening their equity capital.
5. Please note that in our sample partial nationalization mostly occurred through the preference shareholding at distressed banks.
6. For more information about the estimation method, please see Abadie (2005).

REFERENCES

Abadie, A., 2005. Semiparametric difference-in-differences estimators. *Review of Economic Studies*, 72, 1–19.

Aït-Sahalia, Y., Andritzky, J., Jobst, A., Nowak, S., Tamirisa, N., 2012. Market response to policy initiatives during the global financial crisis. *Journal of International Economics*, 87, 162–77.

Barnes, D.M., 2010. Shotgun weddings: director and officer fiduciary duties in government-controlled and partially-nationalized corporations. *Vanderbilt Law Review*, 63, 1419–39.

Berger, A., Roman, R., 2015. Did TARP banks get competitive advantages? *Journal of Financial and Quantitative Analysis*, 50, 1199–236.

Berger, A., Roman, R., Sedunov, J., 2019. Did TARP reduce or increase systemic risk? The effects of government aid on financial system stability. *Journal of Financial Intermediation*, 43, 100810.

Bernanke, B.S., 2008. "Reducing Systemic Risk." Speech delivered at the Federal Reserve Bank of Kansas City's Annual Economic Symposium, Jackson Hole, Wyoming, August 22.

Bertay, A.C., Demirgüç-Kunt, A., Huizinga, H., 2015. Bank ownership and credit over the business cycle: is lending by state banks less procyclical? *Journal of Banking and Finance*, 50, 326–39.

Brei, M., Gambacorta, L., Lucchetta, M., Parigi, B.M., 2020. Bad bank resolutions and bank lending. BIS Working Paper No. 837.

Caballero, R., Hoshi, T., Kashyap, A., 2008. Zombie lending and depressed restructuring in Japan. *American Economic Review*, 98, 1943–77.

Congressional Oversight Panel, 2009. Valuing Treasury's Acquisitions, February Oversight Report.

Corbett, J., Mitchell, J., 2000. Banking crises and bank rescues: the effect of reputation. *Journal of Money, Credit and Banking*, 32, 474–512.

Cull, R., Martinez Pería, M.S., Verrier, J., 2017. Bank ownership: trends and implications. IMF Working Paper No. 17/60.

Demirgüç-Kunt, A., Kane, E.J., 2002. Deposit insurance around the globe: where does it work? *Journal of Economic Perspectives*, 16, 175–95.

Demirgüç-Kunt, A., Kane, E., Laeven, L., 2008. Determinants of deposit-insurance adoption and design. *Journal of Financial Intermediation*, 17, 407–38.

Dinç, S., 2005. Politicians and banks: political influences on government-owned banks in emerging markets. *Journal of Financial Economics*, 77, 453–79.

Enoch, Ch., Baldwin, B., Frécaut, O., Kovanen, A., 2001. Indonesia: anatomy of a banking crisis. Two years of living dangerously 1997–1999. IMF Working Paper No. 01/52.

European Parliament and Council, 2014. Directive 2014/59/EU of the European Parliament and of the Council of 15 May 2014 Establishing a Framework for the Recovery and Resolution of Credit Institutions and Investment Firms and Amending Council Directive 82/891/EEC, and Directives 2001/24/EC, 2002/47/EC, 2004/25/EC, 2005/56/EC, 2007/36/EC, 2011/35/EU, 2012/30/EU and 2013/36/EU, and Regulations (EU) No 1093/2010 and (EU) No 648/2012, of the European Parliament and of the Council, L 173/190. http://eur-lex. europa.eu/legal-content/EN/TXT/PDF/?uri=CELEX:32014L0059&from=EN.

Gandrud, C., Hallerberg, M., 2014. Bad banks in the EU: the impact of Eurostat rules. Bruegel Working Paper No. 2014/15.

Giannetti, M., Simonov, A., 2013. On the real effects of bank bailouts: micro evidence from Japan. *American Economic Journal: Macroeconomics*, 5, 135–67.

Herring, R., 2009. Has the time come to nationalize struggling banks? Yes, but carefully. Knowledge@Wharton, February 18. https://knowledge.wharton.up enn.edu/article/has-the-time-come-to-nationalize-struggling-banks-yes-but-care fully/.

Hoelscher, D.S., Quintyn, M., 2003. Managing systemic banking crises. IMF Occasional Paper No. 224.

Homar, T. 2016. Bank recapitalizations and lending: a little is not enough. ESRB Working Paper Series No. 16, European Systemic Risk Board.

Homar, T., van Wijnbergen, S.J.G., 2017. Bank recapitalization and economic recovery after financial crises. *Journal of Financial Intermediation*, 32, 16–28.

Hryckiewicz, A. 2014. What do we know about the impact of government interventions in the banking sector? An assessment of various bailout programs on bank behavior. *Journal of Banking & Finance*, 46, 246–65.

Hryckiewicz, A., Kryg, N., Tsomocos, D., 2020. New bank resolution mechanisms: is it the end of the bailout era? Working Paper available at ssrn: https://papers. ssrn.com/sol3/papers.cfm?abstract_id=3639644.

Igan, D., Moussawi, H., Tieman, A.F., Zdzienicka, A., Dell'Ariccia, G., Mauro, P., 2019. The long shadow of the Global Financial Crisis: Public interventions in the financial sector. IMF Working Paper No. WP/19/164.

Ingves, S., Lind, G., Shirakawa, M., Caruana, J., Martinez, G.O., 2009. Lessons learned from previous banking crises: Sweden, Japan, Spain and Mexico, Group of Thirty. Occasional Paper No. 79, Washington, DC.

Jackowicz, K., Kowalewski, O., Kozłowski, Ł., 2013. The influence of political factors on commercial banks in Central European countries. *Journal of Financial Stability*, 4, 759–77.

Jensen, M.C., Meckling, W.H., 1976. Theory of the firm: managerial behavior, agency costs and ownership structure. *Journal of Financial Economics*, 3, 306–60.

Kahan, M., Rock, E.R., 2011. When the government is the controlling shareholder, 89. Faculty Scholarship at Penn Law No. 316.

Keefer, P., 2007. Elections, special interests, and financial crisis. *International Organization*, 61, 607–41.

Kerber, R., 2009. Businesses in N.E. say lenders too strict. The BostonGlobe. com, February 21. http://archive.boston.com/business/articles/2009/02/21/busi nesses_in_ne_say_lenders_too_strict/.

Khwaja, A.I., Mian, A., 2005. Do lenders favor politically connected firms? Rent provision in an emerging financial market. *The Quarterly Journal of Economics*, 1371–411.

Klimek, P., Poledna, S., Farmer, D.J., Thurner, S., 2015. To bail-out or to bail-in? Answers from an agent-based model. *Journal of Economic Dynamics and Control*, 50, 144–54.

Laeven, L., Valencia, F., 2018. Systemic banking crises revisited. IMF Working Papers 18/206.

Landier, A., Ueda, K., 2009. The economics of bank restructuring: understanding the options. IMF Staff Position Note, SPN/09/12.

Laprévote, F. Ch., Coupé, F., 2017. The States' toolkit for rescuing banks in difficulty. In Laprévote, F. Ch., Gray, J. and Coupé, F. (eds), *Research Handbook on State Aid in the Banking Sector*, Cheltenham, UK and Northampton, MA, USA: Elgar Edward Publishing, pp. 107–50.

Liddy, E., 2009. Tug of war over AIG bonuses. CNNMoney.com, March 18. https://money.cnn.com/2009/03/18/news/companies/aig_hearing/.

NAO (National Audit Office) Report, 2015. Financial Institutions Landscape, https://www.nao.org.uk/wp-content/uploads/2015/09/Financial-institutions-lands cape.pdf#page=19.

Parsons, Ch., Nicholas, P., 2009. We will rebuild, we will recover. *L.A. Times*, February 25.

Peek, J., Rosengren, E., 2005. Unnatural Selection: perverse incentives and the misallocation of credit in Japan. *American Economic Review*, 95, 1144–66.

Philippon, T., Schnabl, P., 2013. Efficient recapitalization. *The Journal of Finance*, 68, 1–42.

Rosas, G., 2009. *Curbing Bailouts: Bank Crises and Democratic Accountability in Comparative Perspective*. Ann Arbor, MI: University of Michigan Press.

Sapienza, P., 2004. The effects of government ownership on bank lending. *Journal of Financial Economics*, 72, 357–84.

Schäfer, A., Schnabel, I., Weder di Mauro, B., 2016. Bail-in expectations for European banks: actions speak louder than words. ESRB Working Paper Series 07, European Systemic Risk Board.

Sheng, A., 1996. *Bank Restructuring: Lessons from the 1980s*. World Bank, Washington, DC.

Tanaka, M., Hoggarth, G., 2006. Resolving banking crises—an analysis of policy options. Bank of England Working Paper No. 293, London.

Wilson, L., Wu, Y.W., 2012. Escaping TARP. *Journal of Financial Stability*, 8, 32–42.

Yang, Yueh-Ping (Alex), 2019. Government ownership of banks: a curse or a blessing for the United States? *William and Mary Business Law Review*, 10, 667–735.

Yeyati, E.L., Peria, M.S.M., Schmukler, S., 2011. Triplet crises and the ghost of the new drachma. VOX.EU, June 29. https://voxeu.org/article/bank-run-greece-triplet-crises-and-ghost-new-drachma.

12. The sovereign-bank nexus

Giovanni Ferri and Valerio Pesic

12.1 INTRODUCTION

The Global Financial Crisis (GFC) and, even more, the following Euro sovereign debt crisis have highlighted the close interplay between sovereigns and domestic banks. In the most acute phases of crises, the risk of the sovereign sector and the domestic banking sector has increased considerably, with a high degree of correlation. This interconnectedness of banks and sovereigns is often referred to as the sovereign-bank "nexus", whereby problems originating in one of the two sectors may cause a negative "feedback loop" that further amplifies the effects in each sector (BIS, 2017). This evidence has stimulated an extensive debate. On the one hand, some scholars argue that the link between sovereign and banks is very dangerous for financial stability and therefore must be "broken". On the other hand, other pundits claim that government exposures are very important for banks and, more generally, for the proper functioning of the financial system; thus, breaking the nexus could cause many problems.

The second section of this chapter analyses the risks and the benefits of the sovereign-bank nexus. The third section reviews the regulatory treatment of sovereign exposures. The fourth section illustrates recent proposals to alleviate the negative effects of the nexus. The fifth section offers a discussion of the COVID-19 impact on this topic. Finally, the sixth section concludes.

12.2 LITERATURE ON THE RISKS OF THE SOVEREIGN-BANK NEXUS

The risks of the sovereign-bank nexus are analysed by a large and growing literature, inspired by Brunnermeier et al.'s (2011) seminal paper. In their model, a high amount of public securities held by the domestic banking sector increases the credit risk of both the sovereign and the banking sector, through a diabolic loop that increases the probability of twin crises.

For example, speculative attacks on the solvency of the banking sector weaken the sovereign's soundness which, in turn, further reduces the solvency of the banking sector. This mechanism can also work in the opposite direction: speculative attacks on the solvency of the sovereign weaken the soundness of the banking sector which, in turn, further endangers the sovereign's solvency. This literature identifies different channels that link the two sectors.

Regarding the causal link going from the banking sector to the sovereign, two main channels of contagion have been identified:

- The first channel passes through the credit supply: if an exogenous shock weakens the banking sector, banks reduce the supply of credit to the real economy, causing a slowdown of economic activity. The dip of economic activity may well reduce tax revenues and increase welfare outlays. This combination could weaken public finances and increase the risk of sovereign default.
- The second channel of contagion runs through implicit guarantees: if an exogenous shock undermines the solvency of the banking sector, the sovereign could intervene to avoid bank runs or contractions of the credit supply (see Chapter 11). These interventions, however, could increase the public deficit and, consequently, the risk of sovereign default. For example, Ejsing and Lemke (2011) investigate the effect of bank bailout announcements on sovereign credit risk measured by credit default swaps (CDS) spreads. More precisely, they use bank and government CDS premia of ten major Euro area countries between January 2008 and June 2009. The authors find that government rescue packages led to a decrease in the CDS spreads of the banking sectors mirrored by the increase in credit spreads on the sovereigns. Furthermore, they show that the sensitivity of sovereign CDS spreads to the intensifying financial crisis increases after the bailout of the financial sector (see also Alter and Schüler, 2012; Kallestrup et al., 2013).

Regarding the causal link running from the sovereign to the banking sector, five main channels of contagion have been identified (Angelini et al., 2014; BIS, 2011):

- *Asset holdings channel.* The first channel runs through the assets of the banks: given that domestic banks hold a significant share of national public debt, an increase in the probability of sovereign default causes a reduction in the value of these securities, with a negative effect on the capital of banks holding such positions. This channel is investigated empirically by Angeloni and Wolff (2012) who use data provided by the European Banking Authority to analyse the effect of sovereign bond holdings on banks' stock market performance. They find that this effect varies depending on the period. For example, Greek sovereign debt affected banks' market values between July and October 2011 but not after October 2011 (see also Altavilla et al., 2017; Buch et al., 2013; Correa et al., 2014; De Bruyckere et al., 2013; Frisell, 2016).

- *Collateral channel.* The second channel of contagion passes through the banks' funding: a reduction in the value of government securities held by banks reduces banks' funding capacity as these securities are also used in refinancing operations or as collateral in funding operations (Correa et al., 2014; De Bruyckere et al., 2013; Kaminsky et al., 2003; Kiyotaki and Moore, 2005).
- *Guarantee channel.* The third channel runs through the public guarantees: as the sovereign default risk increases, its ability to intervene to support the troubled banking sector decreases, which increases the credit risk of banks (Bertay et al., 2013; Brown and Dinc, 2011; Demirgüç-Kunt and Huizinga, 2010). However, some authors point out that depending on the specific characteristics of the economy and the nature of banking crises, an increase in the size of guarantees may be beneficial for the sovereign-bank nexus (Leonello, 2018).
- *Rating channel.* The fourth channel of contagion materializes through the rating: given that many rating agencies use the rating of the sovereign as the maximum threshold for domestic banks, a sovereign downgrade can also reduce the judgement on the degree of solvency of domestic banks (Adelino and Ferreira, 2016; Alsakka et al., 2014; Arezki et al., 2011; D'Apice et al., 2016) or, more generally, can have a negative effect on banking activity (Drago and Gallo, 2017).
- *Macroeconomic channel.* The fifth channel considers the real economy: the materialization of sovereign risk could trigger a recession, which in turn could increase borrowers' riskiness and banks' fragility and funding costs, resulting in a spiral of credit tightening that deepens the recession, independently of banks' direct exposures to the sovereign (BIS, 2017).

Given that the risks of contagion can operate in both directions, Acharya et al. (2014) are among the first to identify empirically a two-way feedback between sovereign risk and bank risk. In this literature the contagion essentially runs through the holding of sovereign bonds by the banking sector, which is then identified as the hub of the sovereign-bank nexus.

Moreover, a financing stressed sovereign may try to exert some moral suasion on domestic banks to buy the bonds it issues (Ongena et al., 2016).

12.2.1   Literature on the Benefits of the Sovereign-Bank Nexus

Another stream of literature highlights, instead, the benefits of the sovereign-bank nexus. Indeed, banks hold sovereign exposures for many reasons, including (BIS, 2017):

- Balance sheet management: banks use sovereign bonds to manage their financial statements. For example, in Gennaioli et al.'s (2014) model domestic banks optimally choose to hold sovereign bonds as a way to store liquidity for financing future investments. In fact, in many countries, sovereign bonds are most liquid assets and can be used as collateral in securities financing transactions. Sovereign bonds are also an important tool in the transmission of monetary policy.
- Role in market-making: some banks hold sovereign debt as part of their role as market makers for these securities.
- Legislation and regulation: under the existing regulatory framework, sovereign exposures enjoy a more favourable capital treatment than other exposures and can be used to comply with new liquidity requirements. This can incentivize banks to hold sovereign debt.
- Fragmentation: in periods of financial stress banks can decide to increase their national sovereign holdings. Truly, Battistini et al.'s (2013) factor analysis breaks down Euro area domestic sovereign yields into a country-specific and a systemic component and finds that after country risk factors rose banks boosted domestic sovereign holdings in fiscally stressed countries (Greece, Ireland, Italy, Portugal, Spain) but not in core countries (Austria, Belgium, France, Germany, the Netherlands). This result is consistent with their "moral suasion hypothesis" in which governments urge domestic banks to buy local assets to provide credit domestically rather than internationally.
- Investment opportunities: at times, purchasing sovereign securities can be motivated by a simple risk-return analysis. For example, banks can exploit the opportunity to lease the momentarily higher yields on government bonds to boost the banks' trading profits (Correa and Sapriza, 2014).

  Moreover, sovereign securities are used by banks to assure the well-functioning of the financial system through the role of:
  - Shock absorber: banks can also play the role of shock absorber, which is particularly useful for financial stability in times of

stress (e.g. in the COVID-19 period). In fact, in such a situation domestic banks can act as stable and willing investors in sovereign debt, alleviating funding pressure on the sovereign. The GFC has provided several examples of this role (see Lanotte et al., 2016).

- Commitment device: sovereign default is very expensive for the government because, by acting negatively on the financial system, it reduces the supply of credit, hinders the development of economic activity and, therefore, erodes the tax base. The severity of this cost depends essentially on the degree of exposure of the banking sector to sovereign risk: the greater the amount of securities held by banks, the greater the cost of default for the government. For example, in Gennaioli et al.'s (2014) model sovereign default is expensive, given its negative effect on the balance sheets of domestic banks, and the probability of sovereign default decreases as the banking sector's exposure increases. The authors also offer empirical evidence to support this conclusion. Furthermore, Kohlscheen (2010) and Van Rijckeghem and Weder (2004) find that sovereign default is less likely on domestic rather than foreign creditors.

The main point of this line of research is that the exposure of the banking sector to sovereign risk can act as a disciplinary mechanism for the government. Indeed, this inference could explain the increase in sovereign exposure by the banking sector during times of financial stress. On this aspect, Broner et al. (2014) argue that public securities offer a higher expected return for domestic creditors than foreign ones, especially in times of financial stress. In turn, Podstawski and Velinov (2018) find heterogeneous and time-varying effects of bank exposure on sovereign credit risk in the Euro area. Using a Markov switching structural vector autoregressive in a heteroscedastic framework, they find that rising bank exposure increased default risk for the European Monetary Union (EMU) periphery, but decreased credit risk for the core EMU countries during times of financial stress.

In addition to these aspects, sovereign securities also play a key role for monetary and fiscal policy.

About the former, sovereign exposures are important for the conduct of monetary policy in two main ways. First, they play a role in monetary policy implementation, which typically involves transactions in government debt and central bank liabilities. Second, sovereign debt typically plays a role in the transmission of monetary policy through financial markets, for instance, by serving as collateral in repo markets or through the pricing of financial assets against government debt (BIS, 2017). As to fiscal policy implementation, deep and liquid sovereign bond markets allow governments to finance part of their deficits through debt issuance at low cost.

12.3   REGULATORY TREATMENT OF SOVEREIGN EXPOSURES

Since the first version of the 1988 Basel Capital Accord, the regulatory treatment of sovereign exposures has been preferential and discounted as compared to other banks assets (ESRB, 2015). Indeed, the regulatory framework for sovereign exposures has been largely favourable allowing for low capital requirements, especially for those countries exercising the national discretion that allows jurisdictions to apply a 0 per cent risk weight for sovereign exposures denominated and funded in domestic currency, regardless of their inherent risk (BIS, 2017). Therefore, the regulatory framework has likely encouraged banks to purchase sovereign bonds given the fundamental functions these bonds perform in the financial system, with the undesired consequence, as already emphasized, that this approach in some cases has favoured excessive investment in public debt by financial institutions exposing them to deep vulnerability. For that reason, to avoid situations such as those that arose during the Euro area sovereign crisis, several proposals have come to light in the regulatory debate to reduce the exposure to sovereign risk, especially for European banks.

Before discussing those proposals, we will highlight the most significant features characterizing the current regulatory framework for sovereign exposures, in order to outline the most relevant elements of the preferential treatment reserved to government bonds in the current legislation (BIS, 2017). That framework can be related to five fundamental features, which relate to the treatment of sovereign exposures under the risk-weighted framework, both of credit and market risk, the treatment for large exposures framework, the leverage ratio framework and liquidity standards.

First of all, the risk-weighted framework sets capital requirements for sovereign exposures to mitigate both credit risk and market risk via a favourable treatment. This is particularly relevant for credit risk, both in the case of the Standard approach (SA) and the Internal ratings-based approach (IRBA). In the Basel II framework, a bank is allowed to determine its risk weights by use of the SA, which estimates the risk weights in line with the ratings assigned by a recognized External Credit Assessment Institution (ECAI) or by an export credit agency (ECA). Alternatively, a bank is allowed to calculate its risk weights via their IRBA, which considers the results provided by the bank's rating system – once it is validated by the supervisors – as potential measure of credit risk (BIS, 2004).

According to the general rule, in the SA, the risk weighting factor to be applied in order to calculate the capital requirement against sovereign exposures ranges from a weighting of 0 per cent for countries with high ratings (from AAA to AA-) to 150 per cent for countries with a lower credit rating (below B-), whilst a weighting of 100 per cent is attributed to unrated exposures. Nevertheless, at the European level a discretionary exception has been established, the so-called "carved-out rule", for which a 0 per cent risk weight may be applied to banks' sovereign exposures when denominated in domestic currency and funded in that currency (Lanotte et al., 2016). As a result, since almost all of Basel Committee member countries currently exercise this discretion and set a 0 per cent risk weight, banks' risk weight for central government exposures (including both domestic and foreign currency exposures) has been estimated to be on average under the SA about 3 per cent (BIS, 2017).

That advantageous approach holds also when referring to the degree of credit risk mitigation (CRM) provided by collateralized transactions, since supervisors are allowed, under certain conditions, to apply a zero haircut for repo-style transactions, where the counterparty is a core market participant, as sovereign issuers are generally considered.

Within the IRBA, a bank computes its capital requirement for credit risk using its own estimates of the probability of default (PD), loss given default (LGD), exposure at default (EAD), maturity (M). A difference occurs between the Foundation IRBA and the Advanced IRBA, since within the latter a bank is allowed to calculate its estimates for almost all of those elements. After that, those parameters are fed into a regulatory formula provided by the Basel Committee, which yields the risk weight. The weighting function is not unique but there is one for each different category of counterparty. According to the IRBA, sovereign exposures are treated similarly to exposures against corporates and banks, although the probability of default (PD) of sovereign exposures is not subject to the 0.03 per cent floor, which applies to all other asset classes. Despite that peculiarity, it is important to underline how data estimated through the IRB system derive from historical data of default of the counterparties, which in cases of sovereign exposures show a low – if not zero – default rate. For this reason, in any case, albeit not 0 per cent, sovereign risk parameters are often very low and the weighting based on these estimates is usually quite low.

In addition to these preferential treatments provided in the context of the use of the IRBA, it is possible to distinghuish another feature, still related to the measure of credit risk, which can be considered as a further advantage for sovereigns. The European prudential regulation established the "permanent partial use rule", or the so-called "permanent partial use of the standardized approach", which allows banks to permanently omit the use of internal models for calculating the capital requirement for sovereign exposures under specific circumstances. Pursuant to this regulation, banks using the IRBA are allowed, subject to certain conditions, to consider the SA for sovereign exposures (0 per cent weighting), whilst continuing to use the IRBA for other assets (Lanotte et al., 2016). This rule can be interpreted as deriving from some particular motivations. First of all, a bank can assess that, in relation to its strategies, the number of important counterparties – as sovereign exposures generally are – is limited, so that it becomes burdensome, rather than impossible, for the bank to adopt a rating system for those counterparties. Afterwards, States are considered bankruptcy remote counterparties, with estimated PD considered very low, so that no internal estimate is required to assess it. Finally, it is recognized that models developed by banks would in any case be based on judgmental and qualitative elements, since sovereign defaults have been so infrequent in Europe – at least before the GFC – so to make any meaningful statistical analysis impossible (Lanotte et al., 2016).

Similarly to credit risk, in their market risk framework banks are allowed to consider two alternative methodologies to estimate their capital requirement for financial assets held in the trading book, the Standardized approach (SdA) and the Internal models approach (IMA). Within the SdA, two different charges are considered: systemic market risks and idiosyncratic risks. Systemic risks, which are calculated at the portfolio level, are basically related to interest rate risks, with banks having the possibility to offset long and short positions in different securities or instruments. In contract, idiosyncratic risks are calculated separately for each individual security, and are designed to protect against an adverse movement in the price of an individual security owing to factors relating to the individual issuer, with a possibility to offset positions limited to each class (Lanotte et al., 2016). By this perspective, ad hoc rules are stated for uniform categories of financial instruments, whilst within each category the differentiation of weightings takes place depending on idiosyncratic risks or systemic risks. Finally, the sum between the absorption for idiosyncratic risks and that for systemic risks represents the risk charge related to each financial instrument. As regards debt securities, the weighting classes envisaged for idiosyncratic risks of sovereign exposures range from 0 per cent to 12 per cent, depending on the creditworthiness of the issuing counterparty, whilst for systemic risks the weightings are differentiated in line with the maturity or the duration of each instrument. Nevertheless, despite that general framework, similarly to credit risk, at national discretion, a "carve-out rule" applies to idiosyncratic risks for sovereign exposures, leaving the possibility for banks, "when the government paper is denominated in the domestic currency and funded by the bank in the same currency", to apply a risk weight equal to zero. In contrast, no leniency applies with reference to systemic risks, and also the "permanent partial use rule" is not envisaged for exposures of trading books, so that banks, under the IMA, are required to include trading book sovereign exposures as part of their Value at Risk (VaR) models.

With the aim of reducing concentration risks, which can be related to losses deriving from excessive exposure to a single customer or a group of interconnected customers, the Basel Committee in 2014 introduced the regime of large exposures (BIS, 2014), which provides the obligation for banks to limit their exposure to a single counterparty to 25 per cent of the value of the elegible capital, being the exposure computed at 100 per cent. That obligation is not contemplated for all sovereign exposures, and for all those exposures that are guaranteed by sovereign entities, since those have a credit risk weighting coefficient equal to 0 per cent.

Since the first version of the 1988 Basel Capital Accord, the Basel Committee had worked in order to ameliorate the prudential framework and enrich the financial system's soundness. Despite those intense efforts, the GFC represented a wake-up call for urgent amendments in order to improve the resilience of the whole financial system. Nowadays, it is commonly assumed that the magnitude of the crisis was exarcebated by the condition of the banking sector of many countries which had built up excessive on and off-balance sheet leverage, together with a gradual erosion of the level and quality of the capital base (BIS, 2010). At the same time, many banks – despite adequate capital levels – experienced difficulties because they did not manage their liquidity in a prudent manner, since asset markets were considered buoyant and funding was readily available at low cost. The GFC showed how dramatic changes to market conditions can determine liquidity to evaporate, leaving the banking system under severe stress (BIS, 2010). Those conditions, together with other relevant weaknesses already outlined in the previous period, finally led the Basel Committee to formulate the rules text and timelines to implement the Basel III framework, which took place in Europe from 2015. Among other facets, this framework introduces a leverage ratio requirement that is intended to constrain leverage in the banking sector and to introduce an additional safeguard against the model risk characterizing the capital adequacy ratio. Consistent with its nature, the leverage ratio includes all balance sheet assets in the exposure measure, comprising sovereign exposures, which in this case receive no favourable evaluation, being considered at their nominal value (Lanotte et al., 2016).

A fundamental lesson of the financial crisis has been that the minimum capital requirements, even if considered necessary safeguards, may turn out to be insufficient in certain conditions. Indeed, the evidence of the GFC was that many banks, albeit with high capital ratios in the pre-crisis period, found themselves on the verge of bankruptcy as they did not have sufficient liquidity buffers. For this reason, in the aftermath of the GFC, the Basel Committee in 2008 published the document on Principles for Sound Liquidity Risk Management and Supervision, aiming to provide a new guidance on the risk management and supervision of funding liquidity risk (BIS, 2008). Afterwards, as part of the overall Basel III reform, the Committee defined two new liquidity indicators: the Liquidity Coverage Ratio (LCR) and the Net Stable Funding Ratio (NSFR), which completed the set of first pillar requirements that banks are now required to satisfy, together with the traditional Total Capital Ratio and the new Leverage Ratio, to achieve a suitable level of soundness and stability (BIS, 2009).

As regards the LCR, it entered into force in 2015 with a phase-in method and was established by the regulator in order to ensure banks have a readily available stock of liquidable assets in the event of market and idiosyncratic stress condition involving outflows of liquidity over a short-term period. Thus, the LCR, which is defined as the ratio of High-Quality Liquid Assets (HQLA) to Total Net Cash Outflows over 30 days under stress condition, must be at least 100 per cent. The assets that can be part of the HQLA can be divided into two categories: level 1 and level 2 assets. The former comprises exposures that are free from any obstacle to market-ability and therefore can be readily liquidated, whilst the latter includes the assets that are less easily monetizable. In level 1 assets there are certainly more cash and liquidity, together with sovereign exposures, which indeed are generally the most consistent, given the fact that banks are required to diversify the asset classes that contribute to forming the HQLA, with the exception of the sovereign debt of the country of origin or in which the bank operates. Otherwise, in level 2 are included assets characterized by a slightly lower level of liquidity.

Bearing this clarification in mind, it is also necessary to consider that, in order to compute such assets in the HQLA, level 2 assets are subject to haircuts up to 40 per cent of the entire aggregate, whilst for level 1 assets no haircut is applied, as it is assumed their ability to generate liquidity would remain unchanged even in the face of market stress events.

As regards the NSFR, it entered into force in January 2018 and was provided by the regulator with the aim of ensuring a bank the necessary liquidity within a perspective from medium to long term. It is obtained by the ratio of Available amount of stable funding to Required amount of stable funding, and must be at least 100 per cent. The numerator of the

NSFR includes all liabilities with a duration of at least one year that can therefore be considered stable, which are multiplied by a different weighting coefficient based on the residual maturities of the various liabilities. On the other side, the denominator is constituted by assets whose duration is generally greater than one year, to be multiplied by weighting coefficients capturing the difficulty in disposing of the asset. Therefore, sovereign exposures which have 0 per cent credit risk weight are attractive assets in terms of stable assets required by the NSFR and certainly do not even require the application of a risk weight as these assets are considered easily monetizable at any time, so that they do not need approximations of their value in order to be able to compete for the denominator of this ratio.

12.4 PROPOSALS TO ALLEVIATE THE NEGATIVE EFFECTS OF THE NEXUS

The experience of the sovereign debt crisis and the high exposures to domestic government bonds in banks' balance sheets have led to an intense debate among scholars and practitioners on the need to review the current regulatory framework of sovereign exposures (Andritzky et al., 2016; Bongaerts and Schoenmaker, 2017). In the aftermath of the sovereign debt crisis, the need for a more rigorous and risk-based regulation for sovereign exposures was claimed as a priority, to discourage banks from holding too large amounts of government bonds on their balance sheets, thus limiting the vicious circle between sovereign risk and national banking systems.

The discussion, which originated from the view that the current regulation has been one of the main causes of excessive accumulation of government bonds in European bank balance sheets, culminated in the advancement of some reform proposals which to date, for reasons mentioned later, have not been implemented yet.

Indeed, the debate originated from the European Systemic Risk Board (ESRB) report on "The regulatory treatment of sovereign exposures" of March 2015. Since its publication, the debate on this issue has grown with increasing magnitude. Many authors, shortly thereafter, expressed their views on the subject by advancing possible alternative solutions that would allow us to break the relationship between the financial system and sovereign risk, without involving a change in the current European regulatory framework for sovereign exposures.

For that reason, we briefly review the main reform proposals made in favour of a more rigorous and risk-based regulation of sovereign exposures, together with their fundamental policy implications. Each proposed initiative is briefly discussed, indicating the implications it could have on the banking system, together with its potential negative effects. It is important to underline that, although the initiatives under review commonly have the aim to curb the existing vicious circle between sovereign and banks soundness, they have different characteristics which need a deeper understanding. Furthermore, if, on the one hand, positive results are very often expected from their possible enforcement, on the other hand, those reforms in some cases could lead to new problems. Thus, the possible materialization of those potential spillover effects discouraged the Authorities from implementing the proposed reforms. Not surprisingly, the Systemic Risk Committee in its report specifies that although the proposals aim to reduce sovereign risk in banks and, consequently, to break out of the vicious circles between sovereign and banks, these advanced reforms are applicable in a stable economic context and therefore after a careful evaluation of the latter (ESRB, 2015).

As mentioned, the existing regulatory provisions on sovereign exposures allowed in certain circumstances a favourable weighting factor of 0 per cent for sovereign exposures, which is an implicit valuation of a risk-free prudential treatment for banks that hold government bonds, in case of utilization of the SA for calculating their capital requirements for credit risk. Therefore, one of the first proposals suggested eliminating the "carve-out rule" implied with the application of the SA. The rationale behind this decision derives from considering that, first of all, the 0 per cent rule is at odds with the empirical evidence found during the sovereign debt crisis and second, but not least, it is a harbinger of generating additional potential risks to the banking system. Indeed, in the origin the 0 per cent weight was introduced on the hypothesis that the failure of a sovereigns was an exceptional event, so rare that it considers the sovereign exposures of advanced countries to be free of possible risks, foreseeing for the latter the exemption from the obligation of capital requirements on first pillar risks. However, the GFC has eradicated this original belief, raising the awareness that sovereign default is to be considered neither a rare event nor an episode attributable only to emerging economies. On the contrary, sovereign defaults can happen also in a developed country and in several countries belonging to even a larger economic area, as happened in Europe. Based on this idea, together with the lack of a lender of last resort in the Euro area, the need to reconsider the risk weighting applicable to sovereign exposures took place. A first hypothesis suggested the introduction of positive and non-zero risk weights on government bonds in European bank balance sheets, in order to consider also sovereign risk, by virtue of its belonging to the macro-category of credit or market risk, when determining the level of capital adequacy. In a first instance, it was considered to drop-off the 0 per cent rule, by introducing sovereign risk weights based on the creditworthiness of a sovereigh issuer. That hypothesis appears to be in line with the general approach of the Basel framework, which is generally applied to all exposures that are a harbinger of generating potential credit and market risks. This would entail a weighting of sovereign exposures for a value ranging between 0 per cent and 150 per cent under the SA, based on the ratings assigned by the ECAIs.

Nevertheless, as already highlighted, despite the positive effects which would derive from the increased level of capital necessary for banks to comply with the demands of supervisors, the banking system will not remain still sheltered from some fundamental problems (Lanotte et al., 2016). If, on the one hand, eliminating the "carve-out rule" can have a positive effect, acting as a disincentive for banks in holding sovereign debt, and reduce their exposure to sovereign risk and the probability of a vicious circle between sovereign and banking creditworthiness, on the other hand, it would entail higher capital burdens for financial institutions. Furthermore, banks should liquidate part of these riskier assets to save capital, investing only in highly rated government bonds, but this deleveraging activity would lead to a reduction in the price of those securities, creating funding problems and high financing costs for sovereign issuers. Moreover, last but not least, the decision to refer to the opinions issued by the rating agencies would lead to other problems, as repeatedly highlighted over the years by a broad literature (see, among others, Altman and Rijken, 2004; Ferri et al., 1999; IMF, 2010). It is well known how ratings tend to remain too stable, whilst when the downgrade occurs this is usually abrupt, leading to strong price pro-cyclicality; therefore, the decision to relate sovereign risk weights to rating agency evaluations could lead banks to, promptly and even belatedly, react to substantial and unexpected increase in capital burdens, especially for those securities exiting from the investment grade category (Lanotte et al., 2016).

For that reson, to mitigate the reliance on external credit ratings, the Basel Committee considered two alternative approaches, hypothesizing that banks could perform due diligence on their sovereign exposures, in order to potentially determine a higher risk weight than that determined by the external rating, or, alternatively, it should be possible to distinguish some additional (non-rating) indicators to assess the creditworthiness of sovereign exposures, in order to determine the risk weights throughout those alternative measures of risk (BIS, 2017). Nevertheless, neither of the two proposals seems to be easily feasible, as they both would introduce additional elements of discretion, which again would be difficult to control.

A further alternative to the rating-based approach could be to introduce a limit on investments in government bonds for each bank. This would certainly be easier to introduce as it would avoid risk weights that rely excessively on rating agencies or seek alternative criteria to assign adequate weights that reflect the risk inherent in sovereign exposures. Furthermore, such an initiative would not put European banks at a financial disadvantage against other countries. Indeed, at the moment the Basel regulatory framework provides for a quantitative limit on exposures to a single counterparty, with the scope of preventing concentration risks, although an exception is established for sovereign exposures. Within this perspective, the idea would be to introduce a limit that allows us to reduce sovereign exposures by encouraging the diversification of portfolios. Therefore, if the bank wanted to hold a greater amount of government bonds it could do so only on condition of holding a well-diversified portfolio of sovereign exposures. Although this approach should avoid the reliance on rating agencies, together with the problems summarized above, it would not be free from limitations, especially if considering that it refers to a quantitative approach not based on perceived risks and without any differentiation based on the size and business activity of the different banks. Moreover, as already highlighted by Lanotte et al. (2016), although the limit could be introduced gradually, this would not mitigate the selling pressures on sovereign bonds prices, as markets usually tend to anticipate any regulatory change. Other aspects to consider would be the effect on sovereign yields, the lack of possibility for national banks to support the sovereign debt of their country in the event of market stress phenomena and, last but not least, there is also the need for this rule to be calibrated in relation to the new regulatory obligations for banks' liquidity.

An alternative approach has been hypothesized with a positive weighting assumed only for the exposures of financial intermediaries exceeding a given threshold between total exposures and regulatory capital. In this way, banks should reduce concentration risks, whilst choosing between an increase in capital or the disinvestment only of the part that exceeds this limit, thus avoiding the sale of large quantities of sovereign bonds that could have substantial capital impacts and adverse systemic effects. Nevertheless, this proposal also has a drawback, since it certainly would penalize the banks most exposed to sovereign risk, but, as constructed, this would be to the detriment of banks which, even if holding a high amount of investment grade securities, would still be forced to modify their assets portfolio.

Apart from the hypotheses of changes to be implemented to the SA for sovereign exposures, within the framework of the Basel Committee a debate took place about the hypothesis of removal of the IRBA for sovereign exposures. That scenario appears to be related to the general concern, which came to the fore in recent years, about the difficulty to properly model certain asset classes for the calculation of regulatory capital requirements, especially when insufficient data for the estimation of key risk inputs matches with the lack of robust and generally accepted and validated modelling techniques (BIS, 2017).

As said, the current framework does includes no measure to mitigate the risks associated with excessive holdings of sovereign exposures, since the general limit of 25 per cent of a bank's Tier 1 capital to any single counterparty does not apply in case of sovereign exposures (BIS, 2017). For that reason, at the Basel Committee there has been discussion about the potential introduction of marginal risk weight add-ons, to be introduced in relation to bank's Tier 1 capital, so as to mitigate that risk. Nevertheless, because of the large amounts of exposures owned, together with the roles performed for banks in terms of management of their liquidity, it is widely expected that sovereign exposures will continue to be exempted from any limitation even in the future.

Finally, the Basel Committee discussed the idea of removing the existing CRM discretion for repo-style transactions. To the extent that market participants already apply positive haircuts for such transactions, removing the discretion would bring the regulatory framework more in line with market practices. The Committee noted that, if the discretion to apply a 0 per cent haircut were to be removed, banks would be required to apply one of the CRM approaches as set out in the revised SA for credit risk framework for such transactions.

12.5   IMPACT OF THE COVID-19 PANDEMIC

At the start of the pandemic crisis, the European economy had not yet fully recovered from the double recession provoked by the GFC and Euro sovereign crisis. The financial conditions of households and businesses were overall sound and the banks, which had overcome a long period of difficulty, were strengthening their balance sheets. The number of households vulnerable to economic and financial shocks had fallen sharply. Also the corporate sector was in a much stronger financial condition than in the period before the GFC, with a level of leverage which was generally lower than in 2007. Banks had made significant progress in strengthening their balance sheets, also thanks to regulatory reforms and supervisory action. The high-quality capital in relation to risk-weighted assets had been in some cases more than doubled, despite the large losses incurred as a result of the double recession.

The initial spread of the contagion in China in the early months of 2020 initially led to the collapse of tourist flows from that country and difficulties in procuring some imported intermediate goods. The effects exploded

with the appearance of the virus worlwide and the consequent containment provisions necessary to limit the contagion, with the first effects
of the pandemic manifesting its significant effects on the international
financial markets from March 2020. However, if an important package
of interventions by central banks and governments contributed to a relative stabilization of the conditions of the financial markets, the forecast
is unanimous that the most serious consequences are destined to affect
the real economy, even for a long time, with a magnitude of exceptional
proportions worldwide.

Since the beginning of the emergency phase, the banking sector found
itself playing a critical role, constituting the main channel of financial
support for firms, especially small and medium-sized ones. Financial aids
from European Union and other public Authorities around the world were
for some time delayed, whilst banks had to cope with a large and sudden
demand for loans, which have been encouraged by State guarantees generally provided by each country. This resulted in an increasing pressure to
expand lending to support troubled firms, but banks themselves are subject to the consequences of the pandemic crisis. Banks are therefore asked
to face a particularly demanding effort, also having to safeguard their own
economic sustainability and stability.

The challenge of the economic recovery is difficult and requires time.
The estimates on the trend of the economy for the next years feature
modest growth in world GDP, which is not expected to recover the drop
suffered in 2020 very shortly. Therefore, companies will find themselves
in a recessionary context, also because of the protracted containment
provisions necessary to limit the contagion, whilst burdened by greater
debts contracted to face the liquidity crisis. Many companies may find
themselves in a state of insolvency, and, with the increase of distressed
companies, banks will experience a new deterioration in the quality of
their loans. So, if the priority problem created by the pandemic crisis was
a liquidity crisis, which the banks helped to mitigate, the banks will find
themselves managing a crisis due to the downturn of economic activity.
At this juncture, the counter-cyclical role played by sovereigns appears
absolutely decisive. But the speed of exiting the emergency phase is equally
critical, because the faster this speed, the less likely will be entering a
prolonged recession or even a depression. Accordingly, there is broad
consensus on the need for the losses of the private sector to be absorbed,
in large part, by public budgets and by increasing sovereign debts. For
that reason, in many countries subsidies have been granted to those who
lost their jobs and governments have bolstered guarantees to companies
to avoid bankruptcies and unemployment. In addition to subsidies, tax
moratoria have also been envisaged. At the same time, banks continued

to provide liquidity to distressed companies, allowing current account overdrafts or by opening lines of credit and granting loans. But if banks are called upon to support firms in difficulty, they must be enabled to play this role in conditions of stability. Banks have actually been asked for an important commitment, both for the objective difficulty faced by various economic sectors, but also for their own difficulties. It can well be understood how the increase in loans to distressed companies makes credit management more problematic, despite these loans being partly covered by public guarantees.

Although the granting of loans to companies for liquidity reasons constitutes one of the distinctive activities of banks and therefore it is normal to provide companies with credit for temporary cash needs, in situations of protracted economic crisis and in adverse economic times, immediate liquidity needs situations of potential default of deadlines with the need for renewals but also situations in which potential insolvency may underlie. The difficulty of estimating the credit risk of loans to companies in liquidity crisis due to the pandemic can lead to credit rationing and rising interest rates. Therefore, in a context of high uncertainty, most governments have implemented schemes to provide public guarantees for bank loans, to help banks accommodate the surge in loan demand at favourable conditions. These schemes transfer some of the credit risk and potential credit losses from banks to governments, thereby mitigating the costs for banks. Nevertheless, since during the same period there has been also a dramatic increase of sovereign debts, it is possible to argue that those "State guarantee schemes" should result in a "new channel of transmission in the sovereign-bank nexus".

By this perspective, despite the high-coverage State guarantee that the credit risk can be considered zero, in reality it substantially corresponds to that of the sovereign debt, which, especially in circumstance of sharply increasing public debts and economic turmoil, is not necessarily equal to zero. This leads to the affirmation, on one hand, that a positive collaboration has been generated between banks and the State, but, on the other hand, it is necessary to consider how States, providing their guarantees, are undertaking risks, which in case of severe losses, should determine further damage to public finance, with negative consequences that would inevitably have a negative impact on banks' soundness.

12.6 CONCLUSIONS

The Global Financial Crisis and the following European sovereign debt crisis have highlighted the close interplay between sovereigns and domestic banks, whereby problems originating in one of the two sectors may cause a negative "feedback loop" that further amplifies the effects in each sector (BIS, 2017). This evidence has stimulated an extensive debate. On the one hand, some scholars argue that the link between sovereign and banks is very dangerous for financial stability and therefore must be "broken". Instead, other pundits claim that government exposures are very important for banks and, more generally, for the proper functioning of the financial system; therefore, breaking the nexus could cause many problems.

Despite a significant debate in the economics literature, together with several proposals of regulatory interventions hypothesized by various Authorities, at the moment it is not possible to establish proposals able to gather general consensus. In particular, it seems that there is no "best way" nor a solution that is equally suitable for all financial intermediaries. The only certainty is that surely, to be adequate and sustainable, proposals should be calibrated from time to time to the specific case, or in relation to the financial and management situation of each financial firm. Moreover, any initiative should be aimed not only at containing sovereign exposure in banks' balance sheets, but should also ensure fair coverage of public debt. Otherwise, in the absence of investors willing to replace European banks, most of the sovereigns of the Euro area would find it difficult in meeting their financial needs, with potential detrimental consequences for investments, public expenditures and economic growth. Therefore, when evaluating any suitable hypothesis, proper consideration must be given in addition to the actual riskiness of sovereign exposures to all the dimensions of the problem, starting from the idiosyncratic characteristics of banks, up to the stability of the financial system as a whole. Within that perspective, it is not easy to find a one-size-fits-all model that, whilst limiting the excessive accumulation of government bonds in bank balance sheets, tackles all these elements without sacrificing any objective. Certainly the proposals analysed so far tend to overlook numerous problems that are potentially harbingers of generating more costs than benefits, without considering the current pandemic crisis which is making the situation even more difficult to manage. That's why the Authorities preferred to temporarily put aside the proposals so far hypothesized.

For this reason, also considering how the current situation is likely to further increase the debt levels of various countries, it could be particularly useful to further investigate potential corrective actions, through further empirical investigations and research. It could be interesting, for example, to better study the ways to regulate these facets of banking activity, without penalizing liquidity management mechanisms, or by evaluating further actions to contain those exposures for banks, without generating a negative impact on the sustainability of countries' debts. Finally, whatever action is taken in the future, it will be necessary to wait for macroeconomic conditions to improve, in such a way as to allow both banks and sovereigns to deal with any regulatory changes without generating any further negative economic and financial shocks.

REFERENCES

Acharya, V., Drechsler, I., Schnabl, P., 2014. A pyrrhic victory? Bank bailouts and sovereign credit risk. *The Journal of Finance* 69(6), 2689–739.

Adelino, M., Ferreira, M.A., 2016. Bank ratings and lending supply: evidence from sovereign downgrades. *Review of Financial Studies* 29, 1709–46.

Alsakka, R., ap Gwilym, O., Vu, T.N., 2014. The sovereign-bank rating channel and rating agencies' downgrades during the European debt crisis. *Journal of International Money and Finance* 49, 235–57.

Altavilla, C., Pagano, M., Simonelli, S., 2017. Bank exposures and sovereign stress transmission. *Review of Finance* 21(6), 2103–39.

Alter, A., Schüler, Y.S., 2012. Credit spread interdependencies of European states and banks during the financial crisis. *Journal of Banking & Finance* 36(12), 3444–68.

Altman, E.I., Rijken, H.A., 2004. How rating agencies achieve rating stability. *Journal of Banking & Finance* 28(11), 2679–714.

Andritzky, J., Gadatsch, N., Körner, T., Schäfer, A., Schnabel, I., 2016. Removing privileges for banks' sovereign exposures – a proposal. *European Economy*, 1, 139.

Angelini, P., Grande, G., Panetta, F., 2014. The negative feedback loop between banks and sovereigns. Banca d'Italia, Questioni di Economia e Finanza, No. 213.

Angeloni, C., Wolff, G.B., 2012. Are banks affected by their holdings of government debt? Bruegel Working Paper 717.

Arezki, R., Candelon, B., Sy, A., 2011. Sovereign rating news and financial markets spillovers: evidence from the European debt crisis. IMF Working Papers, 1–27.

BIS (Bank for International Settlements), 2004. Basel II: International Convergence of Capital Measurement and Capital Standards: a Revised Framework. Standards, Basel Committee on Banking Supervision.

BIS (Bank for International Settlements), 2008. Principles for Sound Liquidity Risk Management and Supervision. Guidelines, Basel Committee on Banking Supervision.

BIS (Bank for International Settlements), 2009. International framework for liquidity risk measurement, standards and monitoring. Consultative document, Basel Committee on Banking Supervision.

BIS (Bank for International Settlements), 2010. Basel III: A global regulatory framework for more resilient banks and banking systems. Standards, Basel Committee on Banking Supervision.

BIS (Bank for International Settlements), 2011. The impact of sovereign credit risk on bank funding conditions. Committee on the Global Financial System Papers No. 43.

BIS (Bank for International Settlements), 2014. Supervisory framework for measuring and controlling large exposures. Standards, Basel Committee on Banking Supervision.

BIS (Bank for International Settlements), 2017. The regulatory treatment of sovereign exposures. Discussion Paper, Basel Committee on Banking Supervision.

Battistini, N., Pagano, M., Simonelli, S., 2013. Systemic risk and home bias in the euro area. European Commission, European Economy, Economic Papers, No. 494.

Bertay, A.C., Demirgüç-Kunt, A., Huizinga, H., 2013. Do we need big banks? Evidence on performance, strategy and market discipline. *Journal of Financial Intermediation* 22, 532–58.

Bongaerts, D., Schoenmaker, D., 2017. A call for uniform sovereign exposure limits. Blog post: http://bruegel.org/2017/03/a-call-for-uniform-sovereign-exposure-limits/.

Broner, F., Erce, A., Martin, A., Ventura, J., 2014. Sovereign debt markets in turbulent times: creditor discrimination and crowding-out effects. *Journal of Monetary Economics* 61, 114–42.

Brown, C.O., Dinc, I.S., 2011. Too many to fail? Evidence of regulatory forbearance when the banking sector is weak. *Review of Financial Studies* 24(4), 1378–405.

Brunnermeier, M., Garicano, L., Lane, P. et al., 2011. European safe bonds: ESBies. Euro-nomics.com.

Buch, C.M., Koetter, M., Ohls, J., 2013. Banks and sovereign risk: a granular view. *Journal of Financial Stability* 25, 1–15.

Correa, R., Sapriza, H., 2014. Sovereign debt crisis. Board of Governors of the Federal Reserve System International Finance Discussion Papers, No. 1104.

Correa, R., Lee, K.H., Sapriza, H., Suarez, G.A., 2014. Sovereign credit risk, banks' government support, and bank stock returns around the world. *Journal of Money, Credit and Banking* 46, 93–121.

D'Apice, V., Ferri, G., Lacitignola, P., 2016. Rating performance and bank business models: is there a change with the 2007–2009 crisis? *Italian Economic Journal* 2(3), 385–420.

De Bruyckere, V., Gerhardt, M., Schepens, G., Vander Vennet, R., 2013. Bank/sovereign risk spillovers in the European debt crisis. *Journal of Banking & Finance* 37(12), 4793–809.

Demirgüç-Kunt, A., Huizinga, H., 2010. Bank activity and funding strategies: the impact on risk and returns. *Journal of Financial Economics* 98(3), 626–50.

Drago, D., Gallo, R., 2017. The impact of sovereign rating changes on the activity of European banks. *Journal of Banking & Finance* 85, 99–112.

Ejsing, J., Lemke, W., 2011. The janus-headed salvation: sovereign and bank credit risk premia during 2008–2009. *Economics Letters* 110(1), 28–31.

ESRB (European Systemic Risk Board), 2015. ESRB report on the regulatory treatment of sovereign exposures, March.

Ferri, G., Liu, L., Stiglitz, J.E., 1999. The procyclical role of rating agencies: evidence from the East Asin crisis. *Economic Notes* 28(3), 335–56.

Frisell, L., 2016. Europe's regulatory treatment of banks' sovereign exposures – how a flawed framework was put to use in the Irish financial crisis. *European Economy* 1, 105.

Gennaioli, N., Martin, A., Rossi, S., 2014. Sovereign default, domestic banks, and financial institutions. *The Journal of Finance* 69(2), 819–66.

IMF (International Monetary Fund), 2010. Chapter III. The Uses and Abuses of Sovereign Credit Ratings. Global Financial Stability Report, Sovereigns, Funding, and Systemic Liquidity.

Kallestrup, R., Lando, D., Murgoci, A., 2013. Financial sector linkages and the dynamics of bank and sovereign credit spreads. *Journal of Empirical Finance* 38(A), 374–93.

Kaminsky, G.L., Reinhart, C., Vegh, C.A., 2003. The unholy trinity of financial contagion. *Journal of Economic Perspectives* 17, 51–74.

Kiyotaki, N., Moore, J., 2005. Liquidity and asset prices. *International Economic Review* 46(2), 317–49.

Kohlscheen, E., 2010. Domestic vs external sovereign debt servicing: an empirical analysis. *International Journal of Finance & Economics* 15(1), 93–103.

Lanotte, M., Manzelli, G., Rinaldi, A., Taboga, M., Tommasino, P., 2016. Easier said than done? Reforming the prudential treatment of banks' sovereign exposures. Banca d'Italia, Occasional Papers, No. 326.

Leonello, A., 2018. Government guarantees and the two-way feedback between banking and sovereign debt crises. *Journal of Financial Economics* 130(3), 592–619.

Ongena, S., Popov, A., Van Horen, N., 2016. The invisible hand of the government: "moral suasion" during the European sovereign debt crisis. ECB Working Paper, No. 1937.

Podstawski, M., Velinov, A., 2018. The state dependent impact of bank exposure on sovereign risk. *Journal of Banking & Finance* 88, 63–75.

Van Rijckeghem, C., Weder, B., 2004. The politics of debt crises. CEPR Discussion Papers (4683).

13. Financial reforms

Alexandre Garel and Arthur Petit-Romec

13.1 INTRODUCTION

This chapter debates the need for financial reforms following the Global Financial Crisis (GFC) of 2007–09 and reflects on regulatory responses worldwide. For reasons of brevity and focus, it concentrates on bank risk-taking and capital requirements. The first section considers a key cause of the crisis that regulation seeks to address: excessive risk-taking. Several reasons have been put forward to explain why banks undertook excessive risk: faulty governance, poorly designed incentive schemes, implicit state guarantees linked to bank size, the underestimation of systemic risk, and so on. The second section examines selected regulatory responses aimed to limit bank risk-taking and learn the lessons of this unprecedented crisis. It reviews the rationale, implementation, and consequences of measures increasing capital requirements. The chapter concludes by exploring some alternative measures suggested by academics and practitioners that can guide future financial reforms. This chapter is an invitation to reflect on the causes and cures of the excessive risk-taking in banks and does not aim to review exhaustively all the empirical and theoretical research produced on financial reforms since the GFC.

13.2 AT THE ROOTS OF THE CRISIS: FACTORS BEHIND EXCESSIVE RISK-TAKING IN BANKS

There is a broad consensus that, prior to the crisis, banks took too much risk, although acting within the legal framework. Exploiting weak regulatory oversight, opaque derivatives and securitization markets, and lax capital requirements, banks were able to take unsafe levels of risks. The GFC (see Chapter 1) also made clear that the underlying sources of risk to the financial systems were insufficiently monitored and that bank capital levels were largely insufficient with respect to the amount of risk banks had accumulated.

Researchers have followed two main avenues to better understand risk-taking in banks and its determinants. Many studies have examined the effect of pre-crisis bank characteristics on shareholder losses or the drop in market valuation during the 2007–09 crisis. The rationale for this approach is that our ability to assess *ex ante* bank risks is inherently limited and risk-taking may seem value-enhancing, albeit as long as risks have not material-ized (Acharya et al., 2016a; Fahlenbrach et al., 2012; Rajan, 2006 – see also Chapter 8). From this perspective, financial crises represent periods during which banks' underlying risks materialize (see Chapter 14). Other studies have focused on the links between a large battery of risk indicators and different bank characteristics over longer periods. They consider a large set of indicators which include both accounting-based risk measures (Z-score, non-performing loans, loan loss provisions, real estate exposure, the ratio of risk-weighted assets to total assets) and market-based risk measures (stock return volatility, marginal expected shortfall, SRISK).

Banks differ from other firms because their risk-taking and subsequent unfolding can have systemic effects and expose the rest of the economy and society at large to material costs (Stulz, 2016). It follows that banks, which do have incentives to internalize these externalities, may have an amount of risk that largely exceeds what would be optimal from the perspective of society. This specificity of banks makes it even more important to under-stand the determinants of bank risk-taking and of their resilience to crises.

13.2.1   Bank Capital and Funding Structures

Bank capital is probably the most established determinant of a bank's ability to resist during periods of economic shocks. A large number of studies have documented that banks with more capital fared much better during the 2007–09 crisis (as well as in previous crises). Based on international samples, Beltratti and Stulz (2012) and Demirgüç-Kunt et al. (2013) document a positive impact of (pre-crisis) bank capital on bank stock performance during the GFC. Focusing on US banks, Berger and Bouwman (2013) show that bank capital increases survival probability and bank market share during crises. Fahlenbrach et al. (2012) show that banks that were poor performers both during the 1998 crisis and the 2007–09 crisis had lower bank capital before both crises. Not only does bank capital help banks to absorb losses *ex post* but *ex ante* it also limits risk-taking incentives (e.g., Admati et al., 2010; Jayaraman and Thakor, 2014; Purnanandam, 2011).

On top of bank capital, many analyses of the crisis emphasize that the excessive reliance of banks on debt, and in particular on short-term fund-ing, contributed to their vulnerability (e.g., Brunnermeier, 2009; Diamond and Rajan, 2009; Gorton, 2010). Empirically, Fahlenbrach et al. (2012) show that banks that relied more on short-term funding were more likely to be banks that performed poorly both in the 1998 crisis and the 2007–09 crisis.

While the (social) benefits of higher bank capital for financial stability are largely recognized, bankers generally oppose higher capital requirements, on the ground that they would damage shareholder value. The banking literature disputes on how capital affects bank performance and shareholder value. One view is that higher bank capital may entail significant costs including lower discipline, lower liquidity creation, leading to lower value creation for shareholders (e.g., Calomiris and Kahn, 1991; DeAngelo and Stulz, 2015; Diamond and Rajan, 2001; Gorton and Winton, 2017). A competing view is that bank capital increases survival probability and improves market share and profitability, thereby contributing to create value for shareholders (e.g., Allen et al., 2011; Berger and Bouwman, 2013; Mehran and Thakor, 2011). Bouwman et al. (2018) show that capital does not affect returns unconditionally, but in bad times high-capital banks have higher risk-adjusted stock returns (alphas) than low-capital banks.

13.2.2 CEO Compensation Structure

Another important issue that has received growing attention after the 2007–09 crisis and is likely to shape regulatory responses to the crisis is the role played by monetary incentives. To the extent that decisions are taken by human beings, not by inanimate institutions, many observers have argued that risk-taking in banks will largely be influenced by the incentives provided to bank managers through the design of their compensation. Poorly designed incentives have been criticized for inducing managers to engage in excessive risk-taking. For example, Bolton (2013) argues that compensation was based on the wrong performance benchmarks and rewarded short-term revenue performance without looking into how performance was achieved.

In the same vein, Admati and Hellwig (2014) depict distortionary compensation practices at large financial institutions as one of the possible elements for the failure of governance in the banking industry. To the extent that CEOs benefit from the upside of increased risk-taking, via performance-related compensation, and do not bear the consequences of a bank failure, one may expect an imbalanced CEO compensation to induce excessive risk-taking. Bebchuk et al. (2010) provide a case study of compensation at Bear Stearns and Lehman Brothers during the pre-crisis period (i.e., 2000–08). They show that the top five executive teams at these firms cashed out large amounts of performance-based compensation during this period. The bonus compensation they managed to cash out was not clawed back when the firms collapsed, and they pocketed large amounts from selling shares. This finding suggests that the structure of pay arrangements provided top executives with excessive risk-taking incentives. Bhagat and Bolton's (2014) results support this finding. They study the executive compensation structure in 14 of the largest US financial institutions during 2000–08 and document that incentives generated by executive compensation programmes correlate with excessive risk-taking by banks.

Several studies have focused on the role played by the sensitivity of CEO compensation to the stock price (i.e., CEO compensation delta) or to the stock volatility (i.e., CEO compensation vega). These analyses are grounded in previous literature in corporate finance showing that the sensitivity of CEO wealth to the stock price helps in aligning the incentives of managers with shareholder interests (Coles et al., 2006; Jensen and Murphy, 1990). DeYoung and Huang (2016) show that CEO pay-performance incentives reduce both positive liquidity creation externalities and negative systemic risk externalities, while pay-risk incentives increase both externalities. Fahlenbrach and Stulz (2011) show that banks for which CEO's incentives were better aligned with shareholder interests had worse stock returns during the GFC and that bank CEOs did not reduce their holdings of shares in anticipation of the crisis or during it. This suggests that bank managers did not foresee the upcoming materialization of risk and that better governance in banks does not imply less risk-taking. Cheng et al. (2015) show that a positive nexus between bank CEO compensation and risk measures does not necessarily imply that the design of executive pay encourages risk-taking. Specifically, they argue that, even in a classical principal-agent setting without entrenchment and with exogenous firm risk, riskier firms may raise total pay as compensation for the extra risk in equity stakes borne by risk-averse managers.

Bennett et al. (2016) comprehensively analyse the design of incentives in financial firms compared to non-financial firms. They show that banks link a larger fraction of top executive pay to short-term accounting metrics like return on equity (ROE) and earnings per share (EPS) and a smaller fraction to (long-term) stock price. Performance targets for bankers are not related to the risk of the bank, and ROE targets are not appropriately adjusted for leverage. Consequently, they argue that the design of executive compensation in banking may bolster both leverage and risk-taking. They find a positive association between the extent of short-term pay for bank CEOs and the risk of the bank before the financial crisis. Bhattacharyya and Purnanandam (2011) document that bank executive compensation was more sensitive to EPS than to the stock price, which induced banks to engage in risky and value-destroying residential mortgage lending and securitization. Related studies show that accounting profits and specially ROE predict well bank risk notably systemic risk, during crisis periods (e.g., Meiselman et al., 2020; Moussu and Petit-Romec, 2017). These results support the idea that linking bank CEO compensation to short-term performance measures, possibly inflated by risk-taking, may be an important driver of risk-taking in banks.

13.2.3   Corporate Governance

In theory, the effect of corporate governance on bank risk-taking is unclear. On the one hand, strong bank governance may increase risk-taking if it ensures that bank managers choose a risk profile that maximizes the value for shareholders. Importantly, a bank that maximizes shareholder value may hold a level of risk that is excessive from society's perspective. On the other hand, strong governance may also induce less risk-taking if it prevents bank managers from engaging in risky activities that boost short-term performance at the expenses of long-term value creation.

Studies focusing on the crisis period show that banks with boards that were more shareholder friendly underperformed other banks (Beltratti and Stulz, 2012; Erkens et al., 2012). Ferreira et al. (2013) find that banks with more entrenched managers were less likely to be bailed out during the crisis. Using a longer sample period, Anginer et al. (2018) show that better governance is associated with lower bank capital and more insolvency risk. Laeven and Levine (2009) find that the presence of large and powerful shareholders couples with more bank risk. Investigating more specifically the role of independent directors of US banks, Minton et al. (2014) show that financial expertise of independent directors of US banks is positively associated with balance sheet and market-based measures of risk in the run-up to the GFC. This suggests that financially expert independent directors enhanced risk-taking prior to the crisis. Though consistent with shareholder value maximization *ex ante*, these actions turn harmful during the crisis.

These studies do not imply that better governance is bad for shareholders; rather, the correct reading is that better governance does not mean less risk (Stulz, 2016). Better governance meant taking risks that would have been rewarding for shareholders had there not been a crisis. Good governance means that the bank has the right amount of risk for its shareholders, which may largely exceed the amount of risk that is appropriate from the perspective of society.

Related studies have focused on risk management-related corporate governance mechanisms. Ellul and Yerramilli (2013) construct a risk management index (RMI) to measure the strength and independence of the risk management function. They find that banks with higher RMI before the onset of the financial crisis have lower tail risk, lower non-performing loans, and better operating and stock return performance during the financial crisis. They also show that over the period 1995 to 2010, banks with a higher lagged RMI have lower tail risk and higher return on assets. Aebi et al. (2012) show that risk management-related governance mechanisms (e.g., the presence of a chief risk officer (CRO) in a bank's executive board and whether the CRO reports to the CEO or directly to the board of directors) are associated with a better bank performance during the 2007–09 financial crisis. Overall, a strong and independent risk management function seems to play an important role in curtailing tail risk exposures.

Finally, other studies have focused on the links between ownership structure and bank risk. In particular, the preferences of institutional investors (which have increased their power over management and monitor their decisions) as to risk-taking are not straightforward. Importantly, institutional investors are far from homogeneous and differ along an important dimension, namely their investment horizon (i.e., how long they expect to hold their shares on average). Garel and Petit-Romec (2017) show that banks with more short-term investor ownership have worse stock returns during the crisis and had taken more risk before the crisis. Further exploration also suggests that short-term investors sold their shares during the crisis, creating greater selling pressure. Using different risk measures, other studies have also documented that bank ownership structure matters to explain risk-taking over longer periods (e.g., Barry et al., 2011; Garel et al., 2018; Iannotta et al., 2007, 2013; see also Chapter 6).

13.2.4 Financial Innovation

Several studies have pointed out that recent financial innovations have made banks and their risk-taking more complex. Specifically, the involvement of banks in complex financial products has eroded the ability to understand and monitor bank risk-taking for both insiders and outsiders. Rajan (2006) was a precursor in raising the concern that financial innovation had led banks to focus on more and more complicated risks. Coval et al. (2009) show that the risk of structured products is much more complicated to assess than traditional "single-name" securities and shed light on the extreme sensibility of their default risk to modest imprecisions in parameter estimates. Brunnermeier and Sannikov (2014) find that securitization and derivative contracts that improve risk sharing may lead to higher leverage and more frequent crises. The prolonged profitability preceding the GFC may have contributed to give bank managers the illusion that they were correctly judging and managing risk (e.g., Thakor, 2014, 2015).

13.2.5   Systemic Risk and Too-Big-to-Fail Guarantees

A noteworthy feature of financial institutions is their connection with systemic risk (see also Chapters 5 and 7). As Thakor (2014) explains, a risk is *systematic* if it is correlated with the economy and hence not diversifiable whereas *systemic* risk threatens the whole system. While systemic risks are typically systematic, not all systematic risks are systemic. Systemic risk results from the fact that banks often hold assets whose risks are highly correlated, which poses a problem of contagion when the failure of a given bank can trigger the failure of other banks.

The incentives of banks to engage in collective risk-taking, that is, to take risks that are highly correlated with those of other banks, result to a large extent from the existence of (implicit) bailout guarantees. Indeed, a bank whose risks turn out badly is much more likely to be bailed out if other banks are also about to fail than in the case of an isolated failure. Taking correlated risks means that banks are likely to be in trouble at the same time and is thus a way to increase the likelihood of government intervention. Acharya et al. (2010) outline that since the collapse of several banks (or of the entire banking system) would disproportionately raise social costs, governments cannot leave several banks to fail and are forced to intervene. Farhi and Tirole (2012) show theoretically that the possibility of bailout assistance by regulators induces banks to make correlated asset choices and become highly levered. Specifically, they consider that regulators and policymakers may adopt active interest-rate policy in order to help banks during a shock. However, since it will affect the entire economy, policymakers will be reluctant to intervene if only a minority of banks is exposed to the shock. They show that this creates incentives for banks to take correlated risks and to choose risky balance sheets with important maturity mismatch to force government intervention in the case of a shock. Acharya and Yorulmazer (2007) make a similar argument and theoretically demonstrate the existence of a potential "too-many-to-fail" problem. Since regulators' decision to intervene and bailout banks depends on the number of bank failures, banks have incentives to herd on asset portfolio choices.

Empirical evidence suggests that banks choose highly correlated risks. Schuermann and Stiroh (2006) show that among S&P500 firms, the stock return correlation across banks is higher than for firms in any other industry. Bhattacharyya and Purnanandam (2011) find a sizable change in the composition of bank risk in the pre-GFC period. They document that banks became individually less risky as idiosyncratic risk fell sharply but held more and more correlated risks. Above all, they find that this alteration of risk was more marked for those banks more involved in securitizing mortgages. Finally, much care has been paid to develop measures of systemic risk (e.g., Acharya et al., 2012; Acharya et al., 2017) that generally depend on the propensity of a bank to be undercapitalized when the whole system is undercapitalized and in distress.

The GFC has witnessed an unprecedented amount of government support to the financial sector (see Chapters 9 and 11). This support resulted from a desire to contain systemic risk and avoid large financial institutions' failure if that would cause major disruptions to the financial system and economic activity. The nature and magnitude of this support have reinforced concerns about moral hazard arising from investor expectations of too-big-to fail (TBTF) guarantees for large financial institutions. Several empirical studies have sought to provide evidence of these TBTF guarantees and measure their magnitude. Acharya et al. (2016a) show that bond credit spreads are sensitive to risk for most financial institutions, but not for the largest ones. In addition, they observe that non-financial sectors do not share this feature. On equity data, Gandhi and Lustig (2015) find that the largest commercial bank stocks, ranked by total size of the balance sheet, have significantly lower risk-adjusted returns than small and medium-sized bank stocks, even though large banks are significantly more levered. These results are consistent with the existence of a size-dependent implicit support of banks. O'Hara and Shaw (1990) study the effect on bank stocks of the deposit insurance granted to TBTF banks. They find positive wealth effects accruing to TBTF banks, with relating negative effects for non-included banks. Other studies suggest that shareholders benefit from M&As promoting a bank to TBTF status (e.g., Kane, 2000). Brown and Dinç (2011) show that a country's ability to support its financial sector, as reflected by its public deficit, affects its treatment of distressed banks. Also, Demirgüç-Kunt and Huizinga (2013) report evidence suggesting that some banks are too large to save.

The importance of systemic risk in the GFC has called for specific regulatory reforms beyond matters of individual incentives and supervision and raise issues of systemic interdependence and transparency (Hellwig, 2009). Notably, bailing out only one bank should already be considered as too much. Hett and Schmidt (2017) analyse the impact of public intervention during and following the 2007–08 financial crisis in the US. They show that first bank rescues increase the bailout expectations of the remaining banks.

13.2.6   Other Factors

Researchers have investigated countless factors likely to have increased bank risk-taking in the run-up to the GFC. While previous subsections tackled specific key factors, for completeness, here we review other factors the literature identifies as causing bank excessive risk-taking.

Beyond rational factors based on governance, monitoring, and incentives, the role of beliefs and behavioural factors have also received some attention. Cheng et al. (2014) analyse whether mid-level managers in securitized finance were aware of a large-scale housing bubble and a looming crisis in 2004–06 using their personal home transaction data. On average, their sample securitization agents neither timed the market nor were cautious in their home transactions and showed no awareness of problems in overall housing markets. Certain groups of securitization agents were particularly aggressive in increasing their exposure to housing during this period, suggesting the need to expand the incentives-based view of the crisis to incorporate a role for beliefs. Ho et al. (2016) highlight the role played by overconfidence. Specifically, they find that, over a period that includes the 1998 Russian crisis and the GFC, banks with overconfident CEOs were more likely to weaken lending standards and increase leverage than other banks before a crisis. During crisis years, overconfident CEOs generally experienced greater increases in loan defaults, greater drops in operating and stock performance, greater increases in expected default probability, and higher likelihood of CEO turnover or failure than other banks.

A growing body of papers in finance investigates the effect of culture on financial decisions (see Karolyi, 2016 for a review). Boubakri et al. (2017) examine whether the prevailing national culture is material in determining bank performance during the crisis. Using a sample of 3,438 banks from 48 countries, they establish that uncertainty avoidance, collectivism, and power distance affect bank performance during crises. Fahlenbrach et al. (2012) show that a bank's stock return performance during the 1998 crisis predicts its stock return performance and probability of failure during the GFC, consistent with persistence in a bank's risk culture and/or aspects of its business model making its performance sensitive to crises.

Other studies have focused on the influence of stock market listing on bank risk-taking and vulnerability to crisis (e.g., Falato and Scharfstein, 2016; Garel et al., 2020). The results of these studies are consistent with short-term pressures from the stock market inducing banks to change important aspects of their business model and risk profile in a way that makes them more vulnerable to crises.

Finally, some studies have investigated the role of political connections and lobbying. Chen et al. (2018) study the effect of the political connections of government bank CEOs on bank performance during the financial crisis. They find that government banks with politically connected CEOs suffered much higher loan default rates and worse operating performance during the crisis than those without politically connected CEOs. However, these politically connected CEOs were less likely than others to be penalized for the poor performance of their banks. Lambert (2019) analyses the relationship between bank lobbying and supervisory decisions and documents moral hazard implications. Specifically, regulators are 44.7 per cent less likely to initiate enforcement actions against lobbying banks. Bunkanwanicha et al. (2019) examine the effect of bank bailouts on bank CEO careers.

13.3 REGULATORY RESPONSES: FOCUS ON CAPITAL REQUIREMENTS AND THEIR EFFECT ON BANKS

Following the GFC, governments and regulators around the world have sought to impose new and tighter regulations to curb bank risk-taking and foster financial stability. A new framework, Basel III, aims to address three main problems revealed by the GFC: inadequate quantity and quality of capital, insufficient liquidity, and interconnectedness of the financial system (Metrick and Rhee, 2018). While they all contribute to lower bank risk-taking, this section focuses on the increase of capital requirements in the US and European Union (EU). It briefly reviews the other reforms launched to end TBTF, boost the financial system's resilience, and curb contagion across banks.

13.3.1 Higher Capital Requirements

Bank capital occupies a central stage in banking regulation, which is easily explained by the fact that, as discussed in the previous section, higher capital improves financial stability. As explained by Thakor (2014), the rationale for imposing capital requirements on banks lies in the fact that the socially efficient capital level generally exceeds banks' privately optimal levels. A noteworthy feature of bank capital requirements is that they are risk-based (i.e., they depend on the risk of the bank's underlying assets). This section starts with a quick recap of the origins of risk-based capital requirements and then discusses several criticisms that have been highlighted by academic studies following the crisis.

More than three decades ago, the introduction of a form of bank regulation based on a system of risk-weights was largely supported by concurrent academic research which considered that constraining leverage via a simple capital to asset ratio was not an effective form of regulation. For example, Koehn and Santomero (1980) point out that imposing a simple capital to asset ratio to control bank risk-taking is likely to have opposite effects and to increase the probability of failure of some institutions. Their argument is that a form of regulation that does not consider asset quality in determining capital requirements would induce banks to increase the risk of their asset portfolio. In the same vein, Kahane (1977) argues that neither imposing a minimum capital requirement nor constraining the portfolio mix of a bank would be effective forms of regulation. Rather, he stresses that effectively limiting banks' probability of default requires combining the two. This need to have a form of regulation that considers asset quality led to introducing a system of risk-weights specifying a minimum capital requirement for each asset.

Following the GFC, several studies have pointed out several flaws in risk-based capital regulation. First, an important issue of bank capital regulation concerns the types of instruments that are counted as capital from a regulatory perspective. As acknowledged by Basel Committee on Banking Supervision (2009), banks were authorized to build up their regulatory capital with long-term debt, subordinated debt, and other hybrid products. Incorporating debt products in regulatory bank capital seems hard to reconcile with the clear distinction existing in corporate finance between debt and equity. In the case of banks, the rationale for including long-term or subordinated debt is that it represents a junior claim compared to deposits that enjoy deposit insurance. For example, Flannery (2017) and Hart and Zingales (2011) point out that counting long-term debt as Tier-2 regulatory capital makes sense if regulators aim to protect depositors. However, as they note, protecting deposits does not ensure financial stability. Indeed, debt claims provide a cushion for deposits but no insurance against bankruptcy because contrary to equity, debt claims have no loss-absorption capacity. Moreover, increased bank capital will hardly deter risk-taking incentives or provide loss-absorbing capacities if it is of too poor quality (Acharya et al., 2011; Admati et al., 2010). Indeed, as noted by Flannery (2010), risk-taking incentives and the associated gains depend on the "true" level of equity and not on the level of regulatory capital.

Second, the pre-crisis risk-based capital requirements created incentives for banks to overinvest in assets with a low capital charge compared to the underlying risk. Since the primary objective of bank capital regulation is to minimize bank insolvency probability or at least keep it below some predetermined levels, capital charges have been designed to protect against the risk of large unexpected losses. Consequently, capital charges generally depend on the total risk of each asset but fail to differentiate between systematic and idiosyncratic risk. Pennacchi (2006) shows theoretically that capital requirement failure to discriminate the nature of the risk creates strong incentives for banks to invest in assets with high systematic risk. Similarly, Iannotta and Pennacchi (2012) show that when capital requirements are based on credit ratings, banks have incentives to select similarly rated loans and bonds with the highest systematic risk to earn a credit spread premium. They confirm empirically that such strategies are possible by documenting that, for a given credit rating, bonds have significantly greater credit spreads when their issuers have higher systematic risk. In the years preceding the crisis, this overinvestment in the assets with the highest systematic risk was accentuated with the development of securitization. Coval et al. (2009) outline that an important feature of securitization is that it substitutes risks that are largely diversifiable for risks that are highly systematic.

Third, aside from its inability to discriminate systematic versus idiosyncratic risk, the system of regulatory risk-weights does not provide a continuous adjustment of bank capital to risk. Indeed, the same risk-weight can be assigned for a class of assets with risk heterogeneity. The mere fact of requiring the same capital charge for a class of assets where asset risk can differ creates the possibility of a shift towards riskier assets without having to increase capital. One of the most telling examples is sovereign bonds to which Basel II assigns a zero risk-weight (see Chapter 12). Despite differences in country ratings and financial situations, banks have been allowed to invest in sovereign bonds posting no capital against these positions. This zero risk-weight for any investment in sovereign debt creates an incentive to invest in the riskiest sovereign bonds. Acharya and Steffen (2015) study European banks' sovereign bond exposures before and during the recent financial crisis. Estimating the sensitivity of bank stock returns to sovereign bond returns, they find that European banks have positive exposures to peripheral sovereigns (Greece, Italy, Ireland, Portugal, Spain) and negative to German sovereign bonds.

Finally, one additional concern of the system of risk-weights is that it may have involuntarily increased systemic risk. Indeed, if all banks respond to risk-based capital regulation in the same way by making the same regulatory arbitrages and investing in the same low risk-weight assets, they will tend to have correlated asset choices and risk exposures.

The GFC has largely exposed the flaws and limitations of Basel II regulation. The reforms in Basel III retain in their core the technical framework for calculation of risk-weighted assets (RWAs) laid out in Basel II, and increase the required amount of capital for a given size of RWAs. The minimum Tier-1 capital requirements were raised from 4 to 6 per cent of RWAs, but additional extra "buffers" were created to adjust for the systemic importance of some institutions, the economic cycle, and to prevent accidental breaches of the minimum. As of September 2010, proposed Basel III norms asked for ratios as: 7–9.5 per cent (4.5% + 2.5% (conservation buffer) + 0–2.5% (seasonal buffer) for common equity and 8.5–11 per cent for Tier-1 capital and 10.5–13 per cent for total capital. Effective requirements for large global banks are now in the double digits as a percentage of RWAs. Now, capital cushions are greater in banks, especially the largest ones. The merits of these Basel reforms have been fiercely debated. A key issue is whether higher capital requirements have lowered risk-taking in banks post Basel III.

To answer this question, it is vital to understand that banks have been allowed to use their own internal risk models, rather than the Basel standard approach, to determine risk-weights and capital charges. The use of internal models was authorized to improve the risk calibration of capital requirements. A first series of papers examines whether the use of internal models to determine risk-weights harms the objective of a reduction of bank risk-taking. Barakova and Palvia (2014) evaluate the alignment of Basel II/III internal ratings-based (IRB) risk estimates with portfolio risk. They use loan performance as a direct measure of portfolio risk as well as less direct market-based measures. Their results show that internal rating-based risk-weights are highly correlated with loan performance. This supports the view that internally generated risk-weights are determined mostly by portfolio risk.

Other papers are more critical. A concern of internal models is that they also give banks the possibility to modify risk-weights to underestimate the riskiness of their assets, which artificially increases their regulatory capital ratios. In other words, the introduction of internal models may further accentuate the discrepancy between bank asset risk and the level of capital. Mariathasan and Merrouche (2014) document that risk-weight density (i.e., the ratio of risk-weighted assets to total assets) decreases once a bank has been granted regulatory approval to use internal models. This effect is not driven by changes in asset structure or by improved risk-measurement alone. By contrast, they find that the decline in risk-weights is stronger among weakly capitalized banks, which suggests a strategic use of risk models by some banks to appear better capitalized without having to increase capital. In a related study, Vallascas and Hagendorff (2013) examine the sensitivity of bank capital requirements and show that they are only loosely sensitive to changes in market measures of risk. Cizel et al. (2017) show that the nexus between risk-weights and bank distress is statistically insignificant in the subset of large banks that mostly apply internal rating-based models, while it is positive and statistically significant for the small banks not applying them. This finding is consistent with a concern that the IRB capital regulation may hamper the association between banks' reported and real risks. Ferri and Pesic (2017) document further evidence of regulatory arbitrage, studying the determinants of RWA/EAD (Exposure-At-Default) on data painstakingly compiled from Basel Pillar-Three for 239 European banks over 2007–13.

Another issue with IRB models relates to the consistency of the approaches adopted by banks, which further raises concerns. Berg and Koziol (2017), using a comprehensive German credit registry dataset from 40 banks and 17,000 corporate borrowers from 2008 to 2012, assess the consistency of internal default probability estimates across banks. They find that the variability of default probability estimates for the same borrower across banks is large. Montes et al. (2018) use European Banking Authority (EBA) 2014 stress test data to study the use of the internal ratings-based approach and the risk-weights of European banks. A simple inspection of data at country level reveals significant differences in the use of the IRB approach by banks and in RWA densities. They find a negative relation between use of the IRB approach and RWA densities, even after controlling for portfolio and bank characteristics.

Proponents of a reduction of capital requirements often argue that they raise banks' costs of funds, thus cutting credit provision and dampening economic activity. Recent studies examine whether the implemented higher capital requirements have reduced post GFC lending activity.

13.3.2 Leverage Ratio

The Basel III accord also introduced a minimum *leverage ratio* (LR) of capital to total assets (i.e., not risk-weighted), as a backstop for the RWA capital requirements that might not sufficiently match the riskiness of the assets. Since it is not based on an internal rating model of risk, the LR does not expose the peril of regulatory arbitrage as risk-weights based capital requirements do. In the US and EU, LRs require bank holding companies (BHCs) to have a minimum ratio of capital to total assets of 5 to 6 per cent.

After the LR was introduced, BHCs have cut back significantly on the intermediation of some lower-risk assets. This is because while under the risk-weighted capital requirements, such assets where not costly for banks, become so with the LR. They prefer using one dollar of equity to finance assets generating more return. The LR has particularly impaired the market for government securities repo intermediation (Duffie, 2018). General Collateral Finance Repo volumes have sunk by about 30 per cent since 2012 (Adenbaum et al., 2016). Allahrakha et al. (2018) show that following the 2012 introduction of the supplementary LR, broker-dealer affiliates of BHCs decreased their repo borrowing but increased their use of repo backed by more price-volatile collateral. In addition, the paper finds that the announcement of the leverage ratio rule has disincentivized those dealers affiliated with BHCs from borrowing in triparty repos. These repo-market distortions may also lower financial stability. Baranova et al.'s (2016) model suggests a loss of liquidity associated with reduced intermediation of securities financing markets due to the leverage ratio rule, especially in times of market stress.

13.3.3   Liquidity Coverage Ratio (LCR)

Under Basel III, the balance sheet liquidity of large banks must meet a minimum liquidity coverage ratio (LCR), designed to ensure that cash outflows that could plausibly occur within 30 days are fully covered by ready cash sources (Duffie, 2018). Kashyap et al. (2014) use a framework where banks face both credit risk and run risk, where the social planner cares about both sides of bank balance sheets and thus needs two different instruments, capital and liquidity.

Because liquidity rules are new, post-reform research on this question is limited. Calomiris et al. (2015) use a general setting to show that liquidity requirements can be optimal but would not necessarily take the form used in Basel III. Duffie (2018) warns that liquidity coverage ratios may have negative consequences if not relaxed in times of stress to allow a bank to access the liquidity sources that it requires.

An early attempt to empirically examine the consequences of liquidity rules is from Bonner and Eijffinger (2016), who use the rollout of an LCR-like rule in the Netherlands, with the main conclusion being that the rule decreased net-interest margins at banks. Rezende et al. (2020) estimate the effects of the LCR on the tenders that banks submit in Term Deposit Facility operations, a Federal Reserve tool created to manage the quantity of central bank reserves. They find that banks subject to the LCR submit tenders more often and of larger size than exempt banks when term deposits qualify for the LCR. These results suggest that liquidity regulation affects bank demand in monetary policy operations.

13.3.4   Stress Tests

Post GFC, regulatory bodies conduct periodic supervisory stress tests to ensure that large banks would remain adequately capitalized even after the losses arising from adverse macroeconomic scenarios. Comprehensive Capital Analysis and Review (CCAR) in the US and the Single Supervisory Mechanism (SSM) in the EU are the bodies in charge of conducting the tests. Stress tests primarily target systemically important financial institutions, the so-called SIFIs.

Annual stress tests have been shown to lead to changes in the risk management practices of BHCs. Acharya et al. (2018) document findings consistent with stress-tested banks reducing credit supply – particularly to relatively risky borrowers – to decrease their credit risk. Sahin et al. (2020) find that banks' systematic risk, as measured by betas, declined in nearly all years after the publication of stress test results. Cornett et al. (2020) examine bank behaviour around Federal Reserve stress tests and find that stress test banks increase capital ratios at the starting point for annual stress testing significantly more than non-stress test banks.

Another series of papers documents more adverse effects of stress testing on banking activities. Cortés et al. (2020) show that regulatory stress tests have altered banks' credit supply to small businesses. More precisely, they find that banks most affected by stress tests reallocate credit away from riskier markets and towards safer ones and raise interest on small loans. Nguyen et al. (2020) show that regulatory stress tests have a negative effect on both on- and off-balance sheet bank liquidity creation and asset-side liquidity creation. Their results suggest that, as banks enter the stress tests, they reduce their liquidity creation to avoid failing the stress tests. On a different note, Acharya et al. (2014) challenge the measure of capital shortfall used in regulatory stress tests by uncovering that risk measures used in RWAs are cross-sectionally uncorrelated with market measures of risk, as they do not account for the "risk that risk will change". They also show that banks that appeared to be best capitalized relative to RWAs did not outperform other banks when the EU economy suffered the sovereign debt crisis in 2011.

13.3.5 Resolution Mechanisms

How to end the moral hazard of bailouts? As highlighted in the first section, a central issue is that financial firms and their creditors seem to anticipate that government bailouts will be offered if needed, inducing too much risk-taking. New resolution mechanisms giving regulators the ability to impose losses on private creditors rather than have those losses borne by taxpayers have been implemented. Regulators have adopted the single-point-of-entry (SPOE) approach. In theory, regulators are now able to restructure the parent firm's liabilities to allow the key operating subsidiaries to continue providing services to the economy without significant or damaging interruption. As highlighted by Duffie (2018), to be successful, this approach requires that the parent company has enough general unsecured liabilities and that the failure resolution process does not trigger the early termination of financial contracts on which the firm and its counterparties rely for stability.[1] Duffie (2018) also points to problems caused by exemption from bankruptcy of qualified financial contracts and the potential need for debtor-in-possession bankruptcy liquidity in amounts larger than might be available during a general crisis. For these reasons, SPOE method for the failure resolution of systematic financial firms may not be yet ready for safe and successful deployment.

Avgouleas and Goodhart (2016) warn that bail-in regimes will not remove the need for public injection of funds unless the risk is idiosyncratic. This suggestion raises concerns for banks in the periphery of the euro area, which present high levels of non-performing assets, crippling credit growth and economic recovery.

For the new resolution mechanisms to be efficient, they must reshape the expectations of financial institutions. Failure resolution should have a predictable outcome. In the first place, do market participants believe that the resolution authorities will attempt to use their new power when failure is about to occur? Ignatowski and Korte (2014) provide empirical evidence, that, on average, those US banks that have become subject to Orderly Liquidation Authority have responded by reducing their riskiness, relative to banks that were already subject to Federal Deposit Insurance Corporation resolution. Another sign of credibility of failure resolutions is found in the results of event studies. Fiordelisi et al. (2020) document negative abnormal stock price reactions to bail-in policy announcements (EU) suggesting that investors perceive the new bail-in regime as a credible tool to decrease government interventions.

Finally, in practice, European authorities have found it difficult to impose bail-in for creditors (Metrick and Rhee, 2018). Another more general concern is that the developed resolution mechanisms are too complex to work. Tröger (2018), among others, makes the case that the European resolution framework is likely ineffective in establishing adequate market discipline through risk-reflecting prices for bank capital.

13.4   POOL OF ALTERNATIVE IDEAS

The Financial Stability Board regularly summarizes progress of financial stability regulation. While significant progress has been made on making financial institutions more resilient and making the derivatives market safer, question marks remain on the ability of governments to end "too-big-to-fail". We briefly discuss below proposals of researchers and practitioners that can complement existing measures to achieve greater financial stability, limit bank risk-taking, and end the moral hazard of TBTF banks.

Numerous observers have proposed dramatically changing the design of managerial incentives in banks. Since structuring bank CEO compensation to reward shareholder value maximization inevitably encourages risk-taking, some attention has been devoted to ways to incentivize bank executives to consider other stakeholders and the soundness of the bank. For example, Bolton et al. (2015) develop a model that proposes to link bank executive pay not just to stock price performance but also to a measure of default risk in order to force them to consider the interests of debtholders. Empirically, they show that the disclosure of a higher share of pension and deferred compensation in CEO total pay is associated with lower credit default swap (CDS) spreads, indicating that debt-like compensation is perceived by the market as reducing risk for financial institutions. Chaigneau (2013) calls for regulation of bank CEOs' compensation in a standard model of CEO compensation that incorporates leverage and investment decisions. Other studies argue that concentrating on bank capital regulation may be insufficient in controlling risk-taking and highlight the need to incorporate top management incentives (John et al., 2000; Kolm et al., 2017). Bhagat and Bolton (2014) recommend that bank executive incentive compensation should only consist of restricted stock and restricted stock options – restricted in the sense that the executive cannot sell the shares or exercise the options for two to four years after their last day in office. Addressing compensation practices for bank CEOs before and after the Financial Stability Board issued post-crisis guidelines on sound compensation, Cerasi et al. (2020) find that CEO pay has become more sensitive to risk, with CEOs in the post-reform period at riskier banks receiving less variable compensation than those at less-risky ones.

Other papers emphasize the role of fiscal incentives, in particular a reduction in tax discrimination between debt and equity funding to limit risk-taking and encourage banks to increase their capital levels (e.g., Martin-Flores and Moussu, 2019; Roe and Troege, 2018; Schepens, 2016). Rochet and Freixas (2013) show how insurance against systemic shocks can be provided without generating moral hazard. Their solution involves levying a systemic tax needed to cover the costs of future crises and more importantly establishing a systemic risk authority endowed with special resolution powers, including the control of bankers' compensation packages during crisis periods.

Other observers have emphasized that financial regulation, and in particular the risk-weights system of Basel, is too complex and call for grounding regulatory responses in simplicity (Admati and Hellwig, 2014; Haldane, 2012; Hoenig, 2012; Jenkins, 2012).

13.5 CONCLUSIONS

The 2007–09 financial crisis, considered as the worst financial crisis since the Great Depression, has imposed gigantic costs on society and forced states to intervene to avoid the collapse of the financial system. Since then, academics, regulators, and policymakers have tried to understand its causes and consequences. Thanks to countless studies and analyses, our collective understanding of the reasons why banks engage in excessive risk-taking and the factors contributing to foster financial stability has significantly improved. Significant financial reforms, in particular, in the form of higher bank capital requirements, have been implemented to avoid the repetition of a crisis of comparable magnitude. While banks and the financial system should now be much more resilient than they were in the period preceding the 2007–09 crisis, a crucial question is left unanswered: are banks ready to cope with a non-financial crisis that a pandemic or a climate catastrophe would cause?

Regarding the COVID-19 crisis, Carmen Reinhart who has documented the strong similarities of financial crises across the past eight centuries (Reinhart and Rogoff, 2009) recently emphasized that the COVID-19 crisis is truly different from prior financial crises with respect to its causes and severity. Acharya and Steffen (2020) use two "stress tests" to demonstrate that the quantum of credit commitments likely to move onto banks' balance sheets should be manageable thanks to the healthier capitalization of banks relative to before the Global Crisis. However, they point out that in a severely adverse scenario, the average Tier-1 capital to risk-weighted assets ratio of banks will likely move closer to the regulatory minimum of 8 per cent and well below for some banks. They further argue that regulators should plan for such a severe stress test by ensuring that banks prevent any further capital depletion through dividend payout or share buyback.

Regarding a potential climate crisis, concerns have risen that the existence of a carbon bubble (i.e., a bubble in the valuation of firms that depend on fossil fuels as factors of production) may affect financial stability (e.g., ESRB, 2016). Delis et al. (2018) show that before 2015 banks did not take into account climate policy risk in the pricing of loans. After 2015, the risk is priced, especially by green banks. Climate risk is now much more salient than it was in 2007–09 and more attention should be placed on better understanding the exposure of banks to climate risk and its implications for financial stability.

NOTE

1. Goodhart and Avgouleas (2015) provide a detailed critical evaluation of the US and EU bail-in approaches.

REFERENCES

Acharya, V., & Steffen, S. (2015). The "greatest" carry trade ever? Understanding eurozone bank risks. *Journal of Financial Economics*, 115, 215–36.

Acharya, V., & Steffen, S. (2020). Stress tests for banks as liquidity insurers in a time of COVID. VoxEU. org, March, 22.

Acharya, V.V., & Yorulmazer, T. (2007). Too many to fail – an analysis of time-inconsistency in bank closure policies. *Journal of Financial Intermediation*, 16(1), 1–31.

Acharya, V.V., Anginer, D., & Warburton, A.J. (2016a). The end of market discipline? Investor expectations of implicit government guarantees. Available at SSRN: 1961656.

Acharya, V.V., Berger, A.N., & Roman, R.A. (2018). Lending implications of US bank stress tests: Costs or benefits? *Journal of Financial Intermediation*, 34, 58–90.

Acharya, V., Engle, R., & Pierret, D. (2014). Testing macroprudential stress tests: The risk of regulatory risk weights. *Journal of Monetary Economics*, 65, 36–53.

Acharya, V., Engle, R., & Richardson, M. (2012). Capital shortfall: A new approach to ranking and regulating systemic risks. *American Economic Review*, 102(3), 59–64.

Acharya, V.V., Mehran, H., & Thakor, A. (2010). Caught between Scylla and Charybdis? Regulating bank leverage when there is rent seeking and risk taking. Working paper. NYU-Stern, New York Fed, and Washington University at St. Louis.

Acharya, V., Pagano, M., & Volpin, P. (2016b). Seeking alpha: Excess risk taking and competition for managerial talent. *The Review of Financial Studies*, 29(10), 2565–99.

Acharya, V.V., Gujral, I., Kulkarni, N., & Shin, H.S. (2011). Dividends and bank capital in the financial crisis of 2007–2009 (No. w16896). National Bureau of Economic Research.

Acharya, V.V., Pedersen, L.H., Philippon, T., & Richardson, M. (2017). Measuring systemic risk. *The Review of Financial Studies*, 30(1), 2–47.

Adenbaum, Jacob, et al. (2016). What's up with GCF Repo®. Liberty Street Economics, 2 May.

Admati, A., & Hellwig, M. (2014). *The Bankers' New Clothes: What's Wrong with Banking and What to Do about It – Updated Edition*. Princeton, NJ: Princeton University Press.

Admati, A.R., DeMarzo, P.M., Hellwig, M., & Pfleiderer, P. (2010). Fallacies, irrelevant facts, and myths in the discussion of capital regulation: Why bank equity is not expensive (Vol. 86). Max Planck Instute for Research on Collective Goods.

Aebi, V., Sabato, G., & Schmid, M. (2012). Risk management, corporate governance, and bank performance in the financial crisis. *Journal of Banking & Finance*, 36(12), 3213–26.

Allahrakha, M., Cetina, J., & Munyan, B. (2018). Do higher capital standards always reduce bank risk? The impact of the Basel leverage ratio on the US triparty repo market. *Journal of Financial Intermediation*, 34, 3–16.

Allen, F., Carletti, E., & Marquez, R. (2011). Credit market competition and capital regulation. *The Review of Financial Studies*, 24(4), 983–1018.

Anginer, D., Demirgüç-Kunt, A., Huizinga, H., & Ma, K. (2018). Corporate governance of banks and financial stability. *Journal of Financial Economics*, 130(2), 327–46.

Avgouleas, E., & Goodhart, C. (2016). An anatomy of bank bail-ins – why the Eurozone needs a fiscal backstop for the banking sector. *European Economy*, 2, 75–90.

Barakova, I., & Palvia, A. (2014). Do banks' internal Basel risk estimates reflect risk? *Journal of Financial Stability*, 13, 167–79.

Baranova, Y., Liu, Z., & Noss, J. (2016). The role of collateral in supporting liquidity. *Journal of Financial Market Infrastructures*, 5(1), 1–26.

Barry, T.A., Lepetit, L., & Tarazi, A. (2011). Ownership structure and risk in publicly held and privately owned banks. *Journal of Banking & Finance*, 35(5), 1327–40.

Basel Committee on Banking Supervision (2009). Strengthening the Resilience of the Banking Sector, Consultative Document, Bank for International Settlements, Basel.

Bebchuk, L.A., Cohen, A., & Spamann, H. (2010). The wages of failure: Executive compensation at Bear Stearns and Lehman 2000–2008. *Yale Journal on Regulation*, 27, 257.

Beltratti, A., & Stulz, R.M. (2012). The credit crisis around the globe: Why did some banks perform better? *Journal of Financial Economics*, 105(1), 1–17.

Bennett, B., Gopalan, R., & Thakor, A.V. (2016). The structure of banker's pay. Available at SSRN: 2795260.

Berg, T., & Koziol, P. (2017). An analysis of the consistency of banks' internal ratings. *Journal of Banking & Finance*, 78, 27–41.

Berger, A.N., & Bouwman, C.H. (2013). How does capital affect bank performance during financial crises? *Journal of Financial Economics*, 109(1), 146–76.

Bhagat, S., & Bolton, B. (2014). Financial crisis and bank executive incentive compensation. *Journal of Corporate Finance*, 25, 313–41.

Bhattacharyya, S., & Purnanandam, A. (2011). Risk-taking by banks: What did we know and when did we know it? In AFA 2012 Chicago Meetings Paper, November.

Bolton, P. (2013). The Good Banker. Columbia University mimeo, November.

Bolton, P., Mehran, H., & Shapiro, J. (2015). Executive compensation and risk taking. *Review of Finance*, 19(6), 2139–81.

Bonner, C., & Eijffinger, S.C. (2016). The impact of liquidity regulation on bank intermediation. *Review of Finance*, 20(5), 1945–79.

Boubakri, N., Mirzaei, A., & Samet, A. (2017). National culture and bank performance: Evidence from the recent financial crisis. *Journal of Financial Stability*, 29, 36–56.

Bouwman, C.H., Kim, H., & Shin, S.O.S. (2018). Bank capital and bank stock performance. Available at SSRN: 3007364.

Brown, C.O., & Dinç, I.S. (2011). Too many to fail? Evidence of regulatory forbearance when the banking sector is weak. *The Review of Financial Studies*, 24(4), 1378–405.

Brunnermeier, M.K. (2009). Deciphering the liquidity and credit crunch 2007–2008. *Journal of Economic Perspectives*, 23(1), 77–100.

Brunnermeier, M.K., & Sannikov, Y. (2014). A macroeconomic model with a financial sector. *American Economic Review*, 104(2), 379–421.

Bunkanwanicha, P., Di Giuli, A., & Salvadè, F. (2019). CEO careers after bank bailouts. Available at SSRN 3173545.

Calomiris, C.W., & Kahn, C.M. (1991). The role of demandable debt in structuring optimal banking arrangements. *American Economic Review*, 497–513.

Calomiris, C.W., Jaremski, M., Park, H., & Richardson, G. (2015). Liquidity risk, bank networks, and the value of joining the Federal Reserve System (No. w21684). National Bureau of Economic Research.

Cerasi, V., Deininger, S.M., Gambacorta, L., & Oliviero, T. (2020). How post-crisis regulation has affected bank CEO compensation. *Journal of International Money and Finance*, 102153.

Chaigneau, P. (2013). Risk-shifting and the regulation of bank CEOs' compensation. *Journal of Financial Stability*, 9(4), 778–89.

Chen, H.K., Liao, Y.C., Lin, C.Y., & Yen, J.F. (2018). The effect of the political connections of government bank CEOs on bank performance during the financial crisis. *Journal of Financial Stability*, 36, 130–43.

Cheng, I.H., Hong, H., & Scheinkman, J.A. (2015). Yesterday's heroes: Compensation and risk at financial firms. *The Journal of Finance*, 70(2), 839–79.

Cheng, I.H., Raina, S., & Xiong, W. (2014). Wall Street and the housing bubble. *American Economic Review*, 104(9), 2797–829.

Cizel, J., Rijken, H.A., Altman, E.I., & Wierts, P. (2017). Assessing Basel III capital ratios: Do risk weights matter? Tinbergen Institute.

Coles, J.L., Daniel, N.D., & Naveen, L. (2006). Managerial incentives and risk-taking. *Journal of Financial Economics*, 79(2), 431–68.

Cornett, M.M., Minnick, K., Schorno, P.J., & Tehranian, H. (2020). An examination of bank behavior around Federal Reserve stress tests. *Journal of Financial Intermediation*, 41, 100789.

Cortés, K.R., Demyanyk, Y., Li, L., Loutskina, E., & Strahan, P.E. (2020). Stress tests and small business lending. *Journal of Financial Economics*, 136(1), 260–79.

Coval, J., Jurek, J., & Stafford, E. (2009). The economics of structured finance. *Journal of Economic Perspectives*, 23(1), 3–25.

DeAngelo, H., & Stulz, R.M. (2015). Liquid-claim production, risk management, and bank capital structure: Why high leverage is optimal for banks. *Journal of Financial Economics*, 116(2), 219–36.

Delis, M., De Greiff, K., & Ongena, S. (2018). Being stranded on the carbon bubble? Climate policy risk and the pricing of bank loans. SFI Research Paper, 8–10.

Demirguc-Kunt, A., & Huizinga, H. (2013). Are banks too big to fail or too big to save? International evidence from equity prices and CDS spreads. *Journal of Banking & Finance*, 37(3), 875–94.

Demirguc-Kunt, A., Detragiache, E., & Merrouche, O. (2013). Bank capital: Lessons from the financial crisis. *Journal of Money, Credit and Banking*, 45(6), 1147–64.

DeYoung, R., & Huang, M. (2016). The external effects of bank executive pay: Liquidity creation and systemic risk. Available at SSRN: 2753759.

Diamond, D.W., & Rajan, R.G. (2001). Liquidity risk, liquidity creation, and financial fragility: A theory of banking. *Journal of Political Economy*, 109(2), 287–327.

Diamond, D.W., & Rajan, R.G. (2009). The credit crisis: Conjectures about causes and remedies. *American Economic Review*, 99(2), 606–10.

Duffie, D. (2018). Financial regulatory reform after the crisis: An assessment. *Management Science*, 64(10), 4835–57.

Ellul, A., & Yerramilli, V. (2013). Stronger risk controls, lower risk: Evidence from US bank holding companies. *The Journal of Finance*, 68(5), 1757–803.

Erkens, D.H., Hung, M., & Matos, P. (2012). Corporate governance in the 2007–2008 financial crisis: Evidence from financial institutions worldwide. *Journal of Corporate Finance*, 18(2), 389–411.

ESRB (2016). Too Late, Too Sudden: Transition to a Low-carbon Economy and Systemic Risk by a Group of the ESRB Advisory Scientific Committee. European Systemic Risk Board, Frankfurt.

Fahlenbrach, R., & Stulz, R.M. (2011). Bank CEO incentives and the credit crisis. *Journal of Financial Economics*, 99(1), 11–26.

Fahlenbrach, R., Prilmeier, R., & Stulz, R.M. (2012). This time is the same: Using bank performance in 1998 to explain bank performance during the recent financial crisis. *The Journal of Finance*, 67(6), 2139–85.

Falato, A., & Scharfstein, D. (2016). The stock market and bank risk-taking (No. w22689). National Bureau of Economic Research.

Farhi, E., & Tirole, J. (2012). Collective moral hazard, maturity mismatch, and systemic bailouts. *American Economic Review*, 102(1), 60–93.

Ferreira, D., Kershaw, D., Kirchmaier, T., & Schuster, E.P. (2013). Shareholder empowerment and bank bailouts. LSE Research Online Documents on Economics 56083, London School of Economics and Political Science, LSE Library.

Ferri, G., & Pesic, V. (2017). Bank regulatory arbitrage via risk weighted assets dispersion. *Journal of Financial Stability*, 33, 331–45.

Fiordelisi, F., Minnucci, F., Previati, D., & Ricci, O. (2020). Bail-in regulation and stock market reaction. *Economics Letters*, 186, 108801.

Flannery, M.J. (2010, May). What to do about TBTF. In *Federal Reserve Bank of Atlanta 2010 Financial Markets Conference – Up from the Ashes: The Financial System after the Crisis*, Atlanta, May (Vol. 12).

Flannery, M.J. (2017). Stabilizing large financial institutions with contingent capital certificates. In *The Most Important Concepts in Finance*. Cheltenham, UK and Northampton, MA, USA: Edward Elgar Publishing, pp. 277–300.

Gandhi, P., & Lustig, H. (2015). Size anomalies in US bank stock returns. *The Journal of Finance*, 70(2), 733–68.

Garel, A., & Petit-Romec, A. (2017). Bank capital in the crisis: It's not just how much you have but who provides it. *Journal of Banking & Finance*, 75, 152–66.

Garel, A., Martín-Flores, J.M., & Petit-Romec, A. (2020). Stock market listing and the persistence of bank performance across crises. *Journal of Banking & Finance*, 105885.

Garel, A., Petit-Romec, A., & Vander Vennet, R. (2018). Institutional shareholders and bank capital. Available at SSRN: 3170898.

Goodhart, C., & Avgouleas, E. (2015). A critical evaluation of bail-in as a bank recapitalization mechanism. *The New International Financial System: Analyzing the Cumulative Impact of Regulatory Reform*, 267–305.

Gorton, G.B. (2010). *Slapped by the Invisible Hand: The Panic of 2007.* New York: Oxford University Press.

Gorton, G., & Winton, A. (2017). Liquidity provision, bank capital, and the macroeconomy. *Journal of Money, Credit and Banking*, 49(1), 5–37.

Haldane, A.G. (2012). The Dog and the Frisbee. Paper speech held at Federal Bank of Kansas City's 36th Economic Policy Symposium, Jackson Hole, WY.

Hart, O., & Zingales, L. (2011). A new capital regulation for large financial institutions. *American Law and Economics Review*, 13, 453–90.

Hellwig, M.F. (2009). Systemic risk in the financial sector: An analysis of the subprime-mortgage financial crisis. *De economist*, 157(2), 129–207.

Hett, F., & Schmidt, A. (2017). Bank rescues and bailout expectations: The erosion of market discipline during the financial crisis. *Journal of Financial Economics*, 126(3), 635–51.

Ho, P.H., Huang, C.W., Lin, C.Y., & Yen, J.F. (2016). CEO overconfidence and financial crisis: Evidence from bank lending and leverage. *Journal of Financial Economics*, 120(1), 194–209.

Hoenig, T. (2012). Back to basics: A better alternative to Basel Capital Rules. Speech to The American Banker Regulatory Symposium, 14 September.

Iannotta, G., & Pennacchi, G. (2012). Bank Regulation, Credit Ratings, and Systematic Risk. SSRN Scholarly Paper, Social Science Research Network, Rochester, NY.

Iannotta, G., Nocera, G., & Sironi, A. (2007). Ownership structure, risk and performance in the European banking industry. *Journal of Banking & Finance*, 31(7), 2127–49.

Iannotta, G., Nocera, G., & Sironi, A. (2013). The impact of government ownership on bank risk. *Journal of Financial Intermediation*, 22(2), 152–76.

Ignatowski, M., & Korte, J. (2014). Wishful thinking or effective threat? Tightening bank resolution regimes and bank risk-taking. *Journal of Financial Stability*, 15, 264–81.

Jayaraman, S., & Thakor, A.V. (2014). Who monitors the monitor? Bank capital structure and borrower monitoring. Available at SSRN: 2537390.

Jenkins, R. (2012). Let's make a deal. Speech, Bank of England, Financial Policy Committee.

Jensen, M.C., & Murphy, K.J. (1990). Performance pay and top-management incentives. *Journal of Political Economy*, 98(2), 225–64.

John, K., Saunders, A., & Senbet, L.W. (2000). A theory of bank regulation and management compensation. *The Review of Financial Studies*, 13, 95–125.

Kahane, Y. (1977). Capital adequacy and the regulation of financial intermediaries. *Journal of Banking & Finance*, 1(2), 207–18.

Kane, E.J. (2000). Incentives for banking megamergers: What motives might regulators infer from event-study evidence? *Journal of Money, Credit and Banking*, 32(2), 671–701.

Karolyi, G.A. (2016). The gravity of culture for finance. *Journal of Corporate Finance*, 41, 610–25.

Kashyap, A.K., Tsomocos, D.P., & Vardoulakis, A. (2014). Principles for macroprudential regulation. Chicago Booth Research Paper 14-19.

Koehn, M., & Santomero, A.M. (1980). Regulation of bank capital and portfolio risk. *The Journal of Finance*, 35(5), 1235–44.

Kolm, J., Laux, C., & Loranth, G. (2017). Regulating bank CEO compensation and active boards. *Review of Finance*, 21(5), 1901–32.

Laeven, L., & Levine, R. (2009). Bank governance, regulation and risk taking. *Journal of Financial Economics*, 93(2), 259–75.

Lambert, T. (2019). Lobbying on regulatory enforcement actions: Evidence from US commercial and savings banks. *Management Science*, 65(6), 2545–72.

Mariathasan, M., & Merrouche, O. (2014). The manipulation of Basel risk-weights. *Journal of Financial Intermediation*, 23(3), 300–21.

Martin-Flores, J., & Moussu, C. (2019). Is bank capital sensitive to a tax allowance on marginal equity? *European Financial Management*, 25(2), 325–57.

Mehran, H., & Thakor, A. (2011). Bank capital and value in the cross-section. *The Review of Financial Studies*, 24(4), 1019–67.

Meiselman, B.S., Nagel, S., & Purnanandam, A. (2020). Judging banks' risk by the profits they report. Available at SSRN: 3169730.

Metrick, A., & Rhee, J. (2018). Regulatory reform. *Annual Review of Financial Economics*, 10, 153–72.

Minton, B.A., Taillard, J.P., & Williamson, R. (2014). Financial expertise of the board, risk taking, and performance: Evidence from bank holding companies. *Journal of Financial and Quantitative Analysis*, 49(2), 351–80.

Montes, C.P., Artigas, C.T., Cristófoli, M.E., & San Segundo, N.L. (2018). The impact of the IRB approach on the risk weights of European banks. *Journal of Financial Stability*, 39, 147–66.

Moussu, C., & Petit-Romec, A. (2017). ROE in banks: Performance or risk measure? Evidence from financial crises. *Finance*, 38(2), 95–133.

Nguyen, T.V.H., Ahmed, S., Chevapatrakul, T., & Onali, E. (2020). Do stress tests affect bank liquidity creation? *Journal of Corporate Finance*, 101622.

O'Hara, M., & Shaw, W. (1990). Deposit insurance and wealth effects: The value of being "too big to fail". *The Journal of Finance*, 45(5), 1587–600.

Pennacchi, G. (2006). Deposit insurance, bank regulation, and financial system risks. *Journal of Monetary Economics*, 53, 1–30.

Purnanandam, A. (2011). Originate-to-distribute model and the subprime mortgage crisis. *The Review of Financial Studies*, 24(6), 1881–915.

Rajan, R.G. (2006). Has finance made the world riskier? *European Financial Management*, 12(4), 499–533.

Reinhart, C.M., & Rogoff, K.S. (2009). *This Time Is Different: Eight Centuries of Financial Folly.* Princeton, NJ: Princeton University Press.

Rezende, M., Styczynski, M.F., & Vojtech, C.M. (2020). The effects of liquidity regulation on bank demand in monetary policy operations. *Journal of Financial Intermediation*, 100860.

Rochet, J.C., & Freixas, X. (2013). Taming systemically important financial institutions. *Journal of Money, Credit, and Banking*, 45(s1), 37–58.

Roe, M.J., & Troege, M. (2018). Containing systemic risk by taxing banks properly. *Yale Journal on Regulation*, 35, 181.

Sahin, C., de Haan, J., & Neretina, E. (2020). Banking stress test effects on returns and risks. *Journal of Banking & Finance*, 105843.

Schepens, G. (2016). Taxes and bank capital structure. *Journal of Financial Economics*, 120(3), 585–600.

Schuermann, T., & Stiroh, K.J. (2006). Visible and hidden risk factors for banks (No. 252). Staff Report.

Stulz, R.M. (2016). Risk management, governance, culture, and risk taking in banks. *Economic Policy Review*, August, 43–60.

Thakor, A.V. (2014). Bank capital and financial stability: An economic trade-off or a Faustian bargain? *Annual Review of Financial Economics*, 6(1), 185–223.

Thakor, A.V. (2015). Corporate culture in banking. Available at SSRN: 2565514.

Tröger, T.H. (2018). Too complex to work: A critical assessment of the bail-in tool under the European bank recovery and resolution regime. *Journal of Financial Regulation*, 4(1), 35–72.

Vallascas, F., & Hagendorff, J. (2013). The risk sensitivity of capital requirements: Evidence from an international sample of large banks. *Review of Finance*, rfs042.

PART IV

Learning from past financial crises to prevent
future ones

14. Looking back: a historical perspective on European crises

Elias Bengtsson

14.1 UNDERSTANDING FINANCIAL CRISES THROUGH EUROPEAN HISTORICAL EXPERIENCES

The previous chapters in this book show that while there are relatively few theoretical explanations of why financial crises occur (see Chapter 2), there is a large variety in how each crisis plays out. How crises are transmitted and the effects they have had on the economy and society differs. Even if financial crises appear to be a regular and recurring phenomenon in both modern market economies and other types of economies, each financial crisis is essentially different – paraphrasing Reinhart and Rogoff (2008). In addition, policy measures (see Chapters 9 and 10) – or indeed sometimes the absence of policy measures – also differ. Ultimately, for better or for worse, they also alter the paths of crises. Even the Global Financial Crisis (GFC) of 2007–09, as illustrated in Chapter 1, was shared by many economies across the world. It was also a kaleidoscope of several crises, each with its own idiosyncrasies, chronology and resonance with global events and developments in other economies.

Understanding crises fully is a daunting task. There is vast complexity and multitudes of perspectives, actors, interrelations and feedback loops involved in financial crises. Contemporary crises are indeed mirrors of the complexity of modern societies. Despite this, there have been several systemic attempts to summarize, compare and contrast financial crises. This chapter does exactly that by providing a historical perspective on financial crises in Europe (European Union (EU) Member States and Norway) in the period 1973–2016. From a financial perspective, this period covers several financial cycles and disruptive political events – from the liberalization in the 1970s and 1980s; the transition of many Central and Eastern European countries towards market economies; the breakdown and resurgence of currency cooperation; the dotcom crisis, the great moderation that followed and ended with the GFC and the Great Recession;

and finally the post crisis adjustment period that followed afterwards. The period of 1973–2016 also represents a long transition towards "becoming" Europe, or at least a new type of Europe where considerable steps towards financial integration have taken place through shared financial regulation, common monetary policy and freedom of movement of capital. The chapter seeks to draw conclusions on the nature of crises by looking backwards at this transitory period in Europe's history in search of patters and more or less generalizable observations (for a forward-looking approach see Chapter 15).

Ninety-three crisis events over the period are discussed in terms of a number of stylized facts on their nature, frequency, economic consequences and how authorities intervened through policy measures. A particular focus, in line with the scope of this book, is on systemic crises and the GFC in particular. But other non-systemic European financial crises or *episodes of financial stress* in the period are also covered, in order to compare and contrast them with the former group. The historical review is based on a dataset which differs from most, if not all, other crises datasets in that it combines a quantitative approach to identifying relevant events with qualitative information.[1] The qualitative information was provided by financial authorities across Europe, using common definitions and criteria. This enables this chapter to make a relatively rich review of the crises events in terms of their nature, length, policy responses and consequences.[2] Among other features, the dataset distinguishes between crisis and post-crisis adjustment periods, as well as to periods until crisis management policies ceased.[3]

The first section of this chapter presents a number of stylized historical facts on European crises. It shows how the number of ongoing systemic crises has changed over time, the underlying nature of these crises, and how certain features of the crises, such as length of crises' acute and recovery phases vary in relation to the crisis type. It also provides a broad overview of how the timing and duration of crisis policy measures differ depending on the type of crisis.

The second section discusses the consequences of the crisis events. It distinguishes two broad types of effects: macroeconomic consequences; and structural and institutional changes. It thereby seeks to understand the patterns of causes, consequences, responses and long-term effects of crises across different types of financial systems in Europe.

14.2 EUROPEAN FINANCIAL CRISES 1973–2016

14.2.1 Number and Type of Events

The historical events of European economies from 1973 to 2016 display considerable variation in terms of what risks led to financial crises or episodes of financial stress. Table 14.1 provides an overview of the frequency of systemic crises and episodes of financial stress, and breaks them down in terms of types of events.[4] These types determine the nature of events, and categorize them based on whether they were related to capital flows (deterioration in foreign currency exchanges and/or balance of payments), sovereign risk, bank risk or significant repricing in asset and real estate markets (see also Chapters 1, 2 and 3).

In this context, it is important to keep in mind that classifications are non-exclusive, meaning a crisis can be characterized by several risk materializations. For example, the crises in the UK and Sweden 1990–91 were combinations of banking crises related to price corrections in the

Table 14.1 Number and types of events

	Systemic crises	Episodes of financial stress
Complex crisis: multiple risks	33 (66%)	12 (28%)
incl. banking crisis	31	5
incl. significant asset price correction	30	9
incl. currency risk	20	8
incl. sovereign debt risk	10	–
Banking crisis	2 (4%)	3 (7%)
Currency crisis / balance of payments / capital flows	–	7 (17%)
Sovereign crisis	1 (2%)	–
Significant asset price corrections	1 (2%)	17 (39%)
Transition	13 (26%)	4 (9%)
Total	**50**	**43**

Note: The dataset distinguishes between a core set of systemic crises and an additional set of episodes of financial stress. Complex events are defined as the simultaneous materialization of multiple risks. With respect to complex events, this table reports the total frequency of all subcategories, which should not be interpreted as a sum. The materialization of one type of risk does not exclude the materialization of others. The share of each crisis type is indicated in brackets, for example, 66 per cent of the 50 identified systemic crises are complex events and relevant for macroprudential analysis. The totals disregard the subcategories for complex events.

Source: Author's calculations based on ECB/ESRB.

real estate sectors, which in turn were related to currency speculations. Similarly, the post-GFC recession was a combination of problems relating to asset price corrections across a broad range of asset classes, banking and sovereign indebtedness. Indeed, the majority (33 events) of the systemic crises in Europe are complex events which reflect the materialization of a combination of several different risks. Generally, the most frequent type of risk across events is banking risk, which materialized 31 times in complex events and twice in isolation (Table 14.1). The second most frequent type of risk is significant asset price corrections, including real estate downturns (30 occurrences in complex crises and one in isolation). The materialization of sovereign risk and currency risk is less frequent (10 and 20 crises, respectively, in complex crises and one materialization of sovereign risk in isolation).

Figure 14.1 presents a Venn diagram that displays how the crisis categories coincide and overlap for systemic crises. In seven of the 50 crises, all of the risk categories materialized and in nine crises all risks except sovereign risk materialized. The most common combination of risks is the occurrence of banking risk and significant asset price corrections (12 crises). Such "twin" crises have been common across the globe, as documented by Kaminsky and Reinhart (1999). Typically, problems in the banking sector precede a currency crisis – which in turn deepens the banking crisis and leads to a "vicious spiral". Often, such twin crises cause sovereign defaults, leading to the type of triple crises of currency, banking and sovereign risk that characterize seven crises in the European dataset.

Reinhart (2002) provides additional discussions on the interaction between currency crashes and external defaults, and Chapter 12 in this book elaborates further on the interconnectedness and feedback loops between public and private (financial) sectors through macrofinancial linkages. Another important characteristic of historical events in Europe is that 13 systemic crises relate to the transition to market economies in Central and Eastern European (CEE) countries, after the fall of the Soviet Union. This led to severance of existing economic ties as well as losses of important and secure foreign markets for these economies, coupled with increased competition from imported goods (Cornia and Paniccià, 2000).

Europe also experienced 43 residual episodes of financial crisis or stress in the period. Among episodes of financial stress, asset price corrections – which are not related to any other risk category – played a particularly large role. This indicates that when there is substantial stress or a crisis in the financial system, it is more often systemic than not. And that complex crises were more likely to be systemic than simple ones.

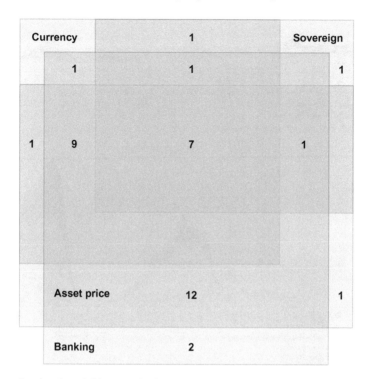

Note: Overlapping of risk categories for systemic crises in a Venn diagram (absolute frequency). This figure only illustrates systemic crises which are deemed relevant for macroprudential analysis and not related to crises relating to transition towards market economies.

Source: ECB/ESRB.

Figure 14.1 Types of risks that materialized during "complex" crises

14.2.2 Evolution of Systemic Crises

The frequency and types of crisis have evolved over time. Figure 14.2 illustrates the evolution of systemic crises (top) and episodes of financial stress (bottom) over time, and by distinguishing between different risk categories.[5] Three major waves of systemic crises can be identified in the charts. A number of crises occurred between the late 1970s and the mid-1980s. These relate in various degrees and shapes to the stagnation following the oil crisis of 1973, and the concurrent breakdown of the Bretton Woods agreement (ELEC, 1975; Ramirez Pérez, 2019; see also Chapter 9).

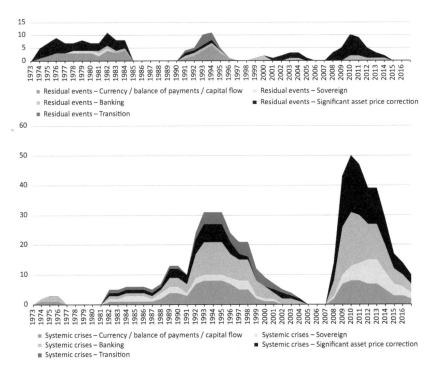

Source: Author's calculations based on ECB/ESRB.

Figure 14.2 *Frequency of systemic crises and episodes of financial stress by type of risk*

Two additional waves of crises occurred in the late 1980s/early 1990s and from 2007 onwards. The first which occurred in the 1990s reflects the Exchange Rate Mechanism (ERM) crisis, the transition in CEE and the transmission of global tensions to European countries due to crises in emerging markets (including the Russian crisis in 1998). This wave also includes crises that related to banking and real estate in a number of countries in North Western Europe, including the UK, Norway and Sweden.

Another big wave, with an even larger number of crises, reflects the transmission of the US subprime crisis and the materialization of bank and sovereign risk in several European countries. Following the subprime crisis that began in the US in mid-2007, 21 European countries experienced systemic crises. These started at different points in time between 2007 and 2011. In the same period, the remaining European countries experienced episodes of elevated financial stress characterized by significant asset price corrections.

Figure 14.2 also illustrates how the frequency of the different risk types has evolved over time. Again, the ERM crisis and the transition of CEE countries to market economies is reflected in the higher frequency of currency and transition crises in the 1980s and 1990s. From 2007, asset price corrections and sovereign crises have tended to play a more prominent role. The dataset of historical European crises also reveals that in most cases, sovereign risk materialized only after bursts of banking crises. This illustrates the interconnectedness of banking systems and government finances as discussed in Chapter 12. Another remark is that episodes of financial stress were quite rare in the 1970s and 1980s but have become much more frequent since the 1990s. Again, this reflects more European economies being more market oriented, and a growing role of financial markets as a source of financing for various economic agents, including non-financial corporations, households and governments.

Table 14.2 illustrates another important feature of systemic crises in Europe between 1973 and 2016 – namely, whether crises were related primarily to economic or social developments within the affected country, or whether they were primarily "imported" in the sense that they were largely caused by cross-border contagion from developments abroad. Clearly, most crises originated in developments inside *and* outside the country (23 crises). These crises also proved to be more complex than crises driven primarily by either domestic or external factors.

Purely domestic events were relatively more common among Western European countries in the 1990s. Externally driven crises occurred more recently. They were also common in Eastern European countries after the fall of the Soviet Union. These episodes can be interpreted as a result of increased financial integration and interconnectedness of the banking sector and real economies across borders, leading to higher risks of international spillovers from economic shocks (Candelon et al., 2011).

14.2.3   Length of Systemic Crises

One may think of crises as evolving processes, beginning with some triggering event, followed by a deterioration of economic conditions typically coupled with some crisis management policies (see also Chapters 2, 9 and 11). These may include liquidity support to banks, guarantees for bank liabilities, recapitalizations, forced/assisted mergers, the creation of bad banks or asset management companies, bank's resolutions. It also covers general debt relief and adoption of emergency fiscal packages and/or unconventional monetary policy (e.g. ECB Security Markets Programme (SMP) and Outright Monetary Transactions (OMT)). Eventually, crisis management policies are phased out and thereafter

Table 14.2   Frequency of crisis by origin of shocks/imbalances

	Domestic	Both	External
Complex crisis: multiple risks	6 (13%)	19 (41%)	6 (17%)
incl. banking crisis	6	16	7
incl. significant asset price correction	5	19	6
incl. currency risk	4	12	4
incl. sovereign debt risk	–	8	2
Banking crisis	1 (2%)	1 (2%)	–
Currency crisis / balance of payments / capital flows	–	–	–
Sovereign crisis	–	1 (2%)	–
Significant asset price correction	1 (2%)	–	–
Transition	2 (4%)	2 (4%)	5 (11%)
Total	**12**	**23**	**13**

Note: This table refers to systemic crises which are deemed relevant for macroprudential analysis. It is important to note that complex events are defined as the simultaneous materialization of multiple risks. The table therefore also reports the total frequency of all subcategories, which should not be interpreted as a sum. The reader should also be aware of the fact that the three classifications of origin are mutually exclusive, that is, a complex event can only be purely domestic, purely external or both external and domestic, but not a combination of these. In two cases sovereign tensions materialized in one country in isolation from "obvious" domestic imbalances. These are complex episodes involving the materialization of several types of risks. One of them was related to the ERM crisis, another episode was driven mainly by external trade imbalances, high foreign interest rates and high government deficits.

Source: ECB/ESRB.

a period of post-crisis adjustment begins (Bussière and Fratzscher, 2008).

Figure 14.3 offers more insight into the length of the different phases of crises experienced in Europe between 1973 and 2016. It shows the breakdown of length of systemic crises by type of financial crisis and origin. In European experiences, significant asset price corrections, sovereign and banking crises do not appear to differ much in terms of their length (between 49 and 68 months). These figures appear to be relatively consistent with other research on the duration of systemic financial crises; on a sample of systemic crises in both advanced and emerging markets between 1899 and 2007, Reinhart and Rogoff (2008) report that crises last on average around 58 months. Currency crises, at least in Europe, seem to be shorter on average. This is not necessarily related to the type of risk that materialized but could be explained by the period when most currency crises occurred. In the 1990s, the ERM crisis caused distress across many European countries, but these crises were relatively quickly

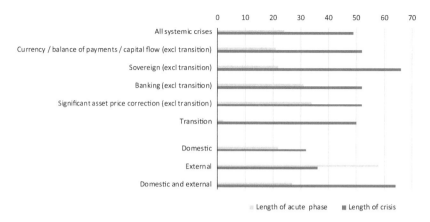

Note: This figure refers to systemic crises which are deemed relevant for macroprudential analysis. Complex events are not separated from single events in this chart, for example, the average is calculated over all events where the currency dummy is activated, including those where another risk materializes for the same event. This results in double counting with respect to complex events. It is further important to note that the classification of crisis types and the origin are not mutually exclusive, that is, the distinctions between crisis types and origins should be interpreted as complements. The length of an acute crisis phase is calculated by taking the time between the start of the crisis and the end of crisis management. The length of the recovery period is defined as being from the end of crisis management policies until the system is "back to normal" (see Appendix for definitions).

Figure 14.3   Length of crisis phases by type of crisis (months in average)

resolved by altered foreign exchange regimes (Buiter et al., 1997). This is also reflected in the relatively short average crisis management phases of such crises. Figure 14.3 also shows that international crises, that is, those which are driven by both domestic and external factors, seem to be the most persistent. This may potentially be driven by the GFC and the Great Recession that followed, but nevertheless illustrate how spillover and contagion effects can amplify domestic risks and weaknesses in financial system resilience.

Figure 14.4 displays the average length in months of the acute and crisis management phases by the year the crisis or crises started. One observation is that the median is lower than the average, implying that average output losses and increases in indebtedness are strongly affected by crises that are exceptionally costly. Moreover, while there appears to be no general pattern of the acute phases between the three major waves of crises, the phase following the acute crisis management phase appears to be lengthier for recent crises than for crises in the 1970s to the 1990s. The underlying reasons for this are uncertain, but an explanation could be that crises have become more synchronized across countries over time (Dungey

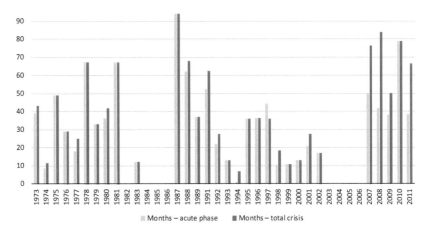

■ Months – acute phase   ■ Months – total crisis

Note: Year is start year of crisis.

Source: Author's calculations based on ECB/ESRB.

Figure 14.4   Average length of crisis phases 1973–2011

and Jacobs, 2015). This may make recovery more difficult, as crisis struck countries can rely less on export-driven recovery that often follow currency devaluations.

14.2.4   Crisis Management Policies

Crisis management policies of various sorts is a common feature of financial crises. Table 14.3 shows how frequently five categories of policy actions were applied in European crises over 1973–2016. One observation is that capital and/or liquidity support is the most commonly used crisis management policy. It was indeed used for all banking crises or complex crises involving banking over the time period. New banking regulation and strengthened financial supervisory authorities (FSAs) was another feature that characterized almost all banking crises. This was also the case for policy measures where banks are restructured, liquidated or consolidated through mergers or acquisitions. In the ERM crises in the 1990s, monetary policy measures were common, such as a change in interest rates and minimum reserve requirements. Measures also involved the introduction of new currencies as many CEE countries transited to market economies after the fall of the Soviet Union. Moreover, during the GFC, many governments were forced to bail out banks or to provide support in the form of capital or liquidity. As discussed in Chapter 9, quantitative monetary easing was also a common policy measure in the GFC.

Table 14.3   Crisis policies in Europe 1973–2016

Breakdown of crisis management policies by crisis type (absolute frequency; percentages)	New banking regulation and strengthening of FSA	Monetary policy measures	Capital or liquidity support and/or funding/deposit guarantee scheme	Restructuring of banks, M&As, liquidations	SPV/bad banks/ AMC
Complex crisis: multiple risks	8 (24%)	16 (48%)	27 (82%)	6 (18%)	7 (21%)
incl. banking crisis	8	14	27	6	7
incl. significant asset price correction	8	15	25	5	7
incl. currency risk	5	10	14	4	5
incl. sovereign debt risk	5	6	7	2	4
Banking crisis	1 (50%)	–	2 (100%)	1 (50%)	–
Currency crisis / balance of payments / capital flows	–	–	1 (100%)	–	–
Sovereign crisis	–	–	–	–	–
Significant asset price correction	–	–	–	–	–
Transition	2 (22%)	3 (33%)	6 (87%)	2 (22%)	2 (22%)
Total	**11**	**19**	**36**	**9**	**9**

Note: Monetary policy measures include new currency and lowering minimum reserve requirements. With respect to complex crises, this table reports the total frequency of policies across all subcategories, which should not be interpreted as a sum, since crises are usually addressed by a variety of measures. This table reports the most frequently named policies. The values denote the percentage shares of systemic crises within the respective subcategory in which the policy was applied, for example, 24 per cent of complex crises are associated with new banking regulation and the strengthening of the financial supervisory authorities (FSA).

Source: ECB/ESRB calculations.

14.3   CONSEQUENCES OF EUROPEAN FINANCIAL CRISES 1973–2016

This section discusses European experiences in terms of the consequences or effects that crises lead to. It distinguishes two broad types of effects: how macroeconomic consequences in terms of output losses and fiscal costs have varied across the types and origins of crisis; and how crises have influenced structural and institutional change. This is accomplished by mapping empirical research on these topics in the European context. The theoretical explanations highlighted in prior research are also briefly covered.

14.3.1   Macroeconomic Consequences

Table 14.4 provides various proxies to estimate the macroeconomic cost of systemic crises in Europe during 1973–2016. Output losses as a percentage of GDP[6] (Column 2) are based on the approach used by Laeven and Valencia (2013) and are calculated as the average cumulative difference between the GDP trend and observed GDP over the crisis period.[7] Table 14.4 also reports a proxy for the fiscal costs of a crisis (Column 3) in the shape of average increases in government debt-to-GDP ratios during

Table 14.4   Costs of systemic crises

	Output loss (% of GDP)			Increase in debt-to-GDP ratio (% of GDP)		
	Mean	Median	Skewness	Mean	Median	Skewness
Total	8%	6%	1.07	21%	16%	1.15
Currency	9%	7%	0.96	25%	18%	0.77
Sovereign	12%	12%	0.5	39%	46%	0.05
Banking	9%	7%	1.02	22%	17%	1.08
Asset price correction	9%	7%	0.93	24%	17%	1.01
External origin	6%	5%	0.76	9%	11%	−0.74
Domestic and external origin	11%	10%	0.58	30%	27%	0.78

Note: Output loss are calculated over a time horizon from start of crisis to end of acute phase. Increase in debt-to GDP ratio are calculated over a time horizon from one year before start of crisis to end of acute phase. Non-complex events are explicitly excluded, as there are too few observations in the dataset. Debt-to-GDP ratio refers to the general government consolidated gross debt as a percentage of GDP. For detailed explanation of the computational methods see Lo Duca et al. (2017).

Source: ECB/ESRB calculations.

the acute phase of the crises.[8] A detailed description of the underlying computational methods and choices is reported in Lo Duca et al. (2017).[9] Also, to complement the averages, Table 14.4 shows the median and distribution skewness and breaks down the results across different types of crises.

The European experiences of systemic crises have on average resulted in output losses of around 8 per cent. The median output loss is 6 per cent, which is relatively close to the average, and indicates that typically crises are very costly events. Comparing the level of government debt-to-GDP ratio one year before the start of the crisis with the level at the end of the crisis, an average increase of 21 percentage points demonstrates how government finances tend to deteriorate with financial crises. As discussed in Chapter 12, this is often a combination of tax revenue decreases from lowered economic activity; increased government expenditures relating to social benefits such as governmental unemployment insurance; and from outright support schemes that could target the financial system or the general economy (or both).

Mean output losses and increases in government indebtedness are relatively similar for crises involving banking, asset price correction and currency/balance of payments turmoil. However, crises relating to sovereign risk are a completely different story; these are associated with output losses of 12 per cent on average and increases in debt-to-GDP ratios of around 39 per cent. Unlike other types of risk, whose median are below their averages, the median increase in indebtedness is 46 per cent. The median output losses of crises that relate to sovereign debt risks are almost twice as high as for other crises. These findings are linked in the sense that a drop in GDP automatically leads to an increase in the debt-to-GDP ratio even without an increase in debt.

In relation to Reinhart and Rogoff's (2008) dataset on systemic crises in both advanced and emerging markets, the output loss estimates are relatively similar; the global crises dataset estimates a −9.3 per cent GDP loss from peak-to-trough over downturns that typically lasts two years. However, Reinhart and Rogoff (2008) report higher figures for increases in public debt, which in their sample averages at 186 per cent. One reason could be that stimulus packages and similar policies in emerging markets have been larger in relation to their relatively lower GDP levels. Also, as put forward by Reinhart and Rogoff, more recent crises (as covered in the European database) may have led to less macroeconomic consequences as a result of different and more flexible monetary policy frameworks.

Turning to the differences in macroeconomic consequences, Table 14.4 also shows that they vary depending on the origin of crises. For domestic crises, average output losses are less compared with crises where external factors play an important role. In crises whose origin is both domestic and international, output losses and impact on government finances are particularly grave. For such crises, GDP drops on average by approximately 11 per cent, whereas government indebtedness rises by 30 per cent.

Table 14.5 shows the differences between particular types of crisis and systemic crises in general. Crises relating to sovereign debt are typically associated with output losses that are 5 per cent higher than for other types of crises. This difference is statistically significant and shows that this pattern is very unlikely to be coincidentally generated.

Similarly, there is a mean difference between domestic events and events that are both domestic and external: 8 per cent higher output losses for crises that are both domestic and external is also statistically significant. If a country experiences domestic and externally generated crises simultaneously, recovery will be more difficult as export-driven recovery is inhibited and domestic competitiveness repressed until structural adjustment changes have taken place.

That financial crises are associated with macroeconomic consequences is beyond doubt, but estimates differ depending on measurement methods, scope in terms of geography and time, and how crises are defined in terms of their type, origin and length. For instance, the output losses reported in this chapter differ somewhat from other crises datasets, where Laeven and Valencia (2013) find that banking or sovereign crises lead to significantly

Table 14.5   Differences in output losses across types of crises

Type of crisis/Origin of crisis	Difference in mean against mean loss of remaining complex events (difference in %)				Difference in mean loss in relation to domestic complex events (difference in %)	
	Currency	Sovereign	Banking	Asset price correction	External	External & domestic
Mean difference	2%	5%	5%	4%	2%	8%
P-value	0.339	0.032	0.263	0.355	0.198	0.012

Note: This table refers to systemic complex crises which are deemed relevant for macroprudential analysis. Non-complex events are explicitly excluded, as there are too few observations in the dataset. Transition events are also excluded due to limited comparability. For the sake of completeness, it should be noted that the mean and median output losses for transition episodes range from 4 per cent to 5 per cent (depending on the calculation approach).

Source: ECB/ESRB calculations.

higher output losses than currency crises, which may be related to different sample sizes and compositions.[10] This also demonstrates the difficulties of drawing general conclusions about the phenomenon of financial crises; each crisis has its own idiosyncrasies, chronology and resonance with international events and domestic developments.

However, research suggests that there may be persistent patterns and differences in how often crises occur and in their consequences. In particular, there have been suggestions that differences arise between different types of economies. Typically, this *Varieties of Capitalism* literature contrasts between market- and bank-based financial systems.[11] In the former, non-financial companies rely more on equity and bond markets for their financing needs, and banks are predominantly providing short-term credit. Countries such as the UK, Ireland and sometimes the Netherlands are often listed as market-based financial systems. In bank-based financial systems, banks provide "patient" capital, mainly in the shape of long-term loans but sometimes, at least traditionally, via shareholdings in non-financial companies. Germany, Austria, Italy and Nordic countries are typically seen as having bank-based financial systems (Amable, 2003; Bijlsma and Zwart, 2013; Hall, 2017; Hancké et al., 2007).

Market-based financial systems generally tend to be related with greater short-run volatility in bank leverage than bank-based systems. However, market-based financial systems are more diversified and have fewer crises in general compared to bank-based systems (Bats and Houben, 2020).[12] Crises also appear to be less severe in market-based financial systems. Using the sample of European crisis, Langfield and Pagano (2016) show that cumulative losses following credit crunches are much larger in bank-based than in market-based financial systems. However, the effects from asset price corrections are not worse in European market-based systems. Moreover, Allard and Blavy (2011) show that countries with market-based financial systems recover faster after economic shocks than bank-based financial systems. One reason could be that the diversified financial systems of such economies provide more scope for substitution of debt securities to compensate reduced availability of bank lending (Darvas et al., 2013). While some of these findings may reflect financial as much as political economy effects, related to the willingness and speed of restructuring, the general pattern tends to hold: in the European historical perspective, market-based financial systems appear to have fewer and less severe financial crises.

However, some research suggests that economies with more market-based financial systems were more severely hit by the GFC and the Great Recession; at least in the earlier stages before it evolved into a European sovereign and currency crisis (Hardie et al., 2013). This contradicts earlier results where bank-based financial systems tend to be more often and worse affected by crisis. It was suggested that this was a result from the crisis having its roots in market-based financing and securitizations (Quaglia and Royo, 2015). Additional studies that consider the different effects from the crisis depending on the nature of national financial systems include Quaglia and Royo (2015) and Howarth (2013). These studies also highlight the role of market-based banking. For instance, in Spain, banks (the *Cajas* in particular) had built up leverage through short-term wholesale funding from international markets. This was coupled with the associated property bubble, which made the Spanish financial system more vulnerable than its more bank-oriented Italian counterpart (Quaglia and Royo, 2015). Similarly, French banks suffered less compared to more market-based banks in the UK, but also compared to banks in the traditionally more bank-based Germany, where banks had embarked on substantial trading activities and built up exposures to securitized assets (Howarth, 2013). On the other hand, in the initial stages France suffered more than less market-based systems in South Europe.

14.3.2   Structural and Institutional Change

Another way of understanding the consequences of crises is to consider the changes they impose on economies and societies. Many of these changes go hand in hand with the macroeconomic effects considered in the previous section. For instance, crisis episodes are typically associated with political upheaval, legal reform or even regulatory regime changes. They also cause structural changes in the corporate and financial sector as well as in the economy as a whole. There is considerable literature that studies how such institutional change is associated with crisis events, both for particular countries and for certain reform areas (social policies, collective bargaining, labour legislation, impact on women, innovation and so on) (Farnsworth and Irving, 2011; Hardy and Sever, 2020; Hermann, 2014; Karamessini and Rubery, 2013).

There is also a strand of literature that explicitly considers the impact of crises, and the GFC in particular, on the institutions and structures of the financial system itself and the overall economy. The *Varieties of Capitalism* framework suggests that country-specific weaknesses, available institutions and comparative advantages determine national responses. Accordingly, the GFC was not expected to lead to fundamental changes in financial systems (Iversen and Soskice, 2012). Instead, Hall (2017) shows that institutional differences among European financial systems were reinforced after the crisis, rather converging through weakening of differences (see Hermann, 2014 for a discussion).

Using the European experience, Figure 14.5 displays post-crisis developments in an aggregate market-based index (MBI) for the EU between 2011
and 2018. This index is based on the actual balance sheets of non-financial
companies (NFCs). It measures the combined unweighted percentage of
market-based credit and publicly listed equity in NFCs. Market-based
credit covers credit securities issues by the NFCs, which are assumed to be
more prone to market pressures through higher extents of market trading,
frequent pricing and transactions compared to bank credit. Publicly listed
equity is similarly assumed to be more sensitive to market factors compared to equity that is privately held.[13] Figure 14.6 portrays how financial
systems in individual EU Member States transformed over 2010–18.

In general, it appears that the transition towards more market-based
financial system was more intense for countries that were (a) more
market-based at the beginning of 2010 (such as Malta and the UK) and
(b) heavily influenced by the GFC (such as Spain, Italy and Greece). On
the other hand, many countries that were also heavily exposed to the crisis
display muted developments towards market-based funding structures.
Moreover, when observing the aggregate adjustment pattern in the EU
over the period, it becomes clear that adjustments are not linear. Taken
together, this raises questions on the influence of underlying determinants
of stability and change following the Great Recession.

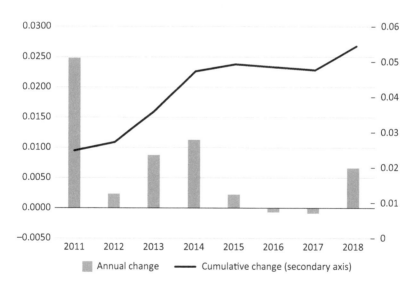

Source: Author's calculations based on OECD, EUROSTAT, BIS and Orbis.

Figure 14.5   European market-based index (MBI) (2011–18)

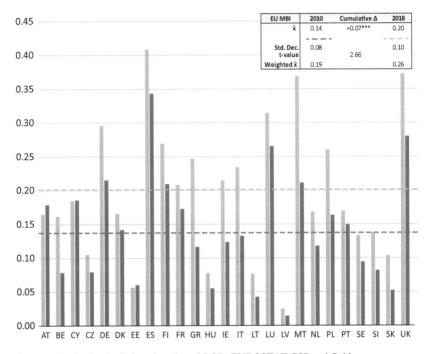

EU MBI	2010	Cumulative Δ	2018
x̄	0.14	+0.07***	0.20
– – –			– – –
Std. Dec.	0.08		0.10
t-value		2.66	
Weighted x̄	0.19		0.26

Source.   Author's calculations based on OECD, EUROSTAT, BIS and Orbis.

Figure 14.6   *European market-based index (MBI) by Member State*
                 (2010 and 2018)

Bengtsson (2019) demonstrates that stronger crisis impact drives transitions towards more market-based financial systems. This effect is significant for many estimates of the magnitude of the crisis; length of crisis, output loss and peak non-performing loans are all positively related to transitions towards more market-based financial systems. These effects are independent of the nature of financial systems prior to the crisis. However, the effect is small and only significant for the initial years following the crisis. But crisis magnitude measures that also capture policy responses, such as fiscal costs (both net and in relation to financial assets), are associated with significant transitions towards market-based financial systems. Perhaps this is the empirical manifestation of adopting neoliberal fiscal policies (Hermann, 2014; Peters, 2012).

Structural changes in the post-crisis economies are most likely a consequence of a manifold of factors: stricter and more regulatory requirements on banks, as well as the process of balance sheet repair at many banks in crisis struck economies, may be one factor; related to this is the continuous growth in the parallel or shadow banking system following the crisis (Grillet-Aubert et al., 2016), which is also promoted through policy initiatives such as the EU Capital Markets Union; a search among non-financial companies for other forms of financing, the relative success of large listed companies taking advantage of global value chains and positions of market dominance. These potential determinants are likely to be stronger in crisis struck economies, where the desire for change is intensified among voters, policymakers and corporate decision-makers. Understanding crises and effects such as those discussed above is key to grasp economic and social transformation of present capitalist societies.

14.4 CONCLUSION

This chapter provides an overview of crises experiences in European countries between 1973 and 2016. In this period, Europe has undergone profound changes – liberalization and integration, geopolitical expansion and several boom and bust cycles. Intricately related to these changes are the recurring crises that also came to pass in this period. While each financial crisis has its idiosyncrasies, the common patterns of these European crises are explored in this chapter.

Crises in Europe have tended to be complex, in the sense that their root causes and transmitters originate in several sectors or market segments. Currency and banking crises have often occurred simultaneously, such as in the wave of crises following the turbulent oil market from 1973 onwards. The crises related to the breakdown of the ERM in the early 1990s is another example. Complex crises have often also led to sovereign crises, frequently caused by the interconnectedness of the financial system to public finances. The GFC and the subsequent Great Recession is a prominent example of this. A number of crises covered in this chapter relate to European geopolitics and the transition crises in CEE.

The consequences of these crises for the citizens of Europe have been detrimental. Especially complex crises involving sovereign fiscal difficulties have been the costliest types of crises in terms of macroeconomic consequences. Crises in general tend to have vast negative macroeconomic consequences, but sovereign crises have been particularly severe. On average output losses for such crises in Europe were 5 percentage points higher than for other types of crises. This has also been the case for European crises that originate in domestic and external events simultaneously – these events are associated with 8 per cent higher output losses than crises that are purely domestic.

Over time, crises relating to sovereign risk and involving both domestic and external sources have become more common in Europe. In addition, crises in Europe appear to have become more synchronized. This may make recoveries more difficult as export-driven recovery is inhibited and domestic competitiveness remains repressed until structural adjustment changes have taken place. Indeed, post-crisis adjustment phases appear to be lengthier for recent crises than for crises in the 1970s to 1990s. It also appears that the post-adjustments following the Great Recession have resulted in transitions towards more market-based financial systems for countries that were heavily influenced by the GFC. Such structural changes in post-crisis economies are likely the consequence of many factors: regulatory reform for and balance sheet repair among banks; the continuous growth in the parallel banking system; policy initiatives such as the EU Capital Markets Union; the relative success of often large and listed companies that take advantage of global value chains and positions of market dominance. This demonstrates the profound impact of financial crises as social forces. European crises have shaped not only our economies but societies generally and even Europe as we know it.

NOTES

1. There are "qualitative" databases, where crises, their characteristics and durations are identified by various forms of qualitative information and expert judgement (Babecký et al., 2012; Detken et al., 2014; Laeven and Valencia, 2008, 2013; Reinhart and Rogoff, 2008, 2009). There are also "quantitative approaches", where particular criteria are used to determine the existence and length of crises (Frankel and Rose, 1996; Lo Duca and Peltonen, 2013). Discussing the advantages and drawbacks of such approaches is beyond the scope of this chapter, and in essence, each approach adopts a different perspective to understand crises.
2. In constructing this crisis dataset, events identified by Laeven and Valencia (2013) and Babecký et al. (2012) were also critically reviewed. In particular, events that were not identified by the approach adopted in this exercise, but were included in Laeven and Valencia (2013) and Babecký et al. (2012), were also submitted to European financial authorities for revision in order to assess whether they should be included in the ECB/ESRB EU crises dataset.
3. For a discussion see Bussière and Fratzscher (2008). This separation facilitates the estimation of early warning models by addressing the "post-crisis bias" and improves the analysis.
4. This chapter is based on a concept of types of crises. Such types relate primarily to the underlying weaknesses that contribute to the crisis, but not necessarily their triggers (reassessment of risk, viruses etc.) or underlying causes (political shift, flawed supervision or regulation, underestimation of risk etc.).
5. The acute phase of the crisis is between the "start date" and the "end of crisis management date". The post-crisis adjustment period is between the "end of crisis management date" and the "system back to normal date" (see Lo Duca et al., 2017).
6. One caveat is that the analysis does not consider contingent liabilities (e.g. in the form of guarantees) resulting from governmental interventions in the banking sector.
7. Trends are computed based on an event's preceding ten years [T-11; T-1], with T being the year in which the crises started.

8. The debt-to-GDP data refers to the general government consolidated gross debt as a share of GDP.
9. For a discussion on possible caveats in the analysis see Lo Duca et al. (2017).
10. The methodological approach, although relatively similar, differs to a certain extent relative to Laeven and Valencia (2013). For details see Lo Duca et al. (2017).
11. Other studies focus on the differences in financial structure between countries within the EU, and in particular between northern and southern countries (Zingales and Rajan, 2003) and between old and new Member States (Allen and Song, 2005).
12. See also Kalemli-Ozcan et al. (2012) for a cross-country analysis of leverage and asset growth. Huang and Ratnovski (2011) show that the degree of wholesale funding can predict financial crises. Since such funding is associated with market-based financial systems, this is a counterargument to bank-based economies being more susceptible to crises.
13. The market-based index displayed in Figures 14.4 and 14.5 is based on book values. This reduces the volatility in the measure, and disregards price fluctuations that are unrelated to the nature of financial systems. Since bank credit is typically reported at historical costs, using book values also implies that all sources of funding are values based on similar principles. The index is calculated on an aggregate and annual basis (one can think of the index as an aggregate national balance sheet of all NFCs), which in turn allows for relative and absolute rankings of countries and the EU as a whole across both time and cross-country dimensions. The balance sheet approach of the index implies that cross-listings or cross-border borrowing are covered in the measure, in contrast to most other measures on financial systems.

REFERENCES

Allard, M.J., and Blavy, M.R. (2011). Market phoenixes and banking ducks are recoveries faster in market-based financial systems? International Monetary Fund.

Allen, F., and Song, W.L. (2005). Financial integration and EMU. *European Financial Management*, 11(1), 7–24.

Amable, B. (2003). *The diversity of modern capitalism.* Oxford University Press on Demand.

Babecký, J., Havránek, T., Matějů, J., Rusnák, M., Šmídková, K., and Vašíček, B. (2012). Banking, debt and currency crises: Early warning indicators for developed countries. Working Paper Series, No. 1485, ECB, Frankfurt am Main, October.

Bats, J.V., and Houben, A.C. (2020). Bank-based versus market-based financing: Implications for systemic risk. *Journal of Banking and Finance*, *114*, 105776.

Bengtsson, E. (2019). Institutional dynamics in EU financial systems. Available at SSRN 3507610.

Bijlsma, M.J., and Zwart, G.T. (2013). The changing landscape of financial markets in Europe, the United States and Japan (No. 2013/02). Bruegel Working Paper.

Buiter, W.H., Corsetti, G.M., and Pesenti, P.A. (1997). *Interpreting the ERM crisis: Country-specific and systemic issues.* CEP Discussion Papers, Centre for Economic Performance, London School of Economics and Political Science.

Bussière, M., and Fratzscher, M. (2008). Low probability, high impact: Policy making and extreme events. *Journal of Policy Modeling*, *30*(1), 111–21.

Candelon, B., Sy, M.A.N., and Arezki, M.R. (2011). Sovereign rating news and financial markets spillovers: Evidence from the European debt crisis (No. 11–68). International Monetary Fund.

Cornia, G.A., and Paniccià, R. (2000). *The mortality crisis in transitional economies.* Oxford: Oxford University Press.

Darvas, Z., Pisani-Ferry, J., and Wolff, G.B. (2013). Europe's growth problem (and what to do about it) (No. 776). Policy brief, Bruegel.

Detken, C., Weeken, O., Alessi, L. et al. (2014). Operationalising the countercyclical capital buffer: Indicator selection, threshold identification and calibration options (No. 5). ESRB Occasional Paper Series.

Dungey, M., and Jacobs, J.P. (2015). The internationalisation of financial crises: Banking and currency crises 1883–2008. *The North American Journal of Economics and Finance, 32*, 29–47.

ELEC (1975). *Europe and the Management of the Crisis: Report of the London Conference organised by the European League for Economic Co-operation,* September.

Farnsworth, K., and Irving, Z. (eds.) (2011). *Social policy in challenging times: Economic crisis and welfare systems.* Bristol: Policy Press.

Frankel, J., and Rose, A. (1996). Currency crashes in emerging markets: An empirical treatment. *Journal of International Economics, 41*(3–4), 351–66.

Grillet-Aubert, L., Haquin, J.B., Jackson, C., Killeen, N., and Weistroffer, C. (2016). Assessing shadow banking – non-bank financial intermediation in Europe (No. 10). ESRB Occasional Paper Series.

Hall, P.A. (2017). Varieties of capitalism in light of the euro crisis. *Journal of European Public Policy, 25*(1), 7–30.

Hancké, B., Rhodes, M., and Thatcher, M. (eds). (2007). *Beyond varieties of capitalism: Conflict, contradictions, and complementarities in the European economy.* Oxford: Oxford University Press.

Hardie, I., Howarth, D., Maxfield, S., and Verdun, A. (2013). Banks and the false dichotomy in the comparative political economy of finance. *World Politics, 65*(4), 691–728.

Hardy, B., and Sever, C. (2020). Financial crises and innovation, *BIS Working Papers* No. 846, Monetary and Economic Department.

Hermannn, C. (2014). Structural adjustment and neoliberal convergence in labour markets and welfare: The impact of the crisis and austerity measures on European economic and social models. *Competition and Change, 18*(2), 111–30.

Howarth, D. (2013). *Market-based banking and the international financial crisis.* Oxford Scholarship Online, September.

Huang, R., and Ratnovski, L. (2011). The dark side of bank wholesale funding. *Journal of Financial Intermediation, 20*(2), 248–63.

Iversen, T., and Soskice, D. (2012). Modern capitalism and the advanced nation state: Understanding the causes of the crisis. In *Coping with crisis: government reactions to the Great Recession* (pp. 35–64). New York: Russel Sage Foundation.

Kalemli-Ozcan, S., Sorensen, B., and Yesiltas, S. (2012). Leverage across firms, banks, and countries. *Journal of International Economics, 88*(2), 284–98.

Kaminsky, G.L., and Reinhart, C.M. (1999). The twin crises: The causes of banking and balance-of-payments problems. *American Economic Review, 89*(3), 473–500.

Karamessini, M., and Rubery, J. (2013). Economic crisis and austerity: Challenges to gender equality. In *Women and Austerity* (pp. 336–73). London: Routledge.

Laeven, L., and Valencia, F. (2008). Systemic banking crises: A new database. IMF Working Paper, No. 08/224, Washington DC, November.

Laeven, L., and Valencia, F. (2013). Systemic banking crises database: An update. *IMF Economic Review*, *61*(2), 225–70.

Langfield, S., and Pagano, M. (2016). Bank bias in Europe: Effects on systemic risk and growth. *Economic Policy*, *31*(85), 51–106.

Lo Duca, M., and Peltonen, T. (2013). Assessing systemic risk and predicting systemic events. *Journal of Banking and Finance*, *37*(7), 2183–95.

Lo Duca, M.L., Koban, A., Basten, M. et al. (2017). A new database for financial crises in European countries: ECB/ESRB EU crises database. ECB Occasional Paper No. 194.

Peters, J. (2012). Neoliberal convergence in North America and Western Europe: Fiscal austerity, privatization, and public sector reform. *Review of International Political Economy*, *19*(2), 208–35.

Quaglia, L., and Royo, S. (2015). Banks and the political economy of the sovereign debt crisis in Italy and Spain. *Review of International Political Economy*, *22*(3), 485–507.

Ramirez Pérez, S.M. (2019). Crises and transformations of European integration: European business circles during the long 1970s. *European Review of History: Revue européenne d'histoire*, *26*(4), 618–35.

Reinhart, C.M. (2002). Default, currency crises, and sovereign credit ratings. *The World Bank Economic Review*, *16*(2), 151–70.

Reinhart, C.M., and Rogoff, K.S. (2008). Is the 2007 US sub-prime financial crisis so different? An international historical comparison. *American Economic Review*, *98*(2), 339–44.

Reinhart, C.M., and Rogoff, K.S. (2009). The aftermath of financial crises. *American Economic Review*, *99*(2), 466–72.

Zingales, L., and Rajan, R. (2003). Banks and markets: The changing character of European finance. Working Paper 9595, National Bureau of Economic Research, Cambridge MA.

APPENDIX: THE ECB/ESRB CRISIS DATASET

The crises dataset covers crises for the period 1970–2016 and consists of the following.

1. A core set of 50 systemic crises. The list of systemic crises (the core part of the dataset) contains (i) systemic crises which were identified by a financial stress index and afterwards reviewed by National authorities (i.e. financial supervisory authorities or central banks) and (ii) other crises episodes flagged by National authorities and/or in the related literature. A crisis is considered systemic when it satisfies a number of the criteria described in detail in the next section. In particular, a systemic crisis entails (i) the financial system acting as a shock originator or amplifier and/or (ii) systemic financial intermediaries experiencing distress or going bankrupt and/or (iii) substantial crisis management policy interventions.

2. A set of 43 residual episodes of financial stress, five of which were, however, not associated with a systemic crisis. These episodes, which are reported for transparency purposes, were either flagged by National authorities or identified by the financial stress index approach, but do not fulfil the criteria for a systemic crisis. Some of these episodes were included in other crises datasets (Babecký, 2012; Laeven and Valencia, 2008, 2013; Reinhart and Rogoff, 2008, 2009).

For all crises and episodes, the database dataset reports the type of risk that materialized (currency/balance of payment capital flows, sovereign risk, bank risk, significant repricing in asset markets). It also contains information on chronology of crises and episodes of financial stress. This includes *starting dates* which relate to either (i) the emergence of systemic financial stress in asset markets, (ii) the first policy response in relation to the crisis or (iii) the first failure of a major market player, depending on which date is earlier and/or considered appropriate by National authorities. This choice reflects the fact that the start date of the event normally coincides with the emergence of systemic financial stress in asset markets. This is normally the moment when economic agents start incorporating the expectations of future bad economic outcomes in relation to the occurrence of a crisis. The *end of the crisis management and resolution phase* is marked by the last of the policy interventions aimed at containing the crisis. This can be considered as the end of the acute phase of the crisis and the start of the period of post-crisis adjustment (Bussière and Fratzscher, 2008). Reviewed policy interventions include: the adoption of liquidity support to banks, the introduction of guarantees for bank liabilities, the recapitalization of banks or forced/assisted mergers, the creation of bad banks or asset management companies, the resolution of banks, general debt relief and the adoption of emergency fiscal packages and/or unconventional monetary policy measures that address market disturbances in connection with the materialization of different types of risk (e.g. ECB Security Markets Programme (SMP) and Outright Monetary Transactions (OMT)). The end of the crisis management and resolution phase should anticipate or coincide with the date when the system is considered "back to normal" (see Subsection 14.2.3). Taking the example of the European sovereign and banking crises, for countries that participated in the EU/IMF economic adjustment programmes, the end of crisis management coincides with the exit from the adjustment programme, unless National authorities suggest a valid alternative date (e.g. sale to private investors of a good bank resulting from the resolution of an earlier entity). The system is considered to be *back to a normal mode* when the recovery is on a firm path and the fiscal and monetary policy become broadly neutral. This is when the overall policy mix in one country is no longer driven by factors related to the crisis and its manifestation, including legacy issues. The crisis dataset also contains information on crisis management and resolution policies, and other qualitative and quantitative information in order to enable its users to better understand underlying choices and to enhance transparency in the construction of event chronologies.

15. Looking ahead: early warning systems

E. Philip Davis and Dilruba Karim

15.1 OVERVIEW

15.1.1 Early Development of Macroprudential Surveillance and Analysis of Banking Crises

Clement (2010) tracks the first usage of the term "macroprudential" to a 1979 Cooke Committee Meeting (the precursor of today's Basel Committee on Banking Supervision). There were concerns that problems in maturity transformation of international bank lending, which were microeconomic (i.e. bank level) were large enough to pose macroeconomic risks and thereby, lead to macroprudential concerns. However, it is important to note that the term macroprudential was used in a very limited context at this stage and in response to very specific global banking flows that were a problem at that time.

By 1986, Clement (2010) notes the word macroprudential was used in the context that we are familiar with today: "the safety and soundness of the broad financial system and payments mechanism". This definition was publicly defined in BIS (1986, p. 2) in the context of rapid financial innovation in the 1980s, including the use of derivatives and securitisation in off-balance sheet accounts (see also Boyd and Gertler, 1993). Several other terms used in the report also strike a familiar chord: under-pricing of risk, overestimation of liquidity and risk concentrations.

Concerns with securitisation were also echoed in BIS (1997a) and BIS (1997b) with the former publication advising a focus on enhanced data collection on derivatives trading and the latter devoting a section to detailing the interlinkages of financial systems as part of macroprudential policy. Given the increasing usage of macroprudential terminology in public policy documents and the coincidence with the Asian Financial Crisis in 1997, it is not surprising that its usage permeated to other international financial institutions (IFIs) around the same time, including the International Monetary Fund (IMF, 1998). Central banks soon followed so that even before the subprime crisis, over 50 were producing "Financial Stability Reports" (Čihák, 2006).

The global fallout from the 1997 Asian Crisis and the increasing awareness of macroprudential risks led to the natural questions: what drives banking crises and can we predict them in order to mitigate their effects via macroprudential tools? In sum, these two questions define the objectives of early warning systems and their design has subsequently evolved over the last three decades, with numerous refinements in the post Global Financial Crisis (GFC) period.

Initial studies on banking crises during the 1980s and 1990s tended to focus on country case studies and indeed, specific macroeconomic factors. As such, they did not develop systematic econometric models that underpin early warning systems (EWSs). Rather, the focus of these papers was an attempt to understand how financial imbalances transmitted to shocks in the real economy, at a time when these transmission mechanisms were relatively unexplored. Nevertheless, these studies began to allude to the importance of macroprudential issues.

For example, Velasco (1987) examined the interaction between banking systems and macroeconomies for the Southern Cone and concluded that fiscal deficits and rises in real interest rates were associated with banking instability. Calvo and Mendoza (1996) contrasted trends in financial flows with current account imbalances in Mexico and concluded that the lessons from the 1994 crisis required policymakers to start focusing on bank balance sheet stability, including higher reserve ratios, swap agreements with central banks and stronger credit lines during periods of distress. Pill and Pradhan (1995) focused on the impact of financial liberalisation in six Asian and six African countries during the 1970s and 1980s using trends in current accounts, fiscal balances, inflation and real exchange rates. They noted that macroeconomic stability was a prerequisite for countries which implemented financial liberalisation but avoided subsequent financial instability and, in particular, the credit-to-GDP ratio had superior signalling ability for financial distress.

Although this body of work did not empirically test the causes of crises, the analysis was usually underpinned by theoretical models (as in Davis, 1995). Hence, by identifying anomalous behaviour in macroeconomic and financial variables, such studies provided the theoretical underpinnings for subsequent cross-country empirical methodologies that formed the basis of EWS design. Still, although they presented a menu of explanatory variables that could be tested, they did not provide a systematic definition of banking crises. This side of the crisis equation evolved in a set of seminal articles which still form the basis of current EWS design.

15.1.2   Key Steps in the Analysis of Banking Crises and Their Prediction

The first generation of multivariate EWSs were developed during the late 1990s in response to the Nordic banking crises in the early 1990s and the subsequent 1997 East Asian Financial Crises. Both sequences of banking crisis events in Finland, Norway and Sweden and across Indonesia, Korea, Malaysia, Philippines and Thailand highlighted common patterns of crisis evolution and transmission and led to a proliferation of articles investigating the taxonomy of banking crises by the IMF and other authors. The IMF strand of research on the classification of banking crises has undergone several revisions since the 1990s and continues to be a major accepted source of international crisis events.

Although Drees and Pazarbasioglu (1995) did not develop an empirical model for the Nordic crises, their detailed analysis of many potential contributory factors paved the way for subsequent studies and highlighted the importance of policy responses in such enquiries. Their focus on macroeconomic behaviour in the run-up to the crises (in particular the business cycle), combined with data on the structure of the financial system (in particular banks' balance sheets) allowed them to conclude that the Nordic crises were not solely driven by macroeconomic imbalances but that, crucially, the coincidence of financial deregulation in a period of expansion, combined with risky bank balance sheets and poor internal risk management, led to systemic banking collapse. The regulatory environment was captured by variables such as quantitative restrictions on lending (reserve ratios, credit ceilings and liquidity ratios), interest rate regulations (leading to limited price competition), insufficient macroprudential oversight on capital requirements, and other structural characteristics such as openness to foreign bank entry. It thus highlighted the differences between microeconomic factors that could cause stability problems and macroeconomic and regulatory factors that affected the entire banking landscape.

This separation was reiterated by Gavin and Hausmann (1998) who made a distinction between individual bank failures and vulnerability of whole banking systems. The latter, they argued, required a different analysis from the former in that they were driven by different factors, namely macroeconomic trends. These could include negative economic shocks that made loan repayments less likely, alongside reductions in money demand and international capital flows that posed financing problems for banks. Conversely, increased demand for bank deposits or influxes of foreign capital could turn problematic if they led to lending booms and, in tandem, increases in non-performing loans (NPLs) that could make the system vulnerable to small shocks. The interactions between macroeconomic factors and bank behaviour were formalised in a theoretical model by Calvo and Mendoza (1996) to explain the Mexican crisis of 1994.

The distinctions made between individual or limited bank failures and collapse of entire systems as a whole are central to the definition of the banking crisis variable which also evolved around this time. Gavin and Hausmann (1998) noted that insolvency in individual banks (such as Barings and BCCI) was mostly explained by poor decision making and lack of oversight by bank management. Collapse of a major bank within the system or a group of smaller banks became known as non-systemic crises. Although these episodes could materially impair the payments system and put depositors' funds at risk, they required specific interventions by policymakers in order to address their balance sheet deficiencies and complete any required restructuring. In such cases, the damage to the banking system and loss of investor confidence could be limited. In contrast, collapse of a substantial part or the entire banking system became known as systemic crises. These could evolve from non-systemic crises where local damage was not contained and spread to the entire system via contagion or they could be triggered by the macroeconomic channels described above due to vulnerability of the entire lending mechanism.

The two types of crises have implications for the banking crisis variable and the empirical methodology required to explain it. Non-systemic crises, which involve a subset of individual banks failures, can be described by two types of independent variable. The most common is a microeconomic or bank balance sheet variable such as the return on equity, z-scores, NPL ratios or even stock prices and in this case, the methodology attempts to explain and predict anomalies using microeconomic data on the right-hand side, often with macroeconomic controls. For example, Li et al. (2014) use a semi-parametric Cox proportional hazard model to assess bank-specific determinants of survival time and failure for commercial and agricultural banks. It was suggested that non-performing consumer and commercial loans aggravated banks' financial health and survival.

The second type of dependent variable is the non-systemic crisis binary variable (see below for further discussion in the context of Caprio and Klingebiel, 1996 and thereafter). This is a variable that takes a value of one if a major bank collapses or a subset if the banking system fails and, in this sense, it aggregates information across banks into a non-systemic "event". For this reason, explanatory models require the use of aggregated micro and macro data as independent variables and since non-systemic crises are relatively uncommon events, the use of this binary dummy usually occurs in conjunction with the systemic crisis variable to develop a country level explanation of financial crises.

The systemic banking crisis dummy variable is the main input to the country level EWS models that we will focus on in this chapter and we discuss its definition and evolution in more detail below. However, there are alternative variables that have been used to characterise financial crises such as high frequency indicators and binary variables based on aggregation of banks' balance sheet variables and we shall also review these studies briefly in the following section.

We now turn to discuss the main binary banking crisis variable definitions that have been used in the literature and underpin the EWS models described in the following section.

15.1.3   Banking Crisis Definitions

The first comprehensive global systematic review of banking crises was conducted by Caprio and Klingebiel (1996) as a World Bank review.[1] The objective was to create a publicly available database of major bank insolvencies (that are not always readily observable) and systemic failures since the 1970s. The authors acknowledged that this first attempt to catalogue crises involved flaws in that they relied on the narratives of country level finance professionals to identify the characteristics of each crisis. Also, the inability to mark banks' portfolios to market, especially in developing countries, meant there was no way of gauging the precise level of insolvency of each institution. Timing (especially start date) was also imperfect since non-systemic insolvencies are often unobservable at the point of outbreak. Despite these limitations, the authors provided a sweeping characterisation of crises in 69 countries, including duration, major causes, magnitude (percentage of banking system assets classed as insolvent), resolution costs (percentage of GDP), resolution mechanisms deployed by the authorities and the impacts on real loan growth and GDP growth. They identified systemic events using country level World Bank Financial Sector reviews and a plethora of academic articles and published press.

The novelty and richness of the Caprio and Klingebiel (1996) dataset not only allowed the construction of a time series of banking crises events (the banking crisis dummy) but also paved the way for the development of EWS design via the use of international panel data. Part of the database focused on the behaviour of macroeconomic trends (e.g. terms of trade) and financial variables (real credit/GDP, real deposit interest rates) around the crises and therefore alluded to leading indicators that could be used in EWSs. The database was subsequently updated in Caprio and Klingebiel (1999, 2003). Another variant of the database emerged with more crisis coverage and longer timespan in Caprio et al. (2005) which covered 126 countries from the 1970s to 2005. It also provided the basis for other banking crisis datasets which are widely used in EWS studies.

Demirgüç-Kunt and Detragiache (1998) utilised the Caprio and Klingebiel studies to create an alternative crisis database. They used a more specific set of four criteria where achievement of at least one of the conditions was a requirement for systemic crises, otherwise bank failure was non-systemic. These include:

1. The proportion of NPLs to total banking system assets exceeded 10 per cent, or
2. the public bailout cost exceeded 2 per cent of GDP, or
3. systemic crisis caused large-scale bank nationalisation, or
4. extensive bank runs were visible and, if not, emergency government intervention was visible.

The authors acknowledged they relied on judgement if there was insufficient evidence to support their crisis criteria; on this basis they established 31 systemic crises in 65 countries over the 1980–94 period. Demirgüç-Kunt and Detragiache (2005) conducted a follow-up study and extended the sample to 1980–2002 and using the same criteria as before, they identified 77 systemic crises over 94 countries.

The source for the binary dependent variable that is currently most used is Laeven and Valencia (2008, 2013, 2018) who also rely on Caprio et al (2005) as the underlying source. The database remained the most comprehensive extant source in that it covered all three types of financial crises (banking, currency and sovereign debt) and extended the time range from 1970 to 2007. In Laeven and Valencia (2008), 124 banking crises were captured. Unlike Caprio et al. (2005), the focus was exclusively on systemic events which were classified if:

1. The crisis year coincided with bank runs (whereby a monthly decline in deposits exceeded 5 per cent), or
2. Deposit freezes or guarantees were introduced or extensive liquidity support or government interventions were enacted,
3. The proportion of NPLs in the banking system was excessively high or most of the banking system's capital was depleted.

Two-thirds of the crises were characterised by factors (1) and (2) while the remainder fell under category (3). The database was revised and increased in scope in Laeven and Valencia (2013) and then again in Laeven and Valencia (2018). The latter database catalogues 151 international systemic crises covering the period 1970–2017 and therefore is one of the most accepted sources used to construct the banking crisis dummy for EWSs. It is included in a major data source for financial sector research, the World Bank Global Financial Development Database (World Bank, 2017).

The crisis dummy definitions in these datasets are imperfect. Boyd et al. (2009) argued that the widely used binary banking crisis dummies constructed by Caprio and Klingebiel (1996, 1999) and Demirgüç-Kunt and Detragiache (2002, 2005) suffered from dating problems. Caprio and Klingebiel (1996, 1999) relied on surveys of finance professionals' opinions to isolate common identification criteria that could be used to date crisis onset. Hence the crisis dummy was inherently based on subjective opinions and the authors acknowledged that the inability to mark banks' balance sheets to market values meant this subjective bias could not be eliminated. In addition, if a banking crisis did not manifest in observable events such as bank runs or exchange rate pressure, then the exact start time became difficult to ascertain. This problem was compounded because regulators and finance professionals might only become aware of financial instability a significant while after actual problems emerged. Since systemic crises were distinguished from non-systemic crises if the former involved depletion of bank capital at the aggregate level, classification of these events could also be considered to be subjective, since no quantitative threshold for bank capital is defined and instead, relies on publicly available information of government interventions or supervisory narratives.

Despite the limitations of the banking crisis dummy, these sources have been accepted as the most comprehensive database of global crisis events which are by nature often opaque, dependent on local banking systems, and labour intensive to catalogue. They are used in the three different types of EWS (logit, Binary Recursive Tree and signal extraction) which we discuss in the next section.

15.2 HISTORIC EVOLUTION OF EWS

15.2.1 Some General Issues Related to EWS Evaluation

EWSs, by definition, are designed to *predict* crises so as to give policymakers time to enact mitigating measures. Hence there is a distinction between EWSs and models whose sole objective is to explain crises. The latter type of model may be extremely valuable in identifying the variables that generate financial instability and therefore require monitoring and regulatory oversight but they will not warn society of impending banking system collapse; this is achieved by forward-looking EWSs.

Econometric explanations of banking crises that are not forward look-ing can be assessed by the standard appropriate diagnostics whereas EWSs must be judged on their out-of-sample performance: if the model is unable to predict crises or repeatedly predicts crises that never materialise, its value as an EWS is eroded. The policymaker's requirement is for a correct "signal" of crises to always be emitted (so that she can take preventative action) and for a low rate of incorrect signals to be released, since preventa-tive action in response to these represents an unnecessary social welfare loss. In the terminology of EWSs, two important errors arise: the type I error occurs when the model is unable to identify an impending crisis (which materialises) and the type II error occurs when the model incor-rectly predicts a future crisis (which never occurs).

The rate at which the errors occur depends on the threshold set by the EWS user which can be a probability threshold in the context of logit and Binary Recursive Tree models or standard deviations in the context of signal extraction. However, in all cases, there is a trade-off between type I and II errors since changing the threshold to reduce one error will neces-sarily increase the occurrence of the other. The relative cost of these errors depends on the individual policymaker's preferences as well as the severity of the crisis: for a highly risk-averse policymaker whose objective is the prevention of any crisis, a type I error is extremely costly and her objective function gives low weight to the welfare losses associated with unnecessary policy intervention, that is, she is willing to accept a high type II error rate in order to ensure all crises are forewarned.

The trade-off between type I and II errors occurs in any model that seeks to predict a binary outcome and as such, there are established per-formance measures that are typically used to evaluate these models. Since the policymakers' preferences are unobservable, EWS models for banking crisis have avoided the use of thresholds based on policymakers' objectives and instead are evaluated using generic performance criteria. In the past, these have included the Noise to Signal Ratio (NTSR) and more recently, Receiver Operating Characteristic Curves (ROCs) and their associated Areas Under the Curve (AUROC) have become the accepted means of EWS evaluation.

The NTSR was used by Kaminsky and Reinhart (1999) and is also described in detail in Davis and Karim (2008). For any model predicting a binary outcome, the signal can be placed in one of four categories:

1. "A": a crisis signal is followed by an actual crisis,
2. "B": a crisis signal does not coincide with an actual crisis,
3. "C": a no-crisis signal is followed by an actual crisis,
4. "D": a no-crisis signal coincides with a non-crisis episode.

Clearly, signals in the "A" and "D" categories are correct and a good EWS will maximise these predictions. A signal in the "C" category represents a type I error since the EWS has failed to forecast the impending crisis. Conversely, a signal in the "B" category represents a type II error since the EWS model predicts a crisis will occur but it never materialises.

The NTSR attempts to jointly minimise the occurrence of type I and II errors together and is defined as:

$$NTSR = \frac{type\ II\ error}{1 - type\ I\ error} \tag{15.1}$$

Since different probability thresholds will yield different proportions of type I and II errors, the "best" EWS is defined as the one whose NTSR is the lowest which in turn will correspond to a unique threshold.

More recently, the ROC and AUROC have been used as alternative criteria for the identification of the optimal EWS. Unlike the NTSR criterion, where the minimum value is tied to a particular threshold, the ROC is a function of all potential thresholds. The curve itself is a plot of the true positive rate (i.e. correct crisis calls in category "A") against the type II error and the integral, the AUROC, captures the informativeness of the EWS. Higher values of the AUROC are associated with a low trade-off between the true call rate and type II error whereas lower AUROC values occur in models where an increase in correct crisis calls can only occur if we accept more false alarms. The ROC approach has been applied inter alia by Schularick and Taylor (2012), Giese et al. (2014) and Barrell et al. (2016, 2020) and is discussed further in Section 15.3.3.

15.2.2   First Generation Logit Models (Demirgüç-Kunt and Detragiache, 1998)

As discussed previously, the Nordic banking crises in the early 1990s and the subsequent 1997 East Asian Financial Crises provided the impetus for International Financial Institutions (World Bank and IMF) to gain a better understanding of the causes of crises within their country member-ship. In this context, the econometric approach of Demirgüç-Kunt and Detragiache (1998) was a major contribution in that it provided a multi-variate explanation of crises in a wide cross-section of countries.

They employed the logit estimator which yields some advantages when explaining the binary banking crisis dummy. Firstly, the probability distri-bution of the dependent variable follows the logistic functional form which does not require the assumption of normally distributed independent vari-ables. Secondly, the estimated outputs have an intuitive interpretation as the probability that a banking crisis will occur. Thirdly, the logit approach allows us to check the effects of several potential contributors to crisis simultaneously, unlike signal extraction (discussed in the following section) where independent variables are typically analysed on a univariate basis.

The probability that the banking dummy takes a value of one (crisis occurs) at a point in time is given by the value of the logistic cumulative distribution evaluated for the data and parameters at that point in time. Thus,

$$Prob\left(Y_{it} = 1\right) = F\left(\beta X_{it}\right) = \frac{e^{\beta' X_{it}}}{1 + e^{\beta' X_{it}}} \tag{15.2}$$

where Y_{it} is the banking crisis dummy for country i at time t, β is the vector of coefficients, X_{it} is the vector of explanatory variables and $F(\beta X_{it})$ is the cumulative logistic distribution. The parameters are obtained by maximum likelihood estimation where each possible value of Y_{it} contributes to the joint likelihood function so that the log likelihood becomes:

$$Log_e L = \sum_{i=1}^{n} \sum_{t=1}^{T} \left(Y_{it} \, log_e \, F\left(\beta'X_{it}\right)\right) + \left(1 - Y_{it}\right)$$
$$log_e \left(1 - F\left(\beta'X_{it}\right)\right) \tag{15.3}$$

The banking crisis dummy (Y_{it}) was defined as described in Section 15.1.3 for the period 1980–94, which yielded 31 systemic crisis events. The selection of explanatory variables was underpinned by theory and three categories were used:

1. Macroeconomic: Real GDP growth, Change in Terms of Trade, Depreciation, Real Interest Rates, Inflation and the Fiscal Surplus/GDP,
2. Financial: M2/ Reserves, Credit to the Private Sector/GDP, Bank Cash plus Reserves/ Bank Assets, Real Domestic Credit Growth,
3. Institutional: GDP per Capita, a Law and Order Index and a binary dummy to capture the presence/absence of deposit insurance.

In the macroeconomic context, GDP growth was found to significantly reduce crisis probabilities, whereas an increase in the real interest rate or inflation was found to raise the likelihood of systemic banking crises. In the second category, only M2/Reserves had a consistently positive impact on the chances of crises occurring, although the growth of credit had a positive effect but only in one particular regression specification. There was an institutional impact on financial stability via a negative and weakly significant coefficient on GDP per capita but this also was not apparent in all regression specifications.

Although the Demirgüç-Kunt and Detragiache (1998) model was novel in its multivariate approach and use of the logit estimator, it was not a true

EWS since the explanatory variables were contemporaneous to the banking crisis dummy.[2] The percentage of non-crisis crisis events which were correctly identified ranged between 84 per cent and 75 per cent, however, the models' performance was worse in terms of their ability to identify crises episodes, with the correct call rate varying between 70 per cent and 55 per cent. Nevertheless, this logit approach provided the basis for subsequent refinements that led to a better EWS design and understanding of crisis determinants which are discussed in Section 15.2.3; prior to this we discuss the signal extraction methodology which emerged around the same time as an alternative approach to crisis prediction.

15.2.3   Signal Extraction (Kaminsky and Reinhart, 1999)

Kaminsky and Reinhart (1999) pioneered the use of high frequency data in an event study analysis of financial crises. They specifically probed the occurrence of "twin crises" – namely events where currency crises are followed by banking crises, or vice versa. Using a dataset spanning the 1970s to 1990s for industrialised and developing countries, they captured both types of crises as follows: a banking crisis "event" started if either (i) bank runs led to the closure, merger or nationalisation of one or more financial institutions, or (ii) in the absence of bank runs, either one large bank or a group of banks were closed, merged or received large-scale government bailouts prior to similar measures undertaken on other financial institutions. Identification of these crisis events and their start dates relied on the extant banking crisis literature and financial press. Currency crises were dated using the high frequency exchange rate pressure index which was constructed as the weighted average of changes in exchange rates and central bank reserves, whereby the weights ensured the two variables had identical conditional volatilities. A currency crisis start date was then recorded if this variable exceeded three standard deviations from the mean.

In contrast to the Demirgüç-Kunt and Detragiache (1998) logit model, the Kaminsky and Reinhart (1999) study provided a very different alternative to the investigation of crises. Whereas the logistic estimator is parametric, the signal extraction approach is non-parametric and falls under the broad category of event studies. Another difference is that it typically uses a univariate approach as opposed the multivariate models described above, although some studies have used combinations of variables as a single composite time series (Borio and Lowe, 2002). Two major advantages of this methodology are that it is relatively easy to execute due to low computational requirements and, because of the univariate nature, the data requirements are less burdensome.

The signal extraction approach is also intuitive in its interpretation: an indicator is tracked against a pre-defined threshold. The latter is chosen to discriminate between tranquil periods, where the indicator behaves according to a reasonable probability distribution and periods of crises, where the variable displays an aberrant trend. Hence, whenever the variable value crosses the threshold, the model is effectively signalling a crisis and if the variable remains within the threshold boundary in any period, this corresponds to a non-crisis signal:

Let, i = a univariate indicator, j = a particular country, S = signal variable and X = indicator.

An indicator variable relating to indicator i and country j is denoted by X_i^j and the threshold for this indicator is denoted as X^{*j}_i. A signal variable relating to indicator i and country j is denoted by S_i^j. This is constructed to be a binary variable where $S_i^j = \{0,1\}$. If the variable crosses the threshold, a signal is emitted and $S_i^j = 1$. This happens when

$$\left\{ S_i^j = 0 \right\} = \left\{ \left|X_i^j\right| > \left|X^{*j}_i\right| \right\} \qquad (15.4)$$

If the indicator remains within its threshold boundary, it behaves normally and does not issue a signal so that $S_i^j = 0$,

$$\left\{ S_i^j = 0 \right\} = \left\{ \left|X_i^j\right| \leq \left|X^{*j}_i\right| \right\} \qquad (15.5)$$

The threshold for each indicator is selected to minimise the NTSR, as described in equation (15.1). Note the variable $S_i^j = \{0,1\}$ is the forecasted banking crisis dummy. In order to assess the accuracy of the signal extraction prediction, S_i^j is compared against the occurrence of actual banking crisis events. Details on the latter have been described in Section 15.2.1 and in the Kaminsky and Reinhart (1999) model; this was constructed using the Caprio and Klingebiel (1996) database, public information and stylised facts of crises chronology described in Kaminsky and Reinhart (1996).

One of the drawbacks of the signal extraction framework is the fact that each individual indicator is likely to possess a low informational content since crises are unlikely to be driven by anomalies in one variable alone. As a result, the correct identification of a banking crisis usually occurs only when several indicators cross their respective thresholds. Kaminsky and Reinhart (1999) assessed 16 indicators (which captured the financial sector, external sector, real sector and fiscal position) and found that if less than 20 per cent of these variables emitted a crisis signal, no actual banking crises would be identified. Even to correctly call 31 per cent of the banking crises in their sample, 80–100 per cent of their indicators would have to cross their respective thresholds. This may partially stem from the fact that the univariate approach fails to take into account the interactions between different sectors which often matter in the chronology of a crisis event. We now describe an alternative approach which accommodates these types of variable interdependencies.

15.2.4 Binary Recursive Trees

The Binary Recursive Tree (BRT) method is another non-parametric approach but unlike signal extraction, it assesses multiple indicators simultaneously. Moreover, it is particularly suited to financial crises investigations because of its ability to detect interactions between multiple explanatory variables which may be endogenous. Another advantage is that this technique is able to discover nonlinear variable anomalies, making it especially useful for the analysis of different crisis events which may display several common vulnerabilities but are actually triggered by different factors.

This approach was applied by Ghosh and Ghosh (2002) in the context of currency crises, Cashin and Duttagupta (2008) who examined banking crises and Manasse et al. (2003) in the investigation of sovereign debt crises. Davis et al. (2011) subsequently applied the BRT methodology to a larger banking crisis dataset and provide a detailed explanation of the estimator.

The intuition behind the BRT is as follows: a recursive algorithm is applied to a set of explanatory variable time series and the corresponding set of banking crisis events (i.e. the banking crisis dummy time series). The sample is split into an in-sample "training" dataset and an out-of-sample "test sample". For each variable (X_i), the algorithm checks all values against all potential thresholds (V_i) to identify the best threshold value (V_i^*) that discriminates between crisis and non-crisis periods.

Each threshold for each variable generates a specific ratio of type I and II errors and the optimal threshold is that which minimises the sum of the two errors, although different error weightings can be applied according to user preferences. This generates a ranking of the variables' predictive power with the "best" variable and its corresponding threshold forming the first "parent node" of the tree with observations lower than the threshold being placed on one side and others being placed on the other side. This segregation rule is then recursively repeated until all variable observations are partitioned at different thresholds. A final tree may take the form as shown in Figure 15.1, which then shows the pathway to each crisis with the corresponding variables of importance and their threshold values. The final tree is calibrated on the "training" dataset as an out-of-sample robustness exercise.

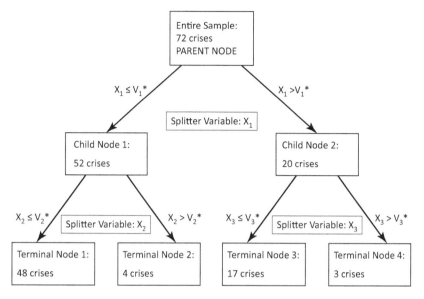

Source: Davis et al. (2011).

Figure 15.1   Schematic diagram of Binary Recursive Tree (BRT)

The output from the BRT methodology differs from the signal extraction and logit approaches in that it provides a context-specific journey towards each crisis, showing the interactions of all the variables that culminate in banking system failure. By identifying the optimal thresholds, the model also provides policymakers with a monitoring benchmark so they can take preventive action if real time data suggests a threshold is being approached. The technique highlights that not all crises are the same and can thus be used to compare events between different economic structures such as developed versus developing economies or market-based versus bank-based financial systems.

There are, however, certain disadvantages associated with the BRT approach. Firstly, the non-parametric estimation means confidence intervals are not attached to forecasts. Secondly, the recursive nature of the algorithm can lead to overfitting and as a result, trees can grow to become extremely complex with little informational gain. It can also be argued that the complexity of the output is counterproductive from the policymakers' perspective since she cannot monitor or influence every variable in a pathway without incurring significant economic disruption. These factors may explain why the BRT approach has not been widely adopted by regulators as part of their macroprudential monitoring and why the logit approach continues to be popular. We discuss recent refinements to the latter in the next section.

15.2.5 Second Generation Logit Models (Barrell et al., 2010)

Although the signal extraction and BRT approaches can provide useful insights into the causes of banking crises, their non-parametric nature has led to limited application in EWS design. In contrast, the logit estimator is a more accepted methodology in the extant literature and in this section, we outline some recent refinements to previous versions.

As described in Section 15.2.2, the Demirgüç-Kunt and Detragiache (1998) model was not an EWS per se, in the sense that the explanatory and dependent variables were contemporaneous. Davis et al. (2011) analysed banking crises in Latin America and Asia and argued that lagged explanatory variables were necessary to avoid endogeneity between banking crises and the independent variables since the occurrence of a systemic crisis is likely to influence the behaviour of the explanatory variables. This was reinforced in Barrell et al. (2010) whose objective was to design an EWS that could explain and forecast the rash of Organisation for Econonomic Co-operation and Development (OECD) banking crises which manifested during the GFC.

The Barrell et al. (ibid) approach involved a sample of 14 banking crises in 14 OECD countries: Belgium, Canada, Denmark, Finland, France, Germany, Italy, Japan, Netherlands, Norway, Sweden, Spain, the UK and the US. This country selection approach differed from previous studies where countries were often pooled despite the fact that there could be significant heterogeneity in their banking system characteristics and thus in the causes of crises (Davis et al., 2011). Heterogeneous pooling was often used as an attempt to overcome the fact that systemic crises are historically relatively rare events and thereby increase the proportion of crisis observations in a sample. However, this approach could lead to EWSs that generated high type I and II errors and poor out-of-sample performance. Barrell et al. (ibid) argued that good EWS design required pooling of countries that were broadly similar in terms of financial structure and economic development.

The sample period (1980–2007) was selected in order to add another innovation to the underlying Demirgüç-Kunt and Detragiache (1998) model. By restricting the start date to 1980, this allowed the authors to test bank-specific macroprudential variables which had not been included in previous models due to lack of consistent historic time series data. The key additions included bank capital adequacy, narrow bank liquidity and property price growth since narratives on the subprime crises cited inadequate capital buffers and liquidity as problems in the face of increasingly risky mortgage lending.

Another refinement was the use of a general to specific approach. Barrell et al. (ibid) argued that well-designed EWSs should not only be robust but also parsimonious since they are designed to be practical tools to support the financial stability objectives of policymakers. While more complex and detailed econometric descriptions of crises may be informative, they may not identify a set of core variables that can be efficiently targeted as part of macroprudential policy. The general to specific approach may also lead to better performance in terms of lower type II error rates since variables that only explain a limited number of crises are eliminated, although a drawback could be a higher type I error rate as some idiosyncratic crises are not captured.

The use of lags combined with the general to specific approach and the inclusion of bank-specific variables generated an EWS that differed substantially from the original Demirgüç-Kunt and Detragiache (1998) model: the three core factors that explained the OECD crises were capital adequacy, liquidity and property price growth. This structure remained stable in the face of a series of robustness tests including country eliminations, alternative specifications of the banking crisis dummy, change of sample period and exclusion of post-crisis observations. The stability of the model supported the argument that EWS design should take into account the nature of the target economies and that models may need to be adapted periodically to reflect evolutions in banking systems and data availability.

15.2.6 Recent Model Comparisons and New Techniques

Davis and Karim (2008) comparing the logit and signalling approach, found that both models are useful, the signal model being better at predicting country-specific crises and the regression model more suitable for detecting global stress. In a recent "horse race" between nine different approaches to crisis prediction in European countries (Alessi et al., 2014) it was suggested that multivariate approaches have added value over simple signalling models, because although signalling was seen as transparent and straightforward, the risk of underestimating the probability of a crisis was high. Logit models may be sensitive to model specification while decision trees' out-of-sample performance is little known. Their recommendation of using a suite of models in policy is shown in practice by the European Central Bank (ECB) work in Section 15.3.2 below.

In another such "horse race", Holopainen and Sarlin (2017) are more categorical in recommending machine learning approaches such as so-called k-nearest neighbours and neural networks, and particularly by model aggregation approaches through ensemble learning. In contrast, results of Beutel et al. (2018) show that machine learning methods are not superior to conventional models in predicting financial crises. In fact, the predictive performance of conventional models often exceeds that of machine learning methods considerably.

Multivariate models tested by Alessi et al. (2014) had features such as addressing uncertainty, choosing indicators by Bayesian techniques and use of random coefficients to allow for cross-country variation. Further developments include models with discrete choice over more than two states such as crisis, post-crisis and tranquil (Bussière and Fratzscher, 2006). Tools based on artificial intelligence may offer some benefits but Alessi et al. (2014) note that the input data has to be chosen by the user, and it is not always clear how risk patterns are detected. Recent work in this area includes the "random forest" of Alessi and Detken (2014), a machine learning method based on decision trees, for detecting systemic risk.

Other recent work looks at alternative dependent variables to the standard banking crisis dummy. Boyd et al. (2009) constructed two sets of systemic bank shock (SBS) indicators using aggregate bank balance sheet data. The first type of indicator focused on the asset side of banks' balance sheets and captured anomalous declines in lending. In this case, the binary dummy became equal to one if real domestic lending growth in a given country fell below the 25th or 10th percentile of the real credit growth variable distribution across all countries in the sample. A similar process was used to create the second binary banking crisis variable which captured anomalies on the liability side of the balance sheet, namely the growth rate of the deposit-to-GDP ratio. These indicators had predictive power when introduced in lagged form into a logit EWS.

There is a burgeoning literature on the use of high frequency data to characterise financial stress which is extensively reviewed in Kliesen et al. (2012). Banking crisis dummies based on observed bank stress or policy responses are inherently backward looking and face criticism of subjectivity in terms of start dates (see below). It is argued that high frequency market data avoids this problem since asset prices should price in expectations of financial instability and its impact on the real economy. Hence, it is expected that anomalous values of these financial stress indicators should coincide with episodes of financial crises and therefore this approach provides an alternative left-hand side variable in EWSs. Typical market information that is embedded includes interest rate spreads on bonds (expected to capture higher rates of firm defaults in the event of crises), stock prices (which via a dividend discount model are expected to capture lower future earnings), and exchange rates.

Babecký et al. (2013) combine continuous (quarterly) information contained in output losses, employment rates and fiscal deficits and discrete (event-based) banking crisis dummies. Vermeulen et al. (2015) use the financial stress index approach to examine 28 OECD countries, although they find a weak relationship between their indicator and actual banking crisis episodes. Kliesen et al. (2012) compare the correlations of nine different financial stress indices in the US against NBER recession dates and find no significant relationship.

15.3   LOOKING AHEAD: USAGE OF EWS IN POLICY FORMATION

This final section of the chapter considers the usage of EWS as developed in the academic literature by policymakers, viewed in the overall context of their mandate to maintain financial stability.

15.3.1   Data Requirements for EWS

The data needs for EWS as estimated in the academic literature and summarised in Section 15.2 are broadly as defined by the results. We note that these typically include a number of macroeconomic and macrofinancial variables. Recent developments have included the focus on aggregate banking sector variables as in Barrell et al. (2010). A further development which has been widely neglected hitherto is the role of banking competition in raising the risk of financial crises, as in Davis et al. (2020). As will be discussed further below, some institutions do indeed use binary estimated model outputs as part of their overall surveillance.

A key variable typically used in practice, not least given its prominence in Basel III and recommendation to be monitored as trigger for the countercyclical buffer, is the credit-to-GDP gap. This is as calculated by the Bank for International Settlements (BIS) to be the difference between the actual total credit/GDP ratio and its trend as calculated by a Hodrick-Prescott filter (BCBS, 2010). As summarised in Davis et al. (2017), a range of studies have shown this indicator to be a useful indicator for financial crises, complementing binary choice models.

In a typical central bank or international organisation, the overall monitoring of vulnerability to financial instability in macroprudential surveillance, which is the function of EWS, goes much wider. Suggested lists of macroprudential indicators date back at least to Davis (1999) of the Bank of England and the IMF's Financial Soundness Indicators. The origin of such lists includes not only the output of empirical studies but also the various academic theories of financial instability and the evidence drawn from actual crises – for example the Asian Crisis showing risks of foreign currency exposures of the non-financial sectors.

In this context, it is suggested by Aikman et al. (2015, 2017) of the Bank of England and the Fed that "no single data series is appropriate for gauging the build-up of risks in a complex and evolving financial system" (Aikman et al., 2017, p. 36). Indeed, their own work highlights the potential role of 46 such indicators for the US, and show (Table 15.1) that this is a typical approach of a central bank or international organisation. They suggest that such indicators come appropriately in three categories – firstly, investor risk appetite and asset price indicators; secondly, non-financial sector leverage and related imbalances; and thirdly, financial sector vulnerabilities linked to leverage, maturity transformation, wholesale funding and shadow banking.

Again, following a typical central bank point of view, they critique the approach of relying on binary probability models given the infrequency of crises and consequent difficulty of highlighting a range of relevant factors. Rather, they focus on a range of indicators showing ability to forecast the credit cycle, highlight growing vulnerability and amplify shocks. They aggregate them in various ways to obtain overall measures of vulnerability. They find that the investor risk appetite leads the other groups of measures – and also the credit-to-GDP gap. But they acknowledge a need to supplement data with structural characteristics (what Davis (1999) calls qualitative information) like the run risk of money market funds. A similar analysis for the UK is given in Aikman et al. (2018).

In this context, Aikman et al. (2017) include a useful chart that shows the use of macroprudential data to monitor risks or to trigger policy decisions. The key points are that each institution does indeed employ a large number of indicators, that they often use summary illustrations of vulnerability such as heat maps, and that they do not generally make explicit reference to overall assessments of vulnerability.

15.3.2   Practical Use of EWS

So what use is made of estimated EWS in practice? It would appear that for many institutions, research may proceed but use in "front line" surveillance is limited. That said, an exception would appear to be the ECB. In the ECB (Constâncio et al., 2018), the quite extensive "analytical apparatus" is said to focus on three areas, firstly, taking stock of the state of financial stress, secondly, measuring the build-up of systemic instability, and thirdly, development of macrofinancial models to assess the potential severity of a financial crisis.

Table 15.1 Use of macroprudential indicators by official institutions

Institution	Purpose	Organising structure	Number of indicators	Visualisation devices
International Monetary Fund[a]	• The "Global Financial Stability Map" is used for monitoring financial stability risks • The aim is to combine economic and financial metrics with judgement based on market intelligence and staff assessment	• Indicators categorised into four "risks" and two underlying "conditions" • Risks include macroeconomic, emerging market, credit and market and liquidity • Conditions include monetary and financial, and risk appetite	• 33 indicators, reflecting a balance of economic, market-based and survey-based information	• The six composite indicators of risks and conditions are shown in a spider chart in each Global Financial Stability Report (GFSR) • A more granular assessment of how specific indicators have changed since previous GFSR is also provided
Office of Financial Research[b]	• The "Financial Stability Monitor" is used to analyse threats to financial stability	• Indicators categorised into five risk groups: macroeconomic; market; credit; funding and liquidity; and contagion	• Multiple indicators – specific indicators not provided	• Heat map table presented in the annual report
European Systemic Risk Board (ESRB)[c]	• Risk dashboard used to monitor vulnerabilities	• Indicators grouped into six risk categories: interlinkages; macro; credit; funding and liquidity; market; profitability/solvency	• 41 distinct indicators	• Charts of each indicator published each quarter

Table 15.1 (*continued*)

Institution	Purpose	Organising structure	Number of indicators	Visualisation devices
Bank of England[d]	• Used to inform decisions on sectoral capital requirements and countercyclical capital buffer • Decisions made by discretion	• Indicators divided into three categories: bank balance sheet stretch; non-bank balance sheet stretch; and conditions and terms in markets	• 25 distinct indicators for countercyclical capital buffer; 22 indicators for sectoral capital requirements	• Indicators routinely published in simple table alongside historical average values, 2006 values and min-max range
Norges Bank[e]	• Core indicators used to guide the Bank's advice to Ministry of Finance on the countercyclical capital buffer • Policy advice made by discretion	• Indicators of imbalances in non-financial sector, property prices and financial institutions' funding	• 4 indicators: (a) the ratio of total credit to GDP; (b) the ratio of house prices to income; (c) commercial property prices; and (d) banks' wholesale funding ratio	• Charts of each indicator published alongside trends and average values
Reserve Bank of New Zealand (RBNZ)[f]	• Core indicators used to guide policy decisions on core funding ratio, countercyclical capital buffers, sectoral capital requirements and LTV restrictions • Policy advice made by discretion	• Indicators divided into three categories: (a) the build-up of risk; (b) the materialisation of stress; and (c) the banking system's capacity to absorb those risks	• 34 distinct indicators	• Charts routinely published of each indicator

| Swiss National Bank[g] | • Used to guide advice on countercyclical capital buffer | • Indicators divided into mortgage credit and real estate prices | • Specific indicators not published | • N/A |

Notes:
a. See Annex 1.1 of the April 2010 Global Financial Stability Report and Dattels et al. (2010) for a description of the methodology underlying the Global Financial Stability Map.
b. See Office of Financial Research (2013, p. 11).
c. The ESRB's risk dashboard is available online at https://www.esrb.europa.eu/pub/rd/html/.
d. See Bank of England (2014), tables C and D, pp. 40–3).
e. See Norges Bank (2013).
f. On the indicators used by the RBNZ, see Wolken (2013); on the macroprudential regime in New Zealand, see also Wolken (2013).
g. See Swiss National Bank (2014).

Source: Aikman et al. (2015).

Concerning the first group, taking stock of financial stress at present, the ECB highlights the probability of default by large and complex banking groups (an EWS called JPoD), the euro-area measure of systemic risk known as the Composite Financial Stress Indicator (CISS) and the corresponding Country Level Index of Financial Stress (CLIFS). They note that these are coincident indicators that do not help predict the near-term incidence of financial instability. This is rather generated by the Financial Stability Risk Index (FSRI) which as in the discussion above, combines 23 macrofinancial indicators (to capture time series risk) with 16 measures of spillover and contagion (cross-section risk). A first step is to filter out noise with four factors, a second is to recursively regress the four factors in a quantile regression on unexplained GDP components. The quantile approach aims to capture nonlinearities around systemic events and focus on amplification mechanisms. Then forecast performance is evaluated with a goodness of fit measure.

Then, as regards the second group measuring the build-up of systemic instability, the focus is on prediction of instability at a usable policy horizon of 2–3 years, again looking both at cross-section and time series levels. Measurement of financial cycles at a country and Eurozone level – as distinct from the business cycle which is much shorter and with a lower amplitude – uses measures based on credit and house prices for a "narrow" measure and then also equity and bond prices at a "broad" level. It is suggested that such composite financial cycle indicators are the best indicators of the start of systemic banking crises and periods of vulnerability, superior to the credit-to-GDP gap for example.

Early warning models are also part of the ECB's armoury and indeed are "a key element of the analytical apparatus supporting macroprudential policy decision making" (Constâncio et al., 2018, p. 37). That said, they note at least three important problems with use of EWS in policy decisions. Firstly, structural breaks may make the signal less effective. Secondly, there are differences between Eurozone countries' financial sectors meaning models require careful interpretation. And thirdly, there could be a difficulty like Goodhart's Law that the use of early warning models for macroprudential policy may blur the future relation between the indicator and crises. The importance of testing out-of-sample is also emphasised.

Five approaches are used, as identified in Section 15.2, namely univariate and bivariate signalling models, a multivariate logit early warning model at the country level, a multivariate logit early warning model using individual bank level data, a random forest, and aggregate risk indicators derived from risk scoreboards. As shown in Table 15.2, a Markov switching model is also employed.

In terms of presentation, for the signalling approach there could be columns for each variable showing the estimated crisis probability for each country (see Constâncio et al., 2018, p. 39) such as residential property price overvaluation but also the illustration of different crisis thresholds and summary conditional crisis probabilities (we discuss these issues further in the following section). This presentation is similar for the multivariate estimates, examples of which are shown in Table 15.2. The different models evidently differ in their intensities of warning signals and the art of surveillance is to interpret them appropriately and deliver useful judgement to decision makers.

The final measure in this group is the cyclical systemic risk indicator (CSRI) based on a scoreboard which seeks to summarise the individual EWS measures whereby "early warning properties or expert judgement are used to select six to ten indicators per risk category, ideally covering different types of vulnerability. The individual indicators are then aggregated into one summary systemic risk indicator where the weights are determined to optimise the in-sample and out-of-sample early warning performance" (Constâncio et al., 2018, p. 41). This measure is considered to signal accurately the likelihood and severity of crises as it includes both domestic and exposure-based SRIs.

The final tool highlighted by the ECB is the macroprudential stress testing apparatus STAMP€, a form of macrofinancial model usable both to assess the impact of given risks on banking sectors and also to consider the effect of policy measures.

The approach of the ECB typifies that of an advanced country or area which has ample research resources and related access to long runs of consistent data. The World Bank (Krishnamurti and Lee, 2014) offers a useful counterpoint for developing and emerging countries. It is suggested that for them an EWS needs to be usable for monitoring build-ups of risk, analysing the signals of risk build-up, interpreting the signals, assessing overall vulnerability, identifying a need for a policy response and communicating warnings and assessments for backing such a response.

Such an approach needs to start at a basic level of ensuring that surveillance covers all relevant financial institutions and markets. Then there is a need for early detection of systemic risk, with the caution that crisis prediction is an inexact art. An EWS, it is suggested, can at best detect a build-up of vulnerabilities but not the feedback effects within the financial system and vis-à-vis the real sector. And data to build indicators are likely to be scarce in developing countries. Hence again, rather than model building, it is recommended that the macroprudential authority seek to identify and monitor leading indicators of financial instability. Aggregation as a composite measure is also recommended. The set of indicators should include non-banking measures both across and outside the financial system

Table 15.2   Identified vulnerabilities based on selected multivariate early warning models

Latest observations	Bank early warning model[1]	Logit model[2]	Random forest[3]	Bivariate signalling[4]		Markov switching model[5]
	Q1 2018	Q4 2017		Bank credit/ GDP gap	Real equity price growth (3 years)	
				Q4 2017		
Country 1	9.2	0.1	13.3	−51.9	11.4	0.5
Country 2	5.5	17.2	24.8	5.5	3.1	3.8
Country 3	4.5	5.2	6.7	−2.4	7.5	2.0
Country 4		6.2	4.5	−5.4	6.7	1.5
Country 5	27.7	0.2	7.1	−54.7	−8.4	1.6
Country 6	15.9	2.1	3.0	−13.8	7.0	1.0
Country 7	4.0	0.2	2.2	−42.1	0.7	0.7
Country 8	7.7	0.6	2.0	−22.5	−15.6	1.0
Country 9		10.3	34.5	3.6	18.3	
Country 10	5.6	7.8	5.9	−7.5	16.6	2.2
Country 11	9.8	12.6	18.2	0.8	10.1	2.7
AUROC	0.85	0.83	0.94	0.84		
High threshold: theta = 0.3	18.08 (CP: 0.46 / T1: 0.44 / T2: 0.07)	15.91 (CP: 0.38 / T1: 0.33 / T2: 0.16)	17.15 (CP: 0.71 / T1: 0.30 / T2: 0.02)	6.12 / 7.93 (CP: 0.49 / T1: 0.42 / T2: 0.06)		
Med-high threshold: theta = 0.4	12.73 (CP: 0.32 / T1: 0.31 / T2: 0.15)	12.46 (CP: 0.33 / T1: 0.23 / T2: 0.22)	12.77 (CP: 0.42 / T1: 0.18 / T2: 0.07)	6.12 / 7.93 (CP: 0.49 / T1: 0.42 / T2: 0.06)		
Medium threshold: theta = 0.5	8.24 (CP: 0.23 / T1: 0.18 / T2: 0.27)	11.99 (CP: 0.32 / T1: 0.20 / T2: 0.24)	12.62 (CP: 0.41 / T1: 0.18 / T2: 0.07)	0.27 / 6.91 (CP: 0.26 / T1: 0.24 / T2: 0.24)		
Med-low threshold: theta = 0.6	7.03 (CP: 0.21 / T1: 0.14 / T2: 0.32)	11.28 (CP: 0.30 / T1: 0.18 / T2: 0.27)	11.09 (CP: 0.29 / T1: 0.13 / T2: 0.13)	0.1 / 7.07 (CP: 0.25 / T1: 0.22 / T2: 0.25)		

Table 15.2 *(continued)*

Latest observations	Bank early warning model[1]	Logit model[2]	Random forest[3]	Bivariate signalling[4]		Markov switching model[5]
	Q1 2018	Q4 2017		Bank credit/ GDP gap	Real equity price growth (3 years)	
				Q4 2017		
Low threshold: theta = 0.7	6.44 (CP: 0.20 / T1: 0.12 / T2: 0.35)	11.28 (CP: 0.30 / T1: 0.18 / T2: 0.27)	10.08 (CP: 0.17 / T1: 0.07 / T2: 0.28)	−0.44 / −10.87 (CP: 0.2 / T1: 0.15 / T2: 0.38)		

Conditional crisis probability > 40%	Conditional crisis probability > 25%
Conditional crisis probability > 35%	Conditional crisis probability > 20%
Conditional crisis probability > 30%	Conditional crisis probability > 15%

Source: ECB and ECB calculations.

Notes: The colour coding is based on the conditional probability that a banking crisis could materialise within the next 12 to 5 quarters (8 to 1 quarters for the bank early warning model) upon a crisis signal being issued. This conditional probability depends on the specific signalling threshold that is being breached. In general, a higher preference for not missing vulnerable states leads to a lower signalling threshold and more false alarms being issued, which is usually associated with a lower conditional distress probability. For each model, five different signalling thresholds are applied based on preference parameters ranging between 0.7 (strong preference for not missing vulnerable states) and 0.3 (strong preference for not issuing false alarms). T1 refers to the type 1 error rate, T2 to the type 2 error rate and CP to the conditional probability associated with each threshold.

1) Aggregation at the country-level of a logit bank early warning model comprising bank-specific, aggregate banking sector and macro-financial variables.

2) Logit models with bank credit-to-GDP gap; residential property price-to-income ratio; three-year real equity price growth; debt service to income ratio (country 5 as of Q3 2017).

3) Random forest comprising 100,000 trees which are grown on six indicators per tree from a total set of 34 indicators.

4) Bivariate signalling model with 1) bank credit-to-GDP gap and 2) two-year real equity price growth.

5) Markov switching model with total credit-to-GDP gap, debt service to income ratio, residential property price-to-rent ratio, annual growth of real residential property prices and annual inflation rate.

Source: Constâncio et al. (2018).

(this is a criticism of the IMF's initial set of financial soundness indicators that they focused too much in the banking sector). The World Bank also mentions qualitative trends relevant to financial stability that are not captured by models such as financial innovations, new products, changes in banks' business models, the type of model used by market participants and the risk of regulatory arbitrage. To provide a forward-looking element, stress tests and scenario analyses are recommended.

The World Bank suggests that many countries with limited resources and data should rely on a small number of Early Warning Indicators whose risk properties are understood and where there are staff resources to analyse them. Then there is a need to identify warning thresholds which trigger a need for policy concern and then trigger thresholds for the introduction of macroprudential policy measures. There is a need to communicate results specifically and sufficiently early for the policy measures to have an effect. The World Bank notes that while external communication is vital, publishing a Financial Stability Review is not a guarantee of protection. Čihák et al. (2012) found 80 countries publishing FSRs at that time but little evidence of a direct link to financial stability, unless there were high quality publications with forward-looking elements. Data gaps, lack of skilled personnel and poor quality modelling may all vitiate efforts.

Meanwhile, the IMF (2013) in its major policy paper on macroprudential policy, suggests in terms of surveillance that "tools exist to assess most sectors and levels of aggregation. However, these tools provide only partial coverage of potential risks and only tentative signals on the likelihood and impact of systemic risk events. As such, they may not provide sufficient comfort to policymakers."

15.3.3   Incorporating Policymakers' Preferences

As noted above and as shown in Table 15.2, there is scope with estimated EWS to incorporate relevant information for policymakers beyond the simple probability of a crisis which is generated by the respective model. Policymakers require an EWS not only to have good forecasting power but also give an early enough signal and be stable. The signal needs to be early enough for macroprudential policies to take effect but also not too early as this would impose unnecessary costs on the economy – and pressure to weaken future policy actions. The signal also needs to be stable since policymakers prefer to react to persistent rather than temporary signals, since this reduces uncertainty over the actual state of the economy and allows for more decisive policy action. The signal should also be robust to sample changes and easy to interpret.

In this context, there needs to be allowance for the policymaker's preference over type I error (failing to forecast a crisis that does occur) and type II error (forecasting crises when they do not occur). Drehmann and Juselius (2014) offer an approach to this issue, incorporating the policy requirements cited above, aspects of which are followed in many recent papers providing estimated EWSs. A key issue is to evaluate the quality of signals in the absence of knowledge of the costs and benefits of policy actions. In particular, they highlight the receiver operating characteristic curve (ROC) which, as noted above, maps the full range of trade-offs of type I and type II error that the EWS provides. It does this by mapping the false positive rate (type II error) to the true positive rate (complement of type I error). They contend that the area under the curve (AUROC) is a helpful summary measure of the signalling quality of the EWS. There is scope to compare the AUROC of two alternative EWSs by, for example, confidence bands and Wald statistics.

Drehmann and Juselius (2014) evaluate the signalling properties of ten EWSs using these AUROCs around the time of crises and find the debt service ratio (over shorter horizons) and the credit-to-GDP gap (over longer horizons) perform best. Evaluations based on them are indeed robust over a range of policymaker preferences, they are well timed and the quality does not deteriorate in the run-up to the crisis. Other indicators often have signalling qualities that vary sharply over time.

Rereading Table 15.2 we can see that the AUROC is shown for each of the EWS shown. A perfect prediction would give an AUROC of 1.0 while an uninformative mode would have one of 0.5, the closer to unity the better (Filippopoulou et al., 2020). There is also information for those willing to accept different levels of probability of a crisis with signalling thresholds between 0.3 and 0.7, and associated type I error rates (T1) and type II error rates (T2) as well as the conditional probability of a crisis (CP). Those most concerned about a crisis would choose 0.7 and those most concerned to avoid overprediction would choose 0.3.

15.3.4 Use of Macroprudential Surveillance (EWS) to Trigger Macroprudential Policy Action

The Bank of England approach to adjusting the countercyclical buffer gives a good example of the use of risk assessments and early warning indicators to guide decision making (Aikman et al., 2013). Constâncio et al. (2018, pp. 51–3) show the equivalent process for the ECB. Aikman et al. point out that "given the complexity and state-contingency of signals from indicators and models, it would not make sense to tie movements in the countercyclical capital buffer (CCB) mechanically to any specific set of indicators or models" (Aikman et al., 2013, p. 18). Rather, use is made of a short list of core financial and economic indicators, which are thought useful inter alia to anchor policy actions, give consistent decision making and a basis for explaining actions externally. Interestingly, it is suggested that simple indicators can outperform in terms of predicting more complex approaches due to their robustness in the face of uncertainty.

The credit-to-GDP gap is indeed used as a starting point but it has to be supplemented due to weaknesses such as the poor ability to signal in deteriorating conditions, ignoring absolute amounts of credit and their sources and quality (Giese et al., 2014). Additional indicators include aggregate risk adjusted capital and leverage ratios (as tested globally in Davis et al., 2020), the loan to deposit ratio as a measure of dependence on wholesale funding, low quality debt spreads, banks' price to book ratios and market value capital ratios, the current account deficit, and global capital market measures such as the VIX, global spreads and long-term interest rates.

It is emphasised that stress tests and output of other models as well as market intelligence are also an input to the decision in the Financial Stability Committee. That is then promulgated via a press release, the meeting minutes and the biannual FSR. International coordination takes place under Basel rules to ensure international banks' exposure to the UK are also subject to the CCB. Banks have 12 months to apply an increase in the CCB, a lag that needs to be taken into account in policymaking. It is finally noted that although there are some calculations of the effect of CCB increases on prices and quantities of credit, and on GDP, these were limited at the time of writing.

15.3.5   Interaction of EWS with Monetary Policy Rules

The interaction of macroprudential and monetary policy is an open question which is very important to macroprudential policy and the usage of EWS. Svensson (2018) argues that monetary policy has a strong effect on price stability and real stability but a small, indirect and unsystematic effect on financial stability, while macroprudential policy has a strong effect on financial stability but a small indirect and unsystematic effect on inflation and resource utilisation.

Accordingly, he argues that the policies are best directed to separate goals – price and real stability for monetary policy and financial stability (ability of the financial system to fulfil its functions with sufficient resilience to disturbances that threaten these functions) for macroprudential policy. Thus, these policies can be best undertaken separately, while taking account of the likely action of the other, as in a Nash equilibrium. Such separate conduct helps both policies to be distinct, transparent and easy to evaluate and hence facilitates accountability for the decision-making body in achieving the relevant goals. A similar argument can be made for separate monetary and fiscal policy.

The implication for macroprudential surveillance and EWS is that they should take into account an expected path of monetary policy that seeks to maintain monetary stability but is not adjusted to also combat financial instability. The same applies to "inflation reports" and other input to monetary policy decisions in respect of anticipated macroprudential policy decisions. Svensson argues that monetary policy should not seek to target financial stability, which it is not capable to achieve; he discounts the "risk taking channel" of monetary policy that some argue requires it to have a financial stability as well as monetary stability focus (Adrian and Liang, 2018; see also Chapters 6 and 9).

Svensson suggests that the main exception to this optimal separation is in a crisis episode per se when both policies along with fiscal policy need to work to return the economy and financial system to balance. He argues strongly against monetary policy seeking to aid macroprudential policy by "leaning into the wind" and raising rates above those warranted by monetary stability to aid financial stability, suggesting this policy can have few benefits and major costs – notably a weaker economy with lower inflation and higher unemployment if there is no crisis, and a higher cost of crisis if one does occur. The only other exception to the Nash equilibrium, he argues, should be when the macroprudential authorities themselves ask for help from the monetary authorities on the basis that they cannot maintain financial stability with their own instruments.

Such a stance is not without critics, in particular BIS economists such as Juselius et al. (2016) have argued for close coordination and leaning into the wind when it is appropriate. And empirical work such as Kim and Mehrotra (2018) for four Asia-Pacific economies that have inflation targets (Australia, Korea, Thailand, Indonesia) shows that the macroeconomic effect of monetary and macroprudential policy is in fact quite comparable, since both lead to reallocation of spending over time by influencing the availability and cost of credit. For contractionary policies of either type there is a decline in GDP, the price level and the stock of credit. They argue accordingly that whereas most of the time monetary and macroprudential policy can operate alongside each other in a beneficial way, there could be important conflicts in the case that there is low inflation and buoyant credit growth. In such cases an EWS needs to consider not only direct risks to financial stability but also the effects of variations of monetary policy from direct targeting of inflation and forms of coordination may be necessary.

Complementing these are a wide range of theoretical papers that seek to trace the interrelation of monetary and macroprudential policy. To give one example, Agur and Demertzis (2015), using a bank-based model (profitability and leverage), saw that with the presence of macroprudential policy, there is at times a partial offsetting of monetary policy (expansionary interest rate policy) and at the same time, monetary policy can affect financial stability (e.g. the Latin debt crisis of the early 1980s and loose monetary policy in the 2000s leading up to the subprime crisis).

15.3.6　Some Open Issues with EWS

Other open issues include (Aikman et al., 2013) the effect of macroprudential policy in a downturn and calibration in the context of uncertainty. There is a need to consider whether policy and surveillance are too narrowly focused on the banking system and whether tools addressing market and non-bank finance are needed (Constâncio et al., 2018). There is the issue whether there should be targeting of asset prices such as house prices by macroprudential policy (Constâncio, 2016). Measurement and control of policy leakages due to regulatory arbitrage within banks, across the financial system and offshore needs more attention.

The issue of shadow banking requires close attention in terms of monitoring and assessing risks, including appropriate monitoring and use of EWS. Then, as discussed in Section 15.2.6, there is the utility or otherwise of machine learning approaches to crises, which remains an open issue. Finally, we note that our own work suggests inter alia a need to focus on the relation of measures of banking competition to crises and use of both leverage ratios and risk adjusted capital in EWS. We also suggest a need to allow for nonlinear relations between capital and crises (Davis et al., 2020).

NOTES

1. World Bank's Finance and Private Sector Division.
2. The exception was the credit growth variable which was lagged by two years.

REFERENCES

Adrian T, and Liang N (2018), "Monetary policy, financial conditions, and financial stability", *International Journal of Central Banking* 14(1), 73–131.
Agur I, and Demertzis M (2015), "Will macroprudential policy counteract monetary policy's effects on financial stability?", IMF Working Paper, No. 15/283.

Aikman D, Bridges J, Burgess S et al. (2018), "Measuring risks to UK financial stability", Bank of England Staff Working Paper No. 738.

Aikman D, Haldane A G and Kapadia S (2013), "Operationalising a macropru-dential regime, goals, tools and open issues", Bank of Spain Working Paper 24.

Aikman D, Kiley M, Lee S J, Palumbo M G and Warusawitharana M (2015), "Mapping heat in the US financial system", Finance and Economics Discussion Paper Series 2015-019, Board of Governors of the Federal Reserve, Washington, DC.

Aikman D, Kiley M, Lee S J, Palumbo M G and Warusawitharana M (2017), "Mapping heat in the US financial system", *Journal of Banking and Finance*, 81, 36–64.

Alessi L and Detken C (2014), "Identifying excessive credit growth and leverage", ECB Working Paper No. 1723.

Alessi L, Antunes A, Babecky J et al. (2014), "Comparing different early warning systems: Results from a horse race competition among members of the macro-prudential research network", ECB, Mimeo.

Babecký J, Havránek T, Matějů J, Rusnák M, Šmídková K and Vašíček B (2013), "Leading indicators of crisis incidence: Evidence from developed countries", *Journal of International Money and Finance*, 35, C, 1–19.

Bank of England (2014), The Financial Policy Committee's powers to supplement capital requirements: a policy statement, January.

Barrell R, Davis E P, Karim D and Liadze I (2010), "Bank regulation, property prices and early warning systems for banking crises in OECD countries", *Journal of Banking and Finance*, 34, 2255–64.

Barrell R, Karim D and Macchiarelli C (2020), "Towards an understanding of credit cycles: Do all credit booms cause crises?", *The European Journal of Finance*, 26(10), 978–93.

Barrell R, Karim D and Ventouri A (2016), "Interest rate liberalization and capital adequacy in models of financial crises", *Journal of Financial Stability*, 33, December, 261–72.

BCBS (Basel Committee on Banking Supervision) (2010), "Guidance for national authorities operating the countercyclical capital buffer", BCBS, Basel.

Beutel J, List S and von Schweinitz G (2018), "An evaluation of early warning models for systemic banking crises: Does machine learning improve predic-tions?", Deutsche Bundesbank Discussion Paper No. 48/2018.

BIS (Bank for International Settlements) (1986), "Recent innovations in inter-national banking, report prepared by a study group established by the central banks of the G10 countries", Basel, April (Cross Report).

BIS (Bank for International Settlements) (1997a), 67th Annual Report, Basel, June.

BIS (Bank for International Settlements) (1997b), Survey of disclosures about trading and derivatives activities of banks and securities firms, Basel, November.

Borio C and Lowe P (2002), "Assessing the risk of banking crisis", *BIS Quarterly Review*, December.

Boyd J H and Gertler M (1993), "U.S. commercial banking: Trends, cycles, and policy", NBER Chapters, in: *NBER Macroeconomics Annual 1993*, Vol. 8, pp. 319–77, Washington, DC: National Bureau of Economic Research.

Boyd J H, De Nicolo G and Loukoianova E (2009), "Banking crises and crisis dating: Theory and evidence", IMF Working Paper No. 09/141.

Bussière M and Fratzscher M (2006), "Towards a new early warning system of financial crises", *Journal of International Money and Finance*, 25(6), 953–73.

Calvo G A and Mendoza E G (1996), "Mexico's balance-of-payments crisis: A chronicle of a death foretold", *Journal of International Economics*, 41, 235–64.

Caprio G and Klingebiel D (1996), "Bank insolvencies: Cross-country experience", Policy Research Working Paper PRWP1620, Washington, DC: World Bank.

Caprio G and Klingebiel D (1999), "Episodes of systemic and borderline financial crises", Washington, DC: World Bank, Mimeo.

Caprio G and Klingebiel D (2003), "Episodes of systemic and borderline financial crises", January, World Bank database.

Caprio G, Klingebiel D, Laeven L and Noguera G (2005), "Appendix: Banking Crisis Database", in: Honohan P and Laeven L (eds), *Systemic Financial Crises: Containment and Resolution*, pp. 341–60, Cambridge: Cambridge University Press.

Cashin, P and Duttagupta, R (2008), "The anatomy of banking crises", IMF Working Paper No. 08/093.

Čihák M (2006), "How do central banks write on financial stability?", IMF Working Paper No. 06/163.

Čihák M, Muñoz S, Sharifuddin S T and Tintchev K (2012), "Financial Stability Reports: What are they good for?", IMF Working Paper No. 12/1.

Clement P (2010), "The term 'macroprudential': Origins and evolution", *BIS Quarterly Review*, January, 59–67.

Constâncio V (2016), "Principles of Macroprudential Policy", Speech given at the ECB-IMF Conference on Macroprudential Policy, Frankfurt am Main, 26 April 2016.

Constâncio V, Cabral I, Detken C et al. (2018), "Macroprudential policy at the ECB: Institutional framework, strategy, analytical tools and policies", ECB Occasional Paper 227.

Dattels P, McCaughrin R, Miyajima K and Puig J (2010), "Can you map global financial stability?" IMF Working Paper No. 10/145.

Davis E P (1995) *Debt, Financial Fragility and Systemic Risk*, Oxford: Oxford University Press.

Davis E P (1999), "Financial data needs for macroprudential surveillance: What are the key indicators of risk to domestic financial stability?", Lecture Series No. 2, Centre for Central Banking Studies, Bank of England.

Davis E P and Karim D (2008), "Comparing early warning systems for banking crises", *Journal of Financial Stability*, 4, 89–120.

Davis E P, Karim D and Liadze I (2011), "Should multivariate early warning systems for banking crises pool across regions?", *Review of World Economics/ Weltwirtschaftliches Archiv*, 147, 693–716.

Davis E P, Karim D and Noel D (2017), "Macroprudential policy and financial imbalances", Brunel Economics and Finance Working Paper 17-22.

Davis E P, Karim D and Noel D (2020), "The bank capital-competition-risk nexus, a global perspective", *Journal of International Financial Markets, Institutions and Money*, 65.

Demirgüç-Kunt, A and Detragiache E (1998), "The determinants of banking crises in developing and developed countries", IMF Staff Papers 45(1).

Demirgüç-Kunt A and Detragiache E (2002), "Does deposit insurance increase banking system stability? An empirical investigation", *Journal of Monetary Economics*, 49, 1373–406.

Demirgüç-Kunt A and Detragiache E (2005), "Cross-country empirical studies of systemic bank distress: A survey", *National Institute Economic Review*, No.192, April.

Drees B and Pazarbasioglu C (1995), "The Nordic banking crises: Pitfalls in financial liberalization?", IMF Working Paper No. 95/61.

Drehmann M and Juselius M (2014), "Evaluating early warning indicators of banking crises, satisfying policy requirements", *International Journal of Forecasting*, 30, 759–80.

Filippopoulou C, Galariotis E and Spyrou S (2020), "An early warning system for predicting systemic banking crises in the Eurozone, a logit regression analysis", *Journal of Economic Behaviour and Organisation*, 172, 344–63.

Gavin M and Hausmann R (1998), "The roots of banking crises: The macroeconomic context", IDB Working Paper No. 262.

Ghosh S and Ghosh A R (2002), "Structural vulnerabilities and currency crises", IMF Working Paper No. 02/9.

Giese J, Andersen H, Bush O, Castro C, Farag F and Kapadia S (2014), "The credit-to-GDP gap and complementary indicators for macroprudential policy: Evidence from the UK", *International Journal of Finance and Economics*, 19: 25–47.

Holopainen M and Sarlin P (2017), "Toward robust early-warning models: A horse race, ensembles and model uncertainty", *Quantitative Finance*, 17(12), 1–31.

IMF (1998), "Towards a framework for financial stability", World Economic and Financial Surveys, Washington, DC: IMF.

IMF (2013), "Key aspects of macroprudential policy", Washington, DC: IMF.

Juselius M, Borio C, Disyatat P and Drehmann M (2016), "Monetary policy, the financial cycle and ultra-low interest rates", Bank for International Settlements Working Paper No. 569.

Kaminsky G L and Reinhart C M (1996), "The twin crises: The causes of banking and balance-of-payments problems", International Finance Discussion Papers 544, Board of Governors of the Federal Reserve System (US), revised 1996.

Kaminsky G L and Reinhart C M (1999), "The twin crises: The causes of banking and balance-of-payments problems", *American Economic Review*, 89(3), 473–500.

Kim S and Mehrotra A (2018), "Effects of monetary and macroprudential policies, evidence from four inflation targeting countries", *Journal of Money, Credit and Banking*, 50, 967–92.

Kliesen K, Owyang M and Vermann E (2012), "Disentangling diverse measures: A survey of financial stress indexes". Federal Reserve Bank of St. Louis Review 94, 369–98.

Krishnamurti D and Lee Y C (2014), "Macroprudential policy, a practice guide", Washington DC: World Bank.

Laeven L and Valencia F (2008), "Systemic Banking Crises: a new database", IMF Working Paper No. 08/224.

Laeven L and Valencia F (2013), "Systemic Banking Crises Database", *IMF Economic Review*, 61 225–70.

Laeven L and Valencia F (2018), "Systemic banking crises revisited", IMF Working Paper No. 18/206.

Li X, Escalante C L and Epperson J E (2014), "Agricultural banking and bank failures of the late 2000s financial crisis: A survival analysis using Cox proportional hazard model", Selected Paper prepared for presentation at the Southern Agricultural Economics Association (SAEA) Annual Meeting, Dallas, Texas, 1–4 February 2014.

Manasse P, Roubini N and Schimmelpfennig A (2003), "Predicting sovereign debt crises", IMF Working Paper No. 03/221.

Norges Bank (2013), "Criteria for an appropriate countercyclical capital buffer", Norges Bank Papers No. 1, Norway.

Office of Financial Research (2013), 2013 Annual Report, Washington, DC.

Pill, H and Pradhan M (1995), "Financial indicators and financial change in Africa and Asia", IMF Working Paper No. 95/123.

Schularick M and Taylor A (2012), "Credit booms gone bust: Monetary policy, leverage cycles and financial crises, 1870–2008", *American Economic Review*, 102, 1029–61.

Svensson L E O (2018), "Monetary policy and macroprudential policy; different but separate?", *Canadian Journal of Economics*, 18, 802–27.

Swiss National Bank (2014), "Implementing the countercyclical capital buffer in Switzerland: concretizing the Swiss National Bank's role", February.

Velasco A (1987), "Financial crises and balance of payments crises: A simple model of the southern cone experience", *Journal of Development Economics*, 27, 263–83.

Vermeulen R, Hoeberichts M, Vašíček B et al. (2015), "Financial stress indices and financial crises", *Open Economic Review*, 26, 383–40.

Wolken, T. (2013), "Measuring systemic risk: the role of macroprudential indicators", Reserve Bank of New Zealand Bulletin, 76(4), December.

World Bank (2017), "Global Financial Development Database", Washington, DC: IBRD, http://www.worldbank.org/en/publication/gfdr/data/global-finan cial-development-database.

Index